What experts say about t

The questions in Practice Tests For The Digital SAT are very close to the actual test.

– **Vaibhav Sharma SAT Math Coach**

I would recommend high school and public libraries to consider purchasing this book for their patrons.

– **Kelley Wilson, School Library Media Specialist, Brandywine High School**

Because of the breadth, depth, and organization, I would recommend this book to students and teachers.

– **Motz Maria, Purchasing Dept School Board Sarasota County**

This page is intentionally left blank

VIBRANT
PUBLISHERS

TEST PREP SERIES

PRACTICE TESTS FOR THE
Digital SAT®

2023

5 full-length tests

Module-wise tests as per the Digital SAT® format

Questions according to the Digital SAT® guidelines

Detailed answer explanations with distractor explanations

Practice Tests For The Digital SAT®

Paperback ISBN 10 : 1-63651-157-0
Paperback ISBN 13 : 978-1-63651-157-3

Library of Congress Control Number: 2022951781

This publication is designed to provide accurate and authoritative information in regard to the subject matter covered. The author has made every effort in the preparation of this book to ensure the accuracy of the information. However, information in this book is sold without warranty either expressed or implied. The Author or the Publisher will not be liable for any damages caused or alleged to be caused either directly or indirectly by this book.

Vibrant Publishers books are available at special quantity discount for sales promotions, or for use in corporate training programs. For more information please write to **bulkorders@vibrantpublishers.com**

Please email feedback/corrections (technical, grammatical or spelling) to **spellerrors@vibrantpublishers.com**

To access the complete catalogue of Vibrant Publishers, visit **www.vibrantpublishers.com**

Table of Contents

Dear Student,

Thank you for purchasing **Practice Tests for the Digital SAT®.** We are committed to publishing books that are content–rich, concise and approachable enabling more students to read and make the fullest use of them. We hope this book provides the most enriching learning experience as you prepare for your **SAT** exam. Should you have any questions or suggestions, feel free to email us at **reachus@vibrantpublishers.com**. Thanks again for your purchase. Good luck for your Digital SAT!

– Vibrant Publishers Team

ACT/SAT
Books in Test Prep Series

Math Practice Tests for the ACT ISBN: 978-1-63651-085-9	**Winning Strategies For ACT Essay Writing: With 15 Sample Prompts** ISBN: 978-1-63651-125-2
Digital SAT Math Practice Questions ISBN: 978-1-63651-159-7	**Digital SAT Reading and Writing Practice Questions** ISBN: 978-1-63651-158-0

For the most updated list of books visit

www.vibrantpublishers.com

This page is intentionally left blank

How To Get The Most Out Of This Book

Having no useful information about how to successfully take the Digital SAT test can make it look like a difficult thing. However, this practice test book is specifically designed to give you a thorough practice of the new SAT. By attempting the practice tests in this book you will become confident to face the real test.

This book includes *5 full-length Digital SAT tests* with a total of *490 practice questions* for your continuous practice. The practice tests in this book follow the modular format for the Reading and Writing and Math sections. Each question has the most appropriate answer explanation and distractor explanation. This is to ensure that you understand the reasoning behind each correct (or incorrect) answer and train your mind to logically answer the questions.

First, read the **About The Digital SAT** chapter in order to fully understand how the test is planned and administered before diving in to give the tests. As the College Board transitions from administering paper-and-pencil SAT tests to digital SAT Suite tests, you need to be aware of all the appropriate information that can increase your chance of passing the test with a high score.

After reading through the information, consider taking one of the complete practice tests first. In the first test, give yourself as much time as you need rather than trying to finish within the allotted SAT time limit. However, write down how long each section and module takes to solve, so you can determine how to budget your time. Then, compare your answers with the correct answers given in the 'Answer Key' section of each test. Understand what went wrong by referring to the detailed solutions given in the 'Answer & Explanations' section. Look over the categories of questions that you consistently had difficulties with or consistently made errors on. This will help you determine your strengths and weaknesses and the areas you need to focus on.

Identify and practice the question types that you found difficult. Familiarize yourself with their pattern. Often refer to the 'How to Use This Book' section for tips on how to solve the problem associated with each section and which resources to use for getting a thorough and focused practice. You can also get ample practice of Reading and Writing and Math questions from *Digital SAT Reading and Writing Practice Questions* and *Digital SAT Math Practice Questions*.

After completing your practice, try another complete practice test. This time, have your timer at hand and take breaks only at the intervals given in the real test. This more realistic testing experience will also show you how well you can concentrate for extended periods. After you complete the second practice test, check your answers and compare them with the answers given in the 'Answer Key' section after each test and look for patterns in the questions you missed. Are they the same style as before, or do you have different weaknesses? Try reviewing these weaknesses before taking the next complete practice test.

Create a study schedule and stick with it. Attempt to take a practice test every week for 6 weeks. This will help you become well-versed with the format of the SAT and also increase your confidence.

Continue alternating review of specific question types with complete practice tests throughout your preparation period. Do not worry if you miss a day on your study plan; just revise your schedule as needed so you can complete every practice test in this book. When the day arrives for your actual SAT, you will be comfortable with the new pattern of the test and will be ready to solve any style of question that might be on it, whether it is related to language or mathematics. You can be confident of getting your best possible score!

More so, practice test questions and their corresponding answers will expose you to the format and structure of real digital SAT. Do not read this book like a textbook; rather, use it as a companion to guide you in understanding every aspect of the digital SAT suite tests.

Good luck on your SAT journey!

Chapter 1

About the Digital SAT®

Introduction

Now that you have made the important decision to head to college/university, there is one last thing you need to do to achieve your goal—taking the SAT. Most universities or colleges, including the IVY league schools such as Yale, Harvard, and others expect you to have a good SAT score to secure admission in any course of your choice.

But, there is a major change in how students will give the SAT. The College Board has decided to transition the famous pencil-and-paper test into a fully digital one. The College Board's decision to go digital is based on giving a fair testing experience to students. The digital test will be easier to take, easier to administer, will be more secure, and more relevant.

For giving the new test, you need to be aware of the format of the test, the time that will be given to you to answer each question, the possible complexity of the questions, and the scoring method employed to assess your performance in the test. In this chapter, you will discover important information all that including the SAT policy of inclusive accessibility, the newly introduced Multistage Adaptive Testing feature, the modular format of the test, and much more.

The College Board has also streamlined the method of delivery of the digital SAT. With the latest test delivery platform for the digital SAT Suite assessments, students can have access to all their tests and their content, as well as enjoy the chance of practicing with the full-length, adaptive practice test offered for free on the platform so that students can be aware of their knowledge levels before taking the real tests. More so, every question on the digital SAT Suite is in a discrete (standalone) format. This indicates that test takers can answer each question independently. They don't necessarily need to refer to a common stimulus such as an extended passage.

If you are attempting the SAT for the first time, it could be scary not knowing exactly what to expect in the test. This is why this book is specifically designed to expose you to everything you need to know about successfully taking the Digital SAT Suite test.

Customized Test Delivery Platform

The College Board sets up a customized test delivery platform for the Digital SAT Suite assessments. This platform is designed according to the principles of UDA (Universal Design for Assessment) and the main goal of it is to make the testing experience accessible to maximum number of students. The most useful features of this platform are that: (i) all test takers can have complete access to the tests and their content; (ii) students will be able to take full-length, adaptive practice tests for free on the platform so that they can assess their knowledge levels or have an understanding of similar test materials before attempting the real tests.

Multistage Adaptive Testing

The College Board is changing from a linear testing mode, which has been the primary mode of SAT administration to an adaptive mode.

The main difference between the linear and adaptive testing modes is that for the linear testing mode, students are given a test form that contains some questions that have already been set before the test day and do not change during testing, irrespective of the student's performance.

On the other hand, the adaptive testing model makes it possible for the test delivery platform to adjust the questions' difficulty level based on the performance of the individual test takers. Therefore, each student will be given test questions that match their level of understanding.

This adaptive test mode used for the Digital SAT Suite is known as **Multistage Adaptive Testing (MST)**. The MST is administered in 2 stages, and each stage comprises a module or set of questions. The first module consists of test questions with different ranges of difficulty levels (easy, medium, and hard). The performance of the test takers in the first module is appropriately assessed, and the results are used to determine the level of difficulty of questions to be administered to them in the second module.

The set of an administered first-stage module and its second-stage module are referred to as a *panel*.

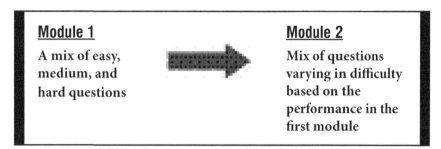

Embedded Pretesting

The digital SAT Suite also includes embedded pretesting in its design. What this means is that a small number of pretest (unscored) questions are incorporated among the operational (scored) questions. Even though they are not administered for a score, students may not be able to distinguish these pretest questions from the operational questions on which their scores are based. It is advisable that students pay maximum attention and effort to these questions, which can be used in estimating their understanding levels to the difficulty of the questions. The number of pretest questions is few so you will not be asked to focus mainly on questions that won't be used to estimate your final SAT score. It is important to note that answers to pretest questions won't contribute to your final score. The pretest questions are mainly used to gather students' performance information so that it can be utilized later to assess if these questions are appropriate for operational use later.

Discrete Questions

One interesting aspect of the Digital SAT is that all their questions are in discreet format; that is they are standalone. You can answer each question on its own, which doesn't necessarily require any reference to a common stimulus such as an extended passage. This is one of the striking differences between the paper-and-pencil SAT and the Digital SAT in the sense that the former uses both discrete and question sets. In practice, the question sets expect you to reference a common stimulus.

Scoring

Students will obtain a section score based on their final performance on the Reading and Writing and Math section. For the SAT, students can get a score between 400-1600. Hence, for each of the tests of the Digital SAT, there will be 3 scores reported: (1) A Reading and Writing section score; (2) A Math section score; (3) A total score, which is the sum of the two section scores. It is important to note that the scales for these scores have the same ranges as for the paper-based SAT Suite. This indicates that the digital SAT total score is on the familiar 400–1600 scale.

Reading and Writing	Math	Total Score
Between 200-800	Between 200-800	Between 400-1600

Overall Test Specifications

The Digital SAT is made up of two sections: A Reading and Writing (RW) section and a Math section. In the linear model, the test has separate sections for Reading and Writing. However, in the Digital SAT, both the Reading and Writing tests are combined in one section. The questions in these two sections concentrate primarily on the skills and knowledge that students need to use in college and/or for getting ready for their careers. The main parts of the digital SAT tests are similar to those of the paper-and-pencil SAT test assessments. More so, all the testing programs within the digital SAT Suite, whether it is the SAT, PSAT 10, PSAT 8/9, or PSAT/NMSQT have similar designs. Although, these tests allow for differences in test takers' ages and levels of understanding.

Digital SAT Suite: Overall Test Specifications

Characteristic	Reading and Writing section	Math section
Administration	Two-stage adaptive design; this section contains two separately timed modules	Two-stage adaptive design; this section contains two separately timed modules
Number of questions	54 questions; 25 questions in each module with 2 pretest ques	44 questions; 20 questions in each module with 2 pretest ques
Time	64 minutes	70 minutes
Time per question	1.19 minutes	1.59 minutes
Time per module	32 minutes	35 minutes
Content domains	Information and Ideas, Craft and Structure, Expression of Ideas, Standard English Conventions	Algebra, Advanced Math, Problem-Solving and Data Analysis, Geometry and Trigonometry

Test Length

There are a total of 54 questions for the Reading and Writing section. These 54 questions are divided into two equal-length modules; that is, one for each of the section's two stages. Out of the 27 questions for each module, **25 questions are operational**—which means that test takers' performance on them is used to calculate their section score, and **2 questions are pretests**.

For the Math section, the first module has 20 operational questions and 2 pretest questions. Then the second module consists of 20 operational questions and 2 pretest questions. In total, the Math section will comprise 44 questions.

Time Per Module

You will have 32 minutes to complete each module of the Reading and Writing section and 35 minutes to complete each module of the Math section. Once the time for the first module has expired, test takers are automatically advanced to the second module. The second module may contain questions that are of higher or lower difficulty, depending on your performance in the first module. You will not have the opportunity to return to the first-module questions.

Total Number of Questions

The Reading and Writing section consists of 54 questions (4 of which are pretest), while the Math section consists of 44 questions (4 of which are, again, pretest questions)

Total Time Allotted

You will have 64 minutes to complete the Reading and Writing section and 70 minutes to complete the Math section.

Average Time Per Question

You will, on average, have 1.19 minutes to answer each Reading and Writing question and 1.59 minutes to answer each Math question.

Question Format(s) used

The Reading and Writing section mostly utilizes four-option multiple-choice questions, and each question has a single best answer (**which is referred to as the keyed response or key**). Roughly 75 percent of questions in the Math section also adopt the same four-option multiple-choice format, while the remaining part of the test utilizes the **student-produced response (SPR) format.** This means that students will be required to answer the latter type of questions by giving their own responses and putting their responses in the field next to the question. These questions measure your ability to be able to solve math problems by yourself. It is possible for the SPR questions to have more than one correct response; however, you are required to provide only one answer.

Text Complexity

It is assumed that the complexity test takers can read is directly related to how ready they are for college and their careers. Therefore, the idea of text complexity is strictly considered when designing and developing the digital SAT Suite. The texts in the Reading and Writing section are given three complexity bands (grades 6–8, grades 9–11, and grades 12–14).

Texts for grades 12-14 have the highest complexity, followed by the texts for grades 9-11, while grades 6-8 have texts with the lowest complexity. While it is possible to use the same texts for grades 12-14 and grades 9-11, those difficult texts cannot be used for grades 6-8 because they don't appropriately assess the literacy knowledge and skills of students in eighth and ninth grades.

On the other hand, text complexity is not an issue in the Math section, because it is not formally measured. It is estimated that about 70 percent of Math questions don't necessarily have a context. You are only required to use the information/data provided to solve some questions that may be related to science, social studies, history, etc.

What is Changing

The College Board continues to maintain fairness and high quality in its administration of SAT Suite, and some aspects of its operations are changing. These changes include:

- Transitioning to digital testing by 2023 or 2024 latest. Once the transition is completed, students can no longer take the paper-and-pencil SAT tests.

- The digital SAT Suite tests are particularly shorter than their paper-and-pencil predecessors—it can be taken in 2 hours 14 minutes instead of 3 hours.

- Test takers now have more time on their hands to answer each question.

- It is now possible for you to receive scores in days instead of weeks, faster than the predecessor paper-and-pencil SAT.

- The SAT Suite now connects students to opportunities based on their scores. They can be connected to information and resources concerning local 2-year colleges, career options, and workforce training programs.

- States, schools, and districts will be given more flexibility concerning when they could give the SAT Suite tests.

- The digital SAT will now have a single Reading and Writing section instead of separate Reading and Writing and Language sections. More importantly, the Reading and Writing section's passages are significantly shorter and more diverse.

- A single (discrete) question is associated with each passage (or passage pair) instead of having several questions associated with a small number of longer passages, as it is for the paper-and-pencil SAT Suite tests.

- You can now use calculators throughout the Math section.

What is Staying the Same

Despite the above-mentioned changes, some aspects of the SAT Suite tests are remaining the same, such as:

- The Digital SAT will still measure skills and knowledge that you are learning in school that can be used in college and/or your future career.

- The test will be scored on the same scales as the paper-and-pencil test.

- The test will be administered in schools and test centers with a proctor.

- You will still be connected to scholarships and the College Board National Recognition Programs.

- Support will be given to all students who need accommodations and/or support to access the tests and their content.

- The Reading/Writing passages will cover a wide range of academic disciplines and text complexities.

- The test will still have both multiple-choice and student-produced response question formats.

1. **When will I be able to register for the digital SAT tests?**

   The first digital SAT administrations at international test centers will start in the fall 2023.

2. **How will students take the digital SAT?**

   You can give the SAT on a laptop or tablet using a custom-built digital exam application that can be downloaded in advance of the test day.

3. **How will the Digital SAT be more secure?**

   At this moment, if one test form is compromised, it can mean that the scores for all the students in that group or at the same test centers will be canceled. However, going digital will make it possible to give every student a unique test form so that it won't be technically possible to share answers.

4. **How will the College Board address test day issues and technical support challenges?**

   The College Board has dedicated customer service resources ready to troubleshoot issues on test day for students and test centers. There is a technology coordinator for each test center to provide additional support and technical help when needed.

5. **What kinds of tools will be available for students taking the digital SAT?**

   You can use the following tools while using the software:

   - Flag questions to come back to them later
   - A countdown clock to know when you are running out of time. You can decide to show or hide it at the top of their testing screen
   - A built-in graphing calculator that you can use on the entire math section (or you can bring their own calculators)
   - A reference sheet, for each math question.

The Reading and Writing Section at a Glance

The table below summarizes the specifications of the types of questions and their distribution in the Reading and Writing section.

Content Domain	Skill/Knowledge	Question distribution
Information and Ideas	• Central Ideas and Details • Command of Evidence ▪ Textual and Quantitative • Inferences	12-14 questions (26%)
Craft and Structure	• Words in Context • Text Structure and Purpose • Cross-Text Connections	13-15 questions (28%)
Expression of Ideas	• Rhetorical Synthesis • Transitions	8-12 questions (20%)
Standard English Conventions	• Boundaries • Form, Structure, and Sense	11-15 questions (26%)

Sample Questions

1. The term "*Anthropocene*" introduced by Dutch scientist Paul Crutzen in the mid-1970s, is often used in the context of pollution caused by human activity since the commencement of the Agricultural Revolution, but also pertains largely to all major human bearings on the environment.

   Various start dates for the Anthropocene have been offered by scientists, ranging from the beginning of the first Agricultural Revolution, also known as the *Neolithic Revolution*, to as recently as the 1960s. However, the _____ has not been completed, and hence, a formal, conclusive date remains to be finalized.

   Which choice completes the text with the most logical and precise word or phrase?

   A) Ratification

   B) Investigation

   C) Legality

   D) Approval

   Key: A

   Level: Hard | **Domain:** CRAFT AND STRUCTURE

   Skill/Knowledge: Words in Context

   Key Explanation: Choice A is the correct option because "ratification" refers to the action of signing or giving formal consent to something, making it officially valid. This word is best suited to the context because the second paragraph of the passage talks about how many scientists have offered dates, but a conclusive date has yet to be finalized. The keywords to focus on are "formal, conclusive date" which points to which option (A) might be most suitable in this context.

Distractor Explanations: Choice B is incorrect because there is no evidence provided that an investigation may have been initiated into the subject. Similarly, **options C** and **D** are incorrect because the passage does not talk about any approval process or legalities that need to be completed for a date to be finalized.

2. Brazil's Atlantic Rainforest is among the most biodiverse regions in the world. But despite its spectacular diversity, _____. To counter this, the Society for the Conservation of Birds in Brazil advocates for birds in Brazil, their habitats, and biodiversity in general, and works towards sustainability in the use of natural resources. Their work focuses on educating local people on the importance of birds, biodiversity, and developing environmentally sustainable economic alternatives, along with good governance tools to empower local communities and improve the quality of life of local people.

What choice most logically completes the underlined space?

A) there are no more birds in the forest

B) the Society for the Conservation of Birds in Brazil cannot do much

C) the rainforest is under extreme threat from human development

D) there are a number of steps that one can take to preserve the Atlantic Rainforest

Key: C

Level: Medium | **Domain:** INFORMATION AND IDEAS

Skill/Knowledge: Command of Evidence (Textual)

Key Explanation: Choice C is the best answer because the first sentence talks about the diversity of the Atlantic Rainforest, while the third sentence talks about what the Society for the Conservation of Birds in Brazil is doing to counter said problem in the second sentence. They work by "educating local people" and "developing environmentally sustainable economic alternatives." Therefore, it may be inferred that the problem denoted in the underlined portion of the text involves humans and economics. Hence, using the process of elimination, choice C is the best answer.

Distractor Explanations: Choice A is incorrect because the text mentions "conservation of birds in Brazil," which means that birds may be endangered but not extinct. **Choice B** is incorrect because there is no information provided that supports this statement. **Choice D** is incorrect because it does not fit in the context of the sentence.

The Math Section at a Glance

The table below summarizes the specifications of the types of questions and their distribution in the Math section.

Content Domain	Skill/Knowledge	Question Distribution
Algebra	<ul><li>Linear equations in one variable</li><li>Linear equations in two variables</li><li>Linear functions</li><li>Systems of two linear equations in two variables</li><li>Linear inequalities in one or two variables</li></ul>	13-15 questions (35%)
Advanced Math	<ul><li>Equivalent expressions</li><li>Nonlinear equations in one variable and systems of equations in two variables</li><li>Nonlinear functions</li></ul>	13-15 questions (35%)
Problem-Solving and Data Analysis	<ul><li>Ratios, rates, proportional relationships, and units</li><li>Percentages</li><li>One-variable data: distributions and measures of center and spread</li><li>Two-variable data: models and scatterplots</li><li>Probability and conditional probability</li><li>Inference from sample statistics and margin of error</li><li>Evaluating statistical claims: observational studies and experiments</li></ul>	5-7 questions (15%)
Geometry and Trigonometry	<ul><li>Area and volume</li><li>Lines, angles, and triangles</li><li>Right triangles and trigonometry</li><li>Circles</li></ul>	5-7 questions (15%)

1. The dog park charges $10 for a membership and $3 per hour for the dog to run around in their park. Mindy brings her dog to the park and spends less than $40. Which of the following inequalities represents Mindy's situation, where h is the number of hours at the park and C is the total amount Mindy paid?

   A) $3h + 10 < 40$

   B) $3C - 10 < 40$

   C) $3h + 10 = 40$

   D) $3h + 10 > 40$

   Key: A

   Level: Easy | **Domain:** ALGEBRA

   Skill/Knowledge: Linear inequalities in one or two variables | **Testing Point:** Create a linear inequality

   Key Explanation: Choice A is correct. To determine the inequality that represents the situation, first create the expression that is equal to the total amount that Mindy paid (C).

   The total amount C is the sum of the membership fee ($10) and the fee for having the dog in the park in h hours. This yields $C = 10 + 3h$ or $C = 3h + 10$.

   Since Mindy spent less than $40 in the dog park, then $C < 40$. Substituting the value of C in terms of h in the inequality yields $3h + 10 < 40$.

   Therefore, the inequality $3h + 10 < 40$ is the correct answer.

   Distractor Explanation: Choice B is incorrect. This option is wrong because C is the total amount paid by Mindy and not the rate per hour for the dog to run around the park. **Choices C** and **D** are incorrect. Mindy spent less than $40. Hence, the correct symbol to use is < not > or =.

2. Which expression is equivalent to $2x^2 + 3x + 1$?

   A) $(2x + 1)(2x + 1)$

   B) $(x + 2)(x + 1)$

   C) $(x - 2)(x - 1)$

   D) $(2x + 1)(x + 1)$

   Key: D

   Level: Easy | **Domain:** ADVANCED MATH

   Skill/Knowledge: Equivalent Expressions | **Testing Point:** Factoring a quadratic equation

   Key Explanation: Choice D is correct.
   To find the equivalent expression, factor the given quadratic equation by splitting the middle term.
   In $2x^2 + 3x + 1$, $a = 2$, $b = 3$ and $c = 1$ using the format $ax^2 + bx + c$.
   Getting the product of a and c yields $ac = (2)(1) = 2$

The factors of 2 whose sum is the value of b (where $b = 3$) is 2 and 1.

Hence, the equation can be written as $2x^2 + 2x + x + 1$.

Grouping the binomials in the equation yields $(2x^2 + 2x) + (x + 1)$.

Factoring $2x$ from the first group yields $2x(x + 1) + (x + 1)$.

Factoring $x + 1$ from the two groups yields $(2x + 1)(x + 1)$.

Therefore, Choice D is the correct answer.

Distractor Explanation: Choices A, B, and C are incorrect and may result from a conceptual or calculation error.

Chapter 2

....

Practice Test 1

You are about to begin a full-length Practice Test. The test has four modules. The time allotted for each module is marked at the beginning of the module. Work on one module at a time. Use a timer to keep track of the time limits for every module.

Try to take the Practice Test under real test conditions. Find a quiet place to work, and set aside enough time to complete the test without being disturbed. At the end of the test, check your answers by referring to the Answer Key and fill in your raw score in the scorecard below. Also, note down the time taken by you for completing each module.

Pay particular attention to the questions that were answered incorrectly. Read the answer explanations and understand how to solve them.

....

My Score Card (Raw Score)

	Reading and Writing		Math	
	Module 1	Module 2	Module 1	Module 2
Out of	27	27	22	22
My Score	_____	_____	_____	_____
Time Taken	_____	_____	_____	_____

TEST BEGINS ON THE NEXT PAGE

Reading and Writing Test

27 QUESTIONS | 32 MINUTES

DIRECTIONS

The questions in this section address a number of important reading and writing skills. Each question includes one or more passages, which may include a table or graph. Read each passage and question carefully, and then choose the best answer to the question based on the passage(s). All questions in this section are multiple–choice with four answer choices. Each question has a single best answer.

1

Allowing goats to graze an area is one potential solution for removing unwanted weeds in terrain that is too rocky and remote to allow for cutting or herbicide spraying. Goats significantly reduce the incidence of the unwanted plants, but must be quickly removed to prevent them from eating everything else as well: goats lack _____.

Which choice completes the text with the most logical and precise word or phrase?

A) bias

B) prejudice

C) discrimination

D) bigotry

2

Anyone interested in a career in business needs superior communications skills. Not only are they essential to convey ideas to colleagues and explain plans clearly to ensure that work is completed effectively in a timely manner, but also they are needed to make proposals _____ to clients and potential investors.

Which choice completes the text with the most logical and precise word or phrase?

A) charismatic

B) irresistible

C) attractive

D) fascinating

3

Explaining the coexistence of various plant and butterfly species is _____ to truly understand the region's biodiversity and the forces that sustain or reduce it. Such an understanding will help ecologists devise an appropriate plan that maximizes the limited funding available for conservation and that still allows for future development of the area.

Which choice completes the text with the most logical and precise word or phrase?

A) critical

B) perilous

C) condemning

D) analytical

4

The Hagia Sophia, built between 532 and 537 in Istanbul under the orders of the Roman Emperor Justinian I, has been alternately used for different religious purposes since that time. The cultural and historical value of the building and its contents are _____, as a wealth of splendid and unique details has been added over the centuries since its construction.

Which choice completes the text with the most logical and precise word or phrase?

A) congenial

B) incalculable

C) cumbersome

D) voluminous

5

By analyzing more than one million surface ocean observations from the Drake Passage, the researchers detected subtle differences between the CO_2 trends in the surface ocean and the atmosphere that suggest a strengthening of the carbon sink that is most pronounced during winter. Although the researchers aren't sure of the exact mechanism driving these changes, it's likely related to winter mixing with deep waters that have not had contact with the atmosphere for several hundred years. These results contrast with previous findings that showed that the Southern Ocean's CO_2 sink had been stagnant or weakening from the early 1990s to the early 2000s. "Given the importance of the Southern Ocean to the global oceans' role in absorbing atmospheric CO_2, these studies suggest that we must continue to expand our measurements in this part of the world despite the challenging environment," says Colm Sweeney, lead investigator on the Drake Passage study.

Which choice best states the main purpose of the text?

A) To emphasize the difficulty of collecting accurate data from the Southern Ocean

B) To illustrate the problems with amassing an adequate database on the Southern Ocean

C) To place the results of the Drake Passage study in the wider context of other studies

D) To highlight the need to correct the problem of CO_2 absorption before it is too late

6

The following text is from Oscar Wilde's 1888 short story "The Selfish Giant."

Every afternoon, as they were coming from school, the children used to go and play in the Giant's garden. <u>It was a large lovely garden, with soft green grass.</u> Here and there over the grass stood beautiful flowers like stars, and there were twelve peach–trees that in the spring–time broke out into delicate blossoms of pink and pearl, and in the autumn bore rich fruit. The birds sat on the trees and sang so sweetly that the children used to stop their games in order to listen to them.

Which choice best states the function of the underlined sentence in the text as a whole?

A) It sets up the description of location presented in the sentences that follow.

B) It establishes a sense of contrast with the description in the previous sentence.

C) It elaborates on the previous sentence's description of the characters.

D) It introduces an ominous undercurrent to the sentences that follow.

7

An antibody–based drug is one candidate for a more effective, longer lasting overdose treatment. To explore this possibility, a team at Scripps Research Institute led by Kim D. Janda first treated mice with a vaccine that stimulated the animals to produce a slew of different antibodies against fentanyl, some of which helped protect the mice from overdoses. In the new work, the team recovered antibodies from the mice, purified them, and screened them for their ability to bind fentanyl. The team evaluated six of these antibodies against nine fentanyl analogs commonly confiscated by law enforcement. One antibody, 6A4, demonstrated the best fentanyl–binding affinity and had a six–day half–life in mice.

Which choice best explains why the author most likely included the information that the drugs were "commonly confiscated by law enforcement"?

A) To explain how the researchers obtained drugs for experimentation

B) To indicate that the research would apply to overdoses in authentic cases

C) To eliminate the argument that the trials were improperly conducted

D) To establish why special permits were needed to experiment with the drugs

Text 1

The views of most individuals are limited to their own happiness; and the workmen whom I beheld so busy in the arsenal of Venice saw nothing but what was good in the labor for which they received... We must have the telescope of philosophy to make us perceive distant ills; further, we know that there are individuals of our species to whom the immediate misery of others is nothing in comparison with their own advantage—for we know that in every age there have been found men very willing to perform the office of executioner.

Text 2

… it is by no means a utopian undertaking to unite the whole world of nations in such a federation … Let men but understand themselves, and the mechanism of their emotions by which they are brought into this perennial catastrophe, and they will be ready enough to take gigantic measures to prevent it.

Which statement made by the author of passage 1 would support the underlined concluding argument made by the author of passage 2?

A) "We must have the telescope of philosophy to perceive distant ills."

B) "The views of most individuals are limited to their own happiness"

C) "there are individuals of our species to whom the immediate misery of others is nothing in comparison with their own advantage"

D) "in every age there have been found men very willing to perform the office of executioner"

9

The following text is adapted from Herman Melville's 1851 novel, *Moby Dick; or The Whale.*

Call me Ishmael. Some years ago—never mind how long precisely—having little or no money in my purse, and nothing particular to interest me on shore, I thought I would sail about a little and see the watery part of the world. It is a way I have of driving off the spleen and regulating the circulation. Whenever I find myself growing grim about the mouth; whenever it is a damp, drizzly November in my soul; whenever I find myself involuntarily bringing up the rear of every funeral I meet—then, I account it high time to get to sea as soon as I can. If they but knew it, almost all men in their degree, some time or other, cherish very nearly the same feelings towards the ocean with me.

Which choice best summarizes the text?

A) A ship captain describes the reasons for embarking on his career.

B) A sailor reminisces about the impetus for setting out on a voyage.

C) A merchant sailor develops an argument about his poor salary.

D) An impoverished man explains how he degenerated to his current condition.

10

The common solution of building more roads may not have the desired effect of reducing rush–hour traffic. For example, the Katy Freeway project in Houston cost millions of dollars and the upshot was that congestion got worse, with travel times increased by 55% during the evening rush hour and by a third in the mornings. The reason for that is something called "induced demand," a term introduced in the 1960s by economists. It relates to the phenomenon that if more of a good is produced, more is consumed. In the same way, if more roads are provided, more people are encouraged to drive.

According to the text, what is induced demand?

A) An idea that contradicts a widespread belief that congestion is the result of road building

B) A phenomenon that is rarely taken into account when road systems are being planned

C) A theory that is understood by city planners and has affected their traditional solutions to traffic congestion

D) A concept that can be mitigated by educating consumers about the potential effects

11

Published in 1794 by William Blake, "The Tyger" is a classic poem from a larger collection titled Songs of Experience. The poem uses the imagery of fire to delve into the question of who might have created such a dangerous creature: _____

Which quotation from "The Tyger" most effectively illustrates the claim?

A) "In what distant deeps or skies, / Burnt the fire of thine eyes?"

B) "In what furnace was thy brain? /What the anvil? what dread grasp / Dare its deadly terrors clasp?"

C) "When the stars threw down their spears, / And water'd heaven with their tears, / Did he smile his work to see?

D) "Did he who made the Lamb make thee?"

12

The following text is adapted from Mother Jones's speech to coal miners picketing in Charlestown, West Virginia, on August 15, 1912.

They wouldn't keep their dog where they keep you fellows. You know that. They have a good place for their dogs and a slave to take care of them. The mine owners' wives will take the dogs up, and say, "I love you, dea–h." My friends, the day for petting dogs is gone; the day for raising children to a nobler manhood and better womanhood is here! You have suffered; I know you have suffered. I was with you nearly three years in this State. I went to jail. I went to the federal courts, but I never took any back water!

In the text, Mother Jones anticipates and addresses which counterargument about her credibility?

A) She is not qualified to speak for the miners because she is not a miner herself.

B) Her involvement could harm the miners' cause because she had been in jail.

C) She does not have adequate contacts in the government to enforce her demands.

D) She has been more caring of pets in the past than she has of human workers.

13

Chili Peppers Exposed to Salt Stress

NaCl concentration (mM)	Average days to first flower	Average days to first fruit	Average number of fruits
0	23.66	48	6
30	23.66	52	3
60	31.66	66	2
90	39.66	0	0
120	40.33	0	0

This study about salt in the soil of growing chili plants indicated that increasing NaCl concentrations significantly delayed flowering and fruit ripening and significantly reduced the fruits' number, size, fresh mass and vitamins B6, B12 and C concentrations, but increased capsaicinoid concentration and consequently the fruit's tangy flavor. For example, plants _____. Thus, salt stress reduced the fruit yields and deteriorated fruit nutritional quality by reducing vitamin concentrations. Further study is necessary to check the implication of capsaicinoid synthetase activity in the increase of the capsaicinoid concentration under salt stress in our local chili cultivar fruits.

Which choice most effectively uses data from the table to complete the example?

A) subjected to high NaCl concentrations were highest in capsaicinoid.

B) subjected to high NaCl concentrations had lower nutritional value.

C) with a NaCl concentration of 90 mM took 16 extra days to flower beyond ones with no salt.

D) with a NaCl concentration of 30 mM averaged 52 chili fruits on the plant.

14

A study led by Sarah Mann aimed to provide a fuller picture of the vegan diet in which no animal products are eaten, encompassing the health of the vegan diet as well as related ethical beliefs by studying scientific and popular literature in tandem. Furthermore, the study aimed to provide an insider's perspective of the vegan diet as a means of combating stereotypes and making the diet more relatable/understandable to those who are not vegan. The research was conducted in two parts – literature review and interview study. The interviews included questions targeting personal history, related health beliefs, factors influencing the decision to become vegan, and diet.

Based on the text, why did Mann include personal interviews in her study?

A) She assumed she would find a conflict between interviews and scientific studies.

B) She expected to resolve an outstanding debate about the health benefits of veganism.

C) She decided that most of the current literature was biased against the subject of veganism.

D) She hoped to better understand the viewpoint of people who opted to become vegan.

15

Scientists studying at a site called Hegra in modern Jordan found the tomb of a woman called Hinat. Her name was identified in an inscription at the entrance which claims the tomb was bought by herself and belonging to her and her descendants. Archaeologists have found the remains of over 80 people buried inside, though none of them are identified. The tomb also contains many well–preserved artifacts that offer insight into the Nabataean culture that flourished in the region about 2,000 years ago.

Based on the passage, what is most likely true about Hinat?

A) She was a royal Nabataean personage.

B) She had her own tomb because she never married.

C) She is buried with many of her ancestors.

D) She was one of the 80 people buried in the tomb.

16

It is inevitable that a world–wide event such as the Olympics has been canceled multiple times since its introduction in 1896. One notable example is when London called _____ the 1944 Summer Olympics due to World War II, as were the Winter Olympics scheduled to be held in Cortina d'Ampezzo, Italy.

Which choice completes the text so that it conforms to the conventions of Standard English?

A) on

B) up

C) off

D) around

17

Yuval Noah Harari is an Israeli historian who regularly discussed global issues with world leaders. Considered one of the foremost thinkers of his time, his current interest is delving into difficult questions combining biology and history, such as asking whether people _____ happier since the Stone Age to the present.

Which choice completes the text so that it conforms to the conventions of Standard English?

A) become

B) are becoming

C) have become

D) will have become

CONTINUE

18

Energy access and gender are deeply entwined components of the global development agenda. The transformative effect on women of access to affordable, reliable, and sustainable modern energy _____ well established by countless research studies.

Which choice completes the text so that it conforms to the conventions of Standard English?

A) are

B) were

C) has been

D) have been

19

Many theories have been proposed for how life originated on Earth, and attention has recently been directed towards hydrothermal vents, _____ occur deep underwater where continental plates diverge. In 2019, scientists from University College London conducted an experiment simulating the concentrated gasses and minerals and created protocells, or the building blocks for living molecules.

Which choice completes the text so that it conforms to the conventions of Standard English?

A) which

B) they

C) that

D) these

20

Attending the cinema allows for the exercise of personal preferences and the human need for distinction. In a nutshell, cinema attendance can be a personally expressive experience, good _____ therapeutic at the same time.

Which choice completes the text so that it conforms to the conventions of Standard English?

A) fun, and,

B) fun, and

C) fun; and

D) fun—and

21

In a 2022 paper written by Kyle Rupp and _____ the researchers explore the complex mechanisms behind the automatic ability that most people have to recognize features of the human voice, even to the point of distinguishing subtleties of emotion and intention.

Which choice completes the text so that it conforms to the conventions of Standard English?

A) associates

B) associates,

C) associates—

D) associates:

22

Even within a single musical tradition, there may be fine distinctions based on the character and color of the voice. _____ a lyric soprano has a light, refined tone and a dramatic soprano has a powerful, emotional tone.

Which choice completes the text so that it conforms to the conventions of Standard English?

A) For example among operatic voices

B) For example, among operatic voices:

C) For example: among operatic voices,

D) For example, among operatic voices,

23

The energy industry has long met demand by varying the rate at which it produces fuel. Controlling the output of an oil–fired power plant is much like changing the speed of a car—press the accelerator and more gas flows to the engine. _____ the wind cannot be turned up or down. Smart software is one solution to make wind farms more efficient and responsive.

Which choice completes the text with the most logical transition?

A) Nevertheless,

B) Despite this,

C) Furthermore,

D) However,

24

Social work can take a toll, but it is deeply rewarding when you can see a positive change in someone else's life. There are many different career paths in social work. _____ there are some administrative roles, most all social workers deal directly with clients. So regardless of the field you choose, you are most likely to interact with people on a regular basis.

Which choice completes the text with the most logical transition?

A) However,

B) While

C) Nevertheless,

D) Therefore,

25

The Paleo diet includes meat, fruit, and vegetables in an attempt to recreate the eating patterns of prehistoric hunter–gatherers. Although it is a popular way to lose weight in the short term, there is no long–term credible research confirming its efficacy. _____ many scientists point out that the diet is misguided because wild grains were consumed well before the advent of farming.

Which choice completes the text with the most logical transition?

A) Subsequently,

B) Nevertheless,

C) Moreover,

D) Therefore,

26

The London and Northwestern Railway War Memorial is a First World War memorial outside Euston Station in London, England. The memorial was designed by Reginald Wynn Owen and _____ employees of the London and Northwestern Railway (LNWR) who were killed in the First World War.

Which word most logically completes the text?

A) commemorates

B) idolizes

C) celebrates

D) overlooks

27

In May, 1992, the Ministry of Forestry in Vietnam and the World Wildlife Federation jointly conducted a survey and came across an astounding discovery: the first new large mammal species identified in half a century. Called a saola, both the males and females have horns. Almost nothing is known of their behavior, though they are classified as critically endangered.

The writer wants to change the underlined portion to emphasize the rarity of the saola. Which choice most effectively achieves that goal?

A) The first indication of a new species was when scientists discovered a skull in a hunter's home.

B) There are currently none in captivity and they live in mountains in Vietnam and Laos.

C) Since the initial sighting, they have only been positively identified on four occasions.

D) They have the fanciful common name of "Asian unicorns," though they have two horns.

No Test Material On This Page

Reading Test

27 QUESTIONS | 32 MINUTES

DIRECTIONS

The questions in this section address a number of important reading and writing skills. Each question includes one or more passages, which may include a table or graph. Read each passage and question carefully, and then choose the best answer to the question based on the passage(s). All questions in this section are multiple–choice with four answer choices. Each question has a single best answer.

1

Any country, city, or rural village could be, in fact, its own unique tourism magnet. The tourism business, though, is <u>broader</u> than just the destination. Considerations need to be made for transportation, hotels and guest accommodations, and services that link the various components of a trip, such as guide services in national parks or city bus tours.

As used in the text, what does the word "broader" most nearly mean?

A) more pronounced

B) more general

C) more spacious

D) more extensive

2

The following text is from Jane Austen's 1811 novel, "Sense and Sensibility."

Many were the tears shed by them in their last adieus to a place so much beloved. "And you, ye well–known trees," said Marianne, "but you will continue the same, unconscious of the pleasure or the regret you occasion, and <u>insensible</u> of any change in those who walk under your shade! But who will remain to enjoy you?"

As used in the text, what does the word "insensible" most nearly mean?

A) comatose

B) negligible

C) unaware

D) insentient

3

The following text is adapted from F. Scott Fitzgerald's 1922 novel, *The Beautiful and the Damned.*

Now Adam J. Patch left his father's farm in Tarrytown early in sixty-one to join a New York cavalry regiment. He came home from the war a major, charged into Wall Street, and amid much fuss, <u>fume</u>, applause, and ill will he gathered to himself some seventy-five million dollars.

As used in the text, what does the word "fume" most nearly mean?

A) exhaust

B) stench

C) pollution

D) ire

4

Sometimes, behaviors have underlying reasons that are not initially apparent, as shown through a classic experiment by Walter Mischel. During the 1960s, Mischel placed a marshmallow piece in front of 600 children aged 4–6. About a third were willing to wait 15 minutes to get a whole marshmallow, and those children got higher SAT scores years later. However, Mischel's theory that willpower contributed to future success was somewhat arbitrary. A later experiment conducted by Tyler Watts and associates included a broader analysis of ethnicity and social status and determined that economic background most closely predicted the demonstrated behavior.

Which choice best states the main purpose of the text?

A) It presents the study by Tyler Watts to show that most behavioral psychology experiments are flawed.

B) It argues that experiments regarding behavior should be performed multiple times in order to determine true correlations.

C) It explains a significant problem in the current understanding of willpower in young children.

D) It discusses the study by Walter Mischel to show that there may be alternate explanations in an apparently obvious situation.

5

The following text is adapted from Abraham Lincoln's last public address, given April 11, 1865.

Some twelve thousand voters in the heretofore slave-state of Louisiana have sworn allegiance to the Union, assumed to be the rightful political power of the State, held elections, organized a State government, adopted a free-state constitution, and empowered the Legislature to confer the elective franchise upon the colored man. Now, if we reject, and spurn them, we do our utmost to disorganize and disperse them. We in effect say to the white men, "You are worthless, or worse--we will neither help you, nor be helped by you." To the blacks we say, "This cup of liberty which these, your old masters, hold to your lips, we will dash from you, and leave you to the chances of gathering the spilled and scattered contents in some vague and undefined when, where, and how."

In the text, what does the imagery of a cup of liberty mainly serve to emphasize?

A) The generosity of the Union in giving freed slaves certain benefits

B) The advances made by the Union in protecting the rights of former slaves

C) The unconscious way in which many people accept their freedoms

D) The precarious nature of the freedoms granted to former slaves in Louisiana

6

The median annual wage for urban and regional planners was $73,050 in May 2018. The median wage is the wage at which half the workers in an occupation earned more than that amount and half earned less. The lowest 10 percent earned less than $45,180, and the highest 10 percent earned more than $114,170. Employment of urban and regional planners is projected to grow 11 percent from 2018 to 2028, much faster than the average for all occupations. Demographic, transportation, and environmental changes will drive employment growth for planners. Within cities, urban planners will be needed to develop revitalization projects and address issues associated with population growth, environmental degradation, the movement of people and goods, and resource scarcity.

Which choice best states the function of the underlined sentence in the text as whole?

A) To define a term provided in the passage

B) To point out that the median wage is an insufficient measurement

C) To suggest a possible reason for the wide range in salaries

D) To provide support for the claim that employment is predicted to grow

Text 1

Depression is an illness of brain circuitry and chemistry that causes and is caused by changes in mood, thinking, and behavior. Behavioral activation is a type of talk therapy that helps patients free themselves from negative mood spirals by identifying a connection between actions and emotions, and gradually add small and enjoyable actions back into their lives. The process decreases avoidance, bolsters peer connection, and improves engagement in activities. This non–intrusive solution takes time, but is much healthier than covering the problem with medications.

Text 2

Studies have shown that a single ketamine infusion can often rapidly relieve depressive symptoms within hours in people who have not responded to conventional antidepressants, which typically take weeks or months to work. However, widespread use of ketamine for treatment–resistant depression has raised concerns about side effects, including feelings of floating, queasiness, visual distortions, and numbness. These conditions occurred in at least half of the participants of one study, but none persisted for more than four hours. To overcome these problems, ongoing research is necessary to develop a more practical rapid–acting antidepressant that works in the brain similarly to ketamine.

Based on the texts, how would the author of Text 1 most likely view the conclusion drawn by the author in the final sentence of Text 2?

A) Agreement, because she knows most depression treatments are insufficient

B) Reservation, because she promotes less invasive ways to address depression

C) Confusion, because she feels that the drug does not need any modification

D) Disapproval, because she contends that drug therapies are unacceptable

The following text is adapted from Jefferson Keel's 2011 statement, "The Indian Reorganization Act—75 Years Later."

Our predecessors had a shared vision. Indian reservations should be places where the old ways are maintained, our languages are spoken, and our children learn our traditions and pass them on. They are places where there are fish in the stream and game in the field, and food grows wild; places where our people can live and be Indian. At the same time, this vision includes modern life, economic development to sustain our people; safety and respectful relationships with our neighbors; and the blessings of education, health care and modern technology. This vision was shared by the U.S. Congress in 1934 when it passed the Indian Reorganization Act. With the IRA, Congress renewed its trust responsibility to protect and restore our tribal homelands and the Indian way of life.

What is the main idea of the text?

A) The Indian Reorganization Act is a policy in keeping with the view of the earlier Indian people themselves.

B) The Indian Reorganization Act was written by Indian predecessors in order to preserve traditional culture.

C) The Indian Reorganization Act was created in the effort to deny Native Americans the basic rights they wished for.

D) The Indian Reorganization Act has been successful in helping Native American cultures to thrive since it was enacted.

The following text is adapted from Fyodor Dostoevsky's 1848 short story collection, "White Nights and Other Stories."

I came back to the town very late, and it had struck ten as I was going towards my lodgings. My way lay along the canal embankment, where at that hour you never meet a soul. It is true that I live in a very remote part of the town. I walked along singing, for when I am happy I am always humming to myself like every happy man who has no friend or acquaintance with whom to share his joy. Suddenly I had a most unexpected adventure.

According to the text, what is the reason the narrator is walking along the embankment late at night?

A) He wanted to avoid meeting other people.

B) He was escaping the pressures of the city.

C) He was returning to his quarters.

D) He sought more excitement in his life.

10

As for tidal devices, the environmental impacts are considered comparably small. Wave devices will represent a much lower collision risk compared to offshore wind devices but they could create a risk of underwater collisions for diving birds. In general, environmental impacts will very much depend on the size of installation and the location selected. Potential positive effects such as the creation of roosting sites and habitat enhancement for marine birds might occur as well. The majority of the studies recommend that commercial–scale installations of ocean energy technology should be accompanied by research studies on local environmental impacts.

According to the text, which of the following will most determine how much a tidal system alters the environment?

A) The placement in the ocean

B) The number of moving parts

C) The number of research studies about it

D) The total energy it generates

11

Over the past 30 years, scientists have discovered many dinosaurs from the group known as Carcharodontosauridae, but a lack of complete fossils led to many assumptions about their structure and movement. However, a recent find in Argentina of a species named *Meraxes gigas* gives new insights. Standing 11 meters (36 feet) and weighing 4 tons, the carnivore probably appeared very much like the unrelated *Tyrannosaurus rex*. This conclusion is partly based on the discovery of an almost intact arm bone that is extremely short like those of *T. rex*.

Which finding, if true, would most strongly support the scientists' conclusion?

A) *M. gigas* and *T. rex* were discovered to have lived in time periods separated by about 20 million years.

B) The skull bones from the *M. gigas* fossil are oversized in proportion to the body, as are those of *T. rex* fossils.

C) The average size of an adult *T. rex* varied greatly, between 5 tons and almost 7 tons.

D) Remains from both *T. rex* and M. gigas show that they both were carnivores which preyed on mostly herbivorous dinosaurs.

12

Biodiversity: Trees in Southern Ontario
(percentage of total trees)

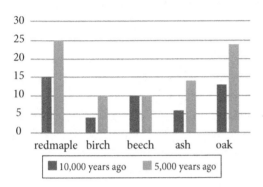

10,000 years ago 5,000 years ago

In 2003, a team of researchers studied ancient forest diversity through analyzing pollen samples in a lakebed. "What we are seeing is huge variability within tree populations over time," said scientist James Clark. For example,_____ He explained that this variability means they overlap in ways that determine which species are going to thrive and which are going to go extinct. He also proposed that the variability might itself represent a stabilizing mechanism. Clark emphasized, however, that even though the role of stabilizing mechanisms remains unknown, the results from the studies offer cautionary lessons.

Which choice most effectively uses data from the table to complete the example?

A) the percent of red maple increased by 10 percent over the time period studied.

B) the populations of beech remained stable over the time period in the study.

C) there were always fewer birch trees than ash trees in the time period studied.

D) the percentage of oak trees decreased by approximately 10 percent over the study period.

13

A seller who makes a claim about how much money a person can earn opening a franchise must provide a document that says in big type: EARNINGS CLAIM STATEMENT REQUIRED BY LAW. This document has to include many statistics including the specifics of the claim; the start and end date those earnings were achieved; the number and percentage of people who got those results or better, and any information about those people that may differ from you – for example, the part of the country where they live. Since the Rule gives the right to see written proof for the seller's earnings claims, savvy buyers exercise that right and study those materials carefully.

Which statement best identifies one of the author's implicit claims about the Earnings Claim Statement Required by Law?

A) Demographic factors may affect a franchise's earnings.

B) The earnings claims must be updated every month.

C) Most sellers do not provide the statement willingly.

D) The document is required with any building purchase.

14

A serious financial investment is needed to bring Sub–Saharan Africa up to par with the global marketplace. Africa has huge potential for growth in its tourism market, but heavy tourism traffic might have a negative impact on the environment, cultural stereotypes could be exploited, and the disparity between wealthy tourists and service workers earning a modest wage may lend itself to divisions and social friction. Tourism demands higher levels of security and public health at all levels. Money spent on tourism development is money not spent on schools or clinics. On the other hand, without tourism income, there are no jobs.

One conclusion that can be drawn about the negative impact of tourism in Africa is that

A) jobs created may not provide adequate employment for all community members.

B) most of the income from tourism will not benefit the local communities at all.

C) an increase in tourism would result in a loss of local culture and traditions.

D) individuals who work in the industry may become resentful of visitors.

15

You must respect copyright laws when composing music. When you sample _____ artist's music without obtaining permission, you're infringing on the copyright to that work, no matter how big or how small a portion of it you actually use.

Which choice completes the text so that it conforms to the conventions of Standard English?

A) another

B) other

C) every

D) others

16

Although many people feel that the court system is too complicated and takes too long to bring a criminal to justice, it is an essential part of a democratic government. Imagine a world in which a _____ guilty person is condemned to death without a trial or any method of recourse.

Which choice completes the text so that it conforms to the conventions of Standard English?

A) presumed

B) presumption

C) presumably

D) presumptive

CONTINUE

17

Known best for his famous *Lord of the Rings* trilogy, author J.R.R. Tolkien also completed a translation of the epic poem "Beowulf" in 1926. His son found the manuscript and had it published in 2014, 40 years after _____ death.

Which choice completes the text so that it conforms to the conventions of Standard English?

A) his

B) Tolkiens

C) Tolkiens'

D) Tolkien's

18

Recently, astronomers discovered two new rocky planets approximately the size of Earth. Smaller than our Sun, _____ making the two planets orbiting it potentially close enough to study their atmospheres in detail. Since the cooler of the two is estimated to be 543 degrees Fahrenheit (284 degrees Celsius), there is little chance of life as we know it, though.

Which choice completes the text so that it conforms to the conventions of Standard English?

A) there are only 33 light years between the red dwarf star HD260655 and our Solar System,

B) only 33 light years separate the red dwarf star HD260655 from our Solar System,

C) our Solar System is only 33 light years away from the red dwarf star HD260655,

D) the red dwarf star HD260655 is only 33 light years away from our solar system,

19

In 1967, Kenyan writer Ngugi wa Thiong'o worked as a lecturer in the department of English at the University of _____ "A Grain of Wheat in July" in the same year. He became instrumental in a movement that advanced African literature.

Which choice completes the text so that it conforms to the conventions of Standard English?

A) Nairobi and published

B) Nairobi, and published

C) Nairobi and published,

D) Nairobi, and published,

20

People often join martial arts such as karate, judo, and taekwondo in order to increase their amount of weekly exercise in an interesting way. Those who participate for extended periods, though, typically cite the development of personal qualities—particularly _____ the reason they continue.

Which choice completes the text so that it conforms to the conventions of Standard English?

A) self-control—

B) self-control—as

C) self-control—which is

D) self-control— they say is

21

Rainwater harvesting is the collection of run-off from a structure or other impervious surface in order to store it for later use. Rainwater collection systems can be as simple _____ rain in a rain barrel or as elaborate as harvesting rainwater into large cisterns to supply your entire household demand.

Which choice completes the text so that it conforms to the conventions of Standard English?

A) as: collecting

B) as, collecting

C) as—collecting

D) as collecting

22

The delicate art of Kamāl ud-Dīn Behzād, who was born circa 1455, is often considered the apogee of Islamic miniature paintings. Director of a workshop in the Herat Academy, Behzād had great influence, and his work was copied extensively both _____ his lifetime.

Which choice completes the text so that it conforms to the conventions of Standard English?

A) during, and after

B) during and after,

C) during—and after

D) during and after

23

Most people have heard of search and rescue dogs, which assist the police and other responders in finding victims of crimes or natural disasters. There are two work methods that the dogs follow.. Trailing dogs follow the specific scent of one person along the path that the person took. _____ air–scent dogs sniff the general vicinity until they find any individual in the search region.

Which choice completes the text with the most logical transition?

A) Because of this,

B) By contrast,

C) Therefore,

D) Moreover,

24

It may seem that all mosquitoes hate the human race, but in reality, only the females require blood to obtain a specific protein needed to produce eggs. Males do not drink blood. _____ even if they wanted to, they do not have the mouthparts to pierce skin. It turns out that mosquitoes get most of their energy from plant nectar and fruit.

Which choice completes the text with the most logical transition?

A) Therefore,

B) Finally,

C) In fact,

D) Namely,

25

The effects of climate change are noticeable now: average temperatures are increasing, storms are more severe, and droughts are more common. In order to protect our planet and life as we know it, we _____ make changes to our daily routines as quickly as possible. If everyone works together, even small alterations such as eating more vegetables or taking public transportation can make a large difference in the long run.

The writer wants to emphasize the necessity of protecting the planet. Which choice most effectively achieves this goal?

A) can

B) will

C) might

D) must

26

As technology evolves apace and more of us work part–time, the trend of skill sets becoming obsolete is _____. For instance, LinkedIn co–founder Reid Hoffman believes that careers are now simply "tours of duty," prompting companies to design organizations that assume people will only stay a few years.

The writer wants to highlight the speed of transition. Which choice best achieves that goal?

A) accelerating in a faster and faster way

B) only accelerating

C) increasingly accelerating

D) accelerating more quickly as time goes by

27

While researching a topic, a student has taken the following notes:

- Cher is a famous musician and performer born in 1946.

- She was known for regularly changing her appearance and musical styles.

- In the 1970s, she starred in a TV series that ran for 3 years.

- She collaborated with her husband on her first pop/rock hit, "I Got You Babe" (1965).

- Her 1979 disco dance song "Take Me Home" brought her fame after a hiatus.

The student wants to emphasize a point using the two songs. Which choice most effectively uses relevant information from the notes to accomplish this goal?

A) "I Got You Babe" was performed in 1965 and "Take Me Home" was performed in 1979.

B) Cher changed styles regularly, using pop/rock for "I Got You Babe" and disco for "Take Me Home."

C) In the 1970s, Cher performed in a television series as well as sang "Take Me Home."

D) Cher both collaborated with her husband and performed a disco dance song.

STOP

No Test Material On This Page

No Test Material On This Page

Math

22 QUESTIONS | 35 MINUTES

The questions in this section address a number of important math skills. Use of a calculator is permitted for all questions.

NOTES

Unless otherwise indicated: • All variables and expressions represent real numbers. • Figures provided are drawn to scale. • All figures lie in a plane. • The domain of a given function is the set of all real numbers x for which $f(x)$ is a real number.

REFERENCE

$A = \pi r^2$
$C = 2\pi r$

$A = \ell w$

$A = \frac{1}{2} bh$

$c^2 = a^2 + b^2$

Special Right Triangles

$V = \ell w h$

$V = \pi r^2 h$

$V = \frac{4}{3}\pi r^3$

$V = \frac{1}{3}\pi r^2 h$

$V = \frac{1}{3}\ell w h$

The number of degrees of arc in a circle is 360.

The number of radians of arc in a circle is 2π.

The sum of the measures in degrees of the angles of a triangle is 180.

For **multiple–choice questions,** solve each problem, choose the correct answer from the choices provided, and then circle your answer in this book. Circle only one answer for each question. If you change your mind, completely erase the circle. You will not get credit for questions with more than one answer circled, or for questions with no answers circled.

For **student–produced response questions,** solve each problem and write your answer next to or under the question in the test book as described below.

- Once you've written your answer, circle it clearly. You will not receive credit for anything written outside the circle, or for any questions with more than one circled answer.

- If you find more than one correct answer, write and circle only one answer.

- Your answer can be up to 5 characters for a positive answer and up to 6 characters (including the negative sign) for a negative answer, but no more.

- If your answer is a fraction that is too long (over 5 characters for positive, 6 characters for negative), write the decimal equivalent.

- If your answer is a decimal that is too long (over 5 characters for positive, 6 characters for negative), truncate it or round at the fourth digit.

- If your answer is a mixed number (such as 3.!. 2), write it as an improper fraction (7/2) or its decimal equivalent (3.5).

- Don't include symbols such as a percent sign, comma, or dollar sign in your circled answer.

1

If $4x + 16 = 24$, what is the value of $x + 4$?

A) 8

B) 6

C) 2

D) 4

2

Cocopine high school conducts annual surveys at its school to find out the number of teachers and students by gender. The results of the survey showed that there were 35 teachers and 245 students in the school.

	Students	Teacher
Male	131	
Female		16

Using the table above, if a person is chosen at random, what is the probability that the person is a male teacher?

A) $\dfrac{19}{280}$

B) $\dfrac{19}{150}$

C) $\dfrac{19}{35}$

D) $\dfrac{19}{131}$

3

If a is a solution to this equation below and $a > 0$, what is the value of a?

$$|2x - 3| = 11$$

4

Line k is a line perpendicular to line m. Given that the equation for line m is $5y = 4x + 15$, which of the following could be the equation for line k?

A) $y = \dfrac{4}{5}x - 12$

B) $y = \dfrac{5}{4}x + 6$

C) $y = -\dfrac{5}{4}x - 2$

D) $y = \dfrac{5}{4}x + 10$

5

What is the center of the circle, given that its equation is $x^2 + y^2 - 6x + 4y = 36$?

A) $(-3, 2)$

B) $(2, -3)$

C) $(3, -2)$

D) $(-2, 3)$

6

If $(8^x)^x \times 4^{2x}$ is equivalent to $\left(\dfrac{2^{ax}}{2^{-b}}\right)^x$, what is the value of a?

7

If (x, y) is a solution to the following system of inequalities, which of the following could be (x, y)?

$$-6x + 3 < y$$

$$y < x + 6$$

A) $(-2, -4)$

B) $(4, 7)$

C) $(-2, 1)$

D) $(-2, -4)$

8

If $f(x) = 2(x-3)^2 + 8$ is transformed to $g(x) = 2(x-5)^2 + 5$, which of the following describes the transformation?

A) The x coordinate moves to the right 2 units and the y coordinate moves 3 units down.

B) The x coordinate moves to the left 2 units and the y coordinate moves 3 units down.

C) The x coordinate moves to the right 2 units and the y coordinate moves 3 units up.

D) The x coordinate moves to the left 2 units and the y coordinate moves 3 units up.

9

Which of the following equation best represents the graph below?

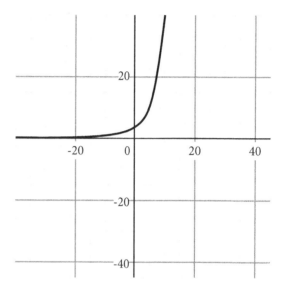

A) $y = 5(0.7)^x$

B) $y = 5(1.3)^x$

C) $y = 3(0.7)^x$

D) $y = 3(1.3)^x$

10

If triangle PQR (not shown) is similar to triangle DEF shown below and DE = 2PQ, what is the value of sin R?

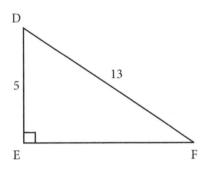

11

The average SAT score of 7 students in a class is 1,320. If a student with an SAT score of 1,460 joins the class, what will be the new average SAT score (rounded off to the nearest 10)?

A) 1,390

B) 1,340

C) 1,300

D) 1,460

12

A researcher studies bacteria in a pond and models a function that shows how the bacteria populate in the pond. Let t be the number of days since the bacteria began to populate the pond. Which of the following is the best interpretation of $(3)^{\frac{t}{14}}$ in the equation: $p(t) = 2,034(3)^{\frac{t}{14}}$?

A) The number of bacteria at the beginning of the study

B) The number of bacteria triples every two weeks

C) The number of bacteria increases by 3 every two weeks

D) The number of bacteria in the pond after two weeks

13

What is the value of p, if the equation below has no solutions?

$$5(x+3) - 3(2-x) = px + 7$$

14

How many solutions does the following system of equations have?

$$3x - 4y = 16$$

$$-6x = -8y + 32$$

A) One solution

B) Two solutions

C) Infinitely many solutions

D) No solution

15

What is the length of the minor arc AB, given that the diameter of the circle is 12 cm and the measure of the angle of sector AOB is 72°?

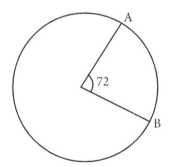

A) 2.4π

B) 28.8π

C) 12π

D) $\dfrac{\pi}{6}$

16

The expression $y = -2(x+3)^2 + 6$ is equivalent to $ax^2 + bx + c$, where $a < 0$ and $b < 0$. What is the value of c?

17

If the coordinates of the midpoint of line segment AB are (8, 10) and the coordinates of point A are (6, 11), which of the following would represent the coordinates of point B?

A) (7, 10.5)

B) (2, 0.5)

C) (10, 9)

D) (7, 11)

18

How many solutions does the equation $|x+3| = 0$ have?

A) 1

B) 2

C) 0

D) There is not enough information to answer the question.

19

What is the value of $|f(2)|$ where

$f(x) = x^2 - 20x + 9$?

A) 27

B) –27

C) 53

D) 35

20

The price of oil increased by 20% at the beginning of May. Some policies were then put in place which reduced the price of oil by 14% two weeks after the initial increase. What is the overall percentage increase or decrease in the oil?

21

A circle is inscribed in a square. If the length of one side of the square is $4\sqrt{2}$ and the area of the circle is $p\pi$, what is the value of p?

A) 32

B) 16

C) 8

D) 64

22

Which of the following is not a solution to the inequality below?

$$-3x + 6 \leq 2 - x$$

A) 2

B) 0

C) 3

D) 4

No Test Material On This Page

Math

22 QUESTIONS | 35 MINUTES

DIRECTIONS

The questions in this section address a number of important math skills. Use of a calculator is permitted for all questions.

NOTES

Unless otherwise indicated: • All variables and expressions represent real numbers. • Figures provided are drawn to scale. • All figures lie in a plane. • The domain of a given function is the set of all real numbers x for which $f(x)$ is a real number.

REFERENCE

$A = \pi r^2$
$C = 2\pi r$

$A = \ell w$

$A = \dfrac{1}{2}bh$

$c^2 = a^2 + b^2$

Special Right Triangles

$V = \ell w h$

$V = \pi r^2 h$

$V = \dfrac{4}{3}\pi r^3$

$V = \dfrac{1}{3}\pi r^2 h$

$V = \dfrac{1}{3}\ell w h$

The number of degrees of arc in a circle is 360.

The number of radians of arc in a circle is 2π.

The sum of the measures in degrees of the angles of a triangle is 180.

For **multiple–choice questions,** solve each problem, choose the correct answer from the choices provided, and then circle your answer in this book. Circle only one answer for each question. If you change your mind, completely erase the circle. You will not get credit for questions with more than one answer circled, or for questions with no answers circled.

For **student–produced response questions,** solve each problem and write your answer next to or under the question in the test book as described below.

- Once you've written your answer, circle it clearly. You will not receive credit for anything written outside the circle, or for any questions with more than one circled answer.

- If you find more than one correct answer, write and circle only one answer.

- Your answer can be up to 5 characters for a positive answer and up to 6 characters (including the negative sign) for a negative answer, but no more.

- If your answer is a fraction that is too long (over 5 characters for positive, 6 characters for negative), write the decimal equivalent.

- If your answer is a decimal that is too long (over 5 characters for positive, 6 characters for negative), truncate it or round at the fourth digit.

- If your answer is a mixed number (such as 3.!. 2), write it as an improper fraction (7/2) or its decimal equivalent (3.5).

- Don't include symbols such as a percent sign, comma, or dollar sign in your circled answer.

1

If m and n are solutions to the equation $f(x) = 3x^2 + 9x - 27$, what is the value of $m + n$?

A) 3

B) -9

C) -3

D) 9

2

Which of the following is equivalent to $3x^2y + 5x - (3x^2y^2 - 2x^2y)$?

A) $6x^2y - 3x^2y^2 + 5x$

B) $x^2y - 3x^2y^2 + 5x$

C) $6x^2y - 2x^2y^2 + 5x$

D) $-3x^2y^2 + 5x^2y + 5x$

3

What is the least integer value of y that satisfies the inequality below?

$$-2y + 2 < 6$$

4

How many solutions does the following system of equations have?

$$y = 2x - 5$$
$$y = 2x^2 - 18x + 45$$

A) 1

B) 2

C) 0

D) Infinite

5

If $3x - y = 11$ and $2x - 2y = 2$, what is the value of $x + y$?

A) 9

B) 5

C) 3

D) 13

6

If $sin\ 32° = 0.551$, what is the value of $cos\ 58°$?

7

If 1 *foot* = 12 *inches*, what is the area of the triangle (not drawn to scale) below in ft^2?

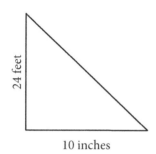

24 feet

10 inches

A) 120

B) 20

C) 1,440

D) 10

8

For all values of $x > 0$, which of the following is equivalent to the following equation $\dfrac{-5}{x} - \dfrac{x}{x-4}$?

A) -6

B) $\dfrac{x^2 + -20}{4}$

C) $\dfrac{-x^2 - 5x + 20}{x^2 - 4x}$

D) $\dfrac{-9 - x}{x - 4}$

9

Which of the following equations best represents the equation of the following graph?

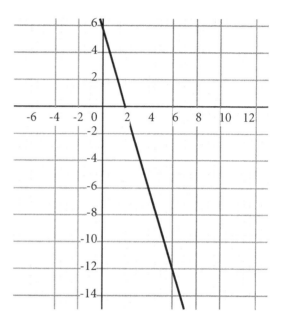

A) $3y - 9x = 18$

B) $3y + 9x = 18$

C) $6y - 12x = 36$

D) $5y + 20x = 30$

10

What is the y–intercept for the equation below?

$$y - 7 = 3^x - 5$$

11

For what value of x does the function

$h(x) = \dfrac{3x-5}{x^2-2x-15}$ become undefined if $x < 0$?

A) 5

B) −5

C) −3

D) −4

12

If $f(3) = -1$ and $f(4) = -3$, what is the x–intercept for the line represented by the function $f(x)$?

A) 2.5

B) 5

C) −2

D) $\dfrac{2}{5}$

13

If $f(x+3) = 5x - 17$, what is the value of $f(2)$?

14

Amber travels from her home to the mall in $1\dfrac{1}{2}$ hours. She completes her errands in one hour and she then travels back home in $2\dfrac{1}{2}$ hours.

If the distance from the mall to her home is x miles, find the average speed of her trip in terms of x.

A) $\dfrac{x}{4}$

B) $\dfrac{x}{2}$

C) $\dfrac{2x}{5}$

D) $2x$

15

Given that the length of a rectangle is 3 *meters* more than its width, what is the perimeter of the rectangle given that the area is 28 *square meters*?

A) 11

B) 22

C) 14

D) 32

16

A study conducted by a school's medical board found that 23 out of the 48 students surveyed practice sanitary routines such as washing their hands before meals. If there are 2,280 students in the school, approximately how many students in the school do not practice sanitary routines (rounded up to the nearest whole number)?

17

Which of the following is the equation of $g(x) = 2x$ when it's moved 1 unit to the left and 1 unit up?

A) $y = 2x - 1$

B) $y = 2x + 1$

C) $y = 2x + 5$

D) $y = 2x + 3$

18

What is the *x coordinate* of the vertex for the parabola represented by the equation $y = 2x^2 + 8x + 12$?

A) 6

B) −4

C) 2

D) −2

19

If $\dfrac{x^2 - 6x + 10}{x + 2} = A + \dfrac{B}{x + 2}$, what is the value of B?

20

If triangle ABC is a right triangle and B is 90° and the longest side of the triangle is 61 and the shortest side is 11, what is the length of the third side of the triangle?

A) 40

B) 60

C) 62

D) 59

21

The psychology department of a school conducted a study on 20 random students in a third grade class of 58 students. 20 of the students were then offered a supplement. The study found that 15 of these students did better in their end–term exams compared to those who did not take the supplements. Which of the following statements can best be concluded from the above study?

A) Students who take supplements do better on exams.

B) Students who do not take supplements do not do well on their exams.

C) Supplements improve students' performance in their exams.

D) No conclusion can be drawn about the cause–and–effect relationship between test taking and supplement taking.

22

If $x+3y=9$ and $2x+2y=14$, what is the value of $y-x$?

A) -5

B) 5

C) 1

D) 6

STOP

No Test Material On This Page

Answer Key

Reading and Writing

Module 1

Questions	Correct	Mark your correct answers
1.	C	
2.	C	
3.	A	
4.	B	
5.	C	
6.	A	
7.	B	
8.	A	
9.	B	
10.	B	
11.	B	
12.	A	
13.	C	
14.	D	
15.	D	
16.	C	
17.	C	
18.	C	
19.	A	
20.	B	
21.	B	
22.	D	
23.	D	
24.	B	
25.	C	
26.	A	
27.	C	

Module 2

Questions	Correct	Mark your correct answers
1.	D	
2.	C	
3.	D	
4.	D	
5.	D	
6.	A	
7.	B	
8.	A	
9.	C	
10.	A	
11.	B	
12.	A	
13.	A	
14.	D	
15.	A	
16.	C	
17.	D	
18.	D	
19.	A	
20.	B	
21.	D	
22.	D	
23.	B	
24.	C	
25.	D	
26.	B	
27.	B	

Math

Module 1

Questions	Correct	Mark your correct answers
1.	B	
2.	A	
3.	7	
4.	C	
5.	C	
6.	3	
7.	B	
8.	A	
9.	D	
10.	$\frac{5}{13}$ or 0.384 or 0.385	
11.	B	
12.	B	
13.	8	
14.	D	
15.	A	
16.	-12	
17.	C	
18.	A	
19.	A	
20.	3.2	
21.	C	
22.	B	

Module 2

Questions	Correct	Mark your correct answers
1.	C	
2.	D	
3.	-1	
4.	A	
5.	A	
6.	0.551	
7.	D	
8.	C	
9.	B	
10.	3	
11.	C	
12.	A	
13.	-22	
14.	B	
15.	B	
16.	1,188	
17.	D	
18.	D	
19.	26	
20.	B	
21.	D	
22.	A	

1. **Level:** Easy | **Domain:** CRAFT AND STRUCTURE
Skill/Knowledge: Words in Context

Key Explanation: Choice C is the best answer because the underlined word is what goats "lack" or "do not have." The first half of the sentence indicates that the goats will eat "everything else" as well as "unwanted weeds." In other words, the goat does not care what it eats. **Choice C** refers to "judgment," or "refinement" about what it chooses, so fits the context of eating anything.

Distractor Explanation: Choices A and **B** are incorrect because they refer to unfairness or partiality towards one thing. However, the goats are not deliberately trying to treat one plant poorly; they eat all without preferences. **Choice D** is incorrect because it refers to an obstinate and unchanging belief about the superiority of one's group over others, but the goats do not feel they are superior to others.

2. **Level:** Easy | **Domain:** CRAFT AND STRUCTURE
Skill/Knowledge: Words in Context

Key Explanation: Choice C is the best answer because the underlined word describes how clients and investors view the proposal that the person with a career in business makes. **Choice C** refers to something that is desirable. The resulting sentence, therefore, indicates that the businessperson helps make the plan desirable to others.

Distractor Explanation: None of the other choices adequately shows how the clients and investors need to view the proposals. **Choice A** refers to a personal quality that inspires others. It does not refer to something inanimate like a

proposal. **Choice B** refers to something that is impossible to avoid the effect of. The clients and investors, though, are not forced to accept the proposal. **Choice D** refers to something that is extremely interesting so that it is impossible to stop paying attention to it. Although a proposal might be fascinating, the key is to make it desirable enough that others buy into it.

3. **Level:** Hard | **Domain:** CRAFT AND STRUCTURE
Skill/Knowledge: Words in Context

Key Explanation: Choice A is the best answer because "critical" is the author's view of what "explaining such coexistence" is. The sentence continues to say that the explanation is needed to "truly understand the region's biodiversity." **Choice A** refers to something absolutely necessary, so fits the context in saying that explaining coexistence is necessary to understand biodiversity and therefore developing an appropriate plan for managing the area.

Distractor Explanation: None of the other choices accurately describes how essential "explaining such coexistence" really is. **Choice B** means "dangerous." **Choice C** refers to expressing criticism and disapproval. **Choice D** refers to using logic and reasoning.

4. **Level:** Medium | **Domain:** CRAFT AND STRUCTURE
Skill/Knowledge: Words in Context

Key Explanation: Choice B is the best answer because the blank portion needs to be a word that describes the "cultural and historical value of the building and its contents," which are described as being full of "splendid and unique details" from over the past 1,500 years. **Choice C** refers to something that is too great to mathematically determine or count. It fits the context that the building's value is so great it cannot be replaced by any money.

Distractor Explanations: None of the other choices adequately describe the precious nature of the "value of the building and its contents." **Choice A** refers to a place or thing that is pleasant and agreeable, not an intangible thing such as "value." **Choices C** and **D** refer to something that is physically large or bulky, not something intangible.

5. **Level:** Hard | **Domain:** CRAFT AND STRUCTURE
   Skill/Knowledge: Text Structure and Purpose

   Key Explanation: Choice C is the best answer because the main point of the paragraph is that "these results contrast with previous findings" and emphasize that more studies are needed, indicating that the Drake Passage study did not provide all the answers. Therefore, the paragraph shows how the results of the Drake Passage study fits into "the wider context" or "bigger picture" of other studies.

   Distractor Explanation: Choice A is incorrect because the paragraph does not suggest that any of the data gathered so far is "inaccurate" or "not correct." Therefore, the paragraph is not being used to show how difficult it is to get correct data. **Choice B** is incorrect because the paragraph does not "illustrate" or "explain" why it is hard to "amass" or "gather" enough data. The paragraph mentions that the conditions are "challenging," but does not give any detail about why. **Choice D** is incorrect because, though the paragraph says that CO_2 absorption is important, it does not talk about "correcting" or "fixing" the problem. It only says that there needs to be more research done to understand the process better.

6. **Level:** Easy | **Domain:** CRAFT AND STRUCTURE
   Skill/Knowledge: Text Structure and Purpose

   Key Explanation: Choice A is the best answer. The underlined sentence shows that the garden was large and "lovely" or "appealing," and the following sentence gives various reasons that the garden was appealing to all the senses.

   Distractor Explanation: Choice B is incorrect because there is no contrast with the previous sentence; the garden was lovely, so that provides a reason for the children to want to play there. **Choice C** is incorrect because the underlined sentence does not refer to "characters" or "people," only to place. **Choice D** is incorrect because there is no "ominous undercurrent" or "scary implication" in the description of the garden. It could be that the giant is very nice and there is no problem with the children playing there.

7. **Level:** Easy | **Domain:** CRAFT AND STRUCTURE
   Skill/Knowledge: Text Structure and Purpose

   Key Explanation: Choice B is the best answer because the phrase is used to describe the "fentanyl analogs" or "drugs comparable to fentanyl." The fact that they were "commonly confiscated" or "often seized" by law enforcement shows that the drugs are ones in common use, and therefore are likely to be illegal drugs that overdose patients had access to and used. If this is true, the research on the drugs is likely to "apply" or "be relevant" to "authentic cases" or "real situations" in which a patient overdoses on an illegal drug.

   Distractor Explanation: Choice A is incorrect because the method of "obtaining" or "getting" the drugs is not mentioned. The researchers could have gotten the drugs from a variety of sources. **Choice C** is incorrect because the fact that the drugs were the kind seized by officers does not show that the trials were "improperly" or "incorrectly" done. **Choice D** is incorrect because there is no indication that the research required special permits to use the drugs. Therefore, the quote is not included to "establish" or "provide a reason" for a point that is not even mentioned.

8. **Level:** Easy | **Domain:** INFORMATION AND IDEAS
Skill/Knowledge: Cross-Text Connections

Key Explanation: Choice A is the best answer because when the author of passage 2 states that if "men but understand themselves . . . they will be ready enough to take gigantic measures to prevent [war]" he is expressing a belief in the ability of wisdom to overcome mankind's tendency towards warfare. This is very similar in intent and belief to the statement made by the author of passage 1 that, "We must have the telescope of philosophy to perceive distant ills." Both authors believe that the key to conquering our urge to ignore the suffering of others and make war is consideration and thoughtfulness.

Distractor Explanation: Choice B is incorrect because it has no relevance to the underlined concluding message in Text 2. The underlined section in Text 2 is expressing a belief in the ability of wisdom to overcome mankind's tendency towards warfare, whereas this choice emphasizes that people only concern themselves with opinions and beliefs that ensure their personal happiness. **Choice C** is incorrect because it doesn't include any information relating to the underlined concluding message in Text 2. The underlined section in Text 2 is expressing a belief in the ability

of wisdom to overcome mankind's tendency towards warfare, whereas this choice emphasizes that there are people that would ignore the misery of others as long as they benefitted. **Choice D** is incorrect because it doesn't include any information relating to the underlined concluding message in Text 2. The underlined section in Text 2 is expressing a belief in the ability of wisdom to overcome mankind's tendency towards warfare, whereas this choice emphasizes that there are men that have no problem with the concept of killing or taking someone else's life.

9. **Level:** Medium | **Domain:** INFORMATION AND IDEAS
Skill/Knowledge: Central Ideas and Details

Key Explanation: Choice B is the best answer because "impetus" refers to a reason or motivation. The passage begins by explaining that the narrator will "take to the ship" whenever he is feeling morbid and needs a change.

Distractor Explanation: Choice A is incorrect because there is no indication that the narrator is a captain. He also does not appear to be a sailor as a steady career, but instead when he feels tired of being on land. **Choice C** is incorrect because the narrator says he had no money, and therefore felt like going sailing; there is no discussion of a sailor's salary. He could have had a large salary aboard ship but spent it all. **Choice D** is incorrect because, while the narrator indicates that he was "impoverished" with "little or no money in my purse," he does not say how he got to that condition

10. **Level:** Medium | **Domain:** INFORMATION AND IDEAS
Skill/Knowledge: Central Ideas and Details

Key Explanation: Choice B is the best answer because the passage says that "induced demand" is a phenomenon in which making more of a product will lead to more people wanting it; in this case, "if more roads are provided, more people are encouraged to drive." However, the passage says that the "common solution" is to build more roads, showing that in the average or common case of wanting to reduce traffic jams, the effect is not considered. If it were "taken into consideration" or "thought about," then planners would probably use a different solution than just building roads.

Distractor Explanation: Choice A is incorrect because, although the passage indicates that congestion continues as more roads are built, it does not say that induced demand "contradicts" or "goes against" that concept. There is also no hint that there is a "widespread belief" or "lots of people thinking" that building roads causes congestion; if so, the common solution would not be to build more. **Choice C** is incorrect because there is no hint that city planners are now incorporating the idea into their plans; if so, then there would not be situations like the example from Houston. **Choice D** is incorrect because there is no discussion in the passage about how to "mitigate" or "reduce" the effect. The effect is just defined.

11. **Level:** Medium | **Domain:** INFORMATION AND IDEAS
    Skill/Knowledge: Command of Evidence (Textual)

    Key Explanation: Choice B is the best answer. The claim is that "the poem uses the imagery of fire to delve into the question of who might have created such a dangerous creature." In choice B, the words "furnace" and "anvil" are "imagery" or "symbols" that evoke heat and fire; they are tools

used to heat metal to the melting point and form it into a shape. **Choice B** refers to "delving" or "asking" the question of who might have created the "dangerous creature," which causes "deadly terrors: what furnace, anvil, and grasp could create a tiger? These questions are asking who would dare to forge and hold the tiger.

Distractor Explanation: Choice A is incorrect because it touches on the fire imagery in the "fire of thine eyes," but it does not refer to the question of who created such a creature. **Choice C** is incorrect because it only refers to the creator and the danger or fear caused by a tiger: tigers are scary enough that stars "throw down their spears" or "give up" and "water heaven with their tears" or "cry." **Choice C** does not use any fire imagery. **Choice D** also does not give any support to the claim that the poem uses fire imagery; it only wonders if someone who created a lamb could also create a tiger.

12. **Level:** Hard | **Domain:** INFORMATION AND IDEAS
    Skill/Knowledge: Command of Evidence (Textual)

    Key Explanation: Choice A is the best answer because a counterargument is an attack against the writer's main argument. The prompt is asking about a counterargument related to Mother Jones's "credibility" or "believability." Mother Jones "addresses" or "faces" the possible attack that she is not qualified to speak because she is not a miner by saying that she has undergone similar conditions that miners live in and suffer through: "I was with you nearly three years in this State. I went to jail. I went to the Federal courts."

Distractor Explanation: Choice B is incorrect because Mother Jones uses her experience in jail as a reason that she can empathize with the miners. It supports her argument of understanding hard conditions rather than weakens her ability to speak for miners. **Choice C** is incorrect because there is no discussion about how many government contacts she has, so she does not "anticipate" a counter argument on that topic. **Choice D** is incorrect because Mother Jones does not say how she treats pets; she is discussing the behavior of the wives of the mine owners.

13. **Level:** Easy | **Domain:** INFORMATION AND IDEAS

    Skill/Knowledge: Command of Evidence (Quantitative)

    Key Explanation: Choice C is the best answer because the figure lists "39.66" in the column of "average days to first flower" for 90nM of NaCl, and 23.66 days for 0 NaCl. Therefore, the difference is 16 days, which supports the claim that "increasing NaCl concentrations delayed significantly flowering" times.

    Distractor Explanation: Choice A is incorrect because only the passage refers to capsaicinoids; the table does not. **Choice B** is incorrect because only the passage refers to vitamins and minerals. Nutritional value is impossible to determine from the table. **Choice D** is incorrect because for the "NaCl concentration of 30 mM" line, the table says 54 days until the first fruit appeared; that is not the total number of fruits.

14. **Level:** Medium | **Domain:** INFORMATION AND IDEAS

    Skill/Knowledge: Inferences

    Key Explanation: Choice D is the best answer because the passage says that Mann used personal interviews "to provide an insider's perspective." She was trying to get a clearer understanding of veganism from vegans themselves.

Distractor Explanation: Choice A is incorrect because there is no evidence that Mann expected to find a "conflict" or "opposing views" between the interviews and scientific research. She was trying to blend the two to get a more rounded view of the topic as a whole. **Choice B** is incorrect because the health benefits were analyzed through scientific studies found in the literature review; Mann was not trying to "resolve a debate" so much as "combat stereotypes" by sharing different views. **Choice C** is incorrect because there is no evidence that "most" or "the largest percentage" of literature is "biased against" or "opposing" veganism.

15. **Level:** Easy | **Domain:** INFORMATION AND IDEAS

    Skill/Knowledge: Inferences

    Key Explanation: Choice D is the best answer. Since the tomb inscriptions say that the tomb belonged to Hinat, it is a logical assumption that she was buried there.

    Distractor Explanations: Choice A is incorrect. There is no evidence that Hinat was royal; if anything, the act of buying a tomb indicates that the populace did not make one for their ruler. **Choice B** is incorrect because, though she bought her own tomb, she had "descendants," which indicates that she had children. **Choice C** is incorrect because "ancestors" are the people who came before someone, so are the opposite of "descendants." There is no indication that anyone before Hinat was buried with her.

16. **Level:** Easy | **Domain:** STANDARD ENGLISH CONVENTIONS

    Skill/Knowledge: Form, Structure, and Sense

Key Explanation: Choice C is the best answer. "Called off" is a phrasal verb that means "canceled."

Distractor Explanation: All of the other choices can be eliminated because they are phrasal verbs with meanings that do not fit the context of saying that the Olympics were not held. **Choice A** refers to visiting someone. **Choice B** refers to telephoning someone. **Choice D** refers to asking various people questions, often when organizing something or trying to find information.

17. **Level:** Medium | **Domain:** STANDARD ENGLISH CONVENTIONS
    Skill/Knowledge: Form, Structure, and Sense

Key Explanation: Choice C is the best answer. The present perfect verb form using "has/have" is used to show that something started in the past and continues now. It fits the time context of the question that Harari poses, "from the stone age to the present."

Distractor Explanation: Choices A and **B** are incorrect because they are present tenses, so do not include the idea of change from the distant past. **Choice D** is incorrect because it refers to something which has not yet occurred in the future, so does not describe "from the stone age to the present."

18. **Level:** Easy | **Domain:** STANDARD ENGLISH CONVENTIONS
    Skill/Knowledge: Form, Structure, and Sense

Key Explanation: Choice C is the best answer. The subject of the sentence is long, "the transformative effect on women of access to affordable, reliable, and sustainable modern energy." However, it can be reduced to the singular

"the effect." **Choice C** is a singular verb that shows that the studies were done in the past and still continue today.

Distractor Explanation: All of the other choices can be eliminated because they are plural verbs, so cannot be used with the singular subject "the effect."

19. **Level:** Easy | **Domain:** STANDARD ENGLISH CONVENTIONS
    Skill/Knowledge: Form, Structure, and Sense

Key Explanation:Choice A is the best answer. "Which" is a relative pronoun used after a comma to add more description to the noun that precedes the comma. In this case, "occur deep underwater where continental plates diverge" adds more information about the "hydrothermal vents."

Distractor Explanation: Choices B and **D** are incorrect because "they" and "these" are pronouns that are used in place of a noun at the start of a sentence. They create independent clauses that can stand on their own, so the resulting sentence is a comma splice. **Choice C** is incorrect because when "that" is used as the start of a relative clause after a noun, it is not preceded by a comma.

20. **Level:** Medium | **Domain:** STANDARD ENGLISH CONVENTIONS
    Skill/Knowledge: Boundaries

Key Explanation: Choice B is the best answer. When three or more items are included in a list joined by "and," the items are followed by commas, but the "and" is not.

Distractor Explanation: Choice A is incorrect because there should be no comma after "and." **Choices C** and **D** are incorrect because both semicolons and a single dash should be preceded by a complete idea, but the two items before the punctuation would need to be joined by "and" for the idea to be complete.

21. **Level:** Easy | **Domain:** STANDARD ENGLISH CONVENTIONS
Skill/Knowledge: Boundaries

Key Explanation: Choice B is the best answer. "In a 2022 paper written by Kyle Rupp and associates" modifies the main clause, "the researchers explore…" by giving the context of when and where the sentence occurs. Such a modifier at the start of the sentence should be divided from the main clause with a comma.

Distractor Explanation:Choice A is incorrect because with no punctuation, the reader does not know where the main clause begins. **Choices C** and **D** are incorrect because a single dash or a colon should follow an independent clause, but the first person has no active verb ("written" modifies the noun "paper.")

22. **Level:** Easy | **Domain:** STANDARD ENGLISH CONVENTIONS
Skill/Knowledge: Boundaries

Key Explanation: Choice D is the best answer. The main clause starts, "a lyric soprano has…." The other words at the start of the sentence modify the main clause, so need to be divided with commas. "For example" is one separate idea that qualifies that the sentence is an illustration of the previous claim. "Among operatic voices" restricts the discussion to voices that are used in the opera.

Distractor Explanation: Choice A is incorrect because it has no punctuation separating the different elements of the sentence from each

other, so it is hard for the reader to determine how the ideas relate to each other. **Choices B** and **C** are incorrect because a colon should follow a complete clause, but the preceding portion has no verb.

23. **Level:** Medium | **Domain:** EXPRESSION OF IDEAS
Skill/Knowledge: Transitions

Key Explanation: Choice D is the best answer. "The wind cannot be turned up or down" is a contrast with the previous discussion, which explains that oil–powered plants can control output like adjusting the flow of gas to a car. **Choice D** is used to indicate that the following information is different from what has preceded, so it effectively warns the reader of the contrast to come.

Distractor Explanation: Choices A and **B** are incorrect because they show that even though one thing happens, another also happens. They do not establish that the discussion is highlighting a difference between two things which might happen even if the other did not. **Choice C** is incorrect because it is used to add more information along the same idea to the preceding argument, not change to a contrasting thought.

24. **Level:** Easy **Domain:** EXPRESSION OF IDEAS
Skill/Knowledge: Transitions

Key Explanation: Choice B is the best answer. There is a contrast in the sentence between "some administrative roles" and the rest of people who do social work. **Choice B** is used at the start of a dependent clause to show a contrast between the clause it introduces and the main clause of the sentence.

Distractor Explanation: All of the other choices can be eliminated because they do not make the clause that they introduce dependent on a main clause; the clause can still stand on its own as a sentence. As a result, the sentence is left with two main clauses joined by a comma, a type of run-on sentence called a comma splice.

25. **Level:** Easy | **Domain:** EXPRESSION OF IDEAS
Skill/Knowledge: Transitions

Key Explanation: Choice C is the best answer. The passage is structured with the first sentence defining the diet and the second sentence giving a reason to doubt that it is effective, a reason not to follow it. The final sentence gives another reason to question whether the diet should be used. **Choice C** is used to introduce an additional argument for the same topic, so fits the context well.

Distractor Explanation: The other choices can be eliminated because they are not used to add more detail on the same topic. **Choice A** is used for a time series, but there is no indication that the lack of research was followed in time by scientists being concerned. **Choice B** is used to stress that the previous point may be true, but that the following, opposing argument is more reasonable. Therefore, it does not fit the context of two concordant ideas. **Choice D** is used to introduce a logical conclusion based on what information is already given, not to bring up new ideas.

26. **Level:** Medium | **Domain:** INFORMATION AND IDEAS
Skill/Knowledge: Inference

Key Explanation: Choice A is correct because to commemorate something means to remember

the event and by doing so, to honor it. Here, the memorial commemorates the employees of LMWR killed in the First World War.

Distractor Explanations: Choice B is incorrect because to idolize is to respect or admire someone extensively. Here, the memorial has been built to remember martyrs and not only to show respect. **Choice C** is incorrect because "celebrate" is not a word used to describe the purpose of a memorial. **Choice D** is incorrect because the memorial has been built for the fallen LNWR employees and hence, cannot overlook or ignore them.

27. **Level:** Medium | **Domain:** EXPRESSION OF IDEAS
Skill/Knowledge: Rhetorical Synthesis

Key Explanation: Choice C is the best answer. The author wants to emphasize "rarity" or the fact that there are very few of the saola. The idea that they have been seen only four times in thirty years indicates that they are hard to find. In other words, there are probably not many because presumably scientists have been wanting to look for and study them.

Distractor Explanation: Choice A is incorrect because it does not emphasize the "rarity" or "unusual nature" of the animal. It is possible that many hunters have such skulls in their homes and the scientists only recently realized some were unusual. **Choice B** is incorrect because it could just mean saola are hard to raise in captivity. There could be a huge number living in the mountains in that region. **Choice D** is incorrect because it does not say anything about how common the saola are; it only describes their name

1. **Level:** Medium | **Domain:** CRAFT AND STRUCTURE
    Skill/Knowledge: Words in Context

    Key Explanation: Choice D is the best answer because "broader" is a comparative adjective that shows the difference between the tourism business and the destination. The paragraph shows that the tourism business contains many different aspects than just the sites: it also includes "transportation, hotels and guest accommodations, and services that link the various components of a trip." Choice D refers to something that covers a wide range of topics or deals with many elements of something, so accurately shows that tourism deals with many more elements than just the destination.

    Distractor Explanation: None of the other choices effectively establishes the relationship between the tourism business and the destination. **Choice A** refers to something that is more noticeable or clear. **Choice B** refers to something that is not detailed or only covers the main points. **Choice C** refers to something that is wide in physical space.

2. **Level:** Medium | **Domain:** CRAFT AND STRUCTURE
    Skill/Knowledge: Words in Context

    Key Explanation: Choice C is the best answer because "insensible" is a verb that shows what the trees do to the "any change in those who walk" under them. **Choice C** means "not notice," so it correctly shows that the trees do not notice that different people are present.

    Distractor Explanation: Choice A refers to an unconscious state, especially when someone is sick or injured. Therefore, it does not apply to

    trees that do not notice anything. **Choice B** means "trivial" or "unimportant," so does not describe what the trees do to a change in the people under them. **Choice D** is incorrect because it refers to a lack of thinking or perception of the environment around something. Although trees do not think, Marianne is talking to them as if they were animate creatures that might perceive things if they wanted to.

3. **Level:** Hard | **Domain:** CRAFT AND STRUCTURE
    Skill/Knowledge: Words in Context

    Key Explanation: Choice D is the best answer because "fume" refers to one of the things relating to the way that Adam amassed millions of dollars in Wall Street. The other things are "fuss" or "commotion," "applause" or "praise," and "ill will" or "hard feelings." **Choice D** refers to anger that is often related to a conflict, so aptly shows that he was very aggressive or hurt others as he "charged in" and made money.

    Distractor Explanation: None of the other choices fits the list of emotional qualities reflecting what happened to Adam on Wall Street. **Choice A** refers to waste gasses, **Choice B** to an unpleasant smell, and **Choice C** to waste products.

4. **Level:** Medium | **Domain:** CRAFT AND STRUCTURE
    Skill/Knowledge: Text Structure and Purpose

    Key Explanation: Choice D is the best answer. The topic sentence points out that "sometimes behaviors have underlying reasons that are not initially apparent," and then gives Mischel's experiment as an example. The differing results of Watt's experiment show that a fuller analysis might reveal previously unconsidered explanations for a behavior such as deciding to wait to eat a marshmallow.

Distractor Explanation: Choice A is incorrect because, while Watt's experiment revealed a flaw in Mischel's experiment, there is no indication that "most" experiments are flawed. **Choice B** is incorrect because the passage does not say that all experiments should be performed more than once; it only gives an example of a situation where a second experiment revealed more information about a topic. **Choice C** is incorrect because the passage does not say there is a "significant problem" in the way we understand willpower now; the passage points out that a previous problem in understanding was rectified.

5. **Level:** Medium | **Domain:** CRAFT AND STRUCTURE
    Skill/Knowledge: Text Structure and Purpose

    Key Explanation: Choice D is the best answer because the cup of liberty is something that "your old masters" hold for the slaves. The imagery shows that the cup can be "dash[ed] from you" so that it is unclear when the "scattered contents" or "freedoms" will be given back. In other words, the imagery emphasizes the "precarious" or "unstable" nature of the freedoms. It is very easy to throw aside or break the gains that have been made.

    Distractor Explanation: Choice A is incorrect because Lincoln is not saying that the Union is "generous" or "willing to give a lot." He is saying that a poor decision will remove everything that has been given so far. **Choice B** is incorrect because the cup of liberty is what "your old masters," who are slave-owners in Louisiana, hold for slaves. The cup of liberty is not the advances of the Union, only of Louisiana. **Choice C** is incorrect because the imagery does not include

the reaction of people accepting the cup; it says the cup is easy to break.

6. **Level:** Easy | **Domain:** CRAFT AND STRUCTURE
    Skill/Knowledge: Text Structure and Purpose

    Key Explanation: Choice A is the best answer because the definition explains what a median wage is. This definition clarifies that not all planners earned the median figure of $73,050. It also explains why a total of 20% of the planners earned less than $45,180 or more than $114,170. If the reader did not know the definition of median wage, then the reason for the wide range in salaries might not make much sense.

    Distractor Explanation: Choice B is incorrect because the author does not imply that the median wage is "insufficient" or "not good enough." The median wage does not give all the necessary details to know the range of salaries, but offers a valid middle point to use as a point of reference. The definition shows how the data can be used to better understand the salary that could be earned as a planner. **Choice C** is incorrect because there is no "reason" or "cause" given to explain why planners earn different amounts of money. **Choice D** is incorrect because there is no link between salary earned and number of jobs. Therefore, a definition of how the salary in the passage was calculated does not support or prove that there will be more jobs in the future.

7. **Level:** Medium | **Domain:** CRAFT AND STRUCTURE
    Skill/Knowledge: Cross–Text Connections

    Key Explanation: Choice B is the best answer because the conclusion of Text 2 is that researchers need to develop a new drug to treat depression.

The author of Text 1 would probably respond with "reservation" or "some doubt" because she promotes behavioral activation, a non–invasive method that does not use any medications at all, to retrain the brain into positive patterns. She probably would encourage avoiding invasive methods like introducing drugs into the body if possible.

Distractor Explanation: Choice A is incorrect because the author of Text 1 indicates that behavioral activation is successful. She does not discuss any other method of treatment, so it is impossible to tell if she would say that "most" treatments do not work. **Choice C** is incorrect because the author of Text 1 does not refer to drug performance at all. **Choice D** is incorrect because there is not enough information to tell whether the author of Text 1 "contends" or "argues" that drugs are "unacceptable" or "not allowable." She may agree that drug therapies should be attempted when other methods fail.

8. **Level:** Medium | **Domain:** INFORMATION AND IDEAS
    Skill/Knowledge: Central Ideas and Details

    Key Explanation: Choice A is the best answer because Keel describes the "vision" or "dream" of the Indian's "predecessors" or "earlier people," then states that "This vision was shared by the U.S. Congress in 1934 when it passed…the Indian Reorganization Act." In other words, Keel feels that the vision was "shared" or "in keeping"—both mean "the same"—with each other.

    Distractor Explanation: Choice B is incorrect because Keel indicates that the IRA was written by the government, not by the predecessors, even though the goals were the same. **Choice C** is incorrect because the policy matched the

desires of the Indians to "protect and restore our tribal homelands and the Indian way of life." The policy did not "deny" or "remove" rights from the Indians. **Choice D** is incorrect because there is no indication of how well the policy has upheld its goals.

9. **Level:** Easy | **Domain:** INFORMATION AND IDEAS
    Skill/Knowledge: Central Ideas and Details

    Key Explanation: Choice C is the best answer because the passage says that the narrator's "way lay along the canal embankment," which shows that he was on the embankment because it was the "route" or "way" he needed to go. The first line says the reason he was taking that route was, "I was going towards my lodgings." "Quarters" and "lodgings" both refer to the place where one lives, so he was headed towards his quarters.

    Distractor Explanation: None of the other choices are supported by evidence from the passage. **Choice A** is incorrect because, although the embankment was usually deserted, "at that hour you never meet a soul," there is no proof that he was trying to avoid other people. **Choice B** is incorrect because he went on his walk to escape the pressures of the city, but the embankment was on his return trip as he was going home to his lodgings. **Choice D** is incorrect because the embankment was usually deserted, so that is not a place that he would have looked for excitement or adventure.

10. **Level:** Medium | **Domain:** INFORMATION AND IDEAS
    Skill/Knowledge: Central Ideas and Details

    Key Explanation: Choice A is the best answer because "placement" refers to "location." The passage directly states that "environmental impacts will very much depend on… the location selected"

Distractor Explanation: None of the other choices are supported by evidence from the passage. **Choice B** is incorrect because, although the passage does say that moving parts can kill wildlife, it does not say that is the most important factor when determining environmental change. **Choice C** is incorrect because the studies revealed how the system affects the environment, but do not change the effects. There is no discussion at all of **Choice D,** the total energy generated.

11. **Level:** Hard | **Domain:** INFORMATION AND IDEAS
    Skill/Knowledge: Command of Evidence (Textual)

    Key Explanation: Choice B is the best answer. The scientists' conclusion is that "the carnivore probably appeared very much like the unrelated *Tyrannosaurus rex.*" **Choice B** gives a detail about the "appearance" or "how it looks" that show that there is a similarity: both species had a head that was "oversized" or "very large" when compared to the rest of the body. Therefore, they both looked like they had big heads.

    Distractor Explanation: Choice A is incorrect because a long separation of time could mean that the dinosaurs had evolved in different ways and looked very different. **Choice C** is incorrect because it shows a way that the dinosaurs looked different rather than a way that they are similar. Both dinosaurs were large, but *T. rex* would have, in general, been much larger. **Choice D** is incorrect because it only shows a similarity in diet. It is possible that two carnivores have very different physical characteristics or appearances while still eating the same food.

12. **Level:** Easy | **Domain:** INFORMATION AND IDEAS
    Skill/Knowledge: Command of Evidence (Quantitative)

    Key Explanation: Choice A is the best answer because the claim is that there "is huge variability within tree populations over time." In other words, Clark is stressing how much of a change there is. **Choice A** accurately uses information from the graph to explain that one species increased greatly, thus supporting the claim.

    Distractor Explanation: Choice B is incorrect because it shows stability rather than variability or change. **Choice C** is incorrect because it is extremely vague and does not show change within the species' composition. It only shows that there is more of one species than another, and those percentages could have remained constant. **Choice D** is incorrect because it incorrectly says there was a "decrease" rather than an "increase" in the number of oak trees. There were more 5,000 years ago…which is a more recent time than 10,000 years ago.

13. **Level:** Medium | **Domain:** INFORMATION AND IDEAS
    Skill/Knowledge: Inferences

    Key Explanation: Choice A is the best answer because the fact that "any information about those people that may differ from you – for example, the part of the country where they live" must be included implies that the information is essential for interpreting the data. Since the data is related to earnings claims and the percentage of people who actually reached the earnings, then it can be reasonably inferred that differences in environment affects the earnings. Since

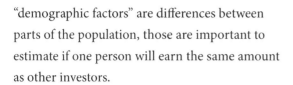

"demographic factors" are differences between parts of the population, those are important to estimate if one person will earn the same amount as other investors.

Distractor Explanation: Choice B is not supported by the passage. The earnings claims must include the dates that earnings were achieved, but there is no evidence regarding how often the document is "updated" or "rewritten." It is possible that the same document could be used for many years. **Choice C** is incorrect because, while some sellers may be happy to provide evidence about their claims, there is no indication that "most" do not want to give the document to the buyer. **Choice D** is incorrect because the paragraph says that any sellers of a franchise must provide the document, not every building for sale.

14. **Level:** Medium | **Domain:** INFORMATION AND IDEAS
    Skill/Knowledge: Inferences

Key Explanation: Choice D is the best answer because the passage says that one problem of tourism is that there could be "divisions and social friction," meaning conflicts, as a result of the "disparity" or "difference" between tourists and the workers who get lower pay. In other words, the local workers could become "resentful" or "dissatisfied" because of the difference in wages.

Distractor Explanation: None of the other choices are supported by evidence from the passage. **Choice A** is incorrect because there is no indication about which members of the community are employed. **Choice B** is incorrect because, while some regions might not benefit immediately from tourism because development money is spent on "schools or clinics," the passage implies that tourism is a good choice for Africa because it creates jobs. **Choice C** is incorrect

because there is no discussion of replacing local cultures and traditions with new ones; if anything, "cultural stereotypes will be exploited" implies that some cultural details will be preserved to share with tourists.

15. **Level:** Easy | **Domain:** STANDARD ENGLISH CONVENTIONS
    Skill/Knowledge: Form, Structure, and Sense

Key Explanation: Choice A is the best answer. It is a singular word which refers to "one more," which in the context refers to "one artist other than yourself." It fits the idea of sampling music from someone who is not yourself.

Distractor Explanation: Choice B is incorrect because, while it can be used to refer to different artists that are not yourself, it needs a plural noun, "artists" as there is no "the" in front of it. **Choice C** is used to describe all other artists, but the context is referring to taking work from one, as seen in the singular "copyright to that work." **Choice D** is incorrect because it is used as an object on its own, not with another noun like "artist."

16. **Level:** Medium | **Domain:** STANDARD ENGLISH CONVENTIONS
    Skill/Knowledge: Form, Structure, and Sense

Key Explanation: Choice C is the best answer. The underline modifies the following word, "guilty," which is an adjective describing "person." **Choice C** is an adverb, so is properly used with an adjective.

Distractor Explanation: Choices A and **D** are

incorrect because they are adjectives, so should not be used to describe another adjective. They are used when referring to nouns. **Choice B** is a noun, so should not be used to modify another part of speech.

17. **Level:** Medium | **Domain:** STANDARD ENGLISH CONVENTIONS
Skill/Knowledge: Form, Structure, and Sense

Key Explanation: Choice D is the best answer. An apostrophe and s are used to show possession for one person; in this case, the death of J.R.R. Tolkien.

Distractor Explanation: Choice A is incorrect because it is too ambiguous; it could refer to either Tolkien or his son. **Choice B** is incorrect because an s forms a plural noun, but does not indicate possession. **Choice C** is used to show the possession of more than one person, but the context implies that Tolkien died and his son was still alive to publish the manuscript.

18. **Level:** Medium | **Domain:** STANDARD ENGLISH CONVENTIONS
Skill/Knowledge: Form, Structure, and Sense

Key Explanation: Choice D is the best answer. "Smaller than our sun" is a modifier that should be followed by the noun it refers to, in this case, "the red dwarf star HD260655."

Distractor Explanation: All of the other choices are incorrect because the modifier at the start of the sentence illogically describes the incorrect noun. In **Choice A**, "smaller than our Sun" refers to the generic "there." In **Choice B**, it refers to "only 33 light years," and in **Choice C** it refers to "our solar system."

19. **Level:** Easy | **Domain:** STANDARD ENGLISH CONVENTIONS
Skill/Knowledge: Boundaries

Key Explanation: Choice A is the best answer. In this text, "and" joins two verb phrases, "worked..." and "published...." Two verbs should not be divided by commas if they share the same subject; in this case, "Kenyan writer Ngugi wa Thiong'o" does both actions. There should also not be a comma between the verb "published" and its object, "A Grain of Wheat in July."

Distractor Explanation: Choices B and **D** are incorrect because there should be no comma after "Nairobi" because the "and" joins two verbs with the same subject. **Choices C** and **D** are incorrect because there should be no comma after "published." A comma is needed between a verb and a quote only when the quoted information is a complete sentence, not when the marks are indicating the title of a book.

20. **Level:** Easy | **Domain:** STANDARD ENGLISH CONVENTIONS
Skill/Knowledge: Boundaries

Key Explanation: Choice B is the best answer. When additional information is included in a sentence using two dashes, then the main part of the sentence should remain grammatically correct. By removing the aside, it is easier to determine that the proper sentence structure uses the idiom "cite XX as YY." **Choice B** completes this structure.

Distractor Explanation: All of the other choices are incorrect because they create a grammatically incorrect main clause. **Choice A** places two nouns in a row without any particle or preposition showing how they relate to each other. **Choices C and D** add an additional subject (which or they) and verb.

21. **Level:** Easy | **Domain:** STANDARD ENGLISH CONVENTIONS
Skill/Knowledge: Boundaries

Key Explanation: Choice D is the best answer. The idiom "as XX as YY" should have no punctuation dividing the elements from each other; they are part of the same idea.

Distractor Explanation: All of the other choices can be eliminated because they divide the standard idiom "as XX as YY" with punctuation. **Choices A and C** are incorrect because a colon and a single dash in a sentence should follow a complete clause, but the idea in front of the punctuation is incomplete. **Choice B** is incorrect because commas are used to divide separate ideas from the main clause.

22. **Level:** Easy | **Domain:** STANDARD ENGLISH CONVENTIONS
Skill/Knowledge: Boundaries

Key Explanation: Choice D is the best answer. "Both" refers to the two ideas "during his lifetime" and "after his lifetime." No punctuation should separate the parts of an idea joined by "both," especially as the shared idea of "lifetime" is included at the end.

Distractor Explanation: All of the other choices include unnecessary punctuation. **Choice A** makes the preposition "during" stand on its own without a noun to clarify it; there needs to be something specifying "during what." **Choice B**

divides "his lifetime" from the two prepositions that refer to it. is incorrect because a single dash should follow a complete sentence, but "during" is dangling.

23. **Level:** Easy| **Domain:** EXPRESSION OF IDEAS
Skill/Knowledge: Transitions

Key Explanation: Choice B is the best answer because the passage is discussing two kinds of dogs that track people in different ways. **Choice B** sets up the idea that the following information is going to be very different from what precedes, so it effectively shows that the two dogs work under two methods that are distinct.

Distractor Explanation: Choices A and C are incorrect because they are used to show the result of an argument. However, the fact that air-scent dogs sniff an area is not the result of the discussion that trailing dogs follow a specific scent. **Choice D** is used to introduce more information on the same topic, so erroneously makes the reader think the discussion will continue with more details about trailing dogs.

24. **Level:** Easy | **Domain:** EXPRESSION OF IDEAS
Skill/Knowledge: Transitions

Key Explanation: Choice C is the best answer. **Choice C** is used to provide emphasis for a preceding claim by adding details that support that claim. **Choice C** therefore fits the context of adding the detail that males are physically not capable of drinking blood to the more general preceding claim that they do not drink blood.

Distractor Explanation: Choice A is used to show a logical conclusion of an argument that is being developed, but the fact that males do not have a special mouth is not necessarily the logical result of not drinking blood; it is more of a cause. It is possible for the males to have the special mouth but not use it. **Choice B** is used to summarize items in a list or conclude a section in a passage, but in this case, there is an additional idea which follows: mosquitos get energy from plants. **Choice D** is incorrect because it is used to add the specific example that illustrates a claim. However, the passage implies that there are more reasons for not drinking blood than the mouth shape. Rather, the reason is that they don't need the protein.

25. **Level:** Easy | **Domain:** EXPRESSION OF IDEAS
    Skill/Knowledge: Rhetorical Synthesis

    Key Explanation: : **Choice D** is the best answer. The writer wants a strong word that shows a strong need to do something, and **Choice D** emphasizes the idea of obligation or necessity.

    Distractor Explanation: Choice A is incorrect because it only shows that something is possible, not that it is necessary to do. **Choice B** indicates that there is no doubt that the act will occur in the future, as opposed to stressing the fact that it needs to be done. **Choice C** is much milder than **Choice D,** giving the indication that making changes is a possibility or option, but not imperative.

26. **Level:** Medium | **Domain:** EXPRESSION OF IDEAS
    Skill/Knowledge: Rhetorical Synthesis

    Key Explanation: Choice B is the best answer. "Accelerating" includes the idea of getting increasingly fast or greater over time, so no additional words are needed.

    Distractor Explanation: All of the other choices

can be eliminated as redundant. They include words with the same meaning as "accelerating," distracting the reader from the point of the sentence.

27. **Level:** Hard | **Domain:** EXPRESSION OF IDEAS
    Skill/Knowledge: Rhetorical Synthesis

    Key Explanation: Choice B is the best answer. The student emphasizes the second bullet that Cher explored different styles by highlighting the point that the two songs are of different styles.

    Distractor Explanation: None of the other choices highlights a common feature. **Choice A** only says that the songs were performed at different times. **Choice C** refers to a song and a television series, but there is no unifying theme about why those are notable. **Choice D** also refers to two unrelated facts: the reader does not know how or why they are significant.

1. **Level:** Easy | **Domain:** ALGEBRA
Skill/Knowledge: Linear equations in one variable
Testing point: Solving equations with one variable

Key Explanation: Choice B is correct. This question can be solved in two ways. The most efficient way to solve the equation is to factor out the 4 from the left side of the equation yielding $4(x+4)=24$. Dividing both sides of the equation by 4 yields $(x+4)=\dfrac{24}{4}$, which equates to $(x+4)=6$, which is **Choice B.**

The second way to solve this equation is to subtract 16 from both sides of the equation. The result is $4x+16-16=24-16$ which in turn translates to $4x=8$. Dividing both sides of the equation by 4 gets $x=2$. However, the question asks for the value of $x+4$, and not x, which will then be 2 + 4, or 6.

Distractor Explanation: Choice A is incorrect as this is the value of $4x$ when 16 is subtracted from both sides of the equation. **Choice C** is incorrect as this is the value of x. **Choice D** is incorrect as this answer may be the result of a conceptual error or miscalculation.

2. **Level:** Medium | **Domain:** PROBLEM–SOLVING AND DATA ANALYSIS
Skill/Knowledge: Probability and conditional probability | **Testing point:** Conditional probability

Key Explanation: Choice A is correct. Given that there are 35 teachers in the school, according to the table, there are 16 female teachers. Thus, the number of male teachers in the school is 35 – 16 = 19. The number of people in the school is found by adding the number of teachers to the number of students as follows: 245 + 35 = 280. Therefore,

of the 280 people in the school, 19 are male teachers and the probability of selecting a male teacher is $\dfrac{19}{280}$.

Distractor Explanation: Choice B is incorrect since it is the probability of choosing a teacher given that he is already male. **Choice C** is incorrect, since it's the probability of choosing a male given that he is already a teacher. **Choice D** is incorrect as it is conceptually incorrect because it mixes students and teachers.

3. **Level:** Easy | **Domain:** ADVANCED MATH
Skill/Knowledge: Nonlinear equations in one variable and systems of equations in two variables
Testing point: Solving absolute value equations

Key Explanation: Absolute value equations usually have two solutions. The first step would be to remove the parentheses and set up two linear equations as follows:

$2x - 3 = 11$ and $2x - 3 = -11$

To solve for x in the first equation, add 3 to both sides of the equation as follows:

$2x - 3 + 3 = 11 + 3$

$2x = 14$

$x = 7$

To find the second solution solve for x in the second equation by adding 3 to both sides of the equation as follows:

$2x - 3 + 3 = -11 + 3$

$2x = -8$

$x = -4$

Thus, the positive solution for x is 7.

4. **Level:** Easy | **Domain:** ALGEBRA
Skill/Knowledge: Linear functions | **Testing point:** Perpendicular lines

Key Explanation: Choice C is correct. Perpendicular lines meet at 90–degree angles and have opposite sign reciprocal slopes. Putting the given equation into slope–intercept form $y = mx + b$ by dividing all terms by 5, yields $y = \frac{4}{5}y + 3$. The m in the slope–intercept form of the equation represents the slope of the line. Therefore, the slope of the line is $\frac{4}{5}$ and the opposite reciprocal slope is $\frac{-5}{4}$, which is the slope of the perpendicular line. This makes **Choice C** the only correct answer.

Distractor Explanation: Choice A is incorrect as the line would be parallel to m rather than perpendicular as the lines have the same slope. **Choices B** and **D** are incorrect as they are the negative of the perpendicular slope.

5. **Level:** Medium | **Domain:** GEOMETRY AND TRIGONOMETRY
    Skill/Knowledge: Circles | **Testing point:** Standard form of the equation of a circle and completing the square

    Key Explanation: Choice C is correct. To find the center of the circle, first transform the equation to its standard form $(x - h)^2 + (y - k)^2 = r^2$, where (h, k) is the center of the circle and r is its radius. To get the equation in standard form, complete the square. To do this, first, rearrange the terms in the equation to have all the x's and y's near each other as follows: $x^2 - 6x + y^2 + 4y = 36$. The standard form of a quadratic equation is $ax^2 + bx + c$ Next, working with just $x^2 - 6x$, with $a = 1$ and $b = -6$, add $\left(\frac{b}{2}\right)^2$ or $\left(\frac{-6}{2}\right)^2$ to both sides of the equation

to get $x^2 - 6x + 9 + y^2 + 4y = 36 + 9$. Next, working with just $y^2 + 4y$, with $a = 1$ and $b = 4$, add $\left(\frac{b}{2}\right)^2$ or $\left(\frac{4}{2}\right)^2$ to both sides of the equation to get $x^2 - 6x + 9 + y^2 + 4y + 4 = 36 + 9 + 4$ or 49. Next, factoring $x^2 - 6x + 9$ yields $(x - 3)^2$, and factoring $y^2 + 4y + 4$ yields $(y + 2)^2$, to get $(x - 3)^2 + (y + 2)^2 = 49$

Therefore, the center of the circle will be (3, –2).

Distractor Explanation: Choice A is incorrect because if the standard form of a circle equation is read incorrectly then $(-h, -k)$ would be incorrectly determined to be the center of the circle. **Choice D** is incorrect as the x and y coordinates have been reversed. **Choice B** is incorrect as this is the negative of incorrect **Choice D**.

6. **Level:** Hard | **Domain:** ADVANCED MATH
    Skill/Knowledge: Equivalent expressions | **Testing point:** Exponents and matching coefficients

    Key Explanation:
    $(8^x)^x \times 4^{2x} = ((2^3)^x)^x \times (2^2)^{2x} = 2^{3x^2} \times 2^{4x}$
    This yields $2^{3x^2 + 4x}$ using exponent rules.
    $\dfrac{2^{ax^2}}{2^{-bx}} = 2^{ax^2 + bx}$ using exponent rules.
    Therefore,
    $3x^2 + 4x = ax^2 + bx$
    $a = 3$

7. **Level:** Medium | **Domain:** ALGEBRA
    Skill/Knowledge: Linear inequalities in one or two variables | **Testing point:** Solving systems of linear inequalities

    Key Explanation: Choice B is correct. The most

efficient way to solve the problem is to substitute the given answer choices into the system of inequalities and see which answer makes both inequalities valid. Plugging in **Choice A** into the first inequality yields

$-6(-2) + 3 < -4$

$12 + 3 < -4$

$15 < -4$, which is false. Plugging in **Choice B** into the first inequality yields $-6(4) + 3 < 7$

$-24 + 3 < 7$

$-21 < 7$, which is true. Next, plug **Choice B** into the second inequality which yields

$7 < 4 + 6$

$7 < 10$. This is true, making **Choice B** the correct option.

Distractor Explanation: Choice A does not work as shown above. Plugging **Choice C** into the first inequality yields

$-6(-2) + 3 < 1$

$12 + 3 < 1$

$15 < 1$, which is not true. Plugging **Choice D** into the first inequality yields

$-6(-2) + 3 < -4$

$12 + 3 < -4$

$15 < -4$, which is not true.

8. **Level:** Hard | **Domain:** ADVANCED MATH
    Skill/Knowledge: Nonlinear functions | **Testing point:** Transformations of quadratic equations

    Key Explanation: Choice A is correct. The vertex form of the equation of a parabola is $y = (x - h)^2 + k$, where (h, k) is the vertex of the parabola. Thus, the vertex of the $f(x)$ equation is (3, 8) and the vertex of the $g(x)$ equation is (5, 5). Therefore, the x coordinate moves to the right 2 units from $f(x)$ to $g(x)$, and the y coordinate moves down 3 units.

Distractor Explanation: Choice B is incorrect as the x coordinate is moving to the right, not the left. A student may pick this option if he or she assumes that since h has reduced by 2 units it is moving to the left. **Choice C** is incorrect because the y coordinate is moving down not up. **Choice D** is incorrect. This incorrect answer may be selected if the student transformed $g(x)$ onto $f(x)$ instead of the other way around.

9. **Level:** Easy | **Domain:** ADVANCED MATH
    Skill/Knowledge: Nonlinear functions | **Testing point:** Identifying the equation of an exponential function from a graph

    Key Explanation: Choice D is correct. The graph depicts an exponential growth equation, which has its standard equation $y = ab^x$, where if in an exponential equation $b > 1$, then the equation represents exponential growth. The value of a in the equation represents the initial value of the equation when $x = 0$. Using the process of elimination, choices A and C can be ruled out as their b values are less than 1 and thus represent exponential decay, not growth. **Choice A** can also be ruled out as it gives an initial value of 5 whereas the graph shows a smaller initial value. **Choice D** is correct as it is the only equation that shows that the graph is increasing exponentially and has a y-intercept of less than 5.

    Distractor Explanation: See the process of elimination answer explanations above.

10. **Level:** Medium | **Domain:** GEOMETRY AND TRIGONOMETRY
    Skill/Knowledge: Right triangles and trigonometry | **Testing point:** Similar triangles and use of SOHCAHTOA

Key Explanation: Since triangle *DEF* and triangle *PQR* are similar, angles *F* and *R* are congruent. Therefore, *sin R = sin F*. Therefore using *SOHCAHTOA* the *sin* of an angle is equal to the length of the opposite side to the angle divided by the length of the hypotenuse of the triangle. Thus, the *Sin* of *F* is $\frac{5}{13}$.

11. **Level:** Easy | **Domain:** PROBLEM-SOLVING AND DATA ANALYSIS
    Skill/Knowledge: One-variable data: distributions and measures of center and spread | **Testing point:** Finding the mean

    Key Explanation: Choice B is correct. To find the average of a set of data, divide the total sum of the values of the data by the number of items. The average of the SAT scores of the 7 students is 1,320. Therefore, the sum of their scores would be 1,320 × 7 = 9,240. Adding in the SAT score of the 8th student, the new sum of the SAT scores will be 9,240 + 1,460 = 10,700. The new average SAT score will be $\frac{10,700}{8} = 1,337.5$, which is 1,340 rounded to the nearest tens place.

    Distractor Explanation: Choice A is incorrect as this is the average of the average SAT scores of the 7 students and the score of the new student $\frac{(1,320 + 1,460)}{2}$. **Choice C** is incorrect as this is the mean score if the new higher score is subtracted from the sum of the current sum of scores and divided by 6. **Choice D** is incorrect as this answer incorrectly assumes that the new score will be the new average SAT score.

12. **Level:** Easy | **Domain:** PROBLEM-SOLVING AND DATA ANALYSIS

    Skill/Knowledge: Two-variable data: models and scatterplots | **Testing point:** Exponential function interpretation

    Key Explanation: Choice B is correct. The 3 in the exponential equation above represents the growth factor. It indicates a tripling of the bacteria. When *t* = 14 the growth factor in the equation becomes $3^{\frac{14}{14}}$, which is 3, and therefore at *t* = 14 days the amount of bacteria triples. There are 14 days in two weeks which makes **Choice B** the correct answer.

    Distractor Explanation: The equation for an exponential model is $y = ab^x$, where *a* represents the initial amount of the data. **Choice A** is incorrect because *a* = 2,034 would represent the amount of bacteria at the beginning of the study and not the given term. **Choice C** is incorrect because it assumes that the model is linear, however, the model is exponential. **Choice D** is incorrect as this answer gives *rp(t)* and not the given term in the equation.

13. **Level:** Easy | **Domain:** ALGEBRA
    Skill/Knowledge: Linear equations in one variable
    Testing point: Linear equation with no solutions

    Key Explanation: The first step is to use the distributive property to expand out the terms on the left side of the equation as follows:

    $5(x + 3) - 3(2 - x)$

    $5x + 15 - 6 + 3x$

    Combining like terms on the left side of the equation yields $8x + 9$

    Therefore, for the equation below to have no solutions, the lines represented by both sides of the equation need to be parallel, and thus have the same slope and different *y*-intercepts. Since the equations are in slope–intercept form $y = mx + b$, with different y-intercepts, the slope of the line represented by $8x + 9$ is 8 and thus $p = 8$.

14. **Level:** Hard | **Domain:** ALGEBRA
Skill/Knowledge: Systems of two linear equations in two variables | **Testing point:** Finding the number of solutions in a system of equations

Key Explanation: Choice D is correct. To compare the equations, do math operations to get the equations in the slope–intercept form $y = mx + b$, where m is the slope of the line and b is the y-intercept. First, simplify the second equation by dividing out a 2 from all terms to get: $-3x = -4y + 16$. Adding $4y$ to both sides of the equation and adding $3x$ to both sides of the equation yields $4y = 3x + 16$. Dividing all terms in the equation by 4 to get it into slope–intercept form yields $y = \dfrac{3}{4} x + 4$. Adding $-3x$ to both sides of the first equation yields $-4y = -3x + 16$. Dividing all terms in the equation by -4 yields $y = \dfrac{3}{4} x - 4$. Looking at the revised equations the lines have the same slope but different y-intercepts, making the lines parallel. Parallel lines do not intersect, and therefore there is no solution to the system of equations.

Distractor Explanation: Choice A is incorrect because to have one solution, the slopes of both equations should not be equal, and they are. **Choice B** is incorrect because linear systems cannot have 2 solutions. **Choice C** is incorrect because to have infinitely many solutions the equations would need to represent the same line and thus be the same (the slopes and y-intercepts of the two lines would be the same); they are not.

15. **Level:** Medium | **Domain:** GEOMETRY AND TRIGONOMETRY
Skill/Knowledge: Circles | **Testing point:** Finding the length of a minor arc

Key Explanation: Choice A is correct. The length of the minor arc is found by using the formula $\dfrac{\theta}{360}\pi d$, where theta is the measure of the central angle and d is the diameter of the circle. Therefore, the length of minor arc AB is $\dfrac{72}{360}\pi(12) = 2.4\pi$, which is **Choice A.**

Distractor Explanation: Choice B is incorrect as it gives the area of the minor sector AOB. **Choice C** is incorrect as it is the circumference of the whole circle. **Choice D** is incorrect as it is $\dfrac{12\pi}{72} = \dfrac{\pi}{6}$ and may be due to a calculation error.

16. **Level:** Medium | **Domain:** ADVANCED MATH
Skill/Knowledge: Equivalent expressions | **Testing point:** Matching coefficients

Key Explanation: $(x + 3)^2$ is equal to $(x + 3) \times (x + 3)$. Using the foiling method to multiply out the terms, yields $x^2 + 3x + 3x + 9$, or $x^2 + 6x + 9$. Using the distributive property, $-2(x^2 + 6x + 9) + 6 = -2x^2 - 12x - 18 + 6$, which is equivalent to $-2x^2 - 12x - 12 = ax^2 + bx + c$. Therefore, $c = -12$.

17. **Level:** Easy | **Domain:** GEOMETRY AND TRIGONOMETRY
Skill/Knowledge: Lines, angles, and triangles | **Testing point:** Midpoint between two points on a line

Key Explanation: Choice C is correct. To find the midpoint between two points on a line (x_1, y_1)

and (x_2, y_2), use the midpoint coordinates formula $\left(\dfrac{x_1 + x_2}{2}, \dfrac{y_1 + y_2}{2} \right)$

Therefore the coordinates of the midpoint of line segment AB can be found from the following equations: $\dfrac{6 + x_2}{2} = 8$ and $\dfrac{11 + y_2}{2} = 10$. Using cross products, solve $x_2 + 6 = 16$, or $x_2 = 10$, and $y_2 + 11 = 20$, or $y_2 = 9$. Therefore, the coordinates of point B are $(10, 9)$.

Distractor Explanation: Choice A is incorrect and is found when the midpoint formula is used incorrectly with $(8, 10)$ and $(6, 11)$ as the points. **Choice B** is incorrect and is found by subtracting in the midpoint formula instead of adding. **Choice D** is incorrect and may be arrived at through a conceptual error.

18. **Level:** Easy | **Domain:** ADVANCED MATH
    Skill/Knowledge: Nonlinear functions | **Testing point:** Finding the number of solutions to an absolute value equation

    Key Explanation: Choice A is correct. Since the absolute value is equal to zero, the only value that makes the absolute value equation equal to zero is $x = -3$. Thus, there is only one solution.

    Distractor Explanation: Choice B is incorrect as to have two solutions the absolute value must be equal to a positive number. Zero is not a positive number. **Choice C** is incorrect because for an absolute value to have 0 solutions, it must be equal to a negative number and zero is not a negative number. **Choice D** is incorrect as there is enough information to answer the question.

19. **Level:** Easy | **Domain:** ADVANCED MATH
    Skill/Knowledge: Nonlinear functions | **Testing point:** Absolute value and value of a function

Key Explanation: Choice A is correct. To find $f(2)$, substitute 2 for all values of x in the equation as follows:

$(2)^2 - 20(2) + 9 = -27$.

To find $|f(2)|$ take the absolute value of -27 which is 27, or **Choice A**.

Distractor Explanation: Choice B is incorrect as the question requires the absolute value of the function value and not the function value itself. **Choices C** and **D** are incorrect and can be arrived at through miscalculations.

20. **Level:** Easy | **Domain:** PROBLEM-SOLVING AND DATA ANALYSIS
    Skill/Knowledge: Percentages | **Testing point:** Percentage increase and decrease

    Key Explanation: Assume that the initial price of the oil was x. The price of oil after the 20% increase would be $1.2x$. This price is then decreased by 14%. Thus, 86% of the oil price remains and thus $0.86 \times 1.2x = 1.032x$. This shows that after the two changes, the price of oil has increased overall by 3.2%.

21. **Level:** Easy | **Domain:** GEOMETRY AND TRIGONOMETRY
    Skill/Knowledge: Circles | **Testing point:** Area of a circle inscribed in a square

    Key Explanation: Choice C is correct. The length of a side of the square is equal to the diameter of the circle. The area of a circle can be found using the formula πr^2, where r is the radius of the circle.

    The radius of a circle is half of its diameter, so the radius of the circle is $\dfrac{4\sqrt{2}}{2}$ or $2\sqrt{2}$. Therefore, the area of the circle is $\left(2\sqrt{2}\right)^2 \times \pi$ or 8π.

Therefore, $p = 8$.

Distractor Explanation: Choice A is incorrect. This is the value of the area of the square and not the circle. **Choice B** is incorrect. This is the value of two times the diameter of the circle. **Choice D** is incorrect. This is the value of the area of the circle if the radius is equal to 8.

22. **Level:** Medium | **Domain:** ALGEBRA
Skill/Knowledge: Linear inequalities in one or two variables | **Testing point:** Solving a linear inequality

Key Explanation: Choice B is correct. To solve, first add x to both sides of the equation to get: $-2x + 6 \leq 2$. Next, subtract 6 from both sides of the equation to get: $-2x \leq -4$ Finally, divide both sides by -2 which flips the inequality sign yielding $x \geq 2x$ is, therefore, greater than or equal to 2. Only Choice B is not in the domain of the equation.

Distractor Explanation: Choices A, C, and **D** are incorrect. These answer choices are solutions to the inequality and answer the opposite of what the question is asking.

1. **Level:** Easy | **Domain:** ADVANCED MATH
   Skill/Knowledge: Nonlinear functions | **Testing point:** Sum of the solutions

   Key Explanation: Choice C is correct. The equation represents a quadratic in the form $ax^2 + bx + c$, where $a=3$, $b=9$, and $c=-27$. The sum of the solutions to a quadratic equation is given by the formula $\left(\dfrac{-b}{a}\right)$, Therefore, the sum of the solutions of the quadratic equation would be $\left(\dfrac{-9}{3}\right)$, or -3.

   Distractor Explanation: Choice A is incorrect as it is $\left(\dfrac{b}{a}\right)$, not $-\left(\dfrac{b}{a}\right)$. **Choice B is incorrect** because it is the product of the solutions to the quadratic equation and not the sum of them. The product of the solutions of a quadratic equation is given by the formula $\left(\dfrac{c}{a}\right)$, which is $\left(\dfrac{-27}{3}\right)$ or -9.

   Choice D is incorrect as it is the negative of the product of the solutions.

2. **Level:** Easy | **Domain:** ADVANCED MATH
   Skill/Knowledge: Equivalent expressions | **Testing point:** Combining like terms

   Key Explanation: Choice D is correct. First, distribute the negative to the terms in the parentheses as follows:

   $3x^2y + 5x - 3x^2y^2 + 2x^2y$. Combining like terms yields $5x^2y + 5x - 3x^2y^2$ which is **Choice D** when the terms are arranged in standard form.

   Distractor Explanation: Choices A and C are incorrect due to miscalculation or lack of concept knowledge. **Choice B is incorrect.** The sign changes of the terms in the parentheses when the negative sign is distributed to these terms and the parenthesis is removed.

3. **Level:** Medium | **Domain:** ALGEBRA
   Skill/Knowledge: Linear inequalities in one or two variables | **Testing point:** Solving for a linear inequality

   Key Explanation: To solve the inequality, first subtract 2 from both sides to get: $\dfrac{-2y + 2 - 2 < 6}{-2}$

   Next, divide both sides by -2 to get: $y > -2$
   Note that multiplying or dividing by a negative number in an inequality flips the inequality sign. -1 is the least possible integer value of y which satisfies the inequality $y > -2$.

4. **Level:** Easy | **Domain:** ADVANCED MATH
   Skill/Knowledge: Nonlinear equations in one variable and systems of equations in two variables
   Testing point: Discriminant and solving for linear and quadratic equations

   Key Explanation: Choice A is correct. Using the substitution method, substitute the first equation for y in the second equation yielding $2x - 5 = 2x^2 - 18x + 45$.

   Next, subtract the $2x$ from both sides to get $-5 = 2x^2 - 20x + 45$. Add 5 to both sides of the equation to get $0 = 2x^2 - 18x + 50$. The discriminant of a quadratic equation is $b^2 - 4ac$, when the quadratic equation is in the form $ax^2 + bx + c$. In the quadratic equation $a = 2$, $b = -20$, and $c = 50$. The value of the discriminant determines the number of solutions for a quadratic equation. Therefore, plugging in the values of a, b, and c into the discriminant, yields $(-20)^2 - 4(2)(50)$ which yields $400 - 400 = 0$ Therefore, the system will have one solution as the discriminant $= 0$.

   Distractor Explanation: Choices A and C are incorrect, most likely due to a miscalculation.

Choice D is incorrect. Quadratic equations can't have an infinite number of solutions.

5. **Level:** Easy | **Domain:** ALGEBRA
   Skill/Knowledge: Systems of two linear equations in two variables | **Testing point:** Solving linear systems using elimination or substitution

   Key Explanation: Choice A is correct. The most efficient way to solve the system of equations is to subtract the two equations resulting in $x + y = 9$.

   The system of equations can also be solved using the elimination or substitution methods to find x and y individually and then adding the values of x and y to find the answer.

   Distractor Explanation: Choice B is incorrect as it is the value of x only and not $x + y$. **Choice D** is incorrect as it is found by the sum of the two equations which instead yields $5x - 3y = 13$, which does not give the value of $x + y$. **Choice C** is incorrect as it is due to a miscalculation or a conceptual error.

6. **Level:** Easy | **Domain:** GEOMETRY AND TRIGONOMETRY
   Skill/Knowledge: Right triangles and trigonometry | **Testing point:** Trigonometric identities

   Key Explanation: There is a trigonometric identity which states that $sin\ x = cos\ (90° - x)$

   Therefore, $sin\ 32° = cos\ 58°$ and thus $cos\ 58° = 0.551$.

7. **Level:** Hard | **Domain:** GEOMETRY AND TRIGONOMETRY
   Skill/Knowledge: Lines, angles, and triangles | **Testing point:** Conversion of measurements and area of triangles

Key Explanation: Choice D is correct. The area of a triangle is found by the formula $A = \frac{1}{2} \times$ base $\times$ height. Since the answer is required in *ft squared*, we will need to convert any lengths of the sides of the triangle that are in *inches* to *feet*.

Therefore, 10 *inches* can be converted to *feet* by multiplying it by $\frac{1}{12}$, which gives $\frac{10}{12}$ feet. This reduces to $\frac{5}{6}$ *ft*.

Using the area of a triangle formula, the area is

$\frac{1}{2} \times \frac{5}{6} \times 24 = 10\ ft.$

Distractor Explanation: Choice A is incorrect as this is the area of the triangle without having converted any of the side *lengths* to *feet*. **Choice B** is incorrect as even though the measurements have been converted to feet, the formula for the area used was *base × height* which is not the correct formula. **Choice C** is incorrect as this is the area if all the side lengths were in inches instead of *feet*.

8. **Level:** Hard | **Domain:** ADVANCED MATH
   Skill/Knowledge: Equivalent expressions | **Testing point:** Subtracting fractions with variable denominators

   Key Explanation: Choice C is correct. All the given answer choices have one term, and not two like the original expression. Thus, the two fractional expressions need to be combined into one fraction by getting them both over the least common denominator. The least common denominator of the two terms is $x\ (x - 4)$. To get both terms over the least common denominator the first term needs to be multiplied by $\frac{(x-4)}{(x-4)}$ and the second term needs to be multiplied by $\frac{x}{x}$, yielding

$$\frac{-5(x-4)}{x(x-4)} = \frac{x(x)}{x(x-4)}$$

Since the denominators of the fractions are equal, the numerators can be combined over a single fraction as follows:

$$\frac{-5(x-4)-x(x)}{x(x-4)} = \frac{-5x+20-x^2}{x^2-4x},$$

which is **Choice C**.

Distractor Explanation: Choice A is incorrect as the question asked to simplify the terms and not solve for anything. **Choices B** and **D** are incorrect and may be due to a conceptual error or miscalculation.

9. **Level:** Easy | **Domain:** ALGEBRA
    Skill/Knowledge: Linear equations in two variables | **Testing point:** Identifying linear equations from graphs

    Key Explanation: Choice B is correct. The slope–intercept equation of a line is $y = mx + b$, where m is the slope and b is the y-intercept of the equation. The slope m of a line can be found using the equation $m = \frac{(y_2 - y_1)}{(x_2 - x_1)}$, where (x_1, y_1) and (x_2, y_2) represent any two points on the line.

    Pick two points on the line that are easy to find on the graph. The x and y intercepts of the line are two good points to use. Using points $(2, 0)$ and $(0, 6)$, the slope of the line can be found by plugging these points into the slope formula, yielding $\frac{(6-0)}{(0-2)}$, or $\frac{6}{-2} = -3$. The y-intercept of the line is 6. Therefore $y = -3x + 6$. All of the answer choices are written in an offset of the standard equation of a line $ax + by = c$. Adding $3x$ to both sides of the slope–intercept form of the equation gives the standard equation of the line as $3x + y$

= 6. Multiplying all terms of the equation by 3 to better match the form of the answer choices yields $9x + 3y = 18$, which matches **Choice B**.

Distractor Explanation: Choice A is incorrect as this equation represents a line with a positive slope. From the graph the slope of the line is negative. **Choice C** is incorrect because the slope of the line is -3 and not 2. **Choice D** is incorrect because the slope of the line is -3 and not -4.

10. **Level:** Easy | **Domain:** ADVANCED MATH
    Skill/Knowledge: Nonlinear functions | **Testing point:** Finding y-intercept

    Key Explanation: The y-intercept occurs where $x = 0$, $y - 7 = 3^0 - 5$. Anything to the power of zero $= 1$, so $y - 7 = 1 - 5$. Adding 7 to both sides of the equation to solve for y yields $y - 7 + 7 = 1 - 5 + 7$, $y = 3$.

11. **Level:** Medium | **Domain:** ADVANCED MATH
    Skill/Knowledge: Nonlinear functions | **Testing point:** Finding the value that makes a function undefined

    Key Explanation: Choice C is correct. A function is undefined when the denominator is equal to 0. To find what values of x make this occur, solve the equation $x^2 - 2x - 15 = 0$ for x. Use the grouping method of factoring to determine what two numbers multiply to -15 but add up to -2. The two numbers would be -5 and 3. Thus, the middle term of the quadratic equation can be written as $-5x + 3x$, instead of $-2x$ as follows: $2 - 5x + 3x - 15 = 0$. Grouping the terms and factoring out the greatest common factor of each group, yields $x(x - 5) + 3(x - 5) = 0$. $(x+3)(x-5) = 0$, $x = -3$, and $x = 5$. Only the solution to the quadratic equation $x = -3$ meets the question condition that x be less than zero. Thus, C is the correct answer.

Distractor Explanation: Choice A is incorrect since this is the positive x value of the solution and the value needs to be less than zero. **Choice B** is incorrect as it gives the negative value 5, which could be the result of factoring incorrectly. **Choice D** is incorrect. It may be due to a miscalculation.

12. **Level:** Medium | **Domain:** ALGEBRA
    Skill/Knowledge: Linear functions | **Testing point:** Finding the x-intercept given two points

    Key Explanation: Choice A is correct. $f(3) = -1$ and $f(4) = -3$ represent the x and y values of two points on a line. The points are $(3, -1)$ and $(4, -3)$. To find the x-intercept of the line represented, the equation of the line first needs to be determined. The slope-intercept form of the equation of the line, $y = mx + b$ is easiest to use. In this equation, m represents the slope of the line and b its y-intercept. The slope of a line can be found using the slope formula $m = \dfrac{(y_2 - y_1)}{(x_2 - x_1)}$. Plugging in the two points into the slope formula yields $m = \dfrac{-3 - (-1)}{4 - 3} = -2$.

    Therefore the equation of the line is $y = -2x + b$.

    To find b, plug either point into the equation and solve for b. Using the point $(3, -1)$ yields

    $-1 = -2(3) + b$, $-1 = -6 + b$, $b = 5$.

    Therefore the equation of the line is $y = -2x + 5$. The x-intercept of a line occurs where $y = 0$. Plugging in zero for y into the equation and solving for x gives the following x-intercept:

    $0 = -2x + 5$, $2x = 5$, $x = 2.5$ or $\dfrac{5}{2}$.

    Distractor Explanation: Choice B is incorrect as this is the y-intercept. **Choice C** is incorrect as this is the slope of the line. **Choice D** is incorrect and

is the result of a miscalculation in solving for the x-intercept.

13. **Level:** Hard | **Domain:** ALGEBRA
    Skill/Knowledge: Linear functions | **Testing point:** Transformations and Solving for function values

    Key Explanation: The function $f(x + 3)$ is moved to the left by 3 units, therefore we should also move the x value in $f(x)$ to the left by 3 units to get $2 - 3$ or $f(-1)$

    Therefore $f(-1)$ is found by substituting -1 into the equation for x as follows:
    $5(-1) - 17 = -22$.

14. **Level:** Hard | **Domain:** PROBLEM-SOLVING AND DATA ANALYSIS
    Skill/Knowledge: Ratios, rates, proportional relationships, and units | **Testing point:** Calculating average speed with unknown variable

    Key Explanation: Choice B is correct. Average speed is calculated by taking the total distance traveled divided by the total time to travel that distance.

    The total distance traveled would be $x + x = 2x$

    The total time taken would be $2.5\ hrs + 1.5\ hrs = 4\ hrs$

    Therefore, the average. speed $= \dfrac{2x}{4} = \dfrac{x}{2}$

    Distractor Explanation: Choice A is incorrect as it does not account for the fact that there is a return trip. **Choice C** is incorrect as it incorrectly accounts for the time it took Amber to do her errands. **Choice D** is incorrect as it may be due to a conceptual error or the student incorrectly found the total distance traveled.

15. **Level:** Easy | **Domain:** GEOMETRY AND TRIGONOMETRY
    Skill/Knowledge: Area and volume | **Testing point:** Perimeter of a rectangle

    Key Explanation: Choice B is correct. If the width of the rectangle is w, the length would be $w+3$. The area of a rectangle can be found by multiplying the width of the rectangle by its length.

    Therefore the area of the rectangle would be $w(w+3)=28$. Using the distributive property, the equation can be expanded out to:

    $$w^2+3w=28$$

    $$w^2+3w-28=0$$

    Factoring the equation yields $(w+7)(w-4)=0$

    Setting both factors of the equation equal to 0 results in $w=-7$ and $w=4$. Since the width of a rectangle cannot be negative, –7 is not a valid width for the rectangle. Therefore the width of the rectangle would be 4 and the length would be $4+3$ or 7. The perimeter of a rectangle is found by the formula $P=2(l+w)$. Plugging in the determined values for w and l yields

    $2(7+4)=22$ or **Choice B**.

    Distractor Explanation: Choice A is incorrect as this value is the sum of the length and the width and not two times the sum. **Choice C** is incorrect as this is half the area. **Choice D** is incorrect and may be due to conceptual error.

16. **Level:** Easy | **Domain:** PROBLEM–SOLVING AND DATA ANALYSIS
    Skill/Knowledge: Inference from sample statistics and margin of error | **Testing point:** Inference from sample statistics

    Key Explanation: The students surveyed who do not practice sanitary routines are (48 – 23) =

25. It can therefore be extrapolated that $\frac{25}{48}$ of all the students in the school donot practice sanitary routines. Therefore $\left(\frac{25}{48}\right)\times 2,280$ or 1,187.5 students. This rounds up to 1,188 students.

17. **Level:** Medium | **Domain:** ALGEBRA
    Skill/Knowledge: Linear functions | **Testing point:** Linear transformations

    Key Explanation: Choice D is correct. To move one unit up, 1 is added to the equation. To move 1 unit to the left, 1 is added to the x term in the equation as follows

    $y = 2 (x +1) + 1$

    $y = 2x + 2 + 1$

    $y = 2x + 3$

    Distractor Explanation: Choice A is incorrect as this is moving the line to the right 1 unit and up by 1 unit. **Choice B** is incorrect as this is moving the line only up by one unit and not moving it to the left. **Choice C** is incorrect as this answer may be due to a conceptual issue.

18. **Level:** Medium | **Domain:** ADVANCED MATH
    Skill/Knowledge: Nonlinear equation in one variable and systems of equations in two variables
    Testing point: Finding the vertex of a parabola

    Key Explanation: Choice D is correct. The standard form of a parabola is represented by the equation $y = ax^2 + bx + c$. In the equation given, $a = 2$, $b = 8$, and $c = 12$. The x coordinate of the vertex is found using the formula $\left(\frac{-b}{2a}\right)$. Thus, $\left(\frac{-8}{2(2)}\right)=-2$

Distractor Explanation: Choice A is incorrect as this is the product of the solutions to the quadratic equation. **Choice B** is incorrect as this is the sum of the solutions to the quadratic equation. **Choice C** is incorrect and is found by incorrectly using $\left(\dfrac{b}{a}\right)$.

19. **Level:** Easy | **Domain:** ADVANCED MATH
    Skill/Knowledge: Equivalent expressions | **Testing point:** Long division and remainder theorem

    Key Explanation: B is the remainder when $x^2 - 6x + 10$ is divided by $x + 2$. When the divisor is equated to 0, we find $x = -2$, we can then find the remainder by substitute -2 in place of x $\left(-2^2 - 6(-2) + 10\right)$ which yields 26, this is the value of B.

20. **Level:** Easy | **Domain:** GEOMETRY AND TRIGONOMETRY
    Skill/Knowledge: Lines, angles, and triangles | **Testing point:** The pythagorean theorem

    Key Explanation: Choice B is correct. The Pythagorean theorem states that the sum of the squares of the lengths of the sides of a right triangle is equal to the square of the length of the hypotenuse of the triangle, or $a^2 + b^2 = c$. Plugging in 11 for a and 61 for c yields $11^2 + b^2 = 61^2$

    $b^2 = 61^2 - 11^2$

    $b^2 = 3,721 - 121$

    $b^2 = 3,600$

    Therefore, $b = 60$.

    Distractor Explanation: Choices A and **D** are incorrect and may be due to conceptual or calculation errors. **Choice C** is incorrect and can be found by adding $61^2 + 11^2$ and finding the square root instead of subtracting the two numbers.

21. **Level:** Easy | **Domain:** PROBLEM-SOLVING AND DATA ANALYSIS
    Skill/Knowledge: Evaluating statistical claims: observational studies, and experiments | **Testing point:** Observational experiments

    Key Explanation: Choice D is correct. This statement is true because it is not certain that taking supplements would directly equate to an improvement in student performance. It is not known if all other variables were kept constant. Therefore, a direct cause-and-effect relationship cannot be determined. Also, the sample size is too small to generalize to a larger population.

    Distractor Explanation: Choices A, **B**, and **C** are incorrect. These statements are false and imply that there is a relationship between student performance and taking supplements.

22. **Level:** Easy | **Domain:** ALGEBRA
    Skill/Knowledge: Systems of two linear equations in two variables | **Testing point:** Solving for system of linear equations

    Key Explanation: Choice A is correct. The most efficient way to answer this question is to not solve the system of equations for x and y individually, but rather to subtract the second equation from the first, yielding $-x + y = -5$. Therefore $y - x = -5$.

    Distractor Explanation: Choice B is incorrect. This is the negative value of option A and is due to a calculation mistake. **Choice C** is incorrect. This is the value of y. **Choice D** is incorrect. This is the value of x.

This page is intentionally left blank

Chapter 3

....

Practice Test 2

You are about to begin a full-length Practice Test. The test has four modules. The time allotted for each module is marked at the beginning of the module. Work on one module at a time. Use a timer to keep track of the time limits for every module.

Try to take the Practice Test under real test conditions. Find a quiet place to work, and set aside enough time to complete the test without being disturbed. At the end of the test, check your answers by referring to the Answer Key and fill in your raw score in the scorecard below. Also, note down the time taken by you for completing each module.

Pay particular attention to the questions that were answered incorrectly. Read the answer explanations and understand how to solve them.

....

My Score Card (Raw Score)

	Reading and Writing		Math	
	Module 1	Module 2	Module 1	Module 2
Out of	27	27	22	22
My Score	_____	_____	_____	_____
Time Taken	_____	_____	_____	_____

TEST BEGINS ON THE NEXT PAGE

Reading and Writing Test

27 QUESTIONS | 32 MINUTES

DIRECTIONS

The questions in this section address a number of important reading and writing skills. Each question includes one or more passages, which may include a table or graph. Read each passage and question carefully, and then choose the best answer to the question based on the passage(s). All questions in this section are multiple-choice with four answer choices. Each question has a single best answer.

1

Hyraxes are small, furry, herbivorous mammals with short tails that live primarily in Africa; one species is also found in the Middle East. These little animals spend time in trees or rocky outcrops. They _____ resemble guinea pigs, but in reality, are much more closely related to sea cows and elephants.

Which choice completes the text with the most logical and precise word or phrase?

A) logically

B) customarily

C) superficially

D) universally

2

The following text is adapted from a publication by Jefferson Keel's 2011 publication, "The Indian Reorganization Act—75 Years Later: Renewing our Commitment to Restore Tribal Homelands and Promote Self-determination."

Today, the Indian Reorganization Act (IRA) is as necessary as it was in 1934. The purposes of the IRA were frustrated first by World War II and then by the termination era. Work did not begin again until the 1970s with the self-determination policy, and since then, Indian tribes are building economies from the ground up.

As used in the text, what does the word "frustrated" most nearly mean?

A) annoyed

B) unfulfilled

C) dissatisfied

D) thwarted

3

The following text is adapted from Mother Jones's speech to coal miners in West Virginia in 1912

The guards of the mining companies beat, abuse, maim, and hold up citizens without process of law; deny freedom of speech, a provision guaranteed by the Constitution; deny the citizens the right to assemble in a peaceable manner for the purpose of discussing questions in which they are concerned.

As used in the text, what does the word "provision" most nearly mean?

A) allocation

B) arrangement

C) contingency

D) requirement

4

The following text is from Frances Hodgson Burnett's 1905 novel "A Little Princess."

If Sara had been older or less punctilious about being quite polite to people, she could have explained herself in a very few words. But, as it was, she felt a flush rising on her cheeks. Miss Minchin was a very severe and imposing person, and she seemed so absolutely sure that Sara knew nothing whatever of French, that she felt as if it would be almost rude to correct her. The truth was that Sara could not remember the time when she had not seemed to know French.

Which choice best states the function of the underlined sentence in the text as a whole?

A) It gives a description of the physical appearance of one of the characters.

B) It establishes why one of the characters was not comfortable in the situation.

C) It reinforces an emotional state alluded to in the previous sentence.

D) It introduces the interaction between two characters in the following sentences.

5

The following text is adapted from Herman Melville's 1851 novel, "Moby Dick; or The Whale."

Now, when I say that I am in the habit of going to sea…I never go as a passenger; nor, though I am something of a salt, do I ever go to sea as a Commodore, or a Captain, or a Cook. I abandon the glory and distinction of such offices to those who like them. No, when I go to sea, I go as a simple sailor, right before the mast, plumb down into the forecastle, aloft there to the royal mast-head. True, they rather order me about some, and make me jump from spar to spar, like a grasshopper in a May meadow. And at first, this sort of thing is unpleasant enough. But this wears off in time.

The narrator brings up the analogy of a grasshopper to anticipate which of the following arguments?

A) A regular crew member does not receive enough compensation.

B) The duties of a simple sailor are sufficient to occupy that person's time.

C) The narrator should try to work his way up to a position as an officer.

D) It is important to obey orders from a superior officer aboard a ship.

6

The following text is adapted from F. Scott Fitzgerald's 1922 novel, "The Beautiful and the Damned."

At fifty-seven years old Adam Patch determined, after a severe attack of sclerosis, to consecrate the remainder of his life to the moral regeneration of the world. He became a reformer among reformers. He levelled a varied assortment of uppercuts and body-blows at liquor, literature, vice, art, patent medicines, and Sunday theatres. From an armchair in the office of his Tarrytown estate he directed against the enormous hypothetical enemy, unrighteousness, a campaign which went on through fifteen years, during which he displayed himself a rabid monomaniac, an unqualified nuisance, and an intolerable bore. The year in which this story opens found him wearying; <u>1861 was creeping up slowly on 1895;</u> his thoughts ran a great deal on the Civil War, somewhat on his dead wife and son, almost infinitesimally on his grandson Anthony.

Which choice best states the function of the underlined portion in the text as a whole?

A) It indicates that Adam Patch was living in the past rather than the present.

B) It provides a reason Adam Patch did not reflect often on the deaths of his wife and son.

C) It offers the reason that Adam Patch dedicated most of his time to campaigning against vices.

D) It clarifies the previous claim that Adam Patch was an intolerable bore.

The following text is adapted from Tien Nguyen's 2019 publication, "Antibodies Reverse Synthetic Opioid Overdoses in Mice."

Medical professionals have only one treatment option, a drug called naloxone, against acute opioid overdoses, which is a growing problem that in 2017 killed more than 47,000 people in the US. The fast–acting treatment, sold as Narcan, races towards the brain where it blocks opioid receptors, denying the drugs access to them. But naloxone breaks down after about an hour, which allows a relapse into overdose unless the drug is re–administered. Naloxone's short lifetime also makes it less effective against powerful synthetic opioids like fentanyl and carfentanil, which are 100– and 10,000–fold stronger than morphine, respectively.

Which choice best explains why naloxone is not completely desirable as a solution for patients who have overdosed on opiates?

A) Naloxone is only able to protect a patient for a limited period.

B) Naloxone is more expensive than other available treatment options.

C) Naloxone offers no results for overdoses of many opiate drugs.

D) Naloxone has harmful side effects which can injure the patient.

Why does the sky turn red at sunrise and sunset? The reason is Rayleigh Scattering, which is actually the same effect that you see in a rainbow when light hits rain. Light travels in waves, with red waves being the longest visible light and blue being the shortest. The shorter the wave, the easier it scatters into different directions. During the day, the Sun shines directly down on the atmosphere, so all wavelengths enter and the sky looks blue to a viewer. However, when the Sun gets lower on the horizon, the light is traveling through a much larger distance of the atmosphere to reach the same place on the Earth's surface. At that angle, many of the shorter blue waves get scattered into outer space, and only the longer, red waves, which travel in a straighter line before being scattered, reach the viewer.

Why does the author mention a rainbow in the text?

A) To explain where waves of light originate

B) To offer an example that the reader might recognize

C) To present an exception to a general rule

D) To show why blue waves scatter more easily than red waves

9

The following text is adapted from Fyodor Dostoevsky's 1848 collection of stories, "*White Nights and Other Stories.*"

Leaning on the canal railing stood a woman with her elbows on the rail, she was apparently looking with great attention at the muddy water of the canal. She was wearing a very <u>charming</u> yellow hat and a <u>jaunty</u> little black mantle. "She's a girl, and I am sure she is dark," I thought. She did not seem to hear my footsteps, and did not even stir when I passed by with bated breath and loudly throbbing heart. I was taken aback when I realized she was not just gazing at the water, but sobbing uncontrollably.

In the text, what is the main function of the words "charming" and "jaunty"?

A) They show that the girl's true age belied her outward appearance.

B) They establish that the girl was not suitably clad for the weather.

C) They identify the reason for the narrator's interest in the girl.

D) They highlight a contrast between the girl's appearance and her actions.

10

Most of the population in Sub-Saharan Africa works in subsistence agriculture to make a living and feed their typically large families. In recent decades, there has been enormous rural-to-urban migration to the major cities, which are extremely overcrowded. At the center of the main business districts are modern high-rise business offices well connected to the global economy, but outside are slums with no services and miserable, unsanitary conditions. The informal sector of the economy—that which is not regulated, controlled, or taxed—has become the primary system of doing business. The lack of government regulation prevents taxes from being assessed or collected, which, in turn, diminishes support for public services or infrastructure.

Based on information from the text, which of the following would best illustrate a transaction that occurs in the informal sector of the Sub-Saharan economy?

A) A farmer trades several chickens for enough wood to build a house for his newly-married son.

B) An international corporation from Denmark invests money in erecting a new school in a rural area.

C) A governor uses tax money to build a bridge, but hires a construction company owned by a good friend.

D) A young man from a rural area moves to a large city because he wants to find a better job.

11

The US Cities with the Greatest Percentage of Residents who Commute by Bicycle

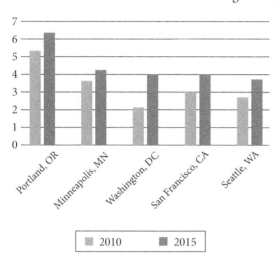

Based on data from the US Census Bureau

Why do people ride bicycles to work? Weather is not everything, as there is an annual average of 156 days of rain in the top commuting city, Portland, Oregon. Making cycling safer by adding protected bike lanes can increase ridership. Another option is making bikes more accessible, such as was done in the District of Columbia, which added 400 bike share depots since 2010. The success of such programs is evident: _____

Which choice most effectively uses data from the graph to complete the example?

A) Ridership in Washington, DC, increased from just over 2 percent in 2010 to 4 percent in 2015.

B) Washington, DC, used to have lower ridership than any other of the top five cities for bicycle commuters in 2010.

C) Portland, Oregon, now boasts over 6 percent of commuters who ride bikes and Washington, DC, has increased to 4 percent.

D) Washington, DC now has more bicycle commuters than San Francisco, California or Seattle, Washington.

12

Cumulative number of battery-electric cars in
the UK (2016 to date)

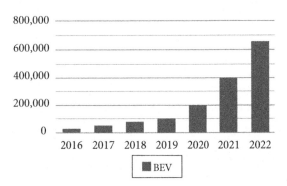

Source: SMMT, December 2002

According to a study released by The Society of Motor Manufacturers and Traders (SMMT), the number of electric cars registered in the United Kingdom has increased dramatically over the years, showing increasing customer preference for battery-electric cars over traditional cars. However, this customer preference for battery-electric cars has not increased uniformly over the years. For instance, _____

Which choice most effectively uses data from the graph to complete the text?

A) between 2016 to 2019, less than 200,000 battery-electric cars were registered in the UK

B) in 2020, less than 300,000 battery-electric cars were registered in the UK

C) by 2022, almost 700,000 electric cars had been registered

D) while the number of registered electric cars rose by 200,00 between the years 2020 and 2021, there was a spike of almost 300,000 additional cars registered in 2022

13

A new species of salamander, *Tylototriton phukhaensis,* was named in 2020. The defining feature is a distinct head ridge, though it also has head horns and a stripe down its back. A molecular examination shows that it is closely related to two of the four other *Tylototriton* species found in Thailand. First identified from a 20–year–old photograph in a travel magazine, biologists speculated whether the species still existed in the wild, but _____

Which choice most logically completes the text?

A) had to base their assessments on the *Tylototriton* species that were more readily available to them.

B) were able to locate living specimens that could provide enough information for a positive identification.

C) spent years vainly scouring the tropical rainforests before determining that it was probably indeed extinct.

D) finally concluded that the photograph might have been inaccurate or was possibly even created as a hoax.

14

Menkes disease is lethal and there is no known cure, so most patients die within the first decade of their lives, most before the age of 3. Because it is so rare, few pharmaceutical companies are investing in research related to the disease. Through the NIH Undiagnosed Diseases program, we evaluated a patient who presented clinically with abnormal hair and cognitive dysfunction. The hair abnormalities observed in our patient resemble those found in Menkes syndrome, but sequence analysis of the ATP7A gene and relevant biochemical testing showed that ATP7A wasn't involved in causing our patient's clinical features.

Which statement regarding Menkes disease can be most reasonably inferred from the passage?

A) Pharmaceutical companies are irresponsible in their attitude towards the disease.

B) Patients are usually not aware that they have the disease until its advanced stages.

C) There are not enough patients to make the development of a cure financially viable.

D) Giving a patient adequate ATP7A supplements can help reduce the effect of the disease.

15

There's nothing like homemade red Thai chili paste to enliven a meal. Most cooks opt for store–bought substitutes, however, because traditionally it takes over 30 minutes of grinding ingredients such as chili pepper, lemongrass, cilantro, _____ in a mortar and pestle.

Which choice completes the text so that it conforms to the conventions of Standard English?

A) shallots and, lime

B) shallots, and lime

C) shallots, and lime,

D) shallots, and, lime

16

William Shakespeare is often misquoted, but at other times, phrases are used in a context very different from what they were intended to be. While "now is the winter of our _____ frequently used to mean a horrible time, it actually signals a time of change for the better in the drama "Richard III."

Which choice completes the text so that it conforms to the conventions of Standard English?

A) discontent." It is

B) discontent," is

C) discontent", is

D) discontent" is

17

Algeria marks its 53rd year of independence this _____ bitter struggle for freedom in the late 1950s and early 1960s became a central focus of the global movement against colonialism. It also influenced the evolving forms of oppression and resistance in apartheid South Africa.

Which choice completes the text so that it conforms to the conventions of Standard English?

A) month, the

B) month—the

C) month: the

D) month. The

18

The Earth's core is _____ a very valuable source of energy, but scientists have only begun to determine how to harness its extreme heat, which may be 10,800 degrees Fahrenheit—about the same temperature as the surface of the Sun.

Which choice completes the text so that it conforms to the conventions of Standard English?

A) potent

B) potency

C) potential

D) potentially

19

The second smallest country by area in the world after Vatican City, Monaco is a mere 2.1 square kilometers. Most famous for the Monte Carlo Casino, _____. In fact, Monaco is a pioneer in marine conservation with one of the first protected marine areas in the world.

Which choice completes the text so that it conforms to the conventions of Standard English?

A) there is also an oceanographic museum in the country which is world–class.

B) the country also is home to a world–class oceanographic museum.

C) a world–class oceanographic museum is also in the country.

D) a museum of oceanography which is world–class is also in the country.

20

Given the number of incidents involving handguns in the past several years, politicians are considering new legislation to regulate the sale and possession of various firearms. Some critics claim that rather than increase the number of laws, police should make more effort to come _____ offenders.

Which choice completes the text so that it conforms to the conventions of Standard English?

A) out of

B) up with

C) down on

D) down with

21

Environmentalists have been trying a variety of solutions to remove plastic waste from the ocean. This serious problem will not be resolved easily, though, because the removal of waste from the ocean is a much slower process _____ the introduction of new plastic pollution.

Which choice completes the text so that it conforms to the conventions of Standard English?

A) as

B) then

C) than

D) to

22

Those who paid attention to the music industry started to notice the decades–long trend of Billboard–topping tracks that directly incorporated inspiration from their predecessors in the form of sampling. _____ Drake sampled Ms. Lauryn Hill, who sampled Wu Tang Clan, who sampled Gladys Knight and the Pips.

Which choice completes the text with the most logical transition?

A) Ultimately,

B) In addition,

C) Furthermore,

D) For example,

23

Since it was completed in 1911, the Stoclet House in Belgium has been among the finest examples of the Vienna Secession of the Art Nouveau style. The integrity of the exterior architecture and garden remains almost untouched, and the interior has undergone few changes. Even much of the furniture is original. _____ the house fulfills the architectural criteria necessary for a UNESCO World Heritage site, which it became in 2009.

Which choice completes the text with the most logical transition?

A) Subsequently,

B) Otherwise,

C) Therefore,

D) However,

24

Messier 47 is a well–known star cluster that contains mostly massive, hot blue stars. It was first identified in 1654 by an Italian astronomer named Giovanni Hodierna. Charles Messier, without knowledge of Hodierna's discovery, independently cataloged the cluster about a hundred years later. _____ he wrote down erroneous coordinates, so the Messier 47 remained lost until its presence was confirmed by T.F. Morris in 1957.

Which choice completes the text with the most logical transition?

A) Finally,

B) Ironically,

C) Specifically,

D) Accordingly,

25

While researching a topic, a student has taken the following notes:

1. The African grey hornbill (Lophoceros nasutus) is a member of the Hornbill family of mainly tropical near-passerine birds found in the Old World.

2. It is a widespread and common resident breeder in much of sub-Saharan Africa and the southwest of the Arabian Peninsula.

3. The African grey hornbill has escaped or been deliberately released into Florida, USA, but there is no evidence that the population is breeding and may only persist due to continuing releases or escapes.

4. At 45–51 cm (18–20 in) in length, the African grey hornbill is a large bird, although it is one of the smaller hornbills.

5. The African grey hornbill is widespread over much of sub-Saharan Africa. It prefers open woodland and savannah.

The student wants to emphasize that it is unlikely that the African grey hornbill will rapidly multiply in Florida. Which choice most effectively uses relevant information from the notes to accomplish this goal?

A) The African grey hornbill is a smaller hornbill and is easier to hunt down

B) It seems likely that the presence of the African grey hornbill is due to a deliberate release or escape, with no proof of breeding

C) The African grey hornbill is only commonly found in sub-Saharan Africa where the climate is highly unlike Florida

D) It is a tropical bird that is only widespread in open woodland and savannah areas

26

"Predictive analytics" is a term that is often used with big data. In essence, the term refers to the use of historical data and statistical techniques such as machine learning to make predictions about the future. An example is how Netflix knows what you want to watch before you do, making suggestions based on your past viewing habits. It is important to note that data doesn't just refer to rows and columns in a spreadsheet, but also to more complex files such as videos, images, and sensor data.

The writer is considering deleting the underlined sentence. Should the writer make this change?

A) Yes, because it disrupts the flow of logic in the paragraph.

B) Yes, because the example would be better placed at the start of the paragraph.

C) No, because it provides a necessary transition to new information.

D) No, because it provides a concrete example to help the reader better understand a concept.

27

Pierre Omidyar became one of the richest men in the world as the founder of eBay. He has invested large amounts of his fortune in antitrust cases <u>against big tech companies. He says that big tech companies are</u> overly powerful and are a danger to democracy.

Which choice most effectively combines the underlined sentences?

A) that he says are

B) against big tech companies, which he says are

C) against big tech companies because big tech companies are, he says,

D) antitrust cases, which are cases against what in his opinion are big tech companies that are

No Test Material On This Page

Reading Test

27 QUESTIONS | 32 MINUTES

DIRECTIONS

The questions in this section address a number of important reading and writing skills. Each question includes one or more passages, which may include a table or graph. Read each passage and question carefully, and then choose the best answer to the question based on the passage(s). All questions in this section are multiple-choice with four answer choices. Each question has a single best answer.

1

Tourism is a growing sector of the global economy. Travel and tourism jobs are increasing worldwide, but Africa as a whole attracts less than 5 percent of total world tourists. However, Sub-Saharan Africa has a strong supply-side potential to attract tourists. Beach resorts alone create a large _____. The coastal waters of the Indian Ocean boast some of the finest beaches in the world, with plenty of opportunities for water sports.

Which choice completes the text with the most logical and precise word or phrase?

A) haul

B) persuasion

C) draw

D) connection

2

Noted for his contributions to understanding seventeenth-century art in the Netherlands, John Montias had a formal education in cultural economics. His studies of art auction sales from the period led to breakthroughs in the understanding of the _____ painter Johannes Vermeer.

Which choice completes the text with the most logical and precise word or phrase?

A) conspicuous

B) eminent

C) radiant

D) absolute

3

The following text is from The Best Plays of the Old Dramatists by Havelock Ellis.

"The earliest known edition of The Tragical History of Doctor Faustus is that of 1604; there is a second edition with date of 1609, agreeing in almost every particular with the first; a third edition with new scenes and many alterations, was published in 1616…

It is very doubtful if any of the additions to the edition of 1616 are by Marlowe; Mr. Bullen thinks that some of them are. They are often ingenious, and sometimes, they are improvements. They appear to be written by a clever and <u>facile</u> imitator of Marlowe's style."

As used in the text, what does the word "facile" most nearly mean?

A) accomplished

B) successful

C) effortless

D) superficial

4

Horses have been demonstrated to possess complex thought processes that involve associations, memories, and recognition of emotions in other species. For example, in one experiment, horses were shown photographs of human faces that were angry or happy. <u>The people in the photographs were all strangers to the horses.</u> Several hours later, the actual person entered the field and stood near the horse with a neutral expression. In every case, the horses avoided approaching the people whose photographs had displayed anger.

What is the purpose of the underlined sentence in the overall structure of the text?

A) It explains how the subjects were selected for the experiment.

B) It points out that horses have a limited range of human contacts.

C) It highlights the importance of expression in communication.

D) It shows the researchers eliminated one possible weakness in the study.

5

While life is a special kind of complex chemistry, the elements involved are nothing special: carbon, hydrogen, oxygen and so on are among the most abundant elements in the universe. Complex organic chemistry is surprisingly common. Amino acids, just like those that make up every protein in our bodies, have been found in the tails of comets. There are other organic compounds in Martian soil. And 6,500 light years away a giant cloud of space alcohol floats among the stars. Habitable planets seem to be common too. The first planet beyond our Solar System was discovered in 1995. Since then astronomers have catalogued thousands.

What technique does the author of the text use to build the argument?

A) Personal anecdotes

B) Comprehensible analogies

C) Unsubstantiated theories

D) Summaries of findings

6

Text 1

Chromosomes were unknown in 1834 when Gregor Mendel proposed his classic concept of heredity. In the late 1880s, scientists finally could stain cell structures with the clarity to see chromosomes. Walter Sutton and Theodor Boveri, in 1902 and 1903 respectively, independently published papers suggesting that genes were located in specific places on the chromosomes, which came in matched pairs except for the male Y chromosome.

Text 2

Thomas Hunt Morgan criticized the Sutton–Boveri chromosome theory of inheritance. However, he noticed some unusual trends while conducting experiments on fruit flies. A few males had white rather than red eyes, so he bred them and observed the results. He determined that white was a recessive mutation which did not appear in any first–generation females, though it might resurface in subsequent generations. After careful documentation, he published his conclusion that eye color genes were located on the X chromosome.

Based on the texts after his experiments, how would Thomas Hunt Morgan (Text 2) most likely describe the view Sutton and Boveri presented in Text 1?

A) It is largely correct, but it required some adjustment concerning minor details.

B) It is not compelling because he had definitive data contradicting the theory.

C) It may seem plausible, but it is not supported by scientific findings.

D) It probably holds true despite his initial skepticism of it.

7

Giant anteaters are neotropical mammals that, as their name suggests, consume ants, termites, and grubs, though they do occasionally eat fruit. Their habitat ranges from Central to South America in swamps, forests, and grasslands where their favored prey is common. The solitary foragers have specialized tongues so they can consume thousands of ants in a few minutes after breaking open a nest, and they quickly abandon the site when soldier ants emerge to protect the colony.

Which choice best states the main idea of the text?

A) Giant anteaters live alone in neotropical areas that have not been disturbed by humans.

B) There are fewer opportunities for giant anteaters to eat since soldier ants are more vigilant.

C) Giant anteaters have adapted so that they are able to gather sufficient food.

D) Despite the danger of soldier ants, giant anteaters prefer to eat ants over other food sources.

8

Scientist James Clark and graduate student Jason McLachlan of Duke University published findings from a study analyzing tree pollen extracted from ancient lake sediments in the journal Nature. According to Clark, the purpose of their study was to address a central scientific problem in explaining the diversity of tree species in a forest. "In the mathematical models ecologists use to describe how different species compete for resources such as light, moisture and nutrients, it can be difficult to get species to coexist," he said. "In models, slight advantages allow one species to 'out-compete' the other, leading to extinction, that is, loss of biodiversity. And so, ecologists have put a lot of effort into trying to understand the differences among species that would allow one species to coexist with another species."

According to the text, what is the primary purpose of analyzing tree pollen extracted from ancient lake sediments?

A) To explore the ramifications of a mathematical model

B) To isolate factors that allow a phenomenon to happen

C) To identify the causes of an unusual incident

D) To isolate the flaws in a common theory

9

Robin Williams (1951–2014) has often been considered one of the best American comedians of all time. Famous for creating engaging characters at the spur of the moment, Williams began his career as a stand–up comic and moved on to win many prestigious awards for his roles in motion pictures. Everyone who knew him described him as full of natural talent and energy:

_____

Which quotation most effectively illustrates the claim?

A) "Williams helped us grow up." (Alyssa Rosenberg)

B) "He gave his…talent freely and generously to those who needed it most—from our troops stationed abroad to the marginalized on our own streets." (Barack Obama)

C) "The world is forever a little darker, less colorful and less full of laughter in his absence." (Zelda Williams)

D) "He came in like a hurricane…there goes my chance in show business." (David Letterman)

10

Figure 1: Deaths from Drug Overdoses in the United States by Year

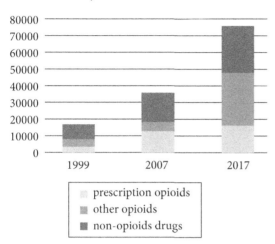

Data from National Institute on Drug Abuse, 2019.

In a potential advance in treating opioid overdose, researchers have developed long–lasting monoclonal antibodies that selectively bind potent synthetic opioids and reverse their effects in mice. The researchers propose that the antibodies could one day be administered as a stand–alone treatment or as part of a more effective combination treatment against opioid overdoses. This is extremely important, given that in 2017 alone, there were approximately _____.

Which choice most effectively uses data from the graph to complete the example?

A) 18,000 deaths caused by any drug overdoses

B) 38,000 deaths caused by any type of opiate drug overdose

C) 48,000 deaths caused by drug overdoses on any opiate

D) 75,000 deaths caused by prescription opiate drug overdoses

CONTINUE

11

Population change in the EU Member States during 2019 *(per 1,000 residents)*

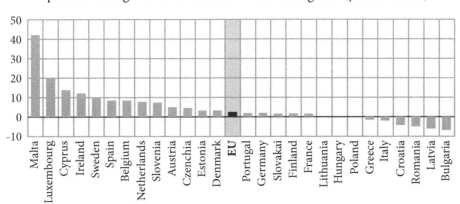

During 2019, there was an increase in population in eighteen member states. By far the highest population increase was recorded in Malta, followed by Luxembourg, Cyprus, Ireland, and Sweden. Conversely, _____

Which choice most effectively uses data from the graph to complete the text?

A) the largest population decreases were recorded in Bulgaria, Latvia, Romania, Croatia, and Italy

B) Italy recorded a negative population growth

C) only a few countries recorded an increase in population

D) 4.7 million deaths were registered in the EU in 2019

12

Studies have shown that a single, subanesthetic–dose (a lower dose than would cause anesthesia) ketamine infusion can often rapidly relieve depressive symptoms within hours in people who have not responded to conventional antidepressants, which typically take weeks or months to work. However, widespread off–label use of intravenous subanesthetic–dose ketamine for treatment–resistant depression has raised concerns about side effects, especially given its history as a drug of abuse. "The most common short–term side effect was feeling strange or loopy," said Acevedo–Diaz, of the Section on the Neurobiology and Treatment of Mood Disorders, part of the NIMH Intramural Research Program (IRP) in Bethesda, Maryland.

According to the text, what is the major concern of doctors about using ketamine to control depression for long periods of time?

A) It may not be effective when used repeatedly.

B) It has serious side effects in conjunction with other drugs.

C) Patients could become addicted to the drug.

D) Patients who take the drug sometimes relapse.

13

Robert Henri (1865–1929) was an American painter and teacher who disliked the conservative restrictions placed on the highly–polished art by artists affiliated with the National Academy of Design. With several colleagues, he introduced a new style that depicted the seedy underside of urban life in a bold, realistic fashion. Critics dubbed the artists with the title of "Ashcan School" because they drew sketches in the streets of New York and depicted dirty snow, laundry hanging out to dry, and other scenes of everyday life.

Based on the text, what is most likely true about artists affiliated with the National Academy of Design?

A) They used a bold, realistic style for their paintings.

B) They did not live or work in New York City.

C) They avoided subjects that were undignified.

D) They preferred to draw scenes related to summertime.

14

Waterfalls come in many shapes. One classic form is the punchbowl, such as at Eagle Falls in Oregon. In such a _____ water flows down a narrow chute into a wide pool at the bottom. It is easy to swim in the tranquil waters at the base.

Which choice completes the text so that it conforms to the conventions of Standard English?

A) waterfall

B) waterfall,

C) waterfall:

D) waterfall;

15

Scott Evans is a golf ball diver. In other words, he dives into the water hazards placed on golf courses to collect and recycle the balls which accidentally landed there. His job may sound fun, but it is not _____ spends hours in murky water and can get trapped by unseen obstacles.

Which choice completes the text so that it conforms to the conventions of Standard English?

A) easy, he

B) easy; because he

C) easy. Since he

D) easy. He

16

Northern New Zealand is home to some of the oldest forests on Earth. Forests filled with kauri, the Maori name for the *Agathis australis* tree, _____ back to the Jurassic period over 135 million years ago.

Which choice completes the text so that it conforms to the conventions of Standard English?

A) date

B) dating

C) they date

D) those forests date

17

While training departments try to give us what we need to stay ahead in the competitive market, research _____ that they are also falling behind: employees rate their Learning & Development departments lower than almost any other product in the consumer landscape.

Which choice completes the text so that it conforms to the conventions of Standard English?

A) are showing

B) will show

C) showed

D) shows

18

Elizabeth Catlett, _____ artwork is Modernist with African and Mexican influences, was a leading figure in portraying images related to race, gender, and class as it was experienced by Black Americans in the twentieth century.

Which choice completes the text so that it conforms to the conventions of Standard English?

A) her

B) who

C) whose

D) which

19

The German pianist Clara Schumann (1819–1896) is considered one of the finest performers of the Romantic period. Her career spanned over sixty years, much of which was spent traveling around Europe. In addition to giving concert performances, _____ composed many works for the piano.

Which choice completes the text so that it conforms to the conventions of Standard English?

A) she

B) her

C) hers

D) she's

20

Many organizations are turning to a policy called "job sharing" in an effort to retain good employees. Dividing one full–time job between two employees _____ a company to recruit talented workers who do not have the time or inclination to work 40 hours every week.

Which choice completes the text so that it conforms to the conventions of Standard English?

A) allow

B) allows

C) allowing

D) to allow

21

The collection of rainwater is known by many names throughout the world. _____ from rainwater collection to rainwater harvesting to rainwater catchment. Rainwater harvesting is a viable technology in an urban setting, as all that is needed to take advantage of this resource is to capture the free water falling onto a roof and direct it to a storage tank.

Which choice completes the text so that it conforms to the conventions of Standard English?

A) They ranges

B) Their range

C) These range

D) The names ranges

22

Dandelions are usually considered to be useless weeds. _____ they can be used in many recipes, as the leaves are edible and perfect for salads. Mature flowers are bitter, but young buds are sweet and taste slightly like honey.

Which choice completes the text with the most logical transition?

A) Therefore,

B) Nevertheless,

C) In particular,

D) Moreover,

23

Guernica, a painting in oil on canvas, is one of Pablo Picasso's masterpieces and arguably one of the most influential anti–war paintings of all time. Though Picasso typically painted in private, he allowed influential visitors into his studio to observe the progress in order to promote awareness of the Spanish Civil War. _____ the completed painting was exhibited around the world to raise funds for war relief efforts.

Which choice completes the text with the most logical transition?

A) In addition,

B) By contrast,

C) Consequently,

D) For instance,

24

Ethiopian Prime Minister Abiy Ahmed was awarded the 2019 Nobel Peace Prize for his efforts to end the ongoing stalemate between Ethiopia and Eritrea. At the beginning of his tenure, he was lauded for progressive decisions. _____ he was accused of restricting the freedom of the press and detaining innocent people who held opposing views.

Which choice completes the text with the most logical transition?

A) Additionally,

B) Accordingly,

C) Subsequently,

D) Consequently,

25

_____ there's something inherently appealing about entrepreneurs and the stories of why and how they do what they do. People are attracted to social entrepreneurs like Nobel Peace Prize laureate Muhammad Yunus for many of the same reasons they find business leaders like Steve Jobs so compelling—these people come up with ideas that dramatically improve people's lives.

At this point, the writer wants to show the depth of appeal. Which choice most effectively achieves the writer's goal?

A) On the most basic level,

B) At a basic and fundamental level,

C) At a level and depth that is fundamental,

D) On levels which are fundamental and basic,

26

While researching a topic, a student has taken the following notes:

1. Ludovico Maria Enrico Einaudi is an Italian pianist and composer who trained at the Conservatorio Verdi in Milan.

2. He has composed the scores for a number of films and television productions and has won several awards for his compositions.

3. Einaudi is most known for being the most-streamed classical artist of all time with his music reaching over 1 million streams daily, and 2 billion streams in total.

4. His latest album Seven Days Walking: Day One has become the fastest-streamed classical album of all time since its release on 15 March 2019. The project is a series of digital albums released monthly over seven consecutive months.

5. Day One interweaves piano and string and focuses on several main themes that will recur in different forms on subsequent albums.

The student wants to emphasize Einaudi's most well-known achievement. Which choice most effectively uses relevant information from the notes to accomplish this goal?

A) Among his many achievements, composer Ludovico Maria Enrico Einaudi trained at the Conservatorio Verdi in Milan and has won multiple awards

B) He has composed for multiple films and television shows

C) Einaudi is known as the most-streamed classical artist of all time, with 2 billion streams in total

D) Einaudi has come up with highly innovative projects, including combining recurring notes of piano and string in different albums

27

The term "ghost kitchen" may make you think of a haunted house. In reality, it is just a physical space to prepare food that will be eaten elsewhere. The number of ghost kitchens is actually _____, since multiple brands or restaurants can share a low–rent space to make meals sold on delivery food apps.

The writer wants to emphasize how fast the number is increasing. Which choice completes the text and achieves the writer's goal?

A) multiplying

B) inflating

C) skyrocketing

D) getting bigger

STOP

No Test Material On This Page

Math

22 QUESTIONS | 35 MINUTES

DIRECTIONS

The questions in this section address a number of important math skills. Use of a calculator is permitted for all questions.

NOTES

Unless otherwise indicated: • All variables and expressions represent real numbers. • Figures provided are drawn to scale. • All figures lie in a plane. • The domain of a given function is the set of all real numbers x for which $f(x)$ is a real number.

REFERENCE

    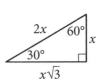

$A = \pi r^2$
$C = 2\pi r$

$A = \ell w$

$A = \frac{1}{2} bh$

$c^2 = a^2 + b^2$

Special Right Triangles

$V = \ell wh$

$V = \pi r^2 h$

$V = \frac{4}{3}\pi r^3$

$V = \frac{1}{3}\pi r^2 h$

$V = \frac{1}{3}\ell wh$

The number of degrees of arc in a circle is 360.

The number of radians of arc in a circle is 2π.

The sum of the measures in degrees of the angles of a triangle is 180.

For **multiple–choice questions,** solve each problem, choose the correct answer from the choices provided, and then circle your answer in this book. Circle only one answer for each question. If you change your mind, completely erase the circle. You will not get credit for questions with more than one answer circled, or for questions with no answers circled.

For **student–produced response questions,** solve each problem and write your answer next to or under the question in the test book as described below.

- Once you've written your answer, circle it clearly. You will not receive credit for anything written outside the circle, or for any questions with more than one circled answer.

- If you find more than one correct answer, write and circle only one answer.

- Your answer can be up to 5 characters for a positive answer and up to 6 characters (including the negative sign) for a negative answer, but no more.

- If your answer is a fraction that is too long (over 5 characters for positive, 6 characters for negative), write the decimal equivalent.

- If your answer is a decimal that is too long (over 5 characters for positive, 6 characters for negative), truncate it or round at the fourth digit.

- If your answer is a mixed number (such as 3.!. 2), write it as an improper fraction (7/2) or its decimal equivalent (3.5).

- Don't include symbols such as a percent sign, comma, or dollar sign in your circled answer.

CONTINUE

1

Ash has a walking and cycling routine. For every minute she walks, she burns 20 calories. And for every minute she cycles, she burns 35 calories. If she burns 340 calories on a particular day after walking for x minutes and cycling for y minutes, which of the following equations best represents her routine?

A) $340 - 20x = 35y$

B) $35y - 20x = 340$

C) $340 - 20y = 35x$

D) $35x - 20y = 340$

2

The graph below shows velocity (y–$axis$) plotted against time (x–$axis$). For how many data points is the actual value higher than the predicted values on the line of best fit?

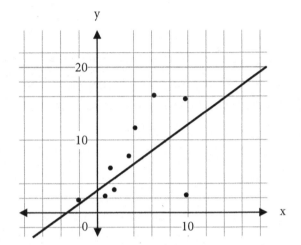

A) 9

B) 6

C) 3

D) 2

3

x	f(x)
−2	30
0	12
3	0
5	2

Which of the following is a factor of $f(x)$?

A) $(x+2)$

B) $(x-3)$

C) x

D) $(x-5)$

4

What is the value of s for the following system of equations?

$$(t-5)+2(s-3)=8$$

$$2(t-5)-3(s-3)=-19$$

5

How many solutions does the equation below have?

$$3(x-2)-2(x-1)=-x+2(x+2)-8$$

A) 0

B) 1

C) 2

D) Infinitely many

6

Which of the following is equivalent to $2g^{\frac{4}{5}}g^{\frac{2}{5}}$?

A) $\sqrt[5]{2g^6}$

B) $\sqrt[5]{32g^6}$

C) $2\sqrt[6]{g^5}$

D) $\sqrt[6]{2g^5}$

7

A researcher found the mean mass of all cheetahs in a park. He found that the mean mass of all cheetahs in the park is between 120 *lbs* and 182 *lbs*. What is the value of the margin of error for the mean mass of the cheetahs in the park?

8

What is the value of $f(6)$, if $f(2x) = 9x - 7$?

A) 20

B) 47

C) 101

D) 11

9

A teacher takes note of the shoe sizes for 21 students in his class and creates the table below. Which of the following statements is true about the data below?

Shoe size	Frequency
1	3
2	4
3	4
4	7
5	2
6	1

A) The mean is greater than the median

B) The mean is the same as the median

C) The median is greater than the mean

D) There isn't enough information to answer the question.

10

What is the value of the given equation $27^x \div 81^{-x} = 3^{ax}$?

11

If the value of the sum of interior angles of the hexagon is $b\pi$, what is the value of b?

A) 0.25

B) 1

C) 4

D) 2

12

What is the value when 80 is increased by 200%?

A) 200

B) 160

C) 240

D) 280

13

If $1 + \dfrac{a\sqrt{2}}{2}$ is a solution to the equation

$2x^2 - 4x - 7 = 0$, what is the possible value of a?

14

A real estate company kept a track of the number of houses it sold in October. Its team came up with the model $h(t) = 262 - 8t$, and t represents the number of days. Which of the following best represents 262?

A) The number of houses at the end of October

B) The number of houses at the beginning of October

C) The number of houses sold per day in October

D) The number of houses sold in the first 8 days of October.

15

ABC is a right–angled triangle, where B is 90° and angle C is 30°. If AC = 32, what is the area of triangle ABC.

A) $128\sqrt{3}$

B) $128\sqrt{2}$

C) $16\sqrt{3}$

D) $16\sqrt{2}$

16

If $(5xy + 3) - (6xy - 2xy^2 + 2) = axy^2 + bxy + c$, what is the value of $a + b$?

17

What is the product of the roots for the equation $3x^2 + 6x - 24 = 0$?

A) 3

B) –8

C) 2

D) –2

18

Which of the following best represents the equation of the graph below?

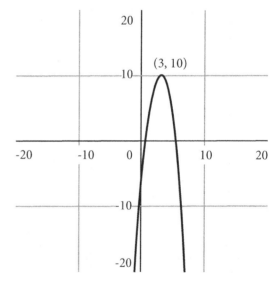

A) $y = 2(x + 3)^2 + 10$

B) $y = -2(x - 3)^2 + 10$

C) $y = 2(x - 3)^2 + 10$

D) $y = -2(x + 3)^2 + 10$

19

If $-3(-2 + 2x) = ax + b$, what is the value of ab?

20

Find the average rate of change when $x = 2$ and $x = 0$.

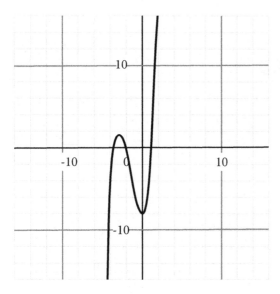

A) 8

B) −8

C) 4

D) −4

21

If $\frac{3}{4}(x-5) = 27$, what is the value of $x - 5$?

A) 41

B) 36

C) $\frac{81}{4}$

D) 31

22

Which of the following coordinates would be true for the following system of inequalities?

$$y > -2x - 1$$

$$3y < x + 9$$

A) (−2, 1)

B) (1, 4)

C) (3 , 1)

D) (−3, 3)

No Test Material On This Page

Math

22 QUESTIONS | 35 MINUTES

DIRECTIONS

The questions in this section address a number of important math skills. Use of a calculator is permitted for all questions.

NOTES

Unless otherwise indicated: • All variables and expressions represent real numbers. • Figures provided are drawn to scale. • All figures lie in a plane. • The domain of a given function is the set of all real numbers x for which $f(x)$ is a real number.

REFERENCE

$A = \pi r^2$
$C = 2\pi r$

$A = \ell w$

$A = \dfrac{1}{2} bh$

$c^2 = a^2 + b^2$

Special Right Triangles

$V = \ell w h$

$V = \pi r^2 h$

$V = \dfrac{4}{3} \pi r^3$

$V = \dfrac{1}{3} \pi r^2 h$

$V = \dfrac{1}{3} \ell w h$

The number of degrees of arc in a circle is 360.

The number of radians of arc in a circle is 2π.

The sum of the measures in degrees of the angles of a triangle is 180.

For **multiple-choice questions,** solve each problem, choose the correct answer from the choices provided, and then circle your answer in this book. Circle only one answer for each question. If you change your mind, completely erase the circle. You will not get credit for questions with more than one answer circled, or for questions with no answers circled.

For **student-produced response questions,** solve each problem and write your answer next to or under the question in the test book as described below.

- Once you've written your answer, circle it clearly. You will not receive credit for anything written outside the circle, or for any questions with more than one circled answer.

- If you find more than one correct answer, write and circle only one answer.

- Your answer can be up to 5 characters for a positive answer and up to 6 characters (including the negative sign) for a negative answer, but no more.

- If your answer is a fraction that is too long (over 5 characters for positive, 6 characters for negative), write the decimal equivalent.

- If your answer is a decimal that is too long (over 5 characters for positive, 6 characters for negative), truncate it or round at the fourth digit.

- If your answer is a mixed number (such as 3.!. 2), write it as an improper fraction (7/2) or its decimal equivalent (3.5).

- Don't include symbols such as a percent sign, comma, or dollar sign in your circled answer.

1

If p and q are solutions to the equation below, which of the following best represents $p+q$?

$$|3x - 1| = 2$$

A) $\dfrac{1}{3}$

B) 1

C) $\dfrac{2}{3}$

D) $-\dfrac{1}{3}$

2

Which of the following coordinates lie on the circle whose equation is $(x-3)^2 + y^2 + 8y = 84$?

A) $(1, 7)$

B) $(-2, 5)$

C) $(-3, 4)$

D) $(3, -6)$

3

If $\sin C = 0.986$ and $\cos 63 = 0.986$, what is the value of C?

4

If $\dfrac{2-2i}{3+4i}$ is equal to $a+bi$. What is the value of a?

A) $\dfrac{-2}{25}$

B) $\dfrac{-14}{25}$

C) $\dfrac{2}{3}$

D) $\dfrac{-1}{2}$

5

Which of the following can be the value of x for the system of equations below?

$$y = 2x^2 - 9x + 7$$
$$y = 2x - 2$$

A) $\dfrac{11}{2}$

B) -1

C) $\dfrac{9}{2}$

D) $\dfrac{7}{2}$

6

What is the positive solution to the following equation?

$$3|3x-2|-|6x-4|=7$$

7

Which of the following represents a *line l* (not shown) which is perpendicular to the *line m* (shown below)?

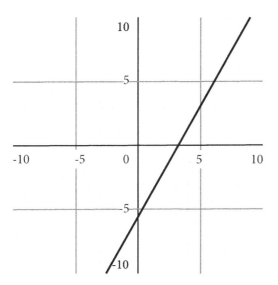

A) $3y = 5x - 15$

B) $5y = 3x + 15$

C) $5y = -3x + 15$

D) $3y = 5x + 10$

8

What is the circumference of the circle whose equation is $x^2 + 6x + y^2 - 4y = 51$

A) 64π

B) 8π

C) 14.28π

D) 16π

9

In the triangle ABC (not drawn to scale) shown below, $\angle ABC = 2x - 2$ and $\angle BAC = x + 3$. If $\angle ACD = 118°$, what is the value of x?

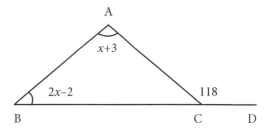

10

It takes 4 carpenters to build a bed in 3 days, how many carpenters will it take to build the bed in 2 days?

A)   12

B)   6

C)   8

D)   24

11

Which of the following is equivalent to $(5xy + 3x)(x - 2y)$?

A) $5x^2y - 6xy$

B) $5x^2y + 3x^2 + 10xy^2 - 6xy$

C) $5x^2y + 3x^2 - 10xy^2 - 6xy$

D) $-5x^2y^2 + 3x^2 - 6xy$

12

What is the value of y, if $7x - 4y = 1$ and $5x + 2y = 8$?

13

Which of the following is NOT a solution to the following equation?

$$-2x \leq 8 - x$$

A) -8

B) -10

C) 2

D) -7

14

If an unfair coin is tossed 20 times, and it lands on heads 14 times. What would be the probability of it landing on heads the 21st time?

A) 0.5

B) 0.20

C) 0.3

D) 0.7

15

What is the value of $x - y$ if $3y - 2x = 16$ and $5x + y = -6$?

A) 6

B) 4

C) -2

D) -6

16

A student conducted research on how many fish there are in a pond after m months and came up with the model, $f(x) = 1{,}200(1.03)^m$.

He wanted to have the time on the model in d days instead, as shown below

(assuming 1 month has 30 days)

$$f(x) = 1{,}200(1.03)^{ad}$$

What is the value of a?

17

If the radius of a circular cylinder is 6, what is the volume of the cylinder if the height is twice its radius?

A) 432π

B) 864π

C) 216π

D) 108π

18

What is the value of the angle EOD, if the angle DRE is 35°?

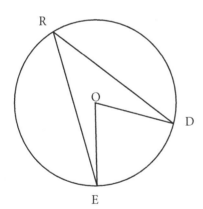

A) 70°

B) 35°

C) 60°

D) 55°

19

Which of the following is equivalent to

$$\frac{4x^2 - 3}{2x + \sqrt{3}}?$$

A) $2x - \sqrt{3}$

B) $2x + \sqrt{3}$

C) $2x - 3$

D) $2x + 3$

20

If the system of equations below has infinite solutions, what is the value of b?

$$9x - 14y = -3$$
$$ax - by = 6$$

21

If $3x + 5y = ax - 4x - by$, what is the value of a?

A) 3

B) 1

C) −5

D) 7

www.vibrantpublishers.com
    129
    CONTINUE

22

Which of the following values is a solution to inequality?

$$3x + 2 < -5(x + 6)$$

A) 4

B) 3

C) −4

D) −5

STOP

No Test Material On This Page

Answer Key

Reading and Writing

Module 1

Questions	Correct	Mark your correct answers
1.	C	
2.	D	
3.	D	
4.	C	
5.	D	
6.	A	
7.	A	
8.	B	
9.	D	
10.	A	
11.	A	
12.	D	
13.	B	
14.	C	
15.	B	
16.	D	
17.	D	
18.	D	
19.	B	
20.	C	
21.	C	
22.	D	
23.	C	
24.	B	
25.	B	
26.	D	
27.	B	

Module 2

Questions	Correct	Mark your correct answers
1.	C	
2.	B	
3.	D	
4.	D	
5.	D	
6.	D	
7.	C	
8.	B	
9.	D	
10.	C	
11.	A	
12.	C	
13.	C	
14.	B	
15.	D	
16.	A	
17.	D	
18.	C	
19.	A	
20.	B	
21.	C	
22.	B	
23.	A	
24.	C	
25.	A	
26.	C	
27.	C	

Math

Module 1

Questions	Correct	Mark your correct answers
1.	A	
2.	B	
3.	B	
4.	8	
5.	D	
6.	B	
7.	31	
8.	A	
9.	A	
10.	7	
11.	C	
12.	C	
13.	3	
14.	B	
15.	A	
16.	1	
17.	B	
18.	B	
19.	−36	
20.	D	
21.	B	
22.	C	

Module 2

Questions	Correct	Mark your correct answers
1.	C	
2.	C	
3.	27°	
4.	A	
5.	C	
6.	3	
7.	C	
8.	D	
9.	39	
10.	B	
11.	C	
12.	$\frac{3}{2}$ or 1.5	
13.	B	
14.	D	
15.	D	
16.	$\frac{1}{30}$ or 0.0333	
17.	A	
18.	A	
19.	A	
20.	−28	
21.	D	
22.	D	

1. **Level:** Medium | **Domain:** CRAFT AND STRUCTURE
    Skill/Knowledge: Words in Context

    Key Explanation: Choice C is the best answer because the blank portion shows how hyraxes resemble guinea pigs. **Choice C** refers to something that is only on the outside or surface, so fits the context of saying that the hyrax and guinea pig look similar, but they are not really related.

    Distractor Explanations: None of the other choices accurately explain how hyraxes resemble guinea pigs. **Choice A** refers to something that makes sense through reasoning, but one would reason that if the hyrax is related to an elephant, then it should look more like one. **Choice B** refers to something that happens by habit or tradition, but appearance is not based on habit. **Choice D** refers to something that happens in all cases or everywhere, so does not establish that some people see a general similarity.

2. **Level:** Medium | **Domain:** CRAFT AND STRUCTURE
    Skill/Knowledge: Words in Context

    Key Explanation: Choice D is the best answer because "frustrated" refers to what World War II and the termination era did to the purposes of the IRA. Choice D means "blocked" or "prevented," which fits the context of showing that events prevented the goals of the IRA from being completely fulfilled; that is why it is still needed today.

    Distractor Explanation: Choices A and C can be eliminated because they are emotional responses, but "the purposes of the IRA" are inanimate and cannot experience emotions. **Choice A** means

"irritated" and **Choice D** means "not happy with something." **Choice B** is incorrect because "fulfilling" refers to something doing the act of making another thing happen. However, it does not fit the context because World War II and the termination era were not things that could "fulfill" or make the IRA's goals happen. They were obstacles that stopped other things from fulfilling the purposes of the IRA.

3. **Level:** Hard | **Domain:** CRAFT AND STRUCTURE
    Skill/Knowledge: Words in Context

    Key Explanation: Choice D is the best answer because "provision" is something that is guaranteed by the Constitution, freedom of speech. **Choice D** refers to something that is necessary or must happen, so it fits the context of saying that freedom of speech is a right or need to be guaranteed by the highest law of the country.

    Distractor Explanation: None of the other choices adequately shows what is guaranteed by the Constitution. **Choice A** refers to the process of sharing something. **Choice B** refers to plans or preparations, but does not include the idea that they must occur. **Choice C** is a future event that might occur but cannot be accurately predicted.

4. **Level:** Medium | **Domain:** CRAFT AND STRUCTURE
    Skill/Knowledge: Text Structure and Purpose

    Key Explanation: Choice C is the best answer. The underlined sentence says that Sara flushed, which typically happens in anger or embarrassment. In this context, she appears embarrassed because she is not old or experienced enough—and was too "punctilious" or "careful"—to explain how she felt in a few words. The fact that she flushes highlights her sense of awkwardness and embarrassment.

Distractor Explanation: Choice A is incorrect because the sentence only says that Sara flushed. It does not explain what she looked like; she could be tall, short, dark–haired or blonde, dressed nicely, etc. **Choice B** is incorrect because the underlined sentence only establishes that Sara blushes. It does not give a reason why; the following sentences show she could speak French but was reluctant to tell Miss Minchin so. **Choice D** is incorrect because there is no interaction between characters in the following sentences. The underlined portion is expanded upon with a reason for blushing, not actions.

5.   **Level:** Hard | **Domain:** CRAFT AND STRUCTURE
     Skill/Knowledge: Text Structure and Purpose

     Key Explanation: Choice D is the best answer because the narrator describes his actions on the boat, "jumping from spar to spar" as similar to the jumping of a grasshopper. This work is because "they rather order me about some"; presumably "they" are the officers that are not "simple sailors." He says that it is true that he has to hop around obeying orders, but says that "at first, this sort of thing is unpleasant enough" but that "this wears off in time." Therefore, the analogy "anticipates" or "defends against" the argument that such work is "distasteful" or "unpleasant" because he says he is used to the role.

     Distractor Explanation: Choice A is incorrect because "compensations" refers to payment, but the text does not contain references to money. **Choice B** is incorrect because the question is asking for an argument that the grasshopper analogy is used to disprove. Since the grasshopper analogy is that sailors are hopping around, or

busy, the argument being disproved should be the opposite, that sailors are not busy. **Choice C** is incorrect because the analogy of the grasshopper does not show that it is necessary or not to obey orders; the narrator merely says he does and that it is distasteful at first but he gets used to it.

6.   **Level:** Hard | **Domain:** CRAFT AND STRUCTURE
     Skill/Knowledge: Text Structure and Purpose

     Key Explanation: Choice A is the best answer because the phrase implies that Adam Patch still felt he was living in 1861, whereas really years had passed the times were changing. The phrase gives a reason for him to "weary" and become tired… he had been so wrapped up in reforms, but his causes were not current or relevant any more. His thoughts were still focused on events such as the Civil War rather than on everyday life or his grandson.

     Distractor Explanation: Choice B is incorrect because the passage implies that Adam focused on things that interested him. The fact that the wife and son died in the past is not the reason that he thinks about them infrequently; he doesn't really care about them as much as he does about things that happened earlier, like the Civil War. **Choice C** is incorrect because the fact that the times changed was the reason that his campaign against vices started to fade. The changing times is not why he started to fight against vice. **Choice D** is incorrect because someone can be interesting even if the times change. The reason that Adam was a bore was his actions during that time.

7.   **Level:** Easy | **Domain:** INFORMATION AND IDEAS
     Skill/Knowledge: Central Ideas and Details

Key Explanation: Choice A is the best answer because the text says that naloxone breaks down quickly, "after about an hour." This is "not completely desirable" or "unwanted" because it means that the drug needs to be carefully administered and the progress of the patient watched or the patient could "relapse" or "return to the original condition."

Distractor Explanation: Choice B is incorrect because there is no discussion of price in the text. **Choice C** is incorrect because the passage does not say that naloxone has "no results" for some drugs. It only claims that it is less effective, meaning it has results that are not as strong, for "powerful synthetic opioids like fentanyl and carfentanil." **Choice D** is incorrect because there is no evidence of side effects related to naloxone. The only negative effect implied is that it needs to be readministered because it wears off quickly.

8. **Level:** Easy | **Domain:** INFORMATION AND IDEAS
    Skill/Knowledge: Central Ideas and Details

    Key Explanation: Choice B is the best answer. The text is summarizing a potentially confusing effect that involves bending light waves. The reader has presumably seen a rainbow, however, so that image might help the reader visualize light bending when it hits the atmosphere as being similar to light bending when it hits rain.

    Distractor Explanations: Choice A is incorrect because "originate" means "begin," but light does not begin in a rainbow. **Choice C** is incorrect because the example of the rainbow shows the rule or effect of Rayleigh Scattering, it is not an "exception" or "not part of" the rule. **Choice D** is incorrect because the idea of a rainbow does not tell the reader "why" or "the reason" blue scatters

more easily; a rainbow just offers an image which shows that colors separate in different ways when they hit something like rain or the atmosphere.

9. **Level:** Hard | **Domain:** INFORMATION AND IDEAS
    Skill/Knowledge: Central Ideas and Details

    Key Explanation: Choice D is the best answer because the words "charming" and "jaunty" are often associated with cute, fun things. They imply that the yellow hat and black mantle were sweet or endearing things that a happy young girl might wear, for example, to a party. However, the girl is crying on a canal railing, so her cheerful clothes form a "contrast" or "opposite" impression.

    Distractor Explanation: Choice A is incorrect because the passage indicates that the girl is relatively young; the narrator starts by calling her a "woman" and shifts to "girl" after he gets a closer look. Clothes described as "charming" and "jaunty" are suitable for a younger person, so do not "belie" or "contradict" that she is young. **Choice B** is not supported by the passage because there is no description of the temperature or that her clothing was inappropriate; for example, she was not shivering because she was too cold. **Choice C** is incorrect because the narrator noticed the woman's action of leaning on a railing before noting her appearance. Her clothing is described as he takes a closer look.

10. **Level:** Medium | **Domain:** INFORMATION AND IDEAS
    Skill/Knowledge: Command of Evidence (Textual)

    Key Explanation: Choice A is the best answer because the passage defines the informal sector of the economy as "that which is not regulated, controlled, or taxed." Therefore, a situation where goods are bartered between people would count as "informal" because there is no money changing hands and no taxes paid on the exchange.

Distractor Explanation: Choice A is incorrect because the projects sponsored by a foreign investor would most likely need to go through an approval process and the school would need to pass at least a basic inspection. **Choice A** would include regulations and controls, so would be considered formal. **Choice C** is incorrect because, while it might not be completely honest, there would still need to be nominal proof about how much tax money was spent and what it was used for. **Choice D** is weak because there is no evidence in the example to elaborate on the young man's situation. For example, he could have filed all the correct paperwork, moved into a new apartment, and been paying income taxes from his new salary.

11. **Level:** Medium | **Domain:** INFORMATION AND IDEAS
    Skill/Knowledge: Command of Evidence (Textual)

    Key Explanation: Choice A is the best answer. The claim is that "such programs" are successful. There are two programs listed, making cycling safer and making bikes accessible. There are no specific examples of increasing safety, but the passage describes the details making bikes accessible by adding bike share depots in DC. **Choice A** shows that the program in DC, which started in 2010, probably has strong results, as ridership increased by over a percent in the five years after that policy was started.

    Distractor Explanation: Choice B is incorrect because it only says that DC had low ridership, but there is no indication of change. The reader does

not know that the ridership increased after the program started. **Choice C** is incorrect because it focuses on Portland, but there is no indication that Portland did anything to make cycling safer or more accessible. **Choice C** also refers to DC, but the percentage of commuters is lower than that of Portland, so it could appear that the program was not very successful. **Choice D** is incorrect because the reader does not know whether the program helped make the number of commuters in DC greater. It is possible that all along, there have been more commuters than the other cities. It is even possible that ridership in DC decreased after the program started.

12. **Level:** Medium | **Domain:** INFORMATION AND IDEAS
    Skill/Knowledge: Command of Evidence (Quantitative)

    Key Explanation: Choice D is correct because it shows an example of the inconsistent growth between the years 2020 to 2022. The previous sentence in the text talks about how the customer preference for electric cars has not increased uniformly. Choice D further illustrates this idea.

    Distractor Explanation: All the other choices are incorrect because the text must be completed with an example that illustrates the uneven rise in customer preference for battery-electric cars. **Choices A** and **B** both only state the number of electric cars registered between 2016-2019 and 2020, respectively. **Choice C** is incorrect because it does not offer a comparison that shows an uneven increase.

13. **Level:** Medium | **Domain:** INFORMATION AND IDEAS
    Skill/Knowledge: Inference

    Key Explanation: Choice B is the best answer. The third sentence refers to "a molecular examination" which established genetic relationships with other

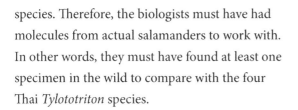
species. Therefore, the biologists must have had molecules from actual salamanders to work with. In other words, they must have found at least one specimen in the wild to compare with the four Thai *Tylototriton* species.

Distractor Explanation: All of the other choices are incorrect because a molecular examination only of the species that were available, not using *T. phukhaensis*, would not be able to determine the molecular characteristics of *T. phukhaensis* well enough to know what species are related or not. The other choices all give scenarios in which the scientists did not find examples of the new species for comparison.

14. **Level:** Easy | **Domain:** INFORMATION AND IDEAS
    Skill/Knowledge: Inference

Key Explanation: Choice C is the best answer because the text establishes that the disease does not have many patients: "Menkes is a rare X–linked disease." As a direct result of that rarity, "few pharmaceutical companies are investing in research related to the disease." In other words, the companies are not "investing" or "putting money" into research because it is rare. The logical implication is that the companies will not get enough profits back from their investment; the process of creating a cure is "not financially viable" or "will lose money."

Distractor Explanation: Choice A is incorrect because the text does not condemn the decision of the pharmaceutical companies. The tone is neutral and stating the fact that companies have not done research on Menkes disease, rather than saying that the company should invest money even though they will not be able to recoup their losses. **Choice B** is incorrect because the text

does not discuss the stages of the disease or when the disease can be diagnosed. It is possible that the disease could be diagnosed from right after birth or even through prenatal testing before any symptoms have appeared. **Choice D** is incorrect because, while the text indicates that the disease is linked to the ATP7A gene, it says there is no cure and there is no mention of supplements.

15. **Level:** Medium | **Domain:** STANDARD ENGLISH CONVENTIONS
    Skill/Knowledge: Boundaries

Key Explanation: Choice B is the best answer. The proper structure for joining a list of over two nouns with "and" is to place a comma after each of the nouns that precedes "and." In this case, there should be a comma after "chili pepper," "lemongrass," "cilantro," and "shallots." No other punctuation is needed because "such as…lime" restricts the type of "ingredients" to specific ones that are ground together.

Distractor Explanation: Choices A and **D** are incorrect because there should be no comma after "and" in a list. The comma after "shallots" is sometimes omitted, but would only be acceptable if there were no other commas in the underlined portion. **Choice C** is incorrect because there should be no comma after "lime." The following portion is necessary to the understanding of the main sentence, so should not be separated with any punctuation.

16. **Level:** Medium | **Domain:** STANDARD ENGLISH CONVENTIONS
    Skill/Knowledge: Boundaries

Key Explanation: Choice D is the best answer. When a phrase is used as part of a sentence, the punctuation aside from the quotation marks should adhere to usual structures. In this case, the quotation is part of a clause subordinated by the conjunction "while." Replacing the quotation with XX, it is easier to see that the quote is the subject and "is used" is the verb, so no punctuation should divide the underlined portion: "While XX is frequently used…"

Distractor Explanation: Choice A is incorrect because the portion before the period is not a complete sentence because there is no active verb. **Choices B** and **D** are incorrect because no comma should divide the subject from the verb in a clause; the placement inside or outside the quote mark is irrelevant in this context.

17. **Level:** Easy | **Domain:** STANDARD ENGLISH CONVENTIONS
    Skill/Knowledge: Boundaries

    Key Explanation: Choice D is the best answer. There are two independent clauses that can stand on their own as sentences on either side of the underlined portion. Therefore, they should be divided into two separate sentences with a period.

    Distractor Explanation: Choice A is incorrect because it is a comma splice between two independent clauses. **Choices B** and **C** can be eliminated because a single dash or colon can follow an independent clause, but the following portion needs to explain or add more detail to the previous sentence. In this case, the following portion changes to a different topic, from the 53rd year of independence to the struggle for freedom.

18. **Level:** Easy | **Domain:** STANDARD ENGLISH CONVENTIONS
    Skill/Knowledge: Form, Structure, and Sense

    Key Explanation: Choice D is the best answer. The underlined portion refers to "is," showing

that the claim has a possibility but not certainty of being true. **Choice D** is an adverb, which can be used to modify a verb.

Distractor Explanation: All of the other choices can be eliminated because they do not modify a verb. **Choices A** and **C** are adjectives, which modify nouns. **Choice B** is a noun.

19. **Level:** Medium | **Domain:** STANDARD ENGLISH CONVENTIONS
    Skill/Knowledge: Form, Structure, and Sense

    Key Explanation: Choice B is the best answer. "Most famous for the Monte Carlo Casino" is a modifier which needs to refer to the following noun. In this case, the modifier describes "the country" and shows what the country is most famous for.

    Distractor Explanation: All of the other choices can be eliminated because the modifier "Most famous for the Monte Carlo Casino" refers to something other than the country. In **Choice A**, the modifier is followed by the generic "there." In addition, "which is world–class" appears to refer to the preceding noun, "the country" rather than the "oceanographic museum." In **Choices C** and **D**, the modifier refers to the museum; the placement of "world–class" does not affect the answer choice.

20. **Level:** Medium | **Domain:** STANDARD ENGLISH CONVENTIONS
    Skill/Knowledge: Form, Structure, and Sense

    Key Explanation: Choice C is the best answer. "To come down on" is a phrasal verb which means "to deal severely with," so fits the context of saying that if police are severe on offenders, there is no need to make more laws.

Distractor Explanation: All of the other choices are incorrect because they are phrasal verbs with meanings that do not fit the context of explaining what police should do to the offenders. **Choice A** refers to leaving a place. **Choice B** refers to creating something. **Choice D** refers to catching an illness.

21. **Level:** Medium | **Domain:** STANDARD ENGLISH CONVENTIONS
    Skill/Knowledge: Form, Structure, and Sense

    Key Explanation: Choice C is the best answer. "Much XX–er than" is a standard idiom of comparison, which in this case shows that the speed of pollution entering the ocean is faster than the speed of pollution being removed from the ocean.

    Distractor Explanation: All of the other choices can be eliminated because they do not complete the idiom "much XX–er than" using a standard word.

22. **Level:** Easy | **Domain:** EXPRESSION OF IDEAS
    Skill/Knowledge: Transitions

    Key Explanation: Choice D is the best answer because it is used to introduce an "example" or "illustration" that supports a claim. The part preceding the underline is a claim that people noticed that sampling occurred. The following portion is a specific illustration of that claim, a list of people who sampled each other's music.

    Distractor Explanation: None of the other choices adequately shows the relationship between the preceding and following sentences. **Choice A** refers to the final statement in a list or the result of an action. **Choices B** and **C** are used to provide different ideas that support the same claim rather than an example of the preceding claim.

23. **Level:** Easy | **Domain:** EXPRESSION OF IDEAS
    Skill/Knowledge: Transitions

    Key Explanation: Choice C is the best answer because it is used to introduce the conclusion of an argument. In this case, the text explains why the Stoclet House is important, and the conclusion is that the house qualifies to be a UNESCO World Heritage site.

    Distractor Explanation: Choice A is incorrect because it is used to introduce something that comes later in a series, but the qualification to be a World Heritage site does not come after the building is created as a classic in its style and in good condition, it is because the building is in good condition. **Choice B** is incorrect because it shows something that would happen in a different situation, but in this case, the qualification and the described situation both occurred. **Choice D** is used to show a contrast or change in ideas, not continue a logical train of thought.

24. **Level:** Medium | **Domain:** EXPRESSION OF IDEAS
    Skill/Knowledge: Transitions

    Key Explanation: Choice B is the best answer because it refers to something that is wryly humorous because it was in error or had something other than the intended result. **Choice B** fits the context of saying that Messier named the cluster but lost it due to writing "erroneous" or "wrong" information about it.

    Distractor Explanation: Choice A is incorrect because it is used to introduce the last item in a list or discussion, but the text continues the story with what happens several hundred years later. **Choice C** is incorrect because it signifies that the following is an example or clarification of the previous claim, but making an error is not an example of cataloging stars. **Choice D** is used to show that the following is done in a way appropriate for the circumstances, so does not fit the context of making an error.

25. **Level:** Medium | **Domain:** EXPRESSION OF IDEAS
    Skill/Knowledge: Rhetorical Synthesis

    Key Explanation: Choice B is the best answer. The notes mention that "there is no evidence that the population is breeding" and that the small population of the African grey hornbill in Florida "may only persist due to continuing releases or escapes."

    Distractor Explanation: Choice A is incorrect because it does not explain why the bird will not rapidly multiply in Florida. **Choice C** is incorrect because the notes offer no comparison between the climate in sub-Saharan Africa and Florida. **Choice D** is incorrect because the notes do not mention that the African grey hornbill is only widespread in open woodland and savannah areas. Instead, it mentions that "it prefers open woodland and savannah."

26. **Level:** Medium | **Domain:** EXPRESSION OF IDEAS
    Skill/Knowledge: Rhetorical Synthesis

    Key Explanation: Choice D is the best answer. The underlined sentence is a specific, probably familiar example of how historical data, in this case, viewing habits, can be used to make predictions or suggestions. The sentence gives the reader an easy point of reference to understand the abstract concept of predictive analysis.

    Distractor Explanation: Choices A and **B** are incorrect because the underlined sentence should

remain in the text. It does not disrupt the logic and would not be better earlier in the paragraph, as it comes after the abstract idea is described. **Choice C** is incorrect because the example is not necessarily related to the following sentence; it elaborates on the previous one.

27. **Level:** Medium | **Domain:** EXPRESSION OF IDEAS
    Skill/Knowledge: Rhetorical Synthesis

    Key Explanation: Choice B is the best answer. "Which is" subordinates the second sentence so it modifies the previous noun, "big tech companies," while at the same time eliminating repeated words.

    Distractor Explanation: Choice A is incorrect because it changes the meaning from big tech companies being overly powerful and a danger to antitrust cases being overly powerful and a danger. **Choice C** is incorrect because it retains the unnecessary repetition of "big tech companies" and complicates the sentence structure with "he says" set aside by commas. **Choice D** is incorrect because it repeats "cases" and adds an element of meaning that is not in the original sentences: "in his opinion" makes the big tech companies ones that he decides are big tech.

1. **Level:** Medium | **Domain:** CRAFT AND STRUCTURE
   Skill/Knowledge: Words in Context

   Key Explanation: Choice C is the best answer because in the sentence, the underlined word is what beach resorts create. Choice C refers to the trait of being attractive and interesting enough to entice people to come. It fits the context of saying that even if there were no other tourist destinations, beach resorts are very attractive and interesting to tourists.

   Distractor Explanation: Choice A is incorrect because it refers to a large number of items collected by someone, but the beach resorts do not have a lot of things that they bought or amassed. **Choice B** refers to the act of convincing someone to do something. However, the beaches do not try to make people come; they are just interesting enough that people want to visit. **Choice D** relates to a link or attachment rather than something that pulls from afar

2. **Level:** Easy | **Domain:** CRAFT AND STRUCTURE
   Skill/Knowledge: Words in Context

   Key Explanation: Choice B is the best answer. The blank needs an adjective that describes the painter named Johannes Vermeer. "Eminent" refers to someone or something famous in a given field. In this context, it shows that the painter Johannes Vermeer is well-known in the field of art.

   Distractor Explanation: None of the other choices create a logical sentence. **Choice A** refers to something that is easy to see. Vermeer is from the seventeenth century, so although his art is famous, he is no longer visible. **Choice C** refers

to something glowing or shining, which does not accurately describe a person. **Choice D** refers to something complete or not modified, so it does not effectively describe a person.

3. **Level:** Hard | **Domain:** CRAFT AND STRUCTURE
   Skill/Knowledge: Words in Context

   Key Explanation: Choice D is the correct option. The author says that of the additions to the 1616 edition, many are clever but only sometimes are they improvements. Therefore, as used in the last sentence of the passage, "facile" refers to a superficial or shallow imitation of Marlowe's style of writing.

   Distractor Explanation: Choice A is incorrect because the sentence does not talk about the accomplishments of the imitator. In fact, the previous sentence points to how only some of the additions are improvements. Choices B and C are incorrect because there is no evidence to point out that all the additions to the 1616 edition are successful or effortless.

4. **Level:** Medium | **Domain:** CRAFT AND STRUCTURE
   Skill/Knowledge: Text Structure and Purpose

   Key Explanation: Choice D is the best answer because the underlined sentence explains that the photographs were of strangers. That detail can eliminate the weakness that the horses already knew the people and were reacting according to their experiences rather than that they were identifying an emotion from a picture of a face.

   Distractor Explanations: Choice A is incorrect because the sentence does not say how the "subjects" or "people in the experiment" were "selected" or "chosen." For example, they could have answered an advertisement or they could have been students in a class. **Choice B** is incorrect because the sentence does not say how many people the horses know; they could know many people. **Choice C** is incorrect because the entire text shows that expression is important for interspecies communication, but the underlined sentence does not stress that point

5. **Level:** Hard | **Domain:** CRAFT AND STRUCTURE
   Skill/Knowledge: Text Structure and Purpose

   Key Explanation: Choice D is the best answer because the author gives many scientific reasons that life may exist, but does not describe the research that went into determining the "findings" or "results." For example, he says, "Amino acids, just like those that make up every protein in our bodies, have been found in the tails of comets," giving the findings of experiments on comets but not explaining how the amino acids were found. The same is true for his discussion of organic compounds in Martian soil, a giant cloud of space alcohol, and the discovery of thousands of habitable planets.

   Distractor Explanation: Choice A is incorrect because "personal anecdotes" are stories from the author's experience, but the author does not discuss any details from his life. **Choice B** is incorrect because there are no "analogies" or "comparisons used to teach" in the text. **Choice C** is incorrect because "unsubstantiated" means that there is no evidence to support the theories. However, the facts that the author brings up, such as the presence of organic compounds in Martian soil, is presumably based on research and supported by facts that are not discussed in the passage.

6. **Level:** Medium | **Domain:** CRAFT AND STRUCTURE
   Skill/Knowledge: Cross–Text Connections

   Key Explanation: Choice D is the best answer. The Sutton–Boveri theory is "that genes were located in specific places on the chromosomes." The passage says that Morgan "criticized the theory" at first or was "initially skeptical," but "after careful documentation," determined that certain genes are located on the X chromosome, showing that he had changed his mind and thought that there were indeed at least some genes in specific places on chromosomes.

   Distractor Explanation: Choice A is incorrect because there is no indication that details needed to be adjusted for the theory to be correct. **Choice B** is incorrect because Morgan found "definitive" or "convincing" data that supported, not "contradicted" or "went against" the theory. **Choice C** is incorrect because Morgan derived scientific findings that supported the theory, even though he originally thought it was not "plausible" or "realistic."

7. **Level:** Medium | **Domain:** INFORMATION AND IDEAS
   Skill/Knowledge: Central Ideas and Details

   Key Explanation: Choice C is the best answer. Giant anteaters have physically adapted by evolving "specialized tongues" that help them eat. They have also adapted behaviorally by living in an area where "their favored prey is common" and by learning to abandon the nest when soldier ants arrive.

   Distractor Explanation: Choice A is incorrect because there is no indication that giant anteaters do not live in areas disturbed by humans; they could still live in swamps, forests, and grasslands around people. **Choice B** is incorrect because the passage does not say that ants are "more vigilant" or that there are "fewer opportunities." The passage only says that the ants are "vigilant" in protecting. **Choice D** is incorrect because the passage does not specify which food the anteaters prefer. It is possible that they might like grubs better, but they have fewer chances to eat them.

8. **Level:** Medium | **Domain:** INFORMATION AND IDEAS
Skill/Knowledge: Central Ideas and Details

Key Explanation: Choice B is the best answer because the text states that "the purpose of their study was to address a central scientific problem in explaining the diversity of tree species in a forest." In other words, the purpose was to "isolate factors" or "determine elements" that permit the "phenomenon" or "situation" of coexisting tree species to occur.

Distractor Explanation: Choice A is incorrect because "ramifications" are "consequences." The study does not establish the consequences of the models; it is trying to explain why in reality there are coexisting species, whereas mathematical models have not solved that question. **Choice C** is incorrect because an "incident" refers to a specific event or occurrence, not an ongoing process. The researchers are trying to find a general explanation that holds valid for more than one specific event. **Choice D** is incorrect because the study does not point to "flaws" or "errors" in proposed theories. It is trying to find an answer to a question that was unexplainable at the time.

9. **Level:** Hard | **Domain:** INFORMATION AND IDEAS
Skill/Knowledge: Command of Evidence (Textual)

Key Explanation: Choice D is the best answer. The claim is that Williams was "full of natural talent and energy." **Choice D** gives the idea of energy through a comparison with a hurricane, a powerful weather phenomenon. The fact that the speaker was worried about his own chances in show business alludes to the idea that Williams was so talented that no one else had a chance.

Distractor Explanation: The other choices can be eliminated because they do not encompass both ideas of talent and energy. **Choice A** is incorrect because it only states that Williams was kind or helpful. **Choice B** shows that he was talented, but not that he was energetic. **Choice C** also implies that he was talented and less exciting when he was around, but does not convey the idea of energy.

10. **Level:** Easy | **Domain:** INFORMATION AND IDEAS
Skill/Knowledge: Command of Evidence (Textual)

Key Explanation: Choice C is the best answer because "any opiate" would include both users of prescription opiates and users of non-prescription opiates. In Figure 1, any opiate refers to the combination of the bottom and middle sections of the column. The right-hand column for 2017 has a combined amount of about 48,000 deaths, since the second section of the bar reaches to just under the 50,000 line.

Distractor Explanation: Choice A is incorrect because there were 18,000 deaths by "any" or "all combined" drug overdoses in 1999, not

2017. In 2017, there were 18,000 deaths caused by prescription opiates, the bottom section, but not all drugs combined; the latter is over 70,000. **Choice B** is incorrect because "any type of opiate" would refer to both prescription and non-prescription, the bottom two sections of the columns. However, none of the columns have those two sections total 38,000. **Choice D** is incorrect because 75,000 is the approximate total number of deaths in 2017, not the total for prescription opiates, which is just the bottom section of the column.

11. **Level:** Medium | **Domain:** INFORMATION AND IDEAS
    Skill/Knowledge: Command of Evidence (Quantitative)

    Key Explanation: Choice A is the best choice. The previous sentence in the text talks about the countries that recorded the highest growth in population. The sentence to be completed begins with "conversely". Thus, an opposite example must be provided which mentions the countries with a decrease in population.

    Distractor Explanation: Choice B is incorrect because it only mentions one country. Since the previous sentence in the text mentions the top 5 countries that recorded a population increase, the ideal choice would be an example that mentions the top 5 countries with a population decrease. **Choice C** is incorrect because it does not provide an example that it is the opposite of the previous sentence. **Choice D** is incorrect because the text does not mention anything about the number of deaths registered.

12. **Level:** Easy | **Domain:** INFORMATION AND IDEAS
    Skill/Knowledge: Inference

    Key Explanation: Choice C is the best answer because the text says, "widespread off-label use of intravenous subanesthetic-dose ketamine for treatment-resistant depression has raised concerns about side effects, especially given its history as a drug of abuse." "Especially" indicates that the main concern is that ketamine is associated with drug abuse or addiction problems.

    Distractor Explanation: None of the other choices are supported by evidence from the passage. **Choice A** is incorrect because there is no discussion of it becoming less effective. **Choice B** is incorrect because, while there is a concern of side effects, there is no mention of the effects "in conjunction with" or "at the same time as" using other drugs. **Choice D** is incorrect because a "relapse" is a return to a former condition. There is no discussion in the passage about whether the patients become depressed again or not.

13. **Level:** Easy | **Domain:** INFORMATION AND IDEAS
    Skill/Knowledge: Inferences

    Key Explanation: Choice C is the best answer because Henri produced work that was "a new style" than that of the National Academy of Design, which he "disliked." The passage says that his style had "depicted the seedy underside of urban life," meaning he painted things that were not considered fashionable or proper; they were "undignified" or "not majestic." Therefore, it is likely that the Academy artists "avoided" or "did not draw" such things.

    Distractor Explanations: Choice A is incorrect because the text says Henri used a "bold, realistic style" and that the Academy artists used a "highly–polished" style. Since Henri was trying to create a new way of painting, the two styles probably have little overlap. **Choice B** is incorrect because the text does not say that the artists were not in New York; it only implies that they did not draw sketches in the streets. **Choice D** is incorrect because "dirty snow" is only one example of Henri's art. It is possible that the artists drew winter scenes, but they avoided the dirt and squalor in their pictures.

14. **Level:** Easy | **Domain:** STANDARD ENGLISH CONVENTIONS
Skill/Knowledge: Boundaries

Key Explanation: Choice B is the best answer. "In such a waterfall" is a prepositional phrase that indicates a situation. Phrases should be divided from the main clause in a sentence by a comma.

Distractor Explanation: Choice A is incorrect because without any punctuation, it is unclear where the prepositional phrase ends and the main clause begins. **Choices C** and **D** are incorrect because colons and semicolons should follow a complete independent clause, but the preceding portion cannot stand on its own as a sentence.

15. **Level:** Easy | **Domain:** STANDARD ENGLISH CONVENTIONS
Skill/Knowledge: Boundaries

Key Explanation: Choice D is the best answer. There are two ideas with subjects and verbs, so they can be divided into separate sentences.

Distractor Explanation: Choice A is incorrect because it is a comma splice between two independent clauses. **Choice B** is incorrect because "because" subordinates the following information. A semicolon should not be followed by a subordinate clause, only an independent

clause. **Choice C** is incorrect because "since" creates a subordinate clause which cannot stand on its own as a sentence.

16. **Level:** Easy | **Domain:** STANDARD ENGLISH CONVENTIONS
Skill/Knowledge: Boundaries

Key Explanation: Choice A is the best answer. The portion between the italics, "the Maori… tree," modifies "kauri." To better see the structure of the main clause, remove the portion between the italics. It is then clear that the subject "Forests filled with kauri" needs to be followed by a verb, in this case, the phrasal verb "date back."

Distractor Explanation: Choice B is incorrect because it leaves the main clause without an active verb—"dating back…" is subordinated, but there is no complete clause before it. **Choices C** and **D** are incorrect because they include an extra noun. Two nouns should not be used in a row within a clause without subordinating one of them.

17. **Level:** Easy | **Domain:** STANDARD ENGLISH CONVENTIONS
Skill/Knowledge: Form, Structure, and Sense

Key Explanation: Choice D is the best answer. Research results are presented in the present tense as "universal truths."

Distractor Explanation: All of the other choices can be eliminated because they do not use the standard form for showing currently accepted research results. **Choice A** is a progressive tense, though "research" can be used in the plural. **Choice B** is a future tense. **Choice C** is the past tense, which is only acceptable if the results have subsequently been proven erroneous.

18. **Level:** Easy | **Domain:** STANDARD ENGLISH CONVENTIONS
Skill/Knowledge: Form, Structure, and Sense

Key Explanation: Choice C is the best answer. The section between the commas, "_____ artwork...influences" is a clause that modifies the previous noun, Elizabeth Catlett. **Choice C** is used to show that the subject of the clause belongs to the preceding noun. Therefore, it effectively shows that the subject "artwork" belongs to "Catlett."

Distractor Explanation: Choice A is incorrect because "her" creates an independent clause rather than a relative clause that modifies the previous word. **Choices B** and **D** are incorrect because they act as the subject of clause, adding more information about the preceding noun; they cannot be followed directly with another subject, "artwork."

19. **Level:** Easy | **Domain:** STANDARD ENGLISH CONVENTIONS
Skill/Knowledge: Form, Structure, and Sense

Key Explanation: Choice A is the best answer. The underlined portion needs to be a subject that is followed by the verb "composed."

Distractor Explanation: Choice B is incorrect because it indicates possession and needs to be followed by a noun. **Choice C** is incorrect because it is an object rather than a subject. **Choice D** is incorrect because it shows possession and needs to be followed by a noun. Alternatively, it could be a contraction for "she is," which does fit the past–tense context or the verb "composed."

20. **Level:** Easy | **Domain:** STANDARD ENGLISH CONVENTIONS
Skill/Knowledge: Form, Structure, and Sense

Key Explanation: Choice B is the best answer. The underlined portion is the main verb of the sentence. The entire preceding portion, "dividing one full–time job between two employees," is the subject. Though it may appear plural, the subject can be simplified to "dividing." When a verb ending in "–ing" is used as a subject, it is considered singular, and **Choice B** is a singular verb.

Distractor Explanation: Choice A is incorrect because it is plural, so does not agree with the singular "dividing." **Choices C** and **D** can be eliminated because they do not create a complete sentence; the underlined portion should be an active verb form.

21. **Level:** Medium | **Domain:** STANDARD ENGLISH CONVENTIONS
Skill/Knowledge: Form, Structure, and Sense

Key Explanation: Choice C is the best answer. "They" is plural, so correctly refers to the plural noun "many names" from the previous sentence. "Range" is plural, so it agrees with the plural noun.

Distractor Explanation: Choices A and **D** can be eliminated because "ranges" is singular, so does not agree with the plural noun. **Choice B** is incorrect because it is a noun rather than a noun and verb. As a result, the sentence is a fragment with no active verb.

22. **Level:** Medium | **Domain:** EXPRESSION OF IDEAS
Skill/Knowledge: Transitions

Key Explanation: Choice B is the best answer because it is used to show a contrast or change in topic. It fits the context of saying that dandelions are viewed as weeds, but in reality, they can be eaten many ways.

Distractor Explanation: None of the other choices are used to indicate that there is a contrast of ideas. **Choice A** is incorrect because it is used to introduce the logical conclusion of an argument, but the idea that dandelions are edible is not a logical reason to view them as weeds. **Choice C** is used to add a specific detail that clarifies the previous claim. **Choice D** is used to add more reasons in support of the previous claim.

23. **Level:** Easy | **Domain:** EXPRESSION OF IDEAS
    Skill/Knowledge: Transitions

Key Explanation: Choice A is the best answer because it is used to add another detail to develop a discussion. In this context, **Choice A** adds what happened to the finished painting after the discussion of what Picasso did while making the painting.

Distractor Explanation: Choice B is incorrect because it is used to introduce an opposing or conflicting idea, but the final sentence continues the theme of the painting being influential for the cause against war. **Choice C** is incorrect because it shows the logical result of a series of actions. Though the final sentence expands on the idea of the anti–war protests, it is not necessarily given that after showing people the painting, Picasso would exhibit the painting to raise funds. **Choice D** is incorrect because it is used to add an example of a previous claim, but the following sentence discusses a time sequence rather than giving more detail about the visitors who entered his studio.

24. **Level:** Medium | **Domain:** EXPRESSION OF IDEAS
    Skill/Knowledge: Transitions

Key Explanation: Choice C is the best answer. The passage is structured with the first two sentences explaining the good that Ahmed did.

The portion following the underline has a different tone from receiving the Nobel Prize. **Choice C** is used to show something that happened at a later time, so fits the context of saying that first he was praised but later he was accused of certain problems.

Distractor Explanation: Choice A is incorrect because it is used to add more information on the same topic, so it does not effectively show that the praise changed to concern over Ahmed's actions. **Choice B** is incorrect because it means that the following is fitting or appropriate given the preceding information, but in this case, being accused of bad things is not appropriate for a winner of a Nobel Prize. **Choice D** is incorrect because it is used to introduce the logical result of the preceding argument, but the following is not a logical result of winning a peace prize.

25. **Level:** Hard | **Domain:** EXPRESSION OF IDEAS
    Skill/Knowledge: Rhetorical Synthesis

Key Explanation: Choice A is the best answer. It concisely shows that the level of the appeal is "basic" or very deep and essential.

Distractor Explanation: All of the other choices can be eliminated as redundant; the extra words distract from the intended meaning. In **Choices B** and **D**, "basic" and "fundamental" are synonyms. In **Choice C**, "level" and "depth" have the same meaning in the context.

26. **Level:** Medium | **Domain:** EXPRESSION OF IDEAS
    Skill/Knowledge: Rhetorical Synthesis

Key Explanation: Choice C is the best answer. The notes mention that is he most known for being the most-streamed classical artist of all time.

Distractor Explanation: Choice A is incorrect because this is not his most significant achievement. **Choice B** is also incorrect as the notes do not mention this as being his most significant achievement. **Choice D** is incorrect because the statement only describes his music projects and not a significant achievement.

27. **Level:** Medium | **Domain:** EXPRESSION OF IDEAS
    Skill/Knowledge: Rhetorical Synthesis

    Key Explanation: Choice C is the best answer. It implies a very fast rate, so indicates that the number of ghost kitchens is increasing extremely fast.

    Distractor Explanation: Choices A and **D** are incorrect because they only indicate an increase; they do not include any hint that the rate is fast. **Choice B** is incorrect because it includes undertones of getting too big too fast, implying that the number may decrease soon, such as when the economy inflates and then collapses.

1. **Level:** Easy | **Domain:** ALGEBRA
   Skill/Knowledge: Linear equations in two variables | **Testing point:** Converting English to Algebra to create a two variable equation

   Key Explanation: Choice A is correct. She burns 20 calories when she walks every minute. Therefore, she burned $20x$ calories after x minutes. She also burns 35 calories every minute she cycles and therefore burns $35y$ calories after y minutes. The equation would therefore be $20x + 35y = 340$. Subtracting $20x$ from both sides of this equation yields
   $35y = 340 - 20x$.

   Distractor Explanation: Choice B is incorrect because it states that the difference between the calories burned from cycling and burned from walking is equal to 340. **Choice C** and **Choice D** are incorrect. The rate of 20 calories per minute can only be multiplied by x minutes of walking. And the rate of 35 calories per minute can only be multiplied by y minutes of cycling.

2. **Level:** Easy | **Domain:** PROBLEM–SOLVING AND DATA ANALYSIS
   Skill/Knowledge: Two–variable data: models and scatterplots | **Testing point:** Identifying points on a scatter plot

   Key Explanation: Choice B is the correct answer because the number of dots that have a higher value than the line of best fit are the dots above the line i.e 6.

   Distractor Explanation: Choice A is incorrect as this is the number of dots on the graph. **Choice C** is incorrect as this is the number of dots below the line of best fit. **Choice D** is incorrect; it may be a conceptual error or lack of understanding of the question.

3. **Level:** Easy | **Domain:** ADVANCED MATH
   Skill/Knowledge: Nonlinear functions | **Testing point:** Using the remainder theorem

   Key Explanation: Choice B is correct. The remainder theorem states that if $f(x)$ is divided by $x-a$, the remainder would be $f(a)$. Therefore when $f(a) = 0$, then $x-a$ is a factor of the function $f(x)$. In this case, $f(3)= 0$, therefore $x-3$ is a factor of the equation $f(x)$.

   Distractor Explanation: Choices A, C, and **D** are incorrect. Based on the table, dividing $(x+2)$, x, or $(x-5)$ from $f(x)$ will not yield a remainder of 0.

4. **Level:** Easy | **Domain:** ALGEBRA
   Skill/Knowledge: System of two linear equations in two variables. | **Testing point:** Solving for one variable in a system of linear equations

   Key Explanation: Simplify the first equation by using the distributive property which yields $t - 5 + 2s - 6 = 8$. Adding 5 and 6 to both sides of the equation yields $t + 2s = 19$. Simplify the second equation by using the distributive property which yields $2t - 10 - 3s + 9 = -19$. Adding 10 and subtracting 9 from both sides of the equation yields $2t - 3s = -18$. To find the value of s, use the elimination method and multiply -2 by the first equation. This yields $-2t -4s = -38$. Then, add the two equations which yield $-7s = -56$. Dividing -7 from both sides of the equation yields $s = 8$.

5. **Level:** Easy | **Domain:** ALGEBRA
   Skill/Knowledge: Linear equations in one variable
   Testing point: Solving linear equations in one variable

   Key Explanation: Choice D is correct. Simplify the equation by using distributive property, which yields
   $3x - 6 - 2x + 2 = -x + 2x + 4 - 8$.
   Combining like terms yields $x - 4 = x - 4$. This

shows that the equation is the same on both sides. So, any value of x makes the equation true. Therefore, the equation has infinitely many solutions.

Distractor Explanation: Choice A is incorrect because to have no solutions, solving the equation will result in a false statement. **Choice B** is incorrect because to have one solution, solving the equation will yield x equal to a number. **Choice C** is incorrect because linear equations do not have 2 solutions.

6. **Level:** Hard | **Domain:** ADVANCED MATH
    Skill/Knowledge: Equivalent expressions |
    Testing point: Converting between exponents and radicals

    Key Explanation: Choice B is correct. To simplify the variable with different exponents, add the exponents of $g^{\frac{4}{5}}$ and $g^{\frac{2}{5}}$ which yields $g^{\frac{6}{5}}$. Making 2 have the same exponent as g yields $32^{\frac{1}{5}} \cdot g^{\frac{6}{5}}$.

    Putting them inside the radical sign yields $\sqrt[5]{32g^6}$

    Distractor Explanation: Choice A is incorrect because the 2 did not have any exponent and thus should have been left outside the root or converted to the fifth. **Choice C** and **Choice D** are incorrect and may result from interchanging the numerator and denominator of the exponent.

7. **Level:** Medium | **Domain:** PROBLEM-SOLVING AND DATA ANALYSIS
    Skill/Knowledge: Inference from sample statistics and margin of error | **Testing point:** Finding the margin of error

    Key Explanation: To find the margin of error, first find the midpoint of the sample mean mass.

This yields $\frac{120+182}{2} = 151$. The margin of error would be the difference between the midpoint and either of the sample mean masses. Subtracting 151 from 182 yields 31.

8. **Level:** Hard | **Domain:** ALGEBRA
    Skill/Knowledge: Linear functions | **Testing point:** Solving a linear function

    Key Explanation: Choice A is correct. To find $f(6)$, first find the value of x which will be plugged into the equation $f(2x)$. Equating $2x$ to 6 and solving for x yields $x = 3$. Plugging 3 to $9x-7$ yields 20. Therefore, $f(6) = 20$.

    Distractor Explanation: Choice B is incorrect and may result from plugging 6 directly into the equation. **Choice C** is incorrect and may result from substituting x with $2x$ and plugging 6 into the equation. **Choice D** is incorrect and may result from plugging 2 directly into the equation.

9. **Level:** Medium | **Domain:** PROBLEM-SOLVING AND DATA ANALYSIS
    Skill/Knowledge: One-variable data: distributions and measures of center and spread | **Testing point:** Finding the mean and median

    Key Explanation: Choice A is correct because. The median of the above data set of 21 students will be the $\frac{21+1}{2}$, which is the 11th shoe size, which is then represented by 3. The mean shoe size can then be calculated by adding the products of the shoe size and their corresponding frequency and dividing the sum by the total number of students. This yields a sum of 67. Dividing the sum by 21 yields a mean of 3.19. Therefore, the mean will be larger than the median.

Distractor Explanation: Choice B and **C** are incorrect as they are both false statements. **Choice D** is incorrect because there is sufficient information to answer the question.

10. **Level:** Medium | **Domain:** ADVANCED MATH
Skill/Knowledge: Equivalent expressions | **Testing point:** Using exponent rules

Key Explanation: To solve for a, first make the bases equal. Converting 27^x to a base 3 yields 3^{3x}. Converting 81^{-x} to a base 3 yields $(3^4)^{-x}$ or 3^{-4x}. The equation will now become $3^{3x} \div 3^{-4x} = 3^{ax}$. On the right side of the equation, the bases are divided, which means that the exponents must be subtracted. Subtracting the exponents yields $3^{(3x-(-4x))} = 3^{ax}$ or simply $3^{7x} = 3^{ax}$. Equating the exponents yields $7x = ax$. Dividing both sides of the equation by x yields $7 = a$.

11. **Level:** Hard | **Domain:** GEOMETRY AND TRIGONOMETRY
Skill/Knowledge: Lines, angles, and triangles | **Testing point:** Finding the sum of the Interior angles of a polygon

Key Explanation: Choice C is correct. The sum of interior angles in a polygon is represented by $180°(n-2)$. A hexagon has 6 sides and therefore the sum of interior angles in the hexagon will be $180(6-2) = 720°$. 720 degrees in radian form will be $\frac{720}{180} = 4\pi$. Therefore $b = 4$.

Distractor Explanation: Choice A is incorrect and may result in calculating $\frac{180}{720}$. **Choice B** is incorrect and may result in calculating $\frac{720}{720}$. **Choice D** is incorrect and may result in

calculating $\frac{720}{360}$.

12. **Level:** Easy | **Domain:** PROBLEM-SOLVING AND DATA ANALYSIS
Skill/Knowledge: Percentages | **Testing point:** Finding the percentage increase

Key Explanation: Choice C is correct. If 80 is increased by 200%, that means that the new value will be 300% of 80 which is 240. An alternative solution is to find 200% of 80 and add it to 80 which yields 240.

Distractor Explanation: Choice A is incorrect because it is the percentage. **Choice B** is incorrect because it is the increase without adding the original. **Choice D** is incorrect because it is the sum of 80 and 200.

13. **Level:** Easy | **Domain:** ADVANCED MATH
Skill/Knowledge: Nonlinear functions | **Testing point:** Using the quadratic formula

Key Explanation: To solve for the quadratic equation, use the quadratic formula $\frac{-b \pm \sqrt{b^2 - 4ac}}{2a}$, where $a = 2$, $b = -4$ and $c = -7$. Substituting the values to the formula yields $\frac{-(-4) \pm \sqrt{(-4)^2 - 4(2)(-7)}}{2(2)}$. Simplifying this yields $\frac{4 \pm \sqrt{72}}{4}$ or $1 \pm \frac{\sqrt{72}}{4}$. Simplifying $\sqrt{72}$ yields $6\sqrt{2}$. Therefore, the expression becomes $1 \pm \frac{6\sqrt{2}}{4}$ or $1 \pm \frac{3\sqrt{2}}{2}$. Since the expression is now in the same format as $1 \pm \frac{a\sqrt{2}}{2}$, then $a = 3$.

14. **Level:** Easy | **Domain:** ALGEBRA
Skill/Knowledge: Linear functions | **Testing point:** Interpretation of terms in a linear function

Key Explanation: Choice B is correct. This is because 262 is the *y-intercept* of the model and represents the number of houses on day 0, which is the beginning of October.

Distractor Explanation: Choice A is incorrect because the number of houses at the end of October is represented by $h(x)$. **Choice C is incorrect** as the number of houses sold per day would be 8. **Choice D is incorrect** as the number of houses sold on the first day of October is represented when $x = 8$.

15. **Level:** Medium | **Domain:** GEOMETRY AND TRIGONOMETRY
Skill/Knowledge: Right triangles and trigonometry | **Testing point:** Working with special triangles

Key Explanation: Choice A is correct. A 90 – 60 – 30 triangle has a hypotenuse of $2x$, a shorter leg of x, and a longer leg of $x\sqrt{3}$. The area of this triangle can then be found by the formula $\frac{1}{2} \times base \times height$. Substituting the base and the height yields $\frac{1}{2} \times x \times x\sqrt{3}$ or $\frac{x^2\sqrt{3}}{2}$. The given side AC is the hypotenuse of the triangle. So, 32 = $2x$ which yields $x = 16$. Substituting 16 to the formula yields $\frac{16^2\sqrt{3}}{2}$ or $128\sqrt{3}$.

Distractor Explanation: Choice B and Choice D are incorrect and may result from using $\sqrt{2}$ instead of $\sqrt{3}$. **Choice C is incorrect** because this is one of the sides of the triangle.

16. **Level:** Easy | **Domain:** ADVANCED MATH
Skill/Knowledge: Equivalent expressions | **Testing point:** Matching coefficients

Key Explanation: Using distributive property on the left side of the equation yields $5xy + 3 – 6xy + 2xy^2 – 2 = axy^2 + bxy + c$. Combining like terms yields $2xy^2 – xy + 1 = axy^2 + bxy + c$. Comparing the coefficients on both sides of the equation, yields $a = 2$, $b = -1$, and $c = 1$ Therefore, $a + b = 1$.

17. **Level:** Easy | **Domain:** ADVANCED MATH
Skill/Knowledge: Nonlinear equations in one variable and systems of equations in two variables **Testing point:** Finding the product of the roots of a quadratic equation

Key Explanation: Choice B is correct. In a quadratic equation $(ax^2 + bx + c = 0)$, the product of the roots can be found by $\frac{c}{a}$, Using the given equation, $c = -24$ and $a = 3$. Thus, the product of the roots will be $\frac{-24}{3}$ or –8.

Distractor Explanation: Choice A is incorrect as this is the value of a. **Choice C is incorrect** and may result from calculating $\frac{b}{a}$. **Choice D is** incorrect and may result from calculating the sum of the roots which is $\left(\frac{-b}{a}\right)$.

18. **Level:** Medium | **Domain:** ADVANCED MATH
Skill/Knowledge: Nonlinear functions | **Testing point:** Using the vertex form of a quadratics equation

Key Explanation: Choice B is correct. The general equation of a parabola is given by $y = a(x - h)^2$

+ k, where (h, k) denotes the coordinate of the vertex. In this case, h = 3 and k = 10. Thus, the equation becomes $y = a(x–3)^2 + 10$. The sign of a denotes the orientation of the parabola. If a is positive, the parabola opens upward. If a is negative, the parabola opens downward. In this case, the parabola opens downward so the value of a must be negative. Therefore, the equation of the parabola is $y = -2(x - 3)^2 + 10$.

Distractor Explanation: Choice A and **Choice C** are incorrect since their a is positive which would suggest that the graph opens upwards however the graph opens downwards. **Choice D** is incorrect and may result from using (–3, 10) as the vertex instead of (3, 10).

19. **Level:** Easy | **Domain:** ALGEBRA
Skill/Knowledge: Linear equations in one variable
Testing point: Matching coefficients

Key Explanation: Using the distributive property, the equation becomes $6 - 6x = ax + b$ or $-6x + 6 = ax + b$. Comparing the coefficient and the constant on both sides of the equation yields $a = -6$ and $b = 6$. Therefore, the product of a and b is –36.

20. **Level:** Easy | **Domain:** ADVANCED MATH
Skill/Knowledge: Nonlinear functions | **Testing point:** Finding the average rate of change

Key Explanation: Choice D is correct. To find the average rate of change between two points on a curve is the same as finding the gradient between the two points. In this case, the points are (0, –8) and (2, –16). $\dfrac{(-16)-(-8)}{0-2}$ which yields the slope as –4.

Distractor Explanation: Choice A is incorrect. This is the value of the difference in the y *coordinates* between the two points. **Choice B** is incorrect as this is the negative value of option A. **Choice C** is incorrect as this is the positive value of option D.

21. **Level:** Medium | **Domain:** ALGEBRA
Skill/Knowledge: Linear equations in one variable
Testing point: Finding the value of x in a linear equation

Key Explanation: Choice B is correct. To find the value of x, multiply both sides of the equation by $\dfrac{4}{3}$.

This yields $(x - 5) = 27 \times \dfrac{4}{3}$ or simply $(x - 5) = 36$.

Distractor Explanation: Choice A is incorrect and may result from calculating the value of x.

Choice C is incorrect and may result from multiplying $\dfrac{3}{4}$ to both sides of the equation instead of $\dfrac{4}{3}$.

Choice D is incorrect and may result from conceptual or calculation errors.

22. **Level:** Hard | **Domain:** ALGEBRA
Skill/Knowledge: Linear inequalities in one or two variables | **Testing point:** Finding solution to a system of linear inequalities

Key Explanation: Choice C is correct. To solve such questions, the best method would be to substitute the points to the inequalities and check if the statements are true or false.
Substituting (3, 1) to the first inequality yields 1 > – 2(3) –1 or 1 > –7, which is true.
Substituting (3, 1) to the second inequality

yields 3(1) < 3 + 9 or 3 < 12, which is also true. Therefore, the coordinate (3, 1) lies inside the intersection of the two inequalities.

Distractor Explanation: Choice A is incorrect. Substituting (–2, 1) to both inequalities will result in one false statement.
Choice B is incorrect. Substituting (1, 4) to both inequalities will result in one false statement.
Choice D is incorrect. Substituting (–3, 3) to both inequalities will result in false statements.

1. **Level:** Easy | **Domain:** ADVANCED MATH
   Skill/Knowledge: Nonlinear equations in one variable and system of equations in two variables | **Testing point:** Solving absolute value equations

   Key Explanation: Choice C is correct. To calculate the two solutions (p & q), equate the contents of the absolute value symbol to both the positive and negative values of the number on the other side of the equation. To obtain the first solution (p), solve for x in the equation $3x - 1 = 2$. Adding 1 to both sides of the equation yields $3x = 3$. Dividing 3 from both sides of the equation yields $x = 1$. Thus, $p = 1$. To obtain the second solution (q), solve for x in the equation $3x - 1 = -2$. Adding 1 to both sides of the equation yields $3x = -1$. Dividing 3 from both sides of the equation yields $x = -\dfrac{1}{3}$. Thus, $q = -\dfrac{1}{3}$. Adding 1 and $-\dfrac{1}{3}$ yields $\dfrac{2}{3}$. Therefore, $p + q = \dfrac{2}{3}$.

   Distractor Explanation: Choice A is incorrect and may result from multiplying the second solution (q) by -1. **Choice B** and **Choice D** are incorrect as these are the two solutions to the equation.

2. **Level:** Medium | **Domain:** GEOMETRY AND TRIGONOMETRY
   Skill/Knowledge: Circles | **Testing point:** Using equation of a circle

   Key Explanation: Choice C is correct. To solve this question, plug each point into the equation of the circle. A coordinate that lies on the circle means that the equation will be equal on both ends. Plugging the point $(-3, 4)$, the equation becomes $(-3 - 3)^2 + 4^2 + 8(4) = 84$. Simplifying the equation, this yields $84 = 84$.
   Therefore, point $(-3, 4)$ lies on the circle.

   Distractor Explanation: Choice A is incorrect. Plugging the point $(1, 7)$ into the equation yields $109 = 84$. Therefore, it lies outside the circle. **Choice B** is incorrect. Plugging the point $(-2, 5)$ into the equation yields $90 = 84$. Therefore, it lies outside the circle. **Choice D** is incorrect. Plugging the point $(3, -6)$ into the equation yields $-12 = 84$. Therefore, it does not lie on the circle.

3. **Level:** Easy | **Domain:** GEOMETRY AND TRIGONOMETRY
   Skill/Knowledge: Right triangles and trigonometry | **Testing point:** Using trigonometry identities

   Key Explanation: $Sin\ x = cos\ (90 - x)$. So, if $sin\ C$ and $cos\ 63$ are equal, then the angles would add up to 90°. Therefore, $63° + C = 90°$. Subtracting 63° from both sides of the equation yields $C = 27°$.

4. **Level:** Hard | **Domain:** ADVANCED MATH
   Skill/Knowledge: Equivalent expressions | **Testing point:** Working with complex numbers

   Key Explanation: Choice A is correct. Rationalize the denominator of $\dfrac{2 - 2i}{3 + 4i}$ by multiplying the fraction by the denominator's conjugate which is $\dfrac{3 - 4i}{3 - 4i}$. This yields $\dfrac{6 - 6i - 8i + 8i^2}{9 - 16i^2}$. Substituting -1 to i^2 yields $-\dfrac{2}{25} - \dfrac{14}{25}i$. Matching the coefficients yields $a = -\dfrac{2}{25}$ and $b = -\dfrac{14}{25}$.

   Distractor Explanations: Choice B is incorrect as this would be the value of b. **Choice C** and **Choice D** are incorrect and may result from miscalculation or conceptual errors.

5. **Level:** Medium | **Domain:** ADVANCED MATH
Skill/Knowledge: Nonlinear equations in one variable and systems of equations in two variables
Testing point: Solving system of linear and quadratic equations

Key Explanation: Choice C is correct. To solve for x, we can equate the two equations.
This yields $2x - 2 = 2x^2 - 9x + 7$.
Subtracting $2x$ and adding 2 to both sides of the equation yields $2x^2 - 9x + 7 - 2x + 2 = 0$.
Combining like terms yields $2x^2 - 11x + 9 = 0$. To solve the quadratic equation use either the factor method or the quadratic formula. Using the factor method, get the two factors of $18x^2$ whose sum is $-11x$.
The two factors are $-2x$ and $-9x$ which makes the equation $2x^2 - 2x - 9x + 9 = 0$.
Grouping the first two terms together and the last two terms together yields $(2x^2 - 2x) - (9x - 9) = 0$
Factoring out the greatest common factor yields $2x(x - 1) - 9(x - 1) = 0$.
Factoring out the common binomial yields $(x - 1)(2x - 9) = 0$. Equating both factors to 0 yields the two solutions, which are $x = 1$ and $x = \dfrac{9}{2}$ or 4.5

Distractor Explanation: Choice A is incorrect and may result from adding the two solutions. **Choice B** is incorrect as it is the negative of one of the solutions. **Choice D** is incorrect and may result from getting the difference between the solutions.

6. **Level:** Hard | **Domain:** ADVANCED MATH
Skill/Knowledge: Nonlinear equations in one variable and systems of equations in two variables
Testing point: Solving absolute equation

Key Explanation: To obtain the solutions, first simplify the equation by factorization. Factoring out 2 from $|6x - 4|$ yields $2|3x - 2|$. Factoring out $|3x - 2|$ from $3|3x - 2| - 2|3x - 2| = 7$ yields

$(3 - 2)|3x - 2| = 7$ or $|3x - 2| = 7$. Then, equate the contents of the absolute value symbol to both the positive and negative values of the number on the other side of the equation. To obtain the first solution, solve for x in the equation $3x - 2 = 7$. Adding 2 to both sides of the equation yields $3x = 9$. Dividing 3 from both sides of the equation yields $x = 3$. To obtain the second solution, solve for x in the equation $3x - 2 = -7$. Adding 2 to both sides of the equation yields $3x = -5$. Dividing 3 from both sides of the equation yields $x = \dfrac{-5}{3}$.

Therefore, the positive solution to the equation is 3.

7. **Level:** Easy | **Domain:** ALGEBRA
Skill/Knowledge: Linear functions | **Testing point:** Creating equations from graphs

Key Explanation: Choice C is correct.
Calculating the slope of the given line using the points $(-5, 0)$ and $(3, 0)$ yields $\dfrac{5}{3}$. A slope of a line perpendicular to this will be the negative reciprocal of the slope of the given line. Therefore, a line perpendicular to this should have a slope of $\left(\dfrac{-3}{5}\right)$.

To get the slope of a line from the equation, convert the equation to slope–intercept form. Dividing both sides of the equation by 5, **Choice C** becomes $y = -\left(\dfrac{3}{5}\right)x + 3$.
Since the coefficient of x is $-\left(\dfrac{3}{5}\right)$, then this line is perpendicular to the given line.

Distractor Explanation: Choice A is incorrect as this is the equation of the line in the graph.

Choice B is incorrect as this is the equation of a line that has a slope of $\frac{3}{5}$. **Choice D** is incorrect as this is the equation of a line that has a slope of $\frac{5}{3}$ making it parallel to the given line.

8. **Level:** Easy | **Domain:** GEOMETRY AND TRIGONOMETRY
   Skill/Knowledge: Circles | **Testing point:** Finding the circumference of a circle given it's equation

   Key Explanation: Choice D is correct. To find the circumference of a circle, first, find the radius of the circle or the diameter. Rewrite the given equation into the standard form for the equation of a circle, by completing the squares. This yields $x^2 + 6x + 9 + y^2 - 4y + 4 = 51 + 9 + 4$. Simplifying the equation yields $(x + 3)^2 + (y - 2)^2 = 64$. Since the equation is now in standard form, then $r^2 = 64$. Solving for r yields 8 as the radius. Using the formula of the circumference which is $2\pi r$ yields 16π.

   Distractor Explanation: Choice A is incorrect and may result from solving for the area of the circle instead of the circumference. **Choice B** is incorrect and may result from using πr instead of $2\pi r$ to solve for the circumference. **Choice C** is incorrect and may result from using $\sqrt{51}$ as the radius of the circle.

9. **Level:** Medium | **Domain:** GEOMETRY AND TRIGONOMETRY
   Skill/Knowledge: Lines, angles and triangles | **Testing point:** Using the exterior angle theorem

   Key Explanation: According to the Exterior Angle Theorem, the exterior angle of a triangle is equal to the sum of the opposite and non-adjacent interior angles.

Therefore, $\angle ABC + \angle BAC = \angle ACD$.
The equation will now become $2x - 2 + x + 3 = 118$.
Combining like terms yields $3x + 1 = 118$.
Subtracting 1 from both sides of the equation yields $3x = 117$.
Dividing 3 from both sides of the equation yields $x = 39$.

10. **Level:** Easy | **Domain:** PROBLEM−SOLVING AND DATA ANALYSIS
    Skill/Knowledge: Ratio, rates, proportional relationships, and units | **Testing point:** Creating and solving rate equation

    Key Explanation: Choice B is correct. The question presents an inverse proportion problem where the number of carpenters (x) is inversely proportional to the number of days it requires to build a bed (y). Using the formula $xy = k$ and the given data $x = 4$ and $y = 3$ yields 12 as the value of k. Thus, the inverse proportion equation becomes $xy = 12$. To solve for the corresponding number of carpenters, substitute 2 with y which then yields $2x = 12$. Solving for x yields 6 as the number of carpenters needed to build the bed in 2 days.

    Distractor Explanation: Choice A is incorrect as this represents the value of the constant k. **Choice C** is incorrect as this is the product of four carpenters and 2 days. **Choice D** is incorrect as this is a miscalculation or conceptual error.

11. **Level:** Easy | **Domain:** ADVANCED MATH
    Skill/Knowledge: Equivalent expressions | **Testing point:** Using the FOILing method to multiply expressions

    Key Explanation: Choice C is correct. Using distributive property yields, $5xy (x - 2y) + 3x (x - 2y)$. Simplifying the expression yields $5x^2y + 3x^2 - 10xy^2 - 6xy$.

Distractor Explanation: Choice A and **Choice D** are incorrect and may result from applying the distributive property incorrectly. **Choice B** is incorrect and may result from a miscalculation error in multiplying $5xy$ and $-2y$.

12. **Level:** Medium | **Domain:** ALGEBRA
    Skill/Knowledge: Systems of two linear equations in two variables | **Testing point:** Solving for a variable in a system of linear equations

    Key Explanation: To solve for y, use the elimination method. Multiplying 2 to the second equation yields $10x + 4y = 16$. Adding the first and second equations yields $7x + 10x - 4y + 4y = 1 + 16$. Combining like terms yield $17x = 17$. Dividing 17 from both sides of the equation yields $x = 1$. Substituting the value of x to the first equation yields $7(1) - 4y = 1$ or $7 - 4y = 1$. Subtracting 7 from both sides of the equation yields $-4y = -6$. Dividing -4 from both sides of the equation yields $y = \frac{3}{2}$ or 1.5.

13. **Level:** Easy | **Domain:** ALGEBRA
    Skill/Knowledge: Linear inequalities in one or two variables | **Testing point:** Solving for x in an inequality

    Key Explanation: Choice B is correct. Adding x to both sides of the equation yields $-2x + x \leq 8 - x + x$ or $-x \leq 8$.
    Dividing both sides of the equation by -1 yields $x \geq -8$. Therefore, x is greater than or equal to -8. And -10 is the only option that is less than -8.

    Distractor Explanation: Choices A, C, and **D** are incorrect. These values will make the inequality true and are considered solutions.

14. **Level:** Easy | **Domain:** PROBLEM–SOLVING AND DATA ANALYSIS
    Skill/Knowledge: Probability and conditional probability | **Testing point:** Finding the probability of an event

    Key Explanation: Choice D is correct. The unfair coin is tossed 20 times and 14 of these land on heads making the probability of the unfair coin landing on heads $\frac{14}{20} = 0.7$. Therefore the probability of the coin landing on heads the 21st time will be 0.7.

    Distractor Explanation: Choice A is incorrect as this is the probability of landing on heads on a fair coin. **Choice B** is incorrect and may result from a miscalculation or conceptual error. **Choice C** is incorrect as it gives the probability of the unfair coin landing on tails.

15. **Level:** Medium | **Domain:** ALGEBRA
    Skill/Knowledge: Systems of two linear equations in two variables | **Testing point:** Solving for x and y in a system of linear equations

    Key Explanation: Choice D is correct. Solve for x and y either by substitution or by elimination. Using the elimination method, multiply 3 by both sides of the second equation. This yields $(5x + y = -6)$ 3 or $15x + 3y = -18$. Subtracting the second equation from the first equation yields $-17x = 34$. Dividing both sides of the equation by -17 yields $x = -2$. Substituting the value of x to the second equation yields $5(-2) + y = -6$. Simplifying the equation yields $y = 4$. Subtracting y from x yields $-2, -4,$ or -6.

    Distractor Explanation: Choice A is incorrect and may result from subtracting x from y. **Choice B** is incorrect because it is the value of y. **Choice C** is incorrect as it is the value of x.

16. **Level:** Easy | **Domain:** ADVANCED MATH
    Skill/Knowledge: Nonlinear functions |
    Testing point: Converting the unit on exponential functions

    Key Explanation: Since the equations are still equal, then $1,200(1.03)^m = 1,200(1.03)^{ad}$. Dividing both sides of the equation by 1,200 yields $(1.03)^m = (1.03)^{ad}$. Since the bases are equal, equate the exponents which yield $m = ad$. Since 1 *month* = 30 *days*, then $1 = a(30)$. Dividing 30 from both sides of the equation yields $\frac{1}{30} = a$.

17. **Level:** Easy | **Domain:** GEOMETRY AND TRIGONOMETRY
    Skill/Knowledge: Area and volume | **Testing point:** Finding the volume of a cylinder

    Key Explanation: Choice A is correct. The volume of a cylinder is given by the formula $\pi r^2 h$. Using the given data, $h = 2r$. Therefore, $h = 2(6) = 12$. Therefore, the volume will be $\pi(6)^2 (12) = 432\pi$.

    Distractor Explanation: Choice B is incorrect and may result from interchanging the values of r and h. **Choice C** is incorrect and may result from calculating the surface area of the cylinder instead of volume. **Choice D** is incorrect and may result from conceptual or calculation errors.

18. **Level:** Easy | **Domain:** GEOMETRY AND TRIGONOMETRY
    Skill/Knowledge: Circles | **Testing point:** Using circle theorems

    Key Explanation: Choice A is correct. An angle subtended at any point of the circle is half the angle subtended at the center. This means that $\angle DOE = 2 \angle DRE$. Therefore, $\angle DOE = 2(35°) = 70°$.

Distractor Explanation: Choice B is incorrect because it implies that the angles are equal. **Choice C** and **D** are incorrect and this maybe due to conceptual or calculation errors

19. **Level:** Easy | **Domain:** ADVANCED MATH
    Skill/Knowledge: Equivalent expressions |
    Testing point: Factoring using the difference of two squares

    Key Explanation: Choice A is correct. This question can be solved using factorization. Using the difference of squares, $x^2 - a^2$ becomes $(x + a)(x - a)$.
    Transforming the numerator of $4x^2 - 3$ to the format $x^2 - a^2$ yields $(2x)^2 - (\sqrt{3})^2$. Factoring the expression yields $(2x + \sqrt{3})(2x - \sqrt{3})$.
    This would result to $\dfrac{(2x + \sqrt{3})(2x - \sqrt{3})}{(2x + \sqrt{3})}$.
    Canceling out the binomial $2x + \sqrt{3}$ from both numerator and denominator yields $2x - \sqrt{3}$.

    Distractor Explanation: Choice B is incorrect and would result if the student mistook the denominator for a minus sign. **Choice C** and **Choice D** are incorrect and may result from conceptual or calculation errors.

20. **Level:** Hard | **Domain:** ALGEBRA
    Skill/Knowledge : Systems of two linear equations in two variables | **Testing point:** Working with systems of equations with Infinite solutions

    Key Explanation: Equations that have infinite solutions are equations that are the same line just written differently. They have the same slope and the same *y-intercept*.
    In the above equation, neither are similar. To

make them similar, multiply the top equation by -2 which yields $-18x + 28y = 6$.

Comparing the coefficients of the first and second equations yields $a = -18$ and $b = -28$.

21. **Level:** Easy | **Domain:** ALGEBRA

    Skill/Knowledge: Linear equations in two variables | **Testing point:** Matching coefficients

    Key Explanation: Choice D is correct. To find the value of a, we have to first group like terms together.

    Adding $4x$ to both sides of the equation yields $3x + 5y + 4x = ax - 4x - by + 4x$

    or simply $7x + 5y = ax - by$. This makes $a = 7$ and $b = -5$

    Distractor Explanation: Choice A is incorrect because this would be the value of a if the $-4x$ had been ignored

    Choice B is incorrect and may result from conceptual or calculation error.

    Choice C is incorrect because this would be the value of b instead.

22. **Level:** Easy | **Domain:** ALGEBRA

    Skill/Knowledge: Linear inequalities in one or two variables | **Testing point:** Solving for x in an inequality

    Key Explanation: Choice D is correct. Using the distributive property yields $3x + 2 < -5x - 30$.

    Adding $5x$ and subtracting 2 from both sides of the equation yields $3x + 5x < -30 - 2$ or $8x < -32$.

    Dividing 8 from both sides of the equation yields $x < -4$. Since -5 is less than -4, then it is a solution to the inequality.

    Distractor Explanation: Choice A and **Choice B** are incorrect because they are both greater than -4. **Choice C** is incorrect because the value of x must be less than and not equal to -4.

Chapter 4

··

Practice Test 3

You are about to begin a full-length Practice Test. The test has four modules. The time allotted for each module is marked at the beginning of the module. Work on one module at a time. Use a timer to keep track of the time limits for every module.

Try to take the Practice Test under real test conditions. Find a quiet place to work, and set aside enough time to complete the test without being disturbed. At the end of the test, check your answers by referring to the Answer Key and fill in your raw score in the scorecard below. Also, note down the time taken by you for completing each module.

Pay particular attention to the questions that were answered incorrectly. Read the answer explanations and understand how to solve them.

··

My Score Card (Raw Score)

	Reading and Writing		Math	
	Module 1	Module 2	Module 1	Module 2
Out of	27	27	22	22
My Score	_____	_____	_____	_____
Time Taken	_____	_____	_____	_____

TEST BEGINS ON THE NEXT PAGE

Reading and Writing Test

27 QUESTIONS | 32 MINUTES

DIRECTIONS

The questions in this section address a number of important reading and writing skills. Each question includes one or more passages, which may include a table or graph. Read each passage and question carefully, and then choose the best answer to the question based on the passage(s). All questions in this section are multiple-choice with four answer choices. Each question has a single best answer.

1

The researchers compiled data on side effects from 163 patients with major depressive disorder or bipolar disorder and 25 healthy <u>controls</u> who participated in one of five placebo-controlled clinical trials conducted at the NIH Clinical Center over 13 years. The study did not address the side effects associated with repeated infusions or long-term use.

As used in the text, what does the word "controls" most nearly mean?

A) authorities

B) restraints

C) benchmarks

D) commands

2

A large percentage of the organisms in the world are parasitic, meaning they derive nutrients from another species, but almost none of them are mammalian. One notable _____ is the vampire bat, which feeds on the blood of cows and other mammals.

Which choice completes the text with the most logical and precise word or phrase?

A) peculiarity

B) exception

C) distortion

D) idiosyncrasy

3

Salt stress, too much salt in the soil for plants to thrive, is one of the major environmental constraints limiting agricultural productivity and influencing the _____ of bioactive compounds of vegetables. In this study, we assessed the effect of NaCl salt stress on flowering, fructification, and fruit nutritional quality of a local cultivar of chili pepper.

Which choice completes the text with the most logical and precise word or phrase?

A) attentiveness

B) dedication

C) concentration

D) centralization

4

How HEPHL1 mechanistically regulates hair growth and development will require in-depth analysis, and the curly whiskers from *HEPHL1* knockout mice could help these investigations. Our preliminary results showed that HEPHL1 regulates the activity of an enzyme, lysyl oxidase, which needs copper for its enzymatic activity. This raises the intriguing possibility that, in addition to playing an iron-related role, HEPHL1 could relate to the copper absorption associated with Menkes disease and its associated hair abnormalities. In conclusion, our study identified HEPHL1 as a novel gene responsible for hair abnormalities and highlights the importance of exploring the role of HEPHL1—and its interconnections with other key regulators—in developing new therapeutic strategies to treat hair disorders and even more insidious genetic diseases.

What is the role of the second sentence in the overall structure of the text?

A) It establishes a potential link between HEPHL1 and the lack of proper copper absorption found in patients with Menkes disease.

B) It explains why patients with hair abnormalities may actually have a condition called Menkes disease.

C) It points out that there is a connection between iron intake and copper intake and an imbalance could cause Menkes disease.

D) It elaborates on the claim that mice are the best source of data about hair growth and development related to Menkes disease.

5

In general, deep ocean habitats may be negatively affected by tidal current energy systems due to the change of water flows, materials on the ocean floor, and movement of sediment. Potential other effects include mortality of fish passing through turbines (blade–strike) and the collision risk of marine mammals with tidal stream farms. A study showed that change in sediment patterns will most likely follow the installation of tidal arrays, impacting the local underwater habitat, and in turn, animal and plant species. However, in their review, Frid et al. conclude that "there is little scientific literature to suggest that operation of underwater tidal energy devices will cause elevated levels of mortality to organisms such as fish and marine mammals." Also, Lewis et al. mention that, "while current technologies have moving parts that may harm marine life, there is no evidence to date of harm from tidal current devices to marine life."

What is the main function of the quotes from Frid et al. and Lewis et al. in the overall structure of the text?

A) They show reputable scientists that hold very different views from each other.

B) They provide authoritative viewpoints that oppose that of the author.

C) They undermine conclusions which emphasize safety of tidal energy systems.

D) They introduce expert opinions that reinforce the authors' primary claim.

6

Extraterrestrial life, that familiar science–fiction trope, that kitschy fantasy, that CGI nightmare, has become a matter of serious discussion, a "risk factor," a "scenario." How has ET gone from sci–fi fairytale to a serious scientific endeavor modeled by macroeconomists, funded by fiscal conservatives, and discussed by theologians? Because, following a string of remarkable discoveries over the past two decades, the idea of alien life is not as far–fetched as it used to seem. Discovery now seems inevitable and possibly imminent.

In the text, what is the primary function of the phrases "science–fiction trope," "kitschy fantasy," and "CGI nightmare"?

A) To point out the ever–changing image of how extraterrestrial creatures appear

B) To encourage readers to imagine the possible variety of extraterrestrial life

C) To interject a lighthearted note into an otherwise serious passage

D) To emphasize that there is credibility in something that once was believed impossible

7

Text 1

A 1979 paper by father–and–son team Luis and William Alvarez identified their discovery of unusual quantities of a rare element called iridium in a layer of sediment about 65 million years ago. They contended that the iridium was indicative of a massive meteor impact that sent clouds of dust into the atmosphere, cooling the Earth enough to trigger the mass extinction of the dinosaurs at the end of the Cretaceous period.

Text 2

Though dramatic, the idea of a meteor strike wiping out the dinosaurs is far–fetched, say modern paleontologists. They agree a strike occurred but claim that there was actually no simultaneous or instantaneous event that could be classified as a mass extinction. Instead, species slowly died out over millions of years, with the last major representatives living to approximately the end of the Cretaceous period.

Based on the texts, which choice would the authors of the text most likely agree about?

A) A massive meteorite impact occurred, though it may not have caused a mass extinction.

B) Though the earth cooled due to a meteor impact, it was not enough to kill the dinosaurs.

C) There was actually no mass extinction of dinosaurs, though eventually they all died.

D) Most dinosaur species died prior to the period after the Cretaceous period.

8

The following text is adapted from Mother Jones's 1912 speech to coal miners picketing in Charlestown, West Virginia.

I want to show you here that the average wages you fellows get in this country is $500 a year. Before you get a thing to eat there is $20 taken out a month, which leaves about $24 a month. Then you go to the "pluck–me" stores (operated by the mine) and want to get something to eat for your wife, and the child comes back and says, "Papa, I can't get anything."

"Why," he says, "there is $24 coming to me?"

The child says, "They said there was nothing coming to you." And the child goes back crying without a mouthful of anything to eat. The father goes to the "pluck–me" store and says to the manager, "there is $24 coming to me," and the manager says, "Oh, no, we have kept $26 for rent."

According to the passage, what is true about the wages of the mine workers?

A) They are lower than the income of mine workers around the country.

B) They are periodically being reduced without explanation.

C) They are not consistent with the minimum wages of other jobs.

D) They are insufficient because of the policies of the mine owners.

The *GRL* paper focuses on one region of the Southern Ocean extending from the tip of South America to the tip of the Antarctic Peninsula. "The Drake Passage is the windiest, roughest part of the Southern Ocean," says Colm Sweeney, lead investigator on the Drake Passage study and co-author on the GRL paper, "The critical element to this study is that we were able to sustain measurements in this harsh environment as long as we have—both in the summer and the winter, in every year over the last 13 years. This data set of ocean carbon measurements is the densest ongoing time series in the Southern Ocean." The team was able to take these long-term measurements by piggybacking instruments on the Antarctic Research Supply Vessel *Laurence M. Gould,* which makes nearly 20 crossings of the Drake Passage each year, transporting people and supplies to and from Antarctic research stations.

According to the text, why are the results of the Drake Passage study unique?

A) They used more complete measurements than any other study of the region.

B) They were derived using equipment that had not previously been used.

C) They incorporated chemical measurements as well as other forms of data.

D) It was the first study to focus only on the Southern Ocean.

10

Emily Dickenson's poems were edited by her friends before publication to match the tastes of the times. Her personal style still shines through, as in the way she personifies books in her poem "In a Library": _____

Which quote from "In a Library" most effectively illustrates the claim?

A) "A precious, mouldering pleasure 't is / To meet an antique book, / In just the dress his century wore;"

B) "What interested scholars most, / What competitions ran / When Plato was a certainty."

C) "When Sappho was a living girl, / And Beatrice wore / The gown that Dante deified."

D) "Facts, centuries before, / He traverses familiar, / As one should come to town"

11

If we manage to separate out a clean signal from a planet outside our solar system and find some features in the light spectrum that might be indicative of life, we will need to work hard to think of any non–biological process that might account for them. "Life is the hypothesis of last resort," noted astronomer Carl Sagan. This requires some understanding of what processes might operate on worlds that we will know relatively little about; what we find on Earth can serve as a guide but also has potential to lead us astray.

Which hypothetical situation is Carl Sagan most likely warning to avoid in his quote?

A) A rover that was sent to Mars discovers a bacteria–like organism when it drills deep into the core of the planet.

B) An astronomer realizes that the atmosphere of a planet is too hot to sustain life even though it has oxygen.

C) A scientist finds a planet with a large amount of oxygen in its atmosphere so claims that the oxygen is produced by living creatures.

D) A new telescope finds a new planet orbiting a star that was previously believed to have no planets.

12

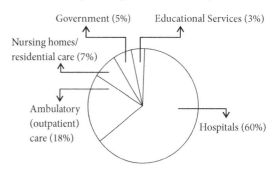

Percentage of Registered Nurses by Field

Data from US Bureau of Labor Statistics, June, 2021

Nursing is one of the fields in most demand, with an anticipated annual growth rate of 7 percent through 2029. Although some nurses work only in hospitals, there are actually many options, especially as the population ages and nurses are needed to tend to the daily needs of seniors. For example, _____

Which choice most effectively uses data from the graph to complete the example?

A) educational services employed about 3 percent of the registered nurses in 2021.

B) fewer registered nurses worked for the government than in ambulatory care.

C) the percentage of registered nurses working in nursing homes increased by 7 percent in 2021.

D) about 7 percent of registered nurses in 2021 worked in nursing or residential homes.

13

Engineering and Computer Science Stereotypes

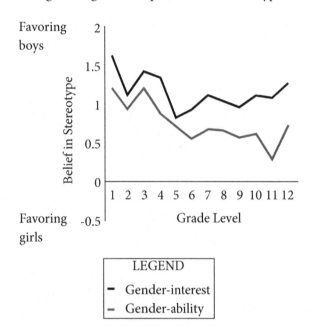

"Scientists ran an experiment where they found that a diverse set of students believed gender-interest stereotypes favoring boys in computer science and engineering. Students developed these stereotypes at a very young age. They also found that: Gender-interest stereotypes were stronger than gender-ability stereotypes. Girls who believed the stereotypes were _____. "

Which choice most effectively uses data from the graph to complete the text?

A) less skilled than interested in computer science and engineering.

B) equally skilled and interested in computer science and engineering.

C) less interested in participating in computer science and engineering.

D) more interested in participating in computer science and engineering.

14

The following text is adapted from Jefferson Keel's 2011 statement, "The Indian Reorganization Act—75 Years Later: Renewing our Commitment to Restore Tribal Homelands and Promote Self-determination."

Two years ago, our shared vision and the Federal responsibility to Indian tribes were threatened by the Supreme Court's interpretation of the IRA in *Carcieri v. Salazar*. There are at least 14 pending cases where tribes and the Secretary of Interior are under challenge. There are many more tribes whose land–to–trust applications have simply been frozen while the Department of Interior works through painstaking legal and historical analysis. We are seeing harassment litigation against tribes who were on treaty reservations in 1934 with a BIA superintendent. Land acquisitions are delayed. Lending and credit are drying up. Jobs are lost or never created. We fear that this will continue to get worse until Congress acts. Even worse, this decision will create two classes of Indian tribes: those who will benefit from Federal trust responsibility and those who will not.

According to the text, why is the Carcieri decision especially problematic?

A) It did not adhere to the exact wording of the original 1934 legislation.

B) It asserted that the 1934 legislation only applies to specific Native Americans.

C) It created new methods by which the Native Americans could regain lands.

D) It set precedents that facilitated the establishment of tribal governments.

15

Behavioral activation is a type of talk therapy that helps a patient get unstuck from negative mood spirals by noticing a connection between what they do and how they feel, and gradually adding more small and enjoyable actions back into life. Behavioral activation has the goal of decreasing avoidance, bolstering peer connection, and improving engagement in rewarding activities. Through behavioral activation, a client works with a counselor to start looking at actions that could help boost the mood. For example, it might start with a goal to get out of one's pajamas and to shower every morning. Feeling a little bit better just by taking that step, the patient then could reach out to get extra support catching up in poor school subjects. In other words, rather than waiting to feel better, the patient does things that align with personal values and that will lead to feeling better.

Based on the text, why is behavioral activation successful in treating depression?

A) It encourages the patient to do what feels most comfortable at the time.

B) It uses incremental steps to form patterns of behavior that alter emotions.

C) it focuses on solving the problems that triggered the depressed behavior.

D) It emphasizes long–term goals that can be attempted when the patient is healthy

16

In the Solomon Islands, cowry shells were sewn into long pieces of cloth as a form of currency, and although _____ use has declined, they have not been completely replaced by modern coinage.

Which choice completes the text so that it conforms to the conventions of Standard English?

A) its

B) their

C) there

D) they're

17

Volcanoes come in all sizes and shapes, but they all fall into three basic structural patterns known as cinder cone, _____ shield formations.

Which choice completes the text so that it conforms to the conventions of Standard English?

A) composite (or stratovolcano), and

B) composite, (or stratovolcano), and

C) composite (or stratovolcano) and,

D) composite, (or stratovolcano) and,

18

Numerous theorists have offered minimum wage as a mechanism for leveling economic inequality by enabling lower-paid workers to earn more money. However, Professor David Neumark, in conjunction with Dr. William Wascher of the Federal Reserve Board, _____ with this view. The results of their literature survey covering over 100 papers revealed that only 10 percent reported positive results and over two-thirds documented increased disparity.

Which choice completes the text so that it conforms to the conventions of Standard English?

A) dissent

B) dissents

C) dissenting

D) have dissented

19

People in developed nations often take water for _____ over 2 billion people in the world do not have access to safe drinking water; 670 million people have no handwashing facilities at all.

Which choice completes the text so that it conforms to the conventions of Standard English?

A) granted but;

B) granted; but

C) granted, but

D) granted but

20

Wheat and rice are the most common cereal crops in the world and are consumed as the staple part of diets in many countries, but there are many other cereal _____ that can be eaten directly or fed to meat animals.

Which choice completes the text so that it conforms to the conventions of Standard English?

A) crops—such as rye and sorghum—

B) crops, such as rye, and sorghum,

C) crops—such as rye and sorghum,

D) crops, such as rye and sorghum—

21

Inuit is the common name for a group of indigenous peoples who live in the arctic and subarctic regions. The term was originally used by the Alaskan Inupiat people, so is not always used in self-reference by all the _____ Labrador, Quebec, Nunavut, and the Northwest Territories.

Which choice completes the text so that it conforms to the conventions of Standard English?

A) sub-groups in Greenland,

B) sub-groups in: Greenland,

C) sub-groups in: Greenland

D) sub-groups; in Greenland,

22

According to _____ the variation among the sites would increase over time, as random chance caused different species to go extinct in some areas but not others.

Which choice completes the text so that it conforms to the conventions of Standard English?

A) Clark the neutral model would predict that:

B) Clark, the neutral model would predict that

C) Clark, the neutral model would predict: that

D) Clark the neutral model would predict, that

23

There are so many sub-fields in science that sometimes the distinctions are hard to determine, and many overlap. _____ paleontology is the study of ancient life, including creatures ranging from as small as microbes to as large as dinosaurs, but paleoichthyology focuses exclusively on the study of prehistoric fish.

Which choice completes the text with the most logical transition?

A) Or else,

B) Even so,

C) For instance,

D) On the whole,

24

Echolocation is a form of sonar in which an animal emits a sound and, using the resulting echo, can locate and identify various objects. Echolocation is highly developed in only a few species, such as bats, whales and dolphins. _____ it is also present in a limited form among shrews and two species of cave–dwelling birds.

Which choice completes the text with the most logical transition?

A) However,

B) Consequently,

C) Accordingly,

D) Clearly,

25

It turns out that 21.6 percent of the population in the United States are bilingual and speak a language other than English in their homes. _____ that may seem like a large percentage, it is far lower than the worldwide average of 43 percent of the population speaking at least two languages.

Which choice completes the text with the most logical transition?

A) Although

B) Because

C) Despite

D) Since

While researching a topic, a student has taken the following notes:

- Maya Angelou was a famous civil rights activist, poet, and author, though she held many other roles throughout her life.

- *I Know Why the Caged Bird Sings* (1969) is one of her most acclaimed books; it publicly reveals details about her private life up to the age of 17.

- She was asked to read the poem "On the Pulse of Morning" at President Bill Clinton's inaugural ceremony in 1993.

- She directed her first movie, *Down the Delta,* in 1996, though she had previously participated in acting and production of other movies.

- Published in 2013 when she was 85 years old, *Mom & Me & Mom* recounts her complex relationship with her own mother.

- At her death in 2014, she was working on a new book about her experiences with different world leaders.

The student wants to emphasize an underlying theme in some of Maya Angelou's books. Which choice most effectively uses relevant information from the notes to accomplish this goal?

A) Maya Angelou wrote a wide variety of works in her later years, including *Down the Delta* and *Mom & Me & Mom.*

B) Many of Maya Angelou's works, such as *I Know Why the Caged Bird Sings* and *Mom & Me & Mom*, are autobiographical.

C) Maya Angelou had close contact with many world leaders, as shown by reading "On the Pulse of Morning" at President Bill Clinton's 1993 inaugural ceremony and writing a book on the subject prior to her death.

D) While some of her books received great critical acclaim, such as *I Know Why the Caged Bird Sings*, others were not popular, such as Mom & Me & Mom.

27

While researching a topic, a student has taken the following notes:

- In 1803, Luke Howard first defined the different categories of clouds.

- Cirro–form clouds are high and wispy, like curls of hair. They usually appear before a change in weather.

- Cumulo–form clouds are tall, reaching from low to high in the sky because they are formed by rising humid air. They have a flat base and distinct shapes, like fluffy cotton balls.

- Strato–form clouds are low, wide, and flat. They often cover the whole sky in a gray or white layer and do not have clear edges.

- Nimbo–form clouds are the type that bring rain or snow. They are actually a combination of the other three cloud forms, so can be similar in shape to any of the others.

The student wants to emphasize how nimbo–form clouds differentiate from the other three types. Which choice most effectively uses relevant information from the notes to accomplish this goal?

A) Unlike other types of clouds, nimbo–form clouds produce precipitation.

B) Nimbo–form clouds are much larger than other types of clouds.

C) Different from other cloud types, nimbo–forms do not have any shape.

D) While other clouds are low in the sky, nimbo–form clouds are high.

No Test Material On This Page

Reading and Writing Test

27 QUESTIONS | 32 MINUTES

1

The cane toad (*Rhinella marina*) was _____ to South America but was transported to Australia in 1935 in an attempt to control the beetle infestations on sugarcane plantation.

Which choice completes the text with the most logical and precise word or phrase?

A) innate

B) congenital

C) pandemic

D) endemic

2

Be aware that some _____ business opportunity promoters have been known to name "insiders" who give glowing—but bogus—recommendations. Don't just talk to the few people they suggest. Choose whom to contact. What if what the seller is telling you is different from what's on the disclosure document or what you hear from another buyer? Step on the brake.

Which choice completes the text with the most logical and precise word or phrase?

A) arguable

B) questionable

C) improbable

D) unresolved

3

The following text is adapted from Abraham Lincoln's last public address, given on April 11, 1965

If this course of rejection has any tendency to bring Louisiana into proper practical relations with the Union, I have, so far, been unable to perceive it. If, on the contrary, we <u>recognize</u>, and sustain the new government of Louisiana the converse of all this is made true.

As used in the text, what does the word "recognize" most nearly mean?

A) identify

B) accept

C) realize

D) appreciate

4

The Business Opportunity Rule governing franchise sales says that a seller has to give you the disclosure document at least seven days before you sign a contract or pay them anything. Use that time to check out the information in the disclosure document, including contacting references. Be aware that some questionable business opportunity promoters have been known to name "insiders" who give glowing—but bogus—recommendations. Don't just talk to the few people they suggest. Choose whom to contact. What if what the seller is telling you is different from what's on the disclosure document or what you hear from another buyer? Step on the brake. An inconsistency could be a tell–tale sign of a business opportunity rip–off. However, it is important to remember that many business investments have a wide range of returns, so not all differences in profit are a deliberate attempt to scam a potential buyer.

What is the purpose of the information that the seller must disclose at least seven days before signing a contract?

A) To point out that there is adequate time to make a decision

B) To emphasize that the buyer is under a lot of pressure

C) To indicate that honest references take time to find

D) To offer the reason that sellers secure bogus recommendations

CONTINUE

5

In order to learn more about the properties of fire in space, scientists aboard the International Space Station have conducted many experiments. Their goal is to gain valuable insight into the mechanisms of fire that will ultimately help prevent fires on spacecraft or offer solutions to quickly extinguish such fires. Flames act very differently in an environment devoid of gravity than they do on Earth. For example, spheres of light form, and the flames can ignite at extremely low temperatures. On Earth, a standard gas stove burns at about 3100 degrees Fahrenheit, but a sustained flame can burn at 900 degrees in the International Space Station.

What is the main purpose of the underlined portion in the overall structure of the text?

A) It highlights the motivation for conducting the experiments.

B) It outlines the methodology the scientists are using to conduct the experiments.

C) It offers a point of comparison for the results of the experiments.

D) It presents an example of the phenomenon viewed in the experiments.

6

This passage is adapted from Emma Lazarus's poem *Spring Star*.

> Over the lamp–lit street,
>
> Trodden by hurrying feet,
>
> Where mostly pulse and beat
>
> Life's throbbing veins,
>
> See where the April star,
>
> Blue–bright as sapphires are,
>
> Hangs in deep heavens far,
>
> Waxes and wanes.

What is the main structure of the text?

A) It establishes a contrast between two images.

B) It shows the futileness of an action.

C) It offers a solution to a problem.

D) It elaborates on an extended metaphor..

7

The following text is adapted from F. Scott Fitzgerald's 1992 novel, *The Beautiful and the Damned.*

Young Anthony had one picture of his father and mother together—so often had it faced his eyes in childhood that it had acquired the impersonality of furniture, but everyone who came into his bedroom regarded it with interest. It showed a dandy of the nineties, spare and handsome, standing beside a tall dark lady with a muff and the suggestion of a bustle. Between them was a little boy with long brown curls, dressed in a velvet Lord Fauntleroy suit. This was Anthony at five, the year of his mother's death.

Which choice best summarizes the text?

A) A young man reminisces about his family.

B) A man's family's appearance is explained.

C) An aristocrat's achievements are outlined.

D) The cause of a tragic event is revealed.

8

The Panama Canal stands as one of the greatest feats of engineering in all time. The idea was not new—in 1534, Charles, King of Spain, ordered a survey of the region—but it took until 1904 for the self-educated engineer John Frank Stevens to solve the technical problems with an intricate lock system and numerous inventions of equipment for the specialized tasks. Equally important were the efforts of Sanitation Engineer William C. Gorgas, who tirelessly oversaw the efforts to keep the work crews healthy. Entire cities of workers and their families needed food, clean water, medical care, and other essential services.

Based on the passage, why is William Gorgas key in building the Panama Canal?

A) He was able to invent equipment that performed different functions.

B) He was a doctor who took care of the workers' medical needs.

C) He was zealous about fulfilling duties regarding the health of workers.

D) He surveyed the area to determine the best way to build cities for workers.

9

George Herman "Babe" Ruth, Jr. (1895–1948) played 22 seasons of Major League baseball. He started as a left-handed pitcher but made his fame as an outfielder and powerful batter, earning the title "Home Run King." Despite the decades that have passed since he stepped off the field, Babe Ruth is still a household name and considered one of the greatest American sports heroes. He was fortunate in that respect, as fans celebrated his triumphs against the background of news from World War I and the 1918 influenza pandemic.

Based on the text, what is one reason why Babe Ruth became so famous?

A) He was an excellent pitcher.

B) He showed people success during a grim time.

C) He fought in World War I.

D) He suffered from the 1918 influenza pandemic.

10

The extreme temperatures on the planet Mercury make it unlikely that there is any life on the planet in a form we would recognize. Mercury is closest to the Sun, and therefore the daytime temperatures are extremely hot, up to 800 degrees Fahrenheit (430 degrees Celsius). Since there is only a residual atmosphere, nights are much colder. In fact, despite its proximity to the Sun, Mercury_____

Which choice most logically completes the text?

A) has an egg-shaped orbit which changes its distance from the Sun.

B) rotates around the Sun faster than any other planet, in only 88 days.

C) is approximately the same size as Earth's moon and covered with craters.

D) might even be cold enough to have permanent water ice near the poles.

11

Median annual wages for urban and regional planners in selected industries in the United States, May, 2019

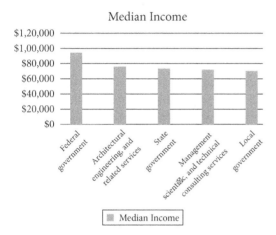

Median Income

The median annual wage for urban and regional planners was $73,050 in May 2018. The median wage is the wage at which half the workers in an occupation earned more than that amount and half earned less. The lowest 10 percent earned less than $45,180, and the highest 10 percent earned more than $114,170. The median rate varies depending on the field of the planning as well. For instance, the median income is _____ .

Which choice most effectively completes the example using information from the graph?

A) higher for state government employees than for local government employees

B) greater for those in architectural, engineering, and related fields than for those in any government position

C) lower for those working in the government than for those who work in private industries such as engineering or related services

D) not as high for management, scientific, and technical consulting service employees as it is for local government employees.

12

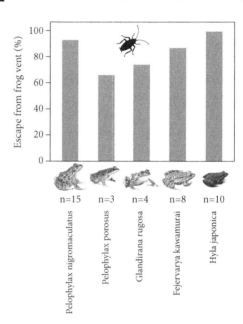

"This study, authored solely by Sugiura Shinji, an ecologist from Kobe University in Japan, describes how the Japanese water scavenger beetle (Regimbartia attenuate) manages to extricate itself from inside several species of frog within 6 hours of being swallowed. Active escape of the aquatic beetle Regimbartia attenuata from the vents of five frog species via the digestive tract. Although adult beetles were easily eaten by frogs, _____."

Which choice most effectively uses data from the graph to complete the text?

A) a maximum of 65% of swallowed beetles were excreted were still alive.

B) on average the swallowed beetles were excreted did not survive.

C) it took less than 6 hours for the swallowed beetles to be extracted.

D) an average of 90% of swallowed beetles were excreted were still alive.

13

The following text is adapted from Herman Melville's 1851 novel, *Moby Dick; or The Whale*.

I always go to sea as a sailor, because of the wholesome exercise and pure air of the fore–castle deck. For as in this world, head winds are far more prevalent than winds from astern (that is, if you never violate the Pythagorean maxim), so for the most part, the Commodore on the quarter-deck gets his atmosphere at second hand from the sailors on the forecastle. He thinks he breathes it first; but not so. In much the same way do the commonalty lead their leaders in many other things, at the same time that the leaders little suspect it. But wherefore it was that after having repeatedly smelt the sea as a merchant sailor, I should now take it into my head to go on a whaling voyage; this the invisible police officer of the Fates.

With which idea about captains would the narrator most likely agree?

A) They have worked hard to earn their position.

B) They are greatly worthy of respect.

C) They do not understand the needs of simple sailors.

D) They are mistaken about the extent of their power.

14

The planet Venus is the second closest to the Sun in our solar system, but is generally hotter than the closest planet, Mercury—the average temperature is 462 degrees Celsius. That is because the atmosphere contains about 96 percent carbon dioxide, creating a greenhouse effect that is like having a giant blanket over the planet that retains the heat. The sulfuric acid in the atmosphere makes it very reflective, so Venus is the second brightest object in the night sky after the Moon.

According to the text, what is most likely true about the planet Mercury?

A) It does not have any sulfuric acid in its atmosphere.

B) Its temperature never exceeds 462 degrees Celsius.

C) It has less than 96 percent carbon dioxide in its atmosphere.

D) It is difficult to locate in the night sky because it is dark.

15

Coffee is the third most consumed beverage in the world, a welcome statistic for the people in Uganda, _____ is the leading cash crop.

Which choice completes the text so that it conforms to the conventions of Standard English?

A) there, it

B) where it

C) which

D) it

16

A classic image of colonial cooperation, _____. Martha kept detailed records of her experiences in the American frontier for over three decades.

Which choice completes the text so that it conforms to the conventions of Standard English?

A) the diary of an 18th–century midwife named Martha Ballard documents several quilting bees

B) an 18th–century midwife named Martha Ballard documented several quilting bees in her diary

C) Martha Ballard, an 18th–century midwife, documented several quilting bees in her diary

D) several quilting bees were documented in the diary of an 18th–century midwife named Martha Ballard

17

Marilyn Monroe, the iconic actress and fashion model from the 1950s and '60s, is attributed as ___ women rarely make history." In reality, the credit should go to Laurel Thatcher Ulrich, who was a student at the time but who later went on to become a professor at Harvard University.

Which choice completes the text so that it conforms to the conventions of Standard English?

A) saying that, "Well-behaved

B) having said that: "well-behaved

C) she said, "Well-behaved

D) saying that "well-behaved

18

Volunteers of America is a non–profit organization which helps homeless, disabled, senior, and other underserved individuals regain a balanced life. Over the past 125 years, the _____ have helped an average of 1.5 million people annually.

Which choice completes the text so that it conforms to the conventions of Standard English?

A) volunteers efforts'

B) volunteer's efforts

C) volunteers' efforts

D) volunteers's efforts'

19

Henry Wadsworth Longfellow's detailed poems greatly influenced the perception of various historical events, such as Paul Revere's nighttime ride during the American Revolutionary war, even though he sometimes sacrificed accuracy for eloquence to make the poems more engaging.

Which choice completes the text so that it conforms to the conventions of Standard English?

A) sacrificed accuracy for eloquence

B) sacrificed—accuracy for eloquence—

C) sacrificed: accuracy for eloquence

D) sacrificed (accuracy for eloquence)

20

Archaeologists determined that a pair of sandals made from sagebrush bark that were found in a cave in Oregon in 1939 are actually the oldest extant example of shoes in the _____ specimens have been dated to between 7,000 and 8,000 BCE.

Which choice completes the text so that it conforms to the conventions of Standard English?

A) world; and the

B) world. Because the

C) world, the

D) world. The

21

Inflation is when the prices of goods and services generally increase, resulting in a decrease in the purchasing power of money. Economists debate about the effects of low levels of _____ high levels of inflation are universally accepted as disruptive to an economy.

Which choice completes the text so that it conforms to the conventions of Standard English?

A) inflation,

B) inflation;

C) inflation:

D) inflation

22

Edward Tingatinga's professional art career only lasted four years. _____ he is considered one of the most influential modern African painters and was the founder of an art style now archetypal in Tanzania.

Which choice completes the text with the most logical transition?

A) Therefore,

B) Even so,

C) Specifically,

D) Moreover,

23

Dogs trained for search and rescue have the same goal of finding humans, but there are actually two main methods that the dogs use to reach this goal. One is called air scent, in which a dog sniffs its surroundings and makes a straight line for the target once the scent is detected. _____ a dog sniffs the ground and follows the specific route that the person took, even if the path is very convoluted. This method is called tracking.

Which choice completes the text with the most logical transition?

A) Furthermore,

B) Precisely,

C) However,

D) Alternatively,

24

Tropical saltwater fish are beautiful to watch, but they take a lot of time and special equipment to maintain properly. That equipment is not cheap, either. A standard tank with fish can easily cost around $2,000 to set up, and there are monthly expenses such as food, salt, and minerals, which can run over $35 a month for a 50–gallon tank. _____ the upkeep alone is equivalent to over two coffee lattes from a specialty store every week.

Which choice completes the text with the most logical transition?

A) On the other hand,

B) Even so,

C) In addition,

D) In other words,

25

While researching a topic, a student has taken the following notes:

- Ada Lovelace (nee Byron) was born 1815 and was very interested in science and math from an early age, so her tutor introduced her to the mathematician Charles Babbage.

- Babbage is considered the "Father of the computer" because he invented an "Analytical Machine," which he used to calculate numbers.

- It is possible that Lovelace wrote the first computer program in the world because she helped design programs for the Analytical Machine.

- In a 1842–1843 Italian translation explaining how the Analytical Machine worked, she wrote down a program in an appendix that was not in the original materials provided by Babbage.

- She realized that the Analytical Machine could be used for non–numerical purposes if other symbols such as letters or musical notes were substituted.

The student wants to emphasize that Ada Lovelace's contributions to mathematics are just as important as Charles Babbage's. Which choice most effectively uses relevant information from the notes to accomplish this goal?

A) Charles Babbage is famous for creating the Analytical Machine, but Ada Lovelace also was interested in explaining how it worked to others, even in different languages.

B) Ada Lovelace wrote a program for the Analytical Machine in 1842–1843, without which Charles Babbage would not have been able to create a working computer.

C) Charles Babbage, Ada Lovelace's tutor, introduced her to the Analytical Machine, and she excelled beyond his abilities at using it.

D) Although Babbage invented the Analytical Machine, Ada Lovelace was able to explain how it worked, create effective programs, and offer additional uses beyond mathematical calculations.

26

While researching a topic, a student has taken the following notes:

- Edward Tingatinga was born in 1932 in a small town called Namochelia in Tanzania.

- An art movement was named after his unique style of cartoon–like animals and landscapes.

- He tried his hand as a musician, and only started painting in 1968. His work was first done using recycled materials like old boards and bicycle paint.

- His work became popular among tourists so he was able to be an artist full time. He started a gallery and studio in 1970.

- In 1972 he was accidentally killed by a policeman who mistook him for someone else.

- His students continue to paint using his style and today his gallery is the largest in Africa.

The student wants to emphasize how influential Edward Tingatinga's painting is in Africa. Which choice most effectively uses relevant information from the notes to accomplish this goal?

A) Edward Tingatinga painted using recycled materials, which started a trend towards using recycled art by a wide range of artists.

B) Though his art career only lasted four years, Edward Tingatinga's art was appealing enough to build a following that carries on the art style today.

C) Edward Tingatinga was the most popular artist of animals and landscapes for tourists to Africa, so his original paintings are highly sought–after today.

D) Despite using recycled materials, Edward Tingatinga became so famous that other artists copied and sold pictures of his artwork.

27

Yellowstone National Park is a popular tourist site, but it is also an active supervolcano. Over the past 2.1 million years, it has erupted with such force that there are layers made of ash and pumice 400 meters thick in places. The most recent giant explosion, about 640,000 million years ago, emitted huge amounts of lava. _____ Now, the park's famous geysers and hot springs are heated by the remaining pools of magma, which are at most 15 percent of their former size.

Which choice most effectively anticipates and addresses a relevant counterargument to the assertion presented in the passage?

A) About 70,000 years ago, there was another eruption, but it was not of the same magnitude and consisted mostly of lava.

B) Geologists have determined that Yellowstone had three supereruptions as well as several lesser eruptions.

C) One might expect a giant peak, but so much magma poured out each time that the underlying reservoirs collapsed and formed a giant caldera.

D) The region to the southwest, the Snake River Plain, had eruptions prior to the supereruptions at Yellowstone.

STOP

No Test Material On This Page

Math

22 QUESTIONS | 35 MINUTES

DIRECTIONS

The questions in this section address a number of important math skills. Use of a calculator is permitted for all questions.

NOTES

Unless otherwise indicated: • All variables and expressions represent real numbers. • Figures provided are drawn to scale. • All figures lie in a plane. • The domain of a given function is the set of all real numbers x for which $f(x)$ is a real number.

REFERENCE

$A = \pi r^2$
$C = 2\pi r$

$A = \ell w$

$A = \frac{1}{2}bh$

$c^2 = a^2 + b^2$

Special Right Triangles

$V = \ell wh$

$V = \pi r^2 h$

$V = \frac{4}{3}\pi r^3$

$V = \frac{1}{3}\pi r^2 h$

$V = \frac{1}{3}\ell wh$

The number of degrees of arc in a circle is 360.

The number of radians of arc in a circle is 2π.

The sum of the measures in degrees of the angles of a triangle is 180.

For **multiple–choice questions,** solve each problem, choose the correct answer from the choices provided, and then circle your answer in this book. Circle only one answer for each question. If you change your mind, completely erase the circle. You will not get credit for questions with more than one answer circled, or for questions with no answers circled.

For **student–produced response questions,** solve each problem and write your answer next to or under the question in the test book as described below.

- Once you've written your answer, circle it clearly. You will not receive credit for anything written outside the circle, or for any questions with more than one circled answer.
- If you find more than one correct answer, write and circle only one answer.
- Your answer can be up to 5 characters for a positive answer and up to 6 characters (including the negative sign) for a negative answer, but no more.
- If your answer is a fraction that is too long (over 5 characters for positive, 6 characters for negative), write the decimal equivalent.
- If your answer is a decimal that is too long (over 5 characters for positive, 6 characters for negative), truncate it or round at the fourth digit.
- If your answer is a mixed number (such as 3.!. 2), write it as an improper fraction (7/2) or its decimal equivalent (3.5).
- Don't include symbols such as a percent sign, comma, or dollar sign in your circled answer.

1

Which of the following describes the transformation of a circle with the equation $(x - 3)^2 + (y + 6)^2 = 49$ to a circle with the equation $(x - 2)^2 + y^2 + 8y = 33$?

A) The circle moves 1 to the right and 2 up

B) The circle moves 1 to the right and 2 down

C) The circle moves 1 to the left and 2 up

D) The circle moves 1 to the left and 2 down

2

How many solutions are there to the equation below?

$$(x - 1)(x + 2) = x (x - 3)$$

A) 0

B) 1

C) 2

D) 4

3

If the system below has an infinite number of solutions, what would be the value of p ?

$$3(x - 6) - 2 (x + 2) = px - 5x - 22$$

4

If the number of weeds on a farm is represented by the function $f(x) = 1,300(1.995)^x$, where x is in weeks, which of the following statements is true about the model?

A) The number of weeds on the farm in the beginning was 1.995

B) The number of weeds on the farm increases by 1.995 every x weeks

C) The number of weeds on the farm increases by 99.5% every x weeks

D) The number of weeds on the farm increases by 1,300 every x weeks

5

Which of the following is equivalent to $(x - 2)^2 (x + 2)^2$?

A) $x^4 - 8x^2 + 16$

B) $x^4 - 16$

C) $x^4 + 8x + 16$

D) $x^4 + 16$

6

A food scientist measures 27 different foods whose calorie content is shown below. What is the difference between the mean and the median of the calorie content of the 27 foods, rounded to the nearest tenth of a calorie?

Calorie content	Frequency
100	6
180	9
280	11
350	1

7

What is the x–intercept for the following equation

$x = 3^{y-1} + \dfrac{5}{3}$?

A) $\dfrac{5}{3}$

B) 3

C) 2

D) $\dfrac{1}{3}$

8

30 Grade 11 students in a summer math class were asked what is the hardest subject for them. 80% of the students said that Statistics was the hardest while the rest chose Physics as the hardest subject. Which of the following statements can best be concluded from this information?

A) 80% of the students in the summer math class think Statistics is the hardest subject.

B) 20% of the Grade 11 students think Statistics is the hardest subject.

C) 80% of the Grade 11 students in the math summer class think Physics is the hardest subject.

D) 20% of the grade 11 students in the math summer class think Physics is the hardest subject.

9

If $-3(x + 3)^2 + 9 + x = ax^2 + bx + c$, what is the value of $a + b + c$?

10

If the maximum point for a quadratic equation $f(x)$ is (3, 2), and it passes through the point (2, 0), which of the following is a solution for x to the quadratic equation?

A) −2

B) 4

C) −16

D) 12

11

What is the value of the slope of a line that passes through the origin and point (3, 5)?

A) $\dfrac{3}{5}$

B) $-\dfrac{3}{5}$

C) $\dfrac{5}{3}$

D) $-\dfrac{5}{3}$

12

If (a , b) is a solution to the following system of inequalities, which of the following represents the minimum value of b?

$$y \geq 2\,(x - 3)^2 + 5$$

$$y \leq x + 3$$

A) 3

B) −3

C) −5

D) 5

13

What is the volume of a sphere with a radius of 3?

14

If the system of equations below has no solution, which of the following would be a possible value of p?

$$3x - 4y = 8$$

$$px + 8y + 6 = 0?$$

A) −6

B) 6

C) 2

D) −2

15

What is the center for the equation of the circle given below

$$x^2 + 6x + y^2 - 6y = 63 ?$$

A) $(3, -3)$

B) $(6, -6)$

C) $(-6, 6)$

D) $(-3, 3)$

16

If one of the solutions for the quadratic equation below is $\dfrac{3 + \sqrt{g}}{3}$, what is the value of g?

$$3x^2 - 6x - 11$$

17

Which of the following is NOT a solution to the following inequality

$$-2x \geq -4 - x ?$$

A) 4

B) 5

C) 3

D) 2

18

What are the possible solutions to the equation below

$$\sqrt{2x + 5} = x - 5 ?$$

A) 2

B) 10

C) 2 and 10

D) -2 and -10

19

If $\dfrac{5}{x} = \dfrac{2}{y}$ and $\dfrac{4}{x} - \dfrac{2}{y} = -\dfrac{1}{5}$, what is the value of xy?

20

If $\dfrac{3x^2 + 7x + 9}{x - 2} = 3x + 13 + \dfrac{A}{x - 2}$. What is the value of A?

A) 19

B) 7

C) 35

D) -23

21

A zookeeper conducted a study on the mass of penguins in the zoo. He found that the mean mass of the penguins in the zoo is 67.9 *kgs*. He estimated that the margin of error for the mean mass is 4.5 *kgs*. Which of the following statements can best be concluded from the study he conducted?

A) The mass of the penguins in the zoo is between 72.4 *kgs* and 63.4 *kgs*.

B) The mass of all penguins is 67.9 *kgs*.

C) The median mass of penguins in the zoo lies between 72.4 *kgs* and 63.4 *kgs*.

D) The mean mass of the penguins in the zoo lies between 72.4 *kgs* and 63.4 *kgs*.

22

How many solutions does the system below have ?
$$3(x - 3) + 2(x + y) = 5x + 2y - 9$$

A) 0

B) Infinitely many

C) 1

D) 2

CONTINUE

No Test Material On This Page

Math

22 QUESTIONS | 35 MINUTES

DIRECTIONS

The questions in this section address a number of important math skills. Use of a calculator is permitted for all questions.

NOTES

Unless otherwise indicated: • All variables and expressions represent real numbers. • Figures provided are drawn to scale. • All figures lie in a plane. • The domain of a given function is the set of all real numbers x for which $f(x)$ is a real number.

REFERENCE

    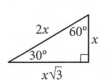

$A = \pi r^2$
$C = 2\pi r$

$A = \ell w$

$A = \frac{1}{2}bh$

$c^2 = a^2 + b^2$

Special Right Triangles

$V = \ell wh$

$V = \pi r^2 h$

$V = \frac{4}{3}\pi r^3$

$V = \frac{1}{3}\pi r^2 h$

$V = \frac{1}{3}\ell wh$

The number of degrees of arc in a circle is 360.

The number of radians of arc in a circle is 2π.

The sum of the measures in degrees of the angles of a triangle is 180.

For **multiple–choice questions,** solve each problem, choose the correct answer from the choices provided, and then circle your answer in this book. Circle only one answer for each question. If you change your mind, completely erase the circle. You will not get credit for questions with more than one answer circled, or for questions with no answers circled.

For **student–produced response questions,** solve each problem and write your answer next to or under the question in the test book as described below.

- Once you've written your answer, circle it clearly. You will not receive credit for anything written outside the circle, or for any questions with more than one circled answer.

- If you find more than one correct answer, write and circle only one answer.

- Your answer can be up to 5 characters for a positive answer and up to 6 characters (including the negative sign) for a negative answer, but no more.

- If your answer is a fraction that is too long (over 5 characters for positive, 6 characters for negative), write the decimal equivalent.

- If your answer is a decimal that is too long (over 5 characters for positive, 6 characters for negative), truncate it or round at the fourth digit.

- If your answer is a mixed number (such as 3.!. 2), write it as an improper fraction (7/2) or its decimal equivalent (3.5).

- Don't include symbols such as a percent sign, comma, or dollar sign in your circled answer.

1

Which of the following equations is equal to
$$3(x + 5)^2 - 2(x - 5)^2 + 2x\ ?$$

A) $x^2 + x + 125$

B) $3x^2 + 52x + 25$

C) $x^2 - 2x - 25$

D) $x^2 + 52x + 25$

2

Which of the following is equivalent to

$\dfrac{1}{x-2} + \dfrac{2x}{5-x}$, for all values of x, where $x \neq 2$ and

$x \neq 5$?

A) $\dfrac{2x^2 - 5x + 5}{-x^2 + 7x - 10}$

B) $\dfrac{2x + 1}{-3}$

C) $\dfrac{2x + 1}{3}$

D) $\dfrac{2x + 1}{(5 - x)(x - 2)}$

3

What is the value of y for the system below?
$$3(x - 2) + 5y = 2$$
$$y = -2(x - 5)$$

4

Which of the following best describes the line of best fit for the graph below?

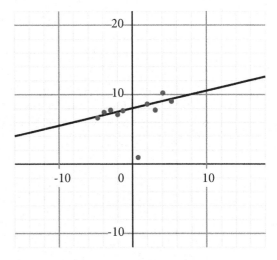

A) $y = \dfrac{1}{4}x + 8$

B) $y = 4x + 8$

C) $y = \dfrac{1}{4}x - 8$

D) $y = \dfrac{-1}{4}x + 8$

5

If angle AOB is $\dfrac{7}{12}\pi$, what is the value of the arc length AB, given that the radius of the circle is 6 *cm*?

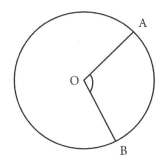

A) $12\pi\ cm$

B) $36\pi\ cm$

C) $\dfrac{7}{2}\pi\ cm$

D) $\dfrac{21}{2}\pi\ cm$

6

What is the sum of the roots for the equation given below

$$2x^2 + 6x + 4 = 0\ ?$$

A) -3

B) -2

C) 2

D) 3

7

If the difference of the sum of the interior angles in a hexagon and that of a heptagon is $a\pi$, what is the value of *a*?

8

Given that $f(3) = 2$ and $f(6) = -3$, which of the following functions best describes $f(x)$?

A) $f(x) = -\dfrac{5}{3}x + 7$

B) $f(x) = \dfrac{2}{3}x - 6$

C) $f(x) = -\dfrac{3}{5}x$

D) $f(x) = \dfrac{3}{5}x + 2$

9

Given that $2(x + 4) = 18$, what is the value of $x + 6$?

A) 9

B) 5

C) −4

D) 11

10

An educational fair is attended by students and parents in a state. If 2,000 students attended the fair, and the ratio of students to parents in the fair is 5:3.5, how many people attended the fair?

11

Find the percent decrease from the actual value y for when $x = 4$ and the predicted value y for when $x = 4$.

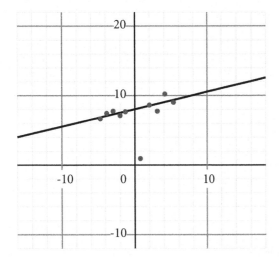

A) 22.22%

B) 33.33%

C) 50%

D) 18.18%

12

Which of the following coordinates represent a solution to the following system of inequalities

$$y > -3x + 5$$

$$y > 2x?$$

A) (2, 4)

B) (1, 4)

C) (4, 3)

D) (2, 1)

13

What is one possible positive solution to the equation below?

$$3 \, |x - 4| = 6$$

14

If AB = DC and segment AD is parallel to segment BC, and AD = 12, DC = 10, and BC = 28, find the area of the figure ABCD below (not drawn to scale).

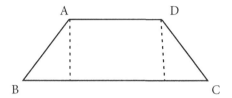

A) 120

B) 60

C) 96

D) 48

15

How many solutions does the equation below have

$$2\,|\,x + 3\,| - 3\,|\,x + 3\,| = -2\ ?$$

A) 0

B) 1

C) 2

D) There isn't sufficient information to answer the question.

16

What is the value of the slope of a line perpendicular to the line $5x - 6y + 30 = 0$

17

Which of the following is equivalent to $cos\ 72°$?

A) $tan\ 18°$

B) $sin\ 72°$

C) $sin\ 18°$

D) $cos\ 18°$

18

The weather channel predicted that there will be a 0.26 chance that it will rain this week. What is the probability that it will not rain this week?

A) 0.62

B) 0.74

C) 0.26

D) 1

19

What is the maximum value of t for the given equation $v(t)$?

$$v(t) = -3t^2 + 9t + 12$$

20

If the semi–circle below has a radius of 7 and angle PQR = 60°, what is the length of side PR?

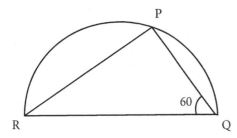

A) 14

B) 7

C) $7\sqrt{2}$

D) $7\sqrt{3}$

21

Which of the following is a solution to the inequality $|x + 3| > 4$?

A) −5

B) −9

C) −2

D) −7

22

If $3x + 4y = 31$ and $2x + 3y = 22$, what is the value of $x + y$?

A) 9

B) 5

C) 4

D) 11

STOP

No Test Material On This Page

Answer Key

Reading and Writing

Module 1

Questions	Correct	Mark your correct answers
1.	C	
2.	B	
3.	C	
4.	A	
5.	B	
6.	D	
7.	D	
8.	D	
9.	A	
10.	A	
11.	C	
12.	D	
13.	C	
14.	B	
15.	B	
16.	B	
17.	A	
18.	B	
19.	C	
20.	A	
21.	A	
22.	B	
23.	C	
24.	A	
25.	A	
26.	B	
27.	A	

Module 2

Questions	Correct	Mark your correct answers
1.	D	
2.	B	
3.	B	
4.	A	
5.	C	
6.	A	
7.	B	
8.	C	
9.	B	
10.	D	
11.	A	
12.	D	
13.	D	
14.	C	
15.	B	
16.	D	
17.	D	
18.	C	
19.	A	
20.	D	
21.	B	
22.	B	
23.	D	
24.	D	
25.	D	
26.	B	
27.	C	

Math

Module 1

Questions	Correct	Mark your correct answers
1.	C	
2.	B	
3.	6	
4.	C	
5.	A	
6.	29.3	
7.	C	
8.	D	
9.	−38	
10.	B	
11.	C	
12.	D	
13.	36π	
14.	A	
15.	D	
16.	42	
17.	B	
18.	B	
19.	10	
20.	C	
21.	D	
22.	B	

Module 2

Questions	Correct	Mark your correct answers
1.	D	
2.	A	
3.	−2	
4.	A	
5.	C	
6.	A	
7.	1	
8.	A	
9.	D	
10.	3,400	
11.	D	
12.	B	
13.	2 or 6	
14.	A	
15.	C	
16.	$\dfrac{-6}{5}$	
17.	C	
18.	B	
19.	$\dfrac{3}{2}$ or 1.5	
20.	D	
21.	B	
22.	A	

1. **Level:** Hard | **Domain:** CRAFT AND STRUCTURE
    Skill/Knowledge: Words in Context

    Key Explanation: Choice C is the best answer because it refers to something that is used as a standard of comparison. It fits the context of saying that 25 healthy people were used as comparisons for the 163 patients with major depressive disorder or bipolar disorder.

    Distractor Explanation: None of the other choices describe the 25 healthy patients. **Choice A** refers to "experts," but the experts on the subject were conducting the experiment, not taking placebos as part of the test. **Choice B** refers to limitations rather than comparisons. **Choice D** refers to orders.

2. **Level:** Easy | **Domain:** CRAFT AND STRUCTURE
    Skill/Knowledge: Words in Context

    Key Explanation: Choice B is the best answer because the text is describing a trend among parasites: almost none are mammals. The blank portion is a noun that describes the vampire bat, which is a parasitic mammal. **Choice B** refers to something that does not follow the general rule, so perfectly describes a parasite that does not fit the usual pattern.

    Distractor Explanations: Choice A is incorrect because it refers to a strange or unusual habit or characteristic that stands out, not to an object that does not fit a rule. **Choice C** is incorrect because it refers to something that is not the same shape or quality, such as sound or appearance. **Choice D** is incorrect because it refers to an individual preference that is unusual.

3. **Level:** Easy | **Domain:** CRAFT AND STRUCTURE
    Skill/Knowledge: Words in Context

    Key Explanation: Choice C is the best answer because C refers to the gradual amassing or acquisition of something. It fits the context of describing what aspect of bioactive compounds—in this case, nutrients—in vegetables is affected by salt stress. The sentence can be paraphrased by saying that salt changes the rate that bioactive compounds amass.

    Distractor Explanation: None of the other choices fits the context of describing what aspect of biological compounds is affected by salt. **Choice A** refers to how well one focuses one's thoughts, so it does not apply to inanimate things. **Choice B** also does not refer to inanimate things, as it describes the emotion of being committed to a purpose. **Choice D** is incorrect because it refers to bringing activities, not things, into one place under one form of control or leadership.

4. **Level:** Hard | **Domain:** CRAFT AND STRUCTURE
    Skill/Knowledge: Text Structure and Purpose

    Key Explanation: Choice A is the best answer because the sentence says that HEPHL1 regulates an enzyme that needs copper. Later, the passage points out that copper is related to Menkes disease. Therefore, the second sentence shows how HEPHL1 might be related: a change in copper changes how lysyl oxidase functions, and that would appear as the copper absorption issues in Menkes disease.

    Distractor Explanation: Choice B is incorrect because the sentence does not refer to hair abnormalities or Menkes disease, only to

HEPHL1. **Choice C** is incorrect because the sentence refers to copper intake, but not iron intake. There is no discussion of whether an "imbalance" or "too much of one compared to the other" causes Menkes disease either. It is possible the syndrome can occur when they are in balance but at too low or high a dose. **Choice D** is incorrect because the second sentence does not relate to mice. It is possible that other creatures are better for study of Menkes disease.

5. **Level:** Medium | **Domain:** CRAFT AND STRUCTURE
   Skill/Knowledge: Text Structure and Purpose

   Key Explanation: Choice B is the best answer because the paragraph is outlining various potential problems to underwater habitats. The author indicates that there are many different potential problems, so "deep ocean habitats may be negatively affected." The quotations come after this discussion and are preceded with "however," which shows that they are a contradiction to the previous idea. Therefore, they are included to show the opposite side of the argument. They indicate that as yet, despite the author's concerns, there has been no "elevated levels of mortality" or "evidence…of harm."

   Distractor Explanation: Choice A is incorrect because the claims made in the quote support the same idea: very little damage occurs to ocean creatures. Therefore, the views are not different from each other. **Choice C** is incorrect because "undermine" refers to weakening an argument. However, the quotes strengthen rather than weaken the idea that systems are safe. **Choice D** is incorrect because the conclusions oppose rather than strengthen the paragraph's main claim that there are risks from tidal energy systems to aquatic habitats and creatures.

6. **Level:** Hard | **Domain:** CRAFT AND STRUCTURE
   Skill/Knowledge: Text Structure and Purpose

   Key Explanation: Choice D is the best answer because the author follows the phrases about extraterrestrial life with a question that asks how such life has changed from "sci-fi fairytale to a serious scientific endeavor." The author is emphasizing the transition in how people perceive extraterrestrial life. In the past, it was viewed as something "impossible" or "not real," and the phrases highlight that image. The phrases provide a strong contrast to the "credible" or "believable" nature of extraterrestrial life today, which the author summarizes in the concept that the search for life is "modeled by macroeconomists, funded by fiscal conservatives, and discussed by theologians."

   Distractor Explanation: Choice A is incorrect because the author never describes the appearance of extraterrestrial life. The phrases may evoke images, but they do not act as a contrast for the current beliefs about what life outside Earth might look like. **Choice B** is incorrect because the images evoked by the phrases are all theatrical forms of aliens. They do not necessarily reflect what scientists think actual extraterrestrial life might look like, and do not "encourage" or "suggest" that the reader think about anything other than the stereotypes. **Choice C** is incorrect because, while the phrases may be "lighthearted," the purpose is not to make the reader laugh. The purpose is to emphasize the important point that the new view of extraterrestrial life is very serious compared to views of such life in the past.

7. **Level:** Medium | **Domain:** CRAFT AND STRUCTURE
   Skill/Knowledge: Cross–Text Connections

Key Explanation: Choice D is the best answer that both authors would agree upon. The author of Text 1 says that there was a mass extinction at the end of the Cretaceous period, indicating that most species did not survive past that time: they died before the next period. The author of Text 2 says that there was no mass extinction, but that the "last major representatives liv[ed] to approximately the end of the Cretaceous period." In other words, they died off slowly over time until the end of the period, and most did not live into the next period.

Distractor Explanations: Choice A is incorrect because the author of Text 1 says that a meteorite "triggered" or "caused" a mass extinction. **Choice B** is incorrect because the author of Text 2 does not say whether the Earth cooled or not; in addition, the author of Text 1 says that the change was enough to cause a mass extinction. **Choice C** is incorrect because Text 1 refers to a mass extinction.

8. **Level:** Medium | **Domain:** INFORMATION AND IDEAS
    Skill/Knowledge: Central Ideas and Details

Key Explanation: Choice D is the best answer because Mother Jones says that the average wage is $500 a year, but that "before you get a thing to eat there is $20 is taken out a month," presumably by the mine owners. Then the "pluck–me" stores, which are owned by the mine owners, take the remaining money for rent. Therefore, the wages are "insufficient" or "not high enough" because the mine owners have the policies of deducting wages and unfairly charging too much.

Distractor Explanation: Choice A is incorrect because the passage says that the "average wages

you fellows get in this country is $500 a year," which indicates that the wages of the miners Mother Jones is addressing is typical of the rest in the country. **Choice B** is incorrect because there is no indication that the wages are "periodically" or "sometimes" lowered or reduced; the problem is that the amount of money is not enough for expenses. **Choice C** is incorrect because there is no reference to the amount of money people earn in other jobs; it could be that miners earn more, but that their expenses are too high to survive.

9. **Level:** Medium | **Domain:** INFORMATION AND IDEAS
    Skill/Knowledge: Central Ideas and Details

Key Explanation: Choice A is the best answer because, according to Sweeney, "The critical element" or "important point" of the study was that the researchers "were able to sustain measurements in this harsh environment as long as [they] have—both in the summer and the winter, in every year over the last 13 years." In other words, the results of the study were "unique" or "one of a kind" because they relied on "measurements" or "data" that did not lack large blocks of time. No previous study had such complete data to work with: the Drake Passage data "is the densest ongoing time series in the Southern Ocean."

Distractor Explanation: Choice B is incorrect because there is no discussion of what equipment or methods the scientists used to collect their data. They could have used very common tools. **Choice C** is incorrect because there is no evidence that previous studies did not "incorporate" or "use" chemical measurements. The only difference brought up is that the period of collection in the Drake Passage study was unbroken for 13 years. **Choice D** is incorrect because it is implied that there have been other studies of the region. If the data set is "the densest," then there is an implied comparison that there were other studies that had data that was not as dense.

10. **Level:** Hard | **Domain:** INFORMATION AND IDEAS
Skill/Knowledge: Command of Evidence (Textual)

Key Explanation: Choice A is the best answer. The claim is that Dickenson "personifies books," which means that she gives books the characteristics of living people. **Choice A** refers to "meeting" a book, like meeting a person, and that the book is "in the dress" or "wearing the clothes" of his time period, just like a person would.

Distractor Explanation: None of the other choices show books in a way that makes them seem like living creatures. **Choice B** only refers to what scholars are interested in, not the way books are. **Choice C** refers to time periods. **Choice D** is a weak choice because books are not mentioned; if "he" refers to a book, it could show that the book is familiar with facts from long ago. However, **Choice A** definitely refers to books having human qualities, so is a much better example of the claim.

11. **Level:** Medium | **Domain:** INFORMATION AND IDEAS
Skill/Knowledge: Command of Evidence (Textual)

Key Explanation: Choice C is the best answer because Sagan's quote is a warning that before assuming that there is life, "we will need to work hard to think of any non-biological process" that could explain "some features in the light spectrum that might be indicative of life." **Choice C** is a case that Sagan would warn against because it

assumes that oxygen is caused by living creatures rather than considering and eliminating all other possible reasons that there may be oxygen present.

Distractor Explanation: Choice A is incorrect because it offers tangible proof of an organism rather than just guessing that there is life based on secondary signs. **Choice B** is incorrect because it shows that the scientist does not rashly assume that oxygen means there is life. Sagan would approve because the scientist indicates there are other options to explain the oxygen. **Choice D** is incorrect because it does not show that anyone is jumping to the conclusion that there is life before enough facts exist to prove that there is life.

12. **Level:** Medium | **Domain:** INFORMATION AND IDEAS
Skill/Knowledge: Command of Evidence (Textual)

Key Explanation: Choice D is the best answer. The example should be one that shows that there are options for nurses other than working in hospitals; particularly, the example should relate to the aging population. **Choice D** focuses on a group of registered nurses who have such an occupation: they work in nursing homes or residential care facilities where seniors often live when their health declines.

Distractor Explanation: Choice A is incorrect because it refers to employment other than working in a hospital, but it does not address the question of an aging population. Nurses in education most likely work with younger people starting out in their careers. **Choice B** is incorrect because it is too vague. It lists two different careers, but does not say what percentage of nurses work in them or how they relate to an aging population. **Choice D** is incorrect because it does not convey the information from the graph correctly. It refers to the percentage change in employment, but the graph refers to the percentage of the registered nurses employed at the time.

13. **Level:** Medium | **Domain:** INFORMATION AND IDEAS
    Skill/Knowledge: Command of Evidence (Quantitative)

Key Explanation: Choice C is the best answer because it uses data from the graph to accurately complete the text. The graph shows Gender-interest stereotypes were stronger than gender-ability stereotypes hence those who believed the stereotypes would be less interested in participating in any courses related to computer science or engineering.

Distractor Explanation: Choice A is incorrect because it doesn't accurately reflect the data from the graph. The graph indicates that girls who believed in the stereotypes would believe that they are less skilled but would also not be interested in participating in any courses related to computer science or engineering. The word "than" suggests that they more interested than skilled however the graph shows that gender-interest stereotypes were stronger than gender-ability stereotypes, meaning that they would be less interested than skilled and not less skilled than interested. **Choice B** is incorrect because it doesn't accurately reflect the data from the graph. The graph indicates that girls who believed in the stereotypes would believe that they are less skilled and not be interested in participating in any courses related to computer science or engineering. The word "equally" suggests that they interested and skilled at the same level however the graph shows that gender-interest stereotypes were stronger than gender-ability stereotypes, meaning that they would be less interested than skilled and not equally

interested and skilled. **Choice D** is incorrect because it doesn't accurately reflect the data from the graph. The graph indicates that gender-interest stereotypes were stronger than gender-ability stereotypes. Hence, girls who believed in the stereotypes would be less interested in participating in any courses related to computer science or engineering.

14. **Level:** Hard | **Domain:** INFORMATION AND IDEAS
    Skill/Knowledge: Inferences

Key Explanation: Choice B is the best answer because Keel complains in the last sentence, "this decision will create two classes of Indian tribes: those who will benefit from Federal trust responsibility and those who will not." In other words, he feels that the decision has problems because some Native Americans qualify and some do not, so the "classes" or "groups" will be unequal in how they are treated.

Distractor Explanation: Choice A is incorrect because Keel does not explain how he felt about the original wording or how the policy varied from the original intent. **Choice C** is incorrect because the decision did not make any "new" methods or laws. It only restricted which groups of people the law applied to. **Choice D** is incorrect because "precedents" are legal cases that act as a guide for deciding future cases. The Carcieri decision, however, did not "facilitate" or "make easier" the process of "establishing" or "creating" tribal governments.

15. **Level:** Easy | **Domain:** INFORMATION AND IDEAS
    Skill/Knowledge: Inferences

Key Explanation: Choice B is the best answer because the process of behavioral activation is described as beginning with simple activities to boost one's mood, such as taking a shower. As the patient improves, more advanced steps can be taken, such as improving in poor school subjects. "Incremental" refers to a series of additions, so accurately describes additional steps taken to alter behavior and feel better using new patterns or routines.

Distractor Explanation: Choice A is incorrect because patients are encouraged to do something positive even when they do not feel comfortable about doing it: "rather than waiting to feel better, the patient does things that align with personal values and that will lead to feeling better." **Choice C** is incorrect because the passage does not refer to solving the problems, only to doing positive steps to get out of a spiral of depression. **Choice D** is incorrect because behavioral activation focuses on a series of short–term goals, such as getting out of pajamas or taking a shower. The short–term goals may be aligned with a larger, long–term goal, but such a process is not discussed in the text.

16. **Level:** Easy | **Domain:** STANDARD ENGLISH CONVENTIONS
    Skill/Knowledge: Form, Structure, and Sense

    Key Explanation: Choice B is the best answer because it is a plural possessive form. It shows that the "use" is something of the "cowry shells."

    Distractor Explanation: Choice A is incorrect because it is a singular possessive word, but "cowry shells" is plural. "Currency" is singular, but it is not the correct referent in the context because "cowry shells" are the subject of the sentence; "they" also give a clue to the proper pronoun.

Choice C is incorrect because it refers to a place rather than possession. **Choice D** is a contraction for "they are," which does not fit the grammatical structure preceding "use has declined."

17. **Level:** Easy | **Domain:** STANDARD ENGLISH CONVENTIONS
    Skill/Knowledge: Form, Structure, and Sense

    Key Explanation: Choice A is the best answer. "(or stratovolcano)" is another name for the composite formation of volcanoes, as shown by the "or." In other words, it is additional information describing the preceding item, "composite." Extra information in parentheses should be treated as part of the word it describes. In this case, there would be a comma after composite if there were no parentheses because it is part of a list joined by "and," so a comma should come after the parentheses.

    Distractor Explanation: All of the other choices have incorrect punctuation for items in a list. For **Choice B**, items in parentheses are included as part of the word they describe, so they should not be divided into a separate item using a comma after "composite." **Choices C** and **D** are incorrect because items in a list should be followed by a comma, but "and" is not. **Choice C** is also missing a comma after "stratovolcano)" and **Choice D** erroneously places the first comma after "composite" rather than after "stratovolcano)".

18. **Level:** Easy | **Domain:** STANDARD ENGLISH CONVENTIONS
    Skill/Knowledge: Form, Structure, and Sense

    Key Explanation: Choice B is the best answer. The subject is the singular "Professor David Neumark," so a singular verb is needed for agreement.

Distractor Explanation: Choices A and **D** are incorrect because "in conjunction with Dr. William Wascher of the Federal Reserve Board" modifies "Professor David Neumark" rather than creates a verb with two people in it. Although it appears that a plural verb is needed, that is not the case. **Choice C** is incorrect because it is only a gerund rather than an active verb (such as "is dissenting,") so the result is a fragment.

19. **Level:** Easy | **Domain:** STANDARD ENGLISH CONVENTIONS
    Skill/Knowledge: Boundaries

    Key Explanation: Choice C is the best answer. "People…granted" is the main idea, and "over…water" is another complete idea with a noun and verb. That idea is made secondary by the word "but." A clause that is secondary needs to be separated from the main idea using a comma.

    Distractor Explanation: It may appear that a semicolon is needed to separate ideas in a list, as there is a semicolon before "670 million." However, **Choices A** and **B** are incorrect because a semicolon must be preceded and followed by complete ideas that can stand on their own. In **Choice A**, "but" is left hanging at the end of the preceding idea, and in **Choice B**, "but" creates a subordinate clause that can not stand alone. **Choice D** is incorrect because there should be a comma separating clauses from each other.

20. **Level:** Medium | **Domain:** STANDARD ENGLISH CONVENTIONS
    Skill/Knowledge: Boundaries

    Key Explanation: Choice A is the best answer. A pair of dashes can be used to add interesting but not essential information to a sentence. In

this case, the names of the crops are not required, but could help the reader know what other cereal crops there are.

Distractor Explanation: Choice B is incorrect because, while commas after "crops" and "sorghum" would also create an aside that describes "cereal crops," there should be no comma after "rye." That punctuation is because "rye and sorghum" forms a list of two items joined by "and," and such a list should not have a comma before the "and." **Choices C** and **D** are incorrect because "that" is the start of a relative clause that should not be divided from its noun with any punctuation. However, a single dash could otherwise be used after a main clause to add more information such as the names of the grains.

21. **Level:** Easy | **Domain:** STANDARD ENGLISH CONVENTIONS
    Skill/Knowledge: Boundaries

    Key Explanation: Choice A is the best answer. A series of nouns joined by "and" should have a comma following each noun. Since "Greenland" is one place on the list where Inuit people live, it should be followed by a comma. No other punctuation is needed.

    Distractor Explanation: Choices B and **C** are incorrect because a colon should follow a complete clause, but the part preceding the colon cannot stand on its own as a sentence. "In" is left dangling. **Choice C** is also incorrect because there should be a comma after "Greenland." **Choice D** is incorrect because the part before and after a semicolon should both be complete clauses, but the following portion has no subject or verb.

22. **Level:** Easy | **Domain:** STANDARD ENGLISH CONVENTIONS
Skill/Knowledge: Boundaries

Key Explanation: Choice B is the best answer because "According to Clark" is a modifier that refers to the main clause, "the neutral model… over time." A modifier should be separated from the main clause with a comma. No other punctuation is needed in the underlined portion.

Distractor Explanation: Choices A and **C** are incorrect because a colon should follow a complete idea, but the portion preceding the colon cannot stand on its own as a sentence. **Choices A** and **D** are incorrect because "according to Clark" needs to be followed by a comma to separate it from the main clause. **Choice D** is also incorrect because there should not be a comma separating "predict" from its object, "that the variation would increase."

23. **Level:** Easy | **Domain:** EXPRESSION OF IDEAS
Skill/Knowledge: Transitions

Key Explanation: Choice C is the best answer. The first sentence explains that some scientific fields overlap, and the following sentence gives a specific example of two fields that have points in common. **Choice C** is used to introduce an example or specific case of a general idea, so fits the context well.

Distractor Explanation: None of the other choices effectively shows that the following information is a particular case that is used to clarify the previous sentence. **Choice A** introduces an alternate possibility, not the same thing. **Choice B** shows that something happens despite something else, so provides an exception rather than a classic example. **Choice D** is used to introduce a summary or preference regarding the previous idea.

24. **Level:** Easy | **Domain:** EXPRESSION OF IDEAS
Skill/Knowledge: Transitions

Key Explanation: Choice A is the best answer. The previous sentence explains that echolocation is highly developed in some species. The following sentence says that other species have echolocation, but it is in a "limited form" or "not developed much at all." **Choice A** is used to qualify an earlier claim, so it fits the context of qualifying the idea that only a few animals have developed echolocation by saying that in reality, others also have it, albeit in a modified form.

Distractor Explanation: Choices B and **C** are used to show the logical result of an argument, so they do not effectively establish the relationship between ideas. A few species having limited echolocation is not necessarily a logical result of some species having echolocation. **Choice D** is used to introduce an idea that the reader might assume; in other words, the author feels it is obvious. However, it is probably not common knowledge that shrews and two bird species have modified echolocation.

25. **Level:** Easy | **Domain:** EXPRESSION OF IDEAS
Skill/Knowledge: Transitions

Key Explanation: Choice A is the best answer because it is used to establish a contrast between clauses in a sentence. In this case, it contrasts what "seems" or "appears" to be a large percentage with the much larger worldwide population. In other words, **Choice A** establishes that the percentage of bilingual speakers in the US is relatively small, as it is half that of the global average.

Distractor Explanation: None of the other choices effectively show the relationship between the first and second halves of the sentence.

Choices **B** and **D** are used to show a reason, but there is no reason given for why different populations are bilingual or not. **Choice C** is grammatically incorrect. Its meaning of "even though" fits the context, but "despite" should be followed by a noun or noun phrase rather than a clause starting with "that."

26. **Level:** Medium | **Domain:** EXPRESSION OF IDEAS
    Skill/Knowledge: Rhetorical Synthesis

    Key Explanation: Choice B is the best answer. The question asks for an "underlying theme" in some of Maya Angelou's books. In other words, it is asking for something that is similar to books that she wrote. The description of *I Know Why the Caged Bird Sings* says that it "reveals details about her private life up to the age of 17," or "tells about her youth," and the notes say that *Mom & Me & Mom* is about her relationship with her mother. In other words, both books tell about her personal life, which makes them "autobiographies."

    Distractor Explanation: Choice A is incorrect because, while it is true, it does not refer to a theme in books. Instead, it refers to a movie, *Down the Delta*. **Choice C** is incorrect because it also does not refer to a theme in books, only a theme in her life. There is no evidence that she actually wrote more than one unfinished book about world leaders. **Choice D** is incorrect because, while *I Know Why the Caged Bird Sings* was received well, there is no indication that her other books were received poorly or were not read by many people.

27. **Level:** Medium | **Domain:** EXPRESSION OF IDEAS
    Skill/Knowledge: Rhetorical Synthesis

    Key Explanation: Choice A is the best answer. The final bullet point refers to the fact that nimbo–form clouds "are the type that bring rain." Therefore, they produce rain, but the others do not.

    Distractor Explanation: Choice B is incorrect because there is no indication that nimbo–forms are larger than the other types. While they combine shapes, they could do so on a small scale. **Choice C** is incorrect because the notes state that nimbo–form combines the shapes of other clouds; therefore, they must have recognizable shapes that can be matched to other forms. **Choice D** is incorrect because the location of nimbo–form clouds is not given. In addition, cirro–forms are described as high.

1. **Level:** Medium | **Domain:** CRAFT AND STRUCTURE
   Skill/Knowledge: Words in Context

   Key Explanation: Choice D is the best answer because the blank shows the cane toad's relationship to South America. **Choice D** means "native to" a specific place, so fits the context of saying that the toad came from South America but was "transported" or "moved" to Australia.

   Distractor Explanations: None of the other choices establishes the toad's relationship to South America. **Choices A** and **B** refer to an inborn or natural trait or characteristic, not a species. **Choice C** refers to an epidemic or wide–spread disease.

2. **Level:** Medium | **Domain:** CRAFT AND STRUCTURE
   Skill/Knowledge: Words in Context

   Key Explanation: Choice B is the best answer because the blank is used to describe the business opportunity promoters who get people to make "glowing—but bogus—recommendations." In other words, the sellers who find people to give fake good reviews. If the reviews are fake, they are dishonest. **Choice B** refers to something which is potentially dishonest or not completely legal, so accurately describes the sellers that do dishonest things.

   Distractor Explanation: None of the other choices fits the context of describing a promoter who uses fraudulent methods to convince someone to buy a product. **Choice A** refers to something that does not have a clear answer. **Choice C** refers to something that is unlikely. **Choice D** refers to something that has not been decided or settled.

3. **Level:** Easy | **Domain:** CRAFT AND STRUCTURE
   Skill/Knowledge: Words in Context

   Key Explanation: Choice B is the best answer because "recognize" is what "we," the Union, could do to the new government of Louisiana that would make true the "converse" or "opposite" of the previous discussion of "discouraging and paralyzing" all the people. The previous discussion is about what happens if the Union does not support Louisiana. Choice B refers to welcoming or integrating something, in this case, Louisiana, so it fits the context of showing the opposite of rejecting Louisiana.

   Distractor Explanation: None of the other choices show the opposite of rejection. **Choice A** refers to indicating what something is or naming it. **Choice C** refers to either fully understanding something or achieving a goal. **Choice D** refers to knowing the value of something.

4. **Level:** Medium | **Domain:** CRAFT AND STRUCTURE
   Skill/Knowledge: Text Structure and Purpose

   Key Explanation: Choice A is the best answer because the reference to the seven–day period is followed by, "Use that time to check out the information in the disclosure document, including contacting references." Therefore, the information about the length of time is given to show that buyers have a full week to research the purchase before agreeing to it.

   Distractor Explanation: Choice B is incorrect because the author does not give any indication that the amount of time is too short. The time is mentioned to show that one even has leeway to contact references. **Choice C** is incorrect because the author suggests using the time to check all the information, not just the references. There is no indication that finding honest references is more time–consuming than any of the other portions. **Choice D** is incorrect because sellers "secure" or "get" bogus recommendations because they want their company to sound good. They do not do it only because of a seven–day period before signing.

5. **Level:** Easy | **Domain:** CRAFT AND STRUCTURE
   Skill/Knowledge: Text Structure and Purpose

   Key Explanation: Choice C is the best answer because the result of the experiment is that "flames can ignite at extremely low temperatures." More specifically, the flames "can burn at 900 degrees in the International Space Station." That piece of information is not very helpful to the average reader, so the author gives a reference that the reader most likely knows, the temperature of something in a house on Earth. The reader can then see that the flame can burn at a third the temperature as one on Earth.

   Distractor Explanations: Choice A is incorrect because "motivation" is a "reason" or "goal." The goal is not a fact about gas stoves on Earth; the goal is described in the second sentence, "to gain valuable insight into the mechanisms of fire." **Choice B** is incorrect because "methodology" is the series of steps taken to perform an experiment. However, there is no indication of how the scientists lit flames in space. **Choice D** is incorrect because the underlined portion shows what happens on Earth, not in the experiments on the International Space Station.

6. **Level:** Hard | **Domain:** CRAFT AND STRUCTURE
   Skill/Knowledge: Text Structure and Purpose

Key Explanation: Choice A is the best answer because the text "contrasts" or "shows the difference" between two different things: the busy street below and the bright star above.

Distractor Explanations: Choice B is incorrect because the passage does not say that any actions are "futile" or "useless." The busy street image is hectic, but there is no claim that it has no point. **Choice C** is incorrect because there is no "problem" or "concern to be solved," and hence, there is also no solution or remedy in the text. **Choice D** is incorrect because while a star or street could be a metaphor, there is no hint about what they might represent in the text.

7. **Level:** Easy | **Domain:** INFORMATION AND IDEAS
   Skill/Knowledge: Central Ideas and Details

   Key Explanation: Choice B is the best answer because the text describes the photograph of Anthony's family, explaining their "appearance" or "how they looked."

   Distractor Explanation: Choice A is incorrect because the passage is written from the point of view of a third–person narrator. Anthony does not "reminisce" or "nostalgically talk about" the people in the picture. **Choice C** is incorrect because, while the characters might be "aristocrats" or "upper class," the passage does not focus on the "achievements" or "successes" of the characters. **Choice D** is incorrect because, while the mother's death might be called "tragic" or "sad," the cause of her death is not "revealed" or "shown."

8. **Level:** Easy | **Domain:** INFORMATION AND IDEAS
   Skill/Knowledge: Central Ideas and Details

Key Explanation: Choice C is the best answer. The next–to–the–last sentence explains that Gorgas "tirelessly" or "did not stop," in other words, was zealous about his "duties" or "tasks," which involved overseeing "the efforts to keep the work crews healthy."

Distractor Explanation: Choice A is incorrect because Stevens, not Gorgas, invented new equipment. **Choice B** is incorrect because there is no indication that Gorgas was a doctor, only a sanitation engineer. **Choice D** is incorrect because the passage does not say the details of building cities for the workers; someone else might have done any necessary surveying.

9. **Level:** Medium | **Domain:** INFORMATION AND IDEAS
   Skill/Knowledge: Central Ideas and Details

Key Explanation: Choice B is the best answer because the passage says he was "fortunate in that respect," meaning that he was lucky in becoming "a household name" or "really famous" because "fans celebrated his triumphs against the background of news from World War I and the 1918 influenza pandemic." In other words, fans liked his "triumphs" or "successes" as a contrast to the "grim" or "bad" times of a war and pandemic.

Distractor Explanations: Choice A is incorrect because the passage says that he started as a pitcher, but became famous when he was "an outfielder and powerful batter." Therefore, his fame was not because of his pitching. **Choices C and D** are incorrect because the passage only refers to the se events as the "background" of Ruth's "triumphs" or "successes." There is no discussion whether he participated in them or not.

10. **Level:** Hard | **Domain:** INFORMATION AND IDEAS
    Skill/Knowledge: Command of Evidence (Textual)

Key Explanation: Choice D is the best answer because the text is discussing the extreme temperatures on Mercury. The transition "in fact" is used to emphasize a point, and in this case, the blank portion needs to emphasize the previous idea of nights being cold. **Choice D** effectively does that by showing that despite the hot days, there may still be ice on the planet.

Distractor Explanations: All of the other choices can be eliminated because they offer a point that is off the topic of temperature and cold. **Choice A** refers to the orbit, **Choice B** to the speed, and **Choice C** to the size and appearance

11. **Level:** Easy | **Domain:** INFORMATION AND IDEAS
    Skill/Knowledge: Command of Evidence (Textual)

Key Explanation: Choice A is the best answer because the graph shows that the median income for state government employees is slightly under the $80,000 mark, at about $75,000. The median income for local government employees is closer to $70,000, which is halfway between the $60,000 and $80,000 lines. Therefore, the median income for state government employees is "higher" or "larger" than that for local government employees.

Distractor Explanation: All of the other choices can be eliminated because they are not supported by the data from the graph. **Choices B and C** are incorrect because "architectural, engineering, and related fields" at just under $80,000 is lower, not greater, than for "federal government employees" at just under $100,000. **Choice D** is incorrect because "management, scientific, and technical consulting service" is slightly higher than for "local government," though both are between $60,000 and $80,000.

12. **Level:** Medium | **Domain:** INFORMATION AND IDEAS
    Skill/Knowledge: Command of Evidence (Quantitative)

    Key Explanation: Choice D is the best answer because the total average of the bar chart values across the 5 species of frogs equates to approximately 90% ($15 \times 94 + 3 \times 64 + 4 \times 70 + 8 \times 88 + 10 \times 100$) / ($15 + 3 + 4 + 8 + 10$). The total average can be estimated by looking at the graph without doing the math.

    Distractor Explanation: Choice A is incorrect because More than 65% of the swallowed beetles survived. **Choice B** is incorrect because more than 50% of the swallowed beetles survived. **Choice C** is incorrect because the results of study was does not use time as variable.

13. **Level:** Medium | **Domain:** INFORMATION AND IDEAS
    Skill/Knowledge: Inferences

    Key Explanation: Choice D is the best answer because the narrator says that the simple sailors breathe the fresh air first, and that the captain "thinks he breathes it first; but not so." The comparison is expanded to say that "In much the same way do the commonalty lead their leaders in many other things, at the same time that the leaders little suspect it." In other words, he is implying that the captain feels he has power, but

really the sailors have influence and can lead or have control about many things in a quiet way.

Distractor Explanation: All of the other choices can be eliminated because they are not supported by any evidence from the passage. For **Choice A**, there is no reference to how captains get appointed. For **Choice B**, the comment that they breathe second-hand air implies that captains do not deserve as much respect as they think they do. For **Choice C**, there is no evidence that captains do not understand the needs of sailors. They order sailors about, but they still could take care of sailors well.

14. **Level:** Hard | **Domain:** INFORMATION AND IDEAS
    Skill/Knowledge: Inferences

    Key Explanation: Choice C is the best answer. The text points out that Venus is warm because it has a "giant blanket" of an atmosphere with so much carbon dioxide holding in the heat. If Mercury had such a blanket, then it would also hold in heat due to the greenhouse effect. Therefore, Mercury probably has less carbon dioxide, which is why it is less hot in general than Venus is, even though Mercury is closer to the Sun.

    Distractor Explanations: Choice A is incorrect because Mercury could have some sulfuric acid in the atmosphere, though it presumably does not have as much as Venus, which is reflective and brighter because of the acid. **Choice B** is incorrect because "never" is too absolute. The passage only says that Venus is "generally hotter," which means that it can sometimes be less hot than Mercury. Plus, the "average" or "middle" temperature is 462 degrees Celsius, so it is possible that Mercury is sometimes hotter than that. **Choice D** is not discussed in the passage; it could be possible to locate Mercury easily. The passage only says that Venus is brighter.

15. **Level:** Medium | **Domain:** STANDARD ENGLISH CONVENTIONS
Skill/Knowledge: Form, Structure, and Sense

Key Explanation: Choice B is the best answer. "Where" is used to start a clause that describes a place, so it fits the context of adding detail about coffee being the leading cash crop in the place of Uganda.

Distractor Explanation: Choices A and **D** are incorrect because they create run–on sentences that join two independent clauses that can stand on their own as sentences. **Choice C** is incorrect because "which" starts a clause that refers to the preceding noun. However, the place of "Uganda" is not a leading cash crop. Instead, coffee is a cash crop in Uganda.

16. **Level:** Medium | **Domain:** STANDARD ENGLISH CONVENTIONS
Skill/Knowledge: Form, Structure, and Sense

Key Explanation: Choice D is the best answer. "A classic image of colonial cooperation" is a modifier that needs to describe the noun that follows it. **Choice D** accurately shows that the image of cooperation refers to quilting bees.

Distractor Explanation: All of the other choices can be eliminated because the modifier "A classic image of colonial cooperation" refers to something illogical. In **Choice A**, it refers to a diary, but a diary is a personal account rather than a classic example of cooperating with other people. **Choices B** and **C** are incorrect because the subject

is Martha Ballard, who is an individual person rather than an image of cooperation.

17. **Level:** Medium | **Domain:** STANDARD ENGLISH CONVENTIONS
Skill/Knowledge: Form, Structure, and Sense

Key Explanation: Choice D is the best answer. When a quote is used as part of a sentence rather than a complete clause, it is only identified with quotation marks. While "said" is followed by a comma and the first word of the quotes is capitalized, in this case, "that" makes the quote part of the sentence itself.

Distractor Explanation: Choice A is incorrect because a comma and capitalization are used after a reporting verb such as "said," not as part of a clause starting with "that." **Choice B** is incorrect because a colon should come after a complete clause, but "that" is left dangling. **Choice C** is incorrect because "is attributed as" is followed by a noun or gerund (the –ing form of a verb) rather than a complete clause with subject or verb.

18. **Level:** Medium | **Domain:** STANDARD ENGLISH CONVENTIONS
Skill/Knowledge: Form, Structure, and Sense

Key Explanation: Choice C is the best answer. An s followed by an apostrophe is the correct way to indicate a plural possessive. It correctly shows that the efforts were made by more than one volunteer.

Distractor Explanation: Choice A is incorrect because "volunteers" is a plural noun that does not show any possession. **Choices A** and **D** are incorrect because "efforts" does not possess anything in the sentence, so should not have an apostrophe. **Choice B** is incorrect because an apostrophe followed by an s is the way to show possession of a singular thing, but the efforts span 125 years, so were done by more than one volunteer.

19. **Level:** Medium | **Domain:** STANDARD ENGLISH CONVENTIONS
Skill/Knowledge: Boundaries

Key Explanation: Choice A is the best answer. "Sacrificed XX for YY" is a standard idiom that refers to doing something at the expense of something else. No punctuation is needed.

Distractor Explanation: Choices B and **D** are incorrect because "accuracy" is the object of "sacrificed;" "for eloquence" is the reason that accuracy was given up. However, dashes and parentheses are used to indicate additional information that is not part of the main clause, so they erroneously divide the object from its verb. **Choice C** is incorrect because a colon should not divide essential parts of the sentence from the main clause. In this case, the portion after the colon is necessary for correct understanding of what Longfellow did.

20. **Level:** Easy | **Domain:** STANDARD ENGLISH CONVENTIONS
Skill/Knowledge: Boundaries

Key Explanation: Choice D is the best answer. The ideas in the preceding and following portions are complete clauses that can stand on their own as sentences, so should be divided by a period and a capital letter "t".

Distractor Explanation: Choice A is incorrect because a semicolon should be preceded and followed by a complete clause that can stand on

its own, but "and" subordinates the following portion. The second part cannot stand on its own. **Choice B** is incorrect because "because" subordinates the following portion, which cannot stand on its own as a sentence. **Choice C** is incorrect because it is a comma splice between two clauses that can each stand on their own.

21. **Level:** Medium | **Domain:** STANDARD ENGLISH CONVENTIONS
Skill/Knowledge: Boundaries

Key Explanation: Choice B is the best answer. The portions before and after the punctuation are both independent clauses, meaning that they could both stand on their own as sentences. Therefore, they should be joined by a semicolon or a period, which is not a given choice.

Distractor Explanation: Choice A is incorrect because it creates a comma splice. **Choice C** is incorrect because a colon is used to add more information clarifying the clause before the colon. In this case, the preceding portion is about low levels of inflation, but the following portion introduces a different topic, high levels of inflation. **Choice D** is incorrect because it is a run–on.

22. **Level:** Easy | **Domain:** EXPRESSION OF IDEAS
Skill/Knowledge: Transitions

Key Explanation: Choice B is the best answer. The first sentence explains that Tingatinga's career was very short. The second sentence offers a contrast: he was one of the most important painters in modern Africa. **Choice B** is used to show that despite one thing happening, another is true. It therefore fits the context of saying that despite the short career, Tingatinga made a great impact.

Distractor Explanation: None of the other choices establishes a contrast between the preceding and following ideas. **Choice A** is used to introduce a logical result of the previous claim, but it is more logical to expect little impact from a short career. **Choices C** and **D** are both used to add more detail to clarify the same topic rather than change tone to something unexpected.

23. **Level:** Easy | **Domain:** EXPRESSION OF IDEAS
    Skill/Knowledge: Transitions

    Key Explanation: Choice D is the best answer. The passage describes two types of search and rescue dog, and the blank is the point at which the topic changes from one type to the other, from air scent to tracking. **Choice D** is used to show that the following method is an "alternate" or "different" case, so it fits the context of introducing a second method.

    Distractor Explanation: None of the other choices shows that the following information is the second of two possible methods. **Choice A** is used to add another point to continue an argument. **Choice B** is used to add specific detail clarifying a general statement. **Choice C** is used to add a qualification or restriction to a previous claim.

24. **Level:** Easy | **Domain:** EXPRESSION OF IDEAS
    Skill/Knowledge: Transitions

    Key Explanation: Choice D is the best answer. The previous sentence describes the price of "monthly expenses" as being over $35. The following sentence describes the "upkeep" or "ongoing expenses," which are the same thing, but uses a different way to express the money: it discusses what alternate things a person could buy, lattes. **Choice D** is used to rephrase or introduce

an idea in different words, so effectively shows that the following is a different way of looking at the figures in the previous sentence.

Distractor Explanation: Choice A is incorrect because it is used to show a contrasting or opposite idea, not rephrase the same point. **Choice B** is used to show that something happens in spite of something else, which does not fit the discussion of equivalent concepts. **Choice C** is used to add more to the same argument, so in the context, would be used to add a new type of expense in caring for tropical fish.

25. **Level:** Medium | **Domain:** EXPRESSION OF IDEAS
    Skill/Knowledge: Rhetorical Synthesis

    Key Explanation: Choice D is the best answer. It gives three valuable contributions that Lovelace made to the field of mathematics: she explained the computer, created programs, and devised uses for it. Therefore, she added to the field in specific and important ways. Creating programs and devising uses, in particular, show the need to manipulate math in order to accomplish certain goals.

    Distractor Explanation: Choice A is incorrect because it only says that Lovelace "explained" or "talked about" the machine. Though that was one valuable addition to help spread information about what it was, on its own that does not show she made mathematical contributions. **Choice B** is incorrect because, while Lovelace wrote a program, the notes do not say that Babbage could not write them himself. It is possible that his computer would have worked without her help, but that she expanded on what it could do. **Choice C** is incorrect because Babbage was not Lovelace's tutor, he was introduced by her tutor. Furthermore, the notes do not say that she exceeded his abilities using it, only that she came up with different uses for it.

26. **Level:** Medium | **Domain:** EXPRESSION OF IDEAS
Skill/Knowledge: Rhetorical Synthesis

Key Explanation: Choice B is the best answer. The notes state that Tingatinga started painting in 1968 and died in 1972, a period of four years. However, his art was "appealing" or "attractive" enough that "an art movement was named after his unique style" and students "continue to paint using his style" even now.

Distractor Explanation: Choice A is incorrect because, while Tingatinga used recycled materials and started a movement, there is no indication that his followers also use recycled materials. His students paint in his style, but they do not represent a "wide range" of other artists, which would include artists in different media or styles. **Choice C** is incorrect because the notes say his artwork, which was of animals and landscapes, was popular among tourists, but not necessarily the "most" popular. The notes also say that his gallery sells works by the students, but not that "his original" or "his own" artworks are still being sold. **Choice D** is incorrect because the passage says that students made pictures "in his style," but not that they "copied" or "made exact replicas" of the works that Tingatinga did.

27. **Level:** Hard | **Domain:** EXPRESSION OF IDEAS
Skill/Knowledge: Rhetorical Synthesis

Key Explanation: Choice C is the best answer. The assertion in the passage is that Yellowstone is a supervolcano. The reader might question that claim by saying that there is no peak, but the passage addresses that question by explaining why

none can be seen: the space where the magma had been collapsed, so the ground dropped down into a caldera or crater.

Distractor Explanation: None of the other choices addresses a counter argument about the park being a supervolcano. **Choices A** and **B** provide more detail about the eruptions, but does not show that the author recognizes that the reader might doubt the claim that there is a supervolcano. **Choice C** expands the discussion to a different area than the park rather than answer a question about the park.

This page is intentionally left blank

1. **Level:** Medium | **Domain:** GEOMETRY AND TRIGONOMETRY
    Skill/Knowledge: Circles | **Testing point:** Working with transformations and the equation of a circle

    Key Explanation: Choice C is correct. The equation of a circle is given by $(x – h)^2 + (y – k)^2 = r^2$, where (h, k) is the center of the circle. In the initial equation, the center of the circle is $(3, –6)$ and in the transformed equation, the center of the circle is $(2, –4)$. To compare the equations, the equation of the second circle must be put into standard form by completing the square as shown below.

    $(x – 2)^2 + y^2 + 8y = 33$
    $(x – 2)^2 + y^2 + 8y + 16 = 33 + 16$
    $(x – 2)^2 + (y + 4)^2 = 33 + 16$
    $(x – 2)^2 + (y + 4)^2 = 49$.

    This yields $(2, –4)$ as the center of the transformed circle.

    Therefore, the transformation will be 1 to the left as the x coordinate moves from 3 to 2 and 2 up as the y coordinate moves from –6 to –4.

    Distractor Explanation: Choice A is incorrect because the x coordinate moves to the left rather than to the right. This answer may have been incorrectly selected if the student misinterpreted the standard form for the equation of a circle and thought that the x-coordinates of the centers of the circles are -3 and -2 . **Choice B is incorrect.** This answer may have been incorrectly selected if the student assumed that the centers were (-3, 6) and (-2 and 4) through misinterpretation of the standard form of the equation of a circle and/or through completing the square incorrectly. **Choice D is incorrect** and may have been incorrectly selected by not completing the square correctly or incorrectly interpreting the center values in the standard equation for a circle

2. **Level:** Hard | **Domain:** ADVANCED MATH
    Skill/Knowledge: Nonlinear equations in one variable and systems of equations in two variables
    Testing point: How many solutions does an equation have

    Key Explanation: Choice B is correct. To solve this equation, first, use the foiling method to expand the left side of the equation and use the distributive property to expand the right side of the equation. Then combine like terms and solve the resulting linear equation as follows:

    $(x – 1) (x + 2) = x(x – 3)$
    $x^2 – x + 2x – 2 = x^2 – 3x$
    $x – 2 = –3x$
    $4x = 2$
    $x = \dfrac{1}{2}$ or 0.5

    This shows that the equation has only one solution.

    Distractor Explanation: Choices A and C are incorrect. These answers may be arrived at due to math miscalculations or conceptual errors. **Choice D is incorrect.** This answer may be arrived at if the student chooses to simply equate each parentheses to zero and finds 1, –2, 0, and 3 as the solutions.

3. **Level:** Easy | **Domain:** Algebra
    Skill/Knowledge: Linear equations in one variable
    Testing point: Solving equations of one variable

    Key Explanation: For a system of equations to have an infinite number of solutions, it means that the equations are identical and have the same slope and y–intercept.
    The first step is to use the distributive property to multiply out the terms on the left side of the equation, resulting in:
    $3x – 18 – 2x – 4 = px – 5x – 22a$
    Combining like terms yields

$x - 22 = px - 5x - 22$

Adding $5x$ to both sides yields:

$6x - 22 = px - 22$

Therefore p is equal to 6.

4. **Level:** Easy | **Domain:** ADVANCED MATH
   Skill/Knowledge: Nonlinear functions | **Testing point:** Determining the meaning in context with exponential equations

   Key Explanation: Choice C is correct. The format for an exponential growth equation is:

   Initial value $\times$ (1+growth rate as a decimal)^x

   The growth factor of the weeds on the farm is defined by 1 + the growth rate r.

   Therefore,

   $$1 + r = 1.995$$
   $$r = 0.995 \text{ or } 99.5\%,$$

   which would then make choice C correct.

   Distractor Explanation: Choice A is incorrect. The number of weeds on the farm, at the beginning, known as the initial value, was 1,300. **Choice B** is incorrect. This choice implies that the model is linear. However, the model is exponential. **Choice D** is incorrect because it implies that the model is linear and that 1,300 is the increase in weeds every x weeks, however, it is the initial number of weeds on the farm.

5. **Level:** Easy | **Domain:** ADVANCED MATH
   Skill/Knowledge: Equivalent expressions | **Testing point:** Binomial expressions

   Key Explanation: Choice A is correct. To solve this problem, first, use the exponent rules to combine both binomials in parentheses with one exponent. $((x - 2)(x + 2))^2$ using the identity $(a + b)(a - b) = a^2 - b^2$, $(x - 2)(x + 2)$ can be simplified to $(x^2 - 4)$ and that would simplify to

$(x^2 - 4)^2$.

Using the identity $(a - b)^2 = a^2 - 2ab + b^2$ the problem can be simplified to $(x^2 - 4)^2 = x^4 - 8x^2 + 16$, making **Choice A** the right option.

Distractor Explanation: Choice B is incorrect. This answer choice may be arrived at due to a common exponent conceptual error. **Choice C** is incorrect as this answer choice may be due to a miscalculation of $8x$ as positive. **Choice D** is incorrect due to both exponent conceptual and miscalculation errors.

6. **Level:** Easy | **Domain:** PROBLEM-SOLVING AND DATA ANALYSIS
   Skill/Knowledge: One-variable data: distributions and measures of center and spread | **Testing point:** Finding mean and median of grouped data

   Key Explanation: To calculate the median of the 27 foods, look for the middle number frequency wise of the data. If there are 27 items then the middle number is the 14th food which, based on the frequency table, has 180 calories. To find the mean number of calories, use the mean formula which can be found by taking the total number of calories divided by the number of food items. To find the total number of calories multiply each calorie content number in the table by its frequency, as follows:

   $(100 \times 6) + (180 \times 9) + (280 \times 11) + (350 \times 1) =$

   $\dfrac{5,650}{27} = 209.3$.

   Therefore the difference of the mean and median of the calorie content of the 27 foods would be $209.3 - 180 = 29.3$.

7. **Level:** Medium | **Domain:** ADVANCED MATH
Skill/Knowledge: Nonlinear functions | **Testing point:** Finding the x-intercept

Key Explanation: Choice C is correct. The x-intercept is found when $y = 0$, therefore:

$$x = 3^{0-1} + \frac{5}{3}$$

$$x = 3^{-1} + \frac{5}{3}$$

$x = \frac{1}{3} + \frac{5}{3}$, which makes $x = 2$ making **Choice C** correct.

Distractor Explanation: Choice A is incorrect. The student might incorrectly think this equation is linear and therefore the $\frac{5}{3}$ represents the y-intercept. However, this is not the case. Also, the question has asked for the x-intercept. **Choices B and D** are incorrect and would be due to a conceptual or miscalculation error.

8. **Level:** Hard | **Domain:** PROBLEM-SOLVING AND DATA ANALYSIS
Skill/Knowledge: Inferences from sample statistics and margin of error |
Testing point: Generalization of data from surveys

Key Explanation: Choice D is correct. 100% – 80% (who think statistics is the hardest subject) = 20%(who chose Physics as the hardest subject. Since only 11th graders in the math summer class were surveyed the data can only be generalized to the 11th graders in the math summer class. This then makes option D, the best option.

Distractor Explanation: Choice A is incorrect. It generalizes the survey to all students in the summer math class. **Choices B and C** are incorrect. They contradict the given information.

9. **Level:** Easy | **Domain:** ADVANCED MATH
Skill/Knowledge: Equivalent expressions |
Testing point: Manipulating quadratic equations

Key Explanation: First, expand out $(x + 3)^2$ to $(x + 3) \times (x + 3)$. Using the foiling method, multiply out the two binomial terms to get the following:
$-3(x^2 + 6x + 9) + 9 + x = ax^2 + bx + c$
Use the distributive property to expand out the left side of the equation and then combine like terms to get the following: $-3x^2 - 17x - 18 = ax^2 + bx + c$
Therefore $a = -3$, $b = -17$ and $c = -18$; $a + b + c = (-3) + (-17) + (-18) = -38$

10. **Level:** Hard | **Domain:** ADVANCED MATH
Skill/Knowledge: Nonlinear functions | **Testing point:** Vertex form of a quadratic equation

Key Explanation: Choice B is correct. The maximum point of a quadratic equation is the vertex. Therefore, $(3, 2)$ is the vertex of the parabola. The vertex form of a parabola is given by $a(x - h)^2 + k$, where (h, k) is the vertex of the parabola. This equation can be used to find the equation for a parabola. Therefore, $y = a(x - 3)^2 + 2$. The quadratic equation passes through the point $(2, 0)$. Plugging this point into the vertex form equation for x and y yields
$0 = a(2 - 3)^2 + 2$
$0 = a + 2$
$a = -2$
$y = -2(x - 3)^2 + 2$
If x is a solution to the quadratic equation, y must equal zero. Plugging in the answer choices into the

vertex form equation is the fastest method. **Choice B** is the only answer that works. $0 = -2(4 - 3)2 + 2$ and thus $0 = 0$ results.

Distractor Explanation: Choice A is incorrect. This is the value of a in the vertex form of a parabola equation. However, this option can also be a miscalculation. **Choice C** is incorrect. This is the *y–intercept* of the equation. **Choice D** is incorrect. This can be the result of a conceptual or miscalculation error.

11. **Level:** Easy | **Domain:** ALGEBRA
    Skill/Knowledge: Linear functions | **Testing point:** Finding the slope of a line given two points

    Key Explanation: Choice C is correct. To find the slope of a line, the formula $\dfrac{y_2 - y_1}{x_2 - x_1}$ is used. Plugging in the x and y coordinates of the two given points $(0, 0)$ and $(3, 5)$ into the slope equation yields $\dfrac{5-0}{3-0} = \dfrac{5}{3}$

    Distractor Explanation: Choice A is incorrect and was determined by finding the change in x over the change in y instead of the change in y over the change in x. **Choices B** and **D** are incorrect and were the result of either miscalculation or conceptual errors.

12. **Level:** Hard | **Domain:** ADVANCED MATH
    Skill/Knowledge: Nonlinear equations in one variable and systems of equations in two variables
    Testing point: System of linear and quadratic inequalities

Key Explanation: Choice D is correct. To solve this problem, graph the system.

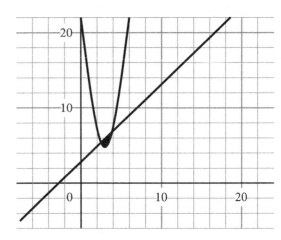

The solution for the system will be the region that is shaded. The minimum value of b can then be found by finding the vertex of the parabola $y = 2(x - 3)^2 + 5$. The vertex form of a parabola is given by $y = a(x - h)^2 + k$. Therefore, the vertex of the parabola is $(3, 5)$. The minimum y value of a concave up parabola can be found at the vertex. Therefore, the minimum value of b is 5.

Distractor Explanation: Choice A is incorrect. It is the minimum value of the system of inequalities. **Choices B** and **C** are incorrect. These answers would be the value of a and b if the vertex was incorrectly found to be $(-3, -5)$.

13. **Level:** Easy | **Domain:** GEOMETRY AND TRIGONOMETRY
    Skill/Knowledge: Area and volume | **Testing point:** Volume of a sphere

Key Explanation: The volume of a sphere is found using the formula $\dfrac{4}{3}\pi r^3 = \dfrac{4}{3}(3)^3\pi = 36\pi$

14. **Level:** Easy | **Domain:** ALGEBRA
    Skill/Knowledge: Systems of two linear equations in two variables | **Testing point:** Systems of equations with no solution

    Key Explanation: Choice A is correct. For a system of equations to have no solution, the system represents parallel lines with the same slope but different y–intercepts.
    $$3x - 4y = 8$$
    $$px + 8y = -6$$
    To easily compare the slopes, the equations should be put into the slope–intercept form of a line $y = mx + b$ where m is the slope. By mathematical manipulation, doing this yields the equations:
    $$y = \frac{3}{4}x - 2$$
    $$y = \frac{-p}{8}x - \frac{3}{4}$$

    Since parallel lines have the same slope, the equation $\frac{-p}{8} = \frac{3}{4}$ can be solved by p. Multiplying both sides of the equation by -8 yields $p = -6$, **Choice A.**

    Distractor Explanation: Choices B, C, and D are incorrect. They would make the system of equations incorrectly have 1 solution. These answer choices are determined by mathematical miscalculations or conceptual errors.

15. **Level:** Easy | **Domain:** GEOMETRY AND TRIGONOMETRY
    Skill/Knowledge: Circles | **Testing point:** Equation of a circle

    Key Explanation: Choice D is correct. To find the center of the circle, we have to write the equation of the circle in its standard form $(x - h)^2 + (y - k)^2 = r^2$. This is done by completing the square for the

x's and the y's in the equation.
$$x^2 + 6x + 9 + y^2 - 6y + 9 = 63 + 9 + 9$$
$$(x + 3)^2 + (y - 3)^2 = 81$$
This then gives the center of the circle as $(-3, 3)$.

Distractor Explanation: Choice A is incorrect. This is the negative of the center of the equation of the circle.
Choices B and **C** are incorrect. They can be determined by incorrectly picking the coefficients of x and y without writing the equation in standard form.

16. **Level:** Hard | **Domain:** ADVANCED MATH
    Skill/Knowledge: Nonlinear equations in one variable and systems of equations in two variables
    Testing point: Solving quadratic equations using the quadratic formula

    Key Explanation: This quadratic equation can be solved using the quadratic formula
    $$x = \frac{-b \pm \sqrt{b^2 - 4ac}}{2a}, \text{ where } a = 3 \text{ and } b = -6 \text{ and }$$
    $c = -11$.

    Therefore:
    $$x = \frac{-(-6) \pm \sqrt{(-6)^2 - 4(3)(-11)}}{2(3)}$$
    $$x = \frac{6 \pm \sqrt{36 + 132}}{6}$$
    $$x = \frac{6 \pm \sqrt{168}}{6}$$
    $$x = \frac{6 \pm \sqrt{42\sqrt{4}}}{6}$$
    $$x = \frac{6 \pm 2\sqrt{42}}{6}$$
    $$x = \frac{3 \pm \sqrt{42}}{3}$$
    Therefore $g = 42$.

17. **Level:** Easy | **Domain:** ALGEBRA
Skill/Knowledge: Linear inequalities in one or two variables | **Testing point:** Solving linear inequalities

Key Explanation: Choice B is correct. To solve the inequality, add x to both sides of the inequality.
$-2x + x \geq -4 - x + x$
$-x \geq -4$, Next, divide both sides of the equation by -1 which flips the inequality sign.
Only 5 is not less than 4.

Distractor Explanation: Choice A is incorrect as it is a solution to the inequality $-4 = -4$. **Choice C** is incorrect as it is also a solution to the inequality $3 \leq 4$. **Choice D** is incorrect as 2 ≤ 4 and is therefore also a solution to the above inequality.

18. **Level:** Easy | **Domain:** ADVANCED MATH
Skill/Knowledge: Nonlinear equations in one variable and systems of equations in two variables
Testing point: Solving square root equations

Key Explanation: Choice B is correct. The problem can be solved in 2 ways. The easiest and quickest way is to just substitute the answer choices and test to see which answer makes the equation true.
Substitute **Choice A**.
$\sqrt{2(2) + 5} = 2 - 5$
$\sqrt{9} = -3$,

This isn't true. Substitute **Choice B**.
$\sqrt{2(10) + 5} = 10 - 5$
$\sqrt{20 + 5} = 10 - 5$
$\sqrt{25} = 5$

This makes **Choice B** the only right option.

Distractor Explanation: Choice A is incorrect mathematically as shown above. **Choice C** is incorrect as it incorrectly states that 2 is one of the solutions. **Choice D** is incorrect. It can be due to a miscalculation error.

19. **Level:** Hard | **Domain:** ALGEBRA
Skill/Knowledge: Systems of two linear equations in two variables | **Testing point:** Solving simultaneous equations

Key Explanation: Cross multiplying $\dfrac{5}{x} = \dfrac{2}{y}$ yields

$5y = 2x$

The next step is to get the two terms on the left side of the second equation of the same common denominator of xy as follows:

$$\frac{4}{x} \times \left(\frac{y}{y}\right) - \frac{2}{y} \times \left(\frac{x}{x}\right) = \frac{4y - 2x}{xy} = -\frac{1}{5}$$

Cross multiplying the condensed second equation yields
$5(4y - 2x) = -xy = 20y - 10x = xy$
Using the first equation, $5y = 2x$, multiply each side by 4, resulting in $20y = 8x$
Substituting $8x$ for $20y$ in the second equation yields
$8x - 10x = xy$ or $-2x = xy$
Dividing both sides of the equation by x yields
$y = -2$
Substituting this value for y in the first equation yields
$5(-2) = 2x$
$-10 = 2x$
$x = -5$
Therefore, $xy = (-2)(-5) = 10$

20. **Level:** Easy | **Domain:** ADVANCED MATH
    Skill/Knowledge: Equivalent expressions |
    Testing point: Remainder theorem

    Key Explanation: Choice C is correct. A is the remainder when the function $3x^2 + 7x + 9$ is divided by $x – 2$. The remainder can be found when $f(2)$ is calculated. Because $– 2 = 0$ yields $x = 2$ as a solution, it can be plugged into the given quadratic function as follows to find A:
    $3(2)^2 + 7(2) + 9 = 12 + 14 + 9 = 35$.

    Distractor Explanation: Choice A is incorrect. This is the answer incorrectly found by adding coefficients together $(3 + 7 + 9)$ of the quadratic equation.
    Choice B is incorrect. This is the answer incorrectly found by plugging in $–2$ instead of 2 into the quadratic equation
    Choice D is incorrect, This is the answer incorrectly found through a conceptual or miscalculation error.

21. **Level:** Easy | **Domain:** PROBLEM–SOLVING AND DATA ANALYSIS
    Skill/Knowledge: Inference from sample statistics and margin of error | **Testing point:** Margin of error

    Key Explanation: Choice D is correct. Given that the sample mean mass is 67.9 *kgs*, the actual mean mass of the penguins in the zoo would lie between 67.9 *kgs* plus or minus 4.5 *kgs*, or 63.4 *kgs* and 72.*kgs*. This then makes **Choice D** correct.

    Distractor Explanation: Choice A is incorrect as the mass of the penguins in the park cannot be found from the data available.
    Choice B is incorrect as the mean mass does not state that the mass of all the penguins is 67.9 kgs.
    Choice C is incorrect. Nothing can be concluded about the median mass of the penguins in the zoo.

22. **Level:** Hard | **Domain:** ALGEBRA
    Skill/Knowledge: Linear equations in two variables | **Testing point:** Number of solutions in a linear system of two variables

    Key Explanation: Choice B is correct. The first step is to use the distributive property to multiply out the terms on the left side of the equation as follows:
    $3x – 9 + 2x + 2y = 5x + 2y – 9$
    Combining like terms on the left side of the equation yields
    $5x + 2y – 9 = 5x + 2y – 9$
    Since the equations on the left and the right are the same, they represent the same line and thus have infinitely many solutions.

    Distractor Explanation: Choice A is incorrect. To have zero solutions the equations would need to be parallel lines and thus have the same slope and different y-intercepts. That would mean that the coefficients of x and y will be equal however the constants will not. This is not the case in this problem. **Choice C** is incorrect. That would mean there would be one (x, y) solution to the system above. That is not the case as they represent the same line. **Choice D** is incorrect. Linear equations with two variables do not have 2 solutions.

1. **Level:** Medium | **Domain:** ADVANCED MATH
   Skill/Knowledge: Equivalent expressions | **Testing point:** Foiling out binomials and combining like terms

   Key Explanation: Choice D is correct. To solve the question, first, distribute out the two binomial expressions. The next step is to combine like terms and put the final expression in standard form.
   $3(x^2 + 10x + 25) -2(x^2 - 10x +25) + 2x$
   $3x^2 + 30x + 75 -2x^2 + 20x - 50 +2x$
   $x^2 + 52x + 25$

   Distractor Explanation: Choices A and C are incorrect. These answers can be arrived at if the foiling expansion is done incorrectly. **Choice B** is incorrect. This answer can be arrived at if a math miscalculation is done after the foiling out expansion is completed.

2. **Level:** Medium | **Domain:** ADVANCED MATH
   Skill/Knowledge: Equivalent expressions |
   Testing point: Finding the least common denominator with binomial terms and combining

   Key Explanation: Choice A is correct. To solve this problem, the fractions need a common denominator to be added. The least common denominator is $(x - 2) (5 - x)$, which multiplies out to a denominator of $-x^2 + 7x - 10$. To get both terms of this expression over the same denominator, the numerator and denominator of the first term each must be multiplied by $(5 - x)$ and the numerator and denominator of the second term each must be multiplied by $(x - 2)$. Since the two terms are now over the same denominator, the numerators can be added as follows:
   $$\frac{5-x+2x(x-2)}{(x-2)(5-x)},$$

Using the foiling and distributive operations to multiply out and combine like terms, the final answer is: $\dfrac{2x^2 - 5x + 5}{-x^2 + 7x - 10}$.

   Distractor Explanation: Choices B and C are incorrect. These answers can be arrived at wrongly by adding the two fractions directly, which is a common conceptual error. **Choice D is incorrect.** This answer may be arrived at by finding the common multiple for the denominator and then just adding the original numerators directly without multiplying them by the binomials needed to get the common multiple for the denominator.

3. **Level:** Easy | **Domain:** ALGEBRA
   Skill/Knowledge: Systems of two linear equations in two variables | **Testing point:** Solving simultaneous equations

   Key Explanation: Solve for y by using the distributing property and the substitution method as follows:
   $3x - 6 + 5(-2(x - 5)) = 2$
   $3x - 6 - 10(x - 5) = 2$
   $3x - 6 - 10x + 50 = 2$
   $-7x + 44 = 2$
   $-7x = -42$
   $x = 6$
   Substitute $x = 6$ into the second equation to find y.
   $y = -2(6 - 5)$
   $y = -2$

4. **Level:** Easy | **Domain:** PROBLEM–SOLVING AND DATA ANALYSIS
   Skill/Knowledge: Two–variable data: models and scatterplots | **Testing point:** Line of best fit

   Key Explanation: Choice A is correct. This question can be solved in several ways. The equation of the line of best fit can be determined by finding the slope and *y–intercept* from the graph directly and plugging those values into the *slope–intercept* equation of a line, $y = mx + b$. The elimination method can also be used. The slope and *y–intercept* of the line of best fit are both positive, which eliminates **Choices C** and **D**. The slope of the line of best fit is not steep so that eliminates **Choice B**.

Distractor Explanation: Choice B is incorrect because the slope of the line of best fit is $\frac{1}{4}$ and not 4. **Choice C** is incorrect because the *y–intercept* of the line of best fit is positive, not negative. **Choice D** is incorrect because the line of best fit has a positive slope and not a negative one.

5.   **Level:** Medium | **Domain:** GEOMETRY AND TRIGONOMETRY
Skill/Knowledge: Circles | **Testing point:** Arc length of a circle

Key Explanation: Choice C is correct. The arc length of the circle can be found by using the equation arc length = $r\theta$, where r is the radius of the circle and theta is the degree in radians of the central angle that subtends the arc length desired.

Therefore the arc length would be $6\left(\frac{7}{12}\pi\right) = \frac{7}{2}\pi$. The arc length can also be found by converting radians to degrees using the formula $\frac{\theta}{360}2\pi r$. This would still give the answer as $\frac{7}{2}\pi$ cm.

Distractor Explanation: Choice A is incorrect. This is the circumference of the whole circle. **Choice B** is incorrect. This is the area of the whole

circle. **Choice D** is incorrect. This is the area of the sector that can be found using the formula $\frac{1}{2}r^2\theta$, where θ is the measure of the central degree in radians.

6.   **Level:** Easy | **Domain:** ADVANCED MATH
Skill/Knowledge: Nonlinear equations in one variable and systems of equations in two variables
Testing point: Finding the sum of the roots in a quadratic equation

Key Explanation: Choice A is correct. The first step is to simplify the equation by dividing out 2, the greatest common factor out of the equation, leaving $x^2 + 3x + 2 = 0$. The equation is in simplified form. The sum of the roots of a quadratic equation is equal to $\frac{-b}{a}$, where $a = 1$, $b = 3$.
Therefore, the sum of the roots of the quadratic equation above would be $\frac{-3}{1} = -3$.

Distractor Explanation: Choice B is incorrect and is the negative of the product of the roots and can be arrived at by using $\frac{-c}{a}$. **Choice C** is incorrect. This is the product of the roots given by $\frac{c}{a}$. **Choice D** is incorrect and is the negative value of the sum of roots i.e $\frac{b}{a}$.

7.   **Level:** Medium | **Domain:** GEOMETRY AND TRIGONOMETRY
Skill/Knowledge: Lines, angles, and triangles
Testing point: Finding the sum of angles in a polygon and converting degrees to radians

Key Explanation: The sum of the interior angles in a polygon is $180 \times (n-2)$, where n is the number of sides in the polygon. A heptagon has 7 sides, so the sum of its interior angles will be $180 \times (7-2) = 900°$.

A hexagon has 6 sides, so the sum of its interior angles will be $180 \times (6-2) = 720°$. The difference between the total number of degrees of the interior angles of the two shapes is $180°$. This number in radians would be π and $a = 1$.

8. **Level:** Medium | **Domain:** ALGEBRA
    Skill/Knowledge: Linear functions | **Testing point:** Finding equations of functions

    Key Explanation: Choice A is correct. The problem gives two points and asks what the function $f(x)$ is that best describes the points. Using points $(3, 2)$ and $(6, -3)$, the slope of the function, which is the change in the y coordinates over the change in the x coordinates, $\dfrac{(y_2 - y_1)}{(x_2 - x_1)}$, can be found as follows:

    $$\frac{2 - (-3)}{3 - 6} = \frac{5}{-3}$$

    The answer choices are in slope–intercept form, $y = mx + b$ where m represents the slope. The only answer choice that has a slope of $\dfrac{-5}{3}$ is **Choice A**.

    Distractor Explanation: Choice B is incorrect most likely due to a conceptual error. **Choice C** is incorrect and incorrectly states the slope formula as the change in x over the change in y. **Choice D** is incorrect as this is the equation of the line that is perpendicular to $f(x)$.

9. **Level:** Easy | **Domain:** ALGEBRA
    Skill/Knowledge: Linear equations in one variable
    Testing point: Solving for x

Key Explanation: Choice D is correct. To solve this problem, first divide both sides of the equation by 2 to get:

$$(x + 4) = \frac{18}{2}$$
$$(x + 4) = 9$$
$$x = 5$$

Therefore $(x + 6) = 5 + 6 = 11$

Distractor Explanation: Choice A is incorrect. This is the value of $(x + 4)$. **Choice B** is incorrect. This is the value of x only. **Choice C** is incorrect. It can be the result of a miscalculation.

10. **Level:** Medium | **Domain:** PROBLEM–SOLVING AND DATA ANALYSIS
    Skill/Knowledge: Ratios, rates, proportional relationships, and units | **Testing point:** Ratios

    Key Explanation: To solve this problem, let x equal the total number of people at the fair. Every group of 5 students and 3.5 parents has a total of 8.5 total people in it. Set up a proportion of ratio students to ratio total people and set it equal to the ratio of the total number of students to the total number of people as follows:

    $$\frac{5}{8.5} = \frac{2,000}{x}$$

    Cross multiplying gives the equation $5x = 2,000 \times 8.5$. Dividing both sides of the equation by 5 gives $x = 3,400$ students.

11. **Level:** Medium | **Domain:** PROBLEM–SOLVING AND DATA ANALYSIS
    Skill/Knowledge: Percentages | **Testing point:** Percent decrease

    Key Explanation: Choice D is correct. The percent decrease can be found by using the formula:

$$\frac{\text{difference between actual and predicted values}}{\text{original value}} \times 100.$$

Looking at the graph, the actual y values when $x = 4$ are 6 and 11. The predicted y value at $x = 4$ is 9. Since the question asked for the percent decrease from the actual value to the predicted value, the actual value needs to be higher and thus we would use the y value of 11 and not 6 at $x = 4$. Plugging in the y values of 11 and 9 into the equation yields $\frac{11-9}{11} \times 100 = 18.18\%$

Distractor Explanation: Choice A is incorrect as this answer is the percent increase from 9 to 11.
Choice B is incorrect as this answer is the percent decrease from 9 to 6.
Choice C is incorrect as this describes the percent increase from 6 to 9.

12. **Level:** Easy | **Domain:** ALGEBRA
Skill/Knowledge: Linear inequalities in one or two variables | **Testing point:** Systems of linear inequalities

Key Explanation: Choice B is correct. To solve the question, the fastest method would be to substitute the x and y coordinates of the answer choices into the system of inequalities and see which coordinate pair satisfies both inequalities. Plugging in the x and y values for **Choice B** makes both inequalities valid as follows:

Inequality 1: $4 > -3(1) + 5$
                 $4 > -3 + 5$
                 $4 > 2$
Inequality 2: $4 > 2(1)$
                 $4 > 2$

Distractor Explanation: Choice A is incorrect. Plugging in this coordinate pair into the second inequality yields $4 > 4$, which is false. **Choice C** is incorrect. Plugging this coordinate pair into the second inequality yields $4 > 2(3) = 4 > 6$, which

is false. **Choice D** is incorrect. Plugging this coordinate pair into the second inequality yields $1 > 2(2) = 1 > 4$, which is false.

13. **Level:** Medium | **Domain:** ADVANCED MATH
Skill/Knowledge: Nonlinear equations in one variable and systems of equations in two variables
Testing point: Finding solutions for an absolute value equation

Key Explanation: To solve this absolute value equation, first divide both sides of the equation by 3 to get: $|x - 4| = 2$. Then remove the absolute value and set up and solve the following 2 equations:
$x - 4 = 2$ and $x - 4 = -2$
$x = 6$ and $x = 2$

14. **Level:** Easy | **Domain:** GEOMETRY AND TRIGONOMETRY
Skill/Knowledge: Area and volume | **Testing point:** Area of a trapezoid

Key Explanation: Choice A is correct. Since segment AD is parallel to segment BC and AB = DC the shape is an isosceles trapezoid. To find the area of a trapezoid the formula $\frac{h}{2}(a+b)$, is used where h is the height of the trapezoid and a and b are the lengths of the two bases of the trapezoid.
The height of the trapezoid can be found by using the Pythagorean theorem $a^2 + b^2 = c^2$, where a and b are the legs of the right triangle and c is its hypotenuse.

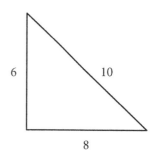

Using the pythagorean theorem $a^2 + 8^2 = 10^2$ or $a^2 = 36$, yielding $a = 6$. Thus the height of the trapezoid is 6. Plugging in the values for a, b, and h into the area of a trapezoid formula, yields

$$\frac{6}{2}(12 + 28) = 120$$

Therefore the area of the trapezoid would be 120.

Distractor Explanation: Choice B is incorrect. This answer is the perimeter of the trapezoid. **Choice C** is incorrect. This answer can be determined if the shape is divided into a rectangle and two triangles. This answer is the area of the rectangle plus one triangle. **Choice D** is incorrect. It is the value of the area of the two triangles alone.

15. **Level:** Easy | **Domain:** ADVANCED MATH
Skill/Knowledge: Nonlinear equations in one variable and systems of equations in two variables
Testing point: Absolute values

Key Explanation: Choice C is correct. The first step is to combine the two absolute value terms into $|x + 3| = -2$. The next step is to divide both sides by -1 to get: $|x + 3| = 2$, The absolute value is equal to a positive number and therefore it has 2 solutions.

Distractor Explanation: Choice A is incorrect. To have 0 solutions in an absolute value equation, the absolute equation value has to be equal to a negative number. **Choice B** is incorrect. For an absolute value equation to have 1 solution it has to be equal to 0. **Choice D** is incorrect. There is sufficient information to answer the question.

16. **Level:** Medium | **Domain:** ALGEBRA
Skill/Knowledge: Linear equations in two variables | **Testing point:** Perpendicular lines

Key Explanation: The slope is found by putting the equation of the line into slope–intercept form of $y = mx + b$ as follows:

$5x - 6y + 30 = 0$

$-6y = -5x - 30$

$y = \frac{5}{6}x + 5$. The slope is then $\frac{5}{6}$, a line perpendicular to this will have the negative inverse of this slope which is $\frac{-6}{5}$.

17. **Level:** Easy | **Domain:** GEOMETRY AND TRIGONOMETRY
Skill/Knowledge: Right triangles and trigonometry
Testing point: Trigonometric identities

Key Explanation: Choice C is correct.
$\sin x = \cos (90° - x)$ and vice versa, therefore $\cos 72° = \sin (90° - 72°)$ This equates to $\sin 18°$.

Distractor Explanation: Choice A is incorrect. This choice may be selected due to a conceptual error. **Choice B** is incorrect as $\sin 72°$ is equal to $\cos 18°$. **Choice D** is incorrect. $\cos 18°$ is equal to $\sin 72°$.

18. **Level:** Easy | **Domain:** PROBLEM–SOLVING AND DATA ANALYSIS
Skill/Knowledge: Probability and conditional probability | **Testing point:** Probability Complement

Key Explanation: Choice B is correct. The sum of the probabilities of an event and its complement must add up to 1. Therefore, if the probability that it will rain is 0.26, the probability of no rain is $1 - 0.26 = 0.74$.

Distractor Explanation: Choices A and **C** are incorrect and can be due to a miscalculation or conceptual error. **Choice D** is incorrect as a probability of 1 means that it is certain that it will not rain.

19. **Level:** Easy | **Domain:** ADVANCED MATH
Skill/Knowledge: Nonlinear functions | **Testing point:** Vertex form of a quadratic and minimum/maximum point

Key Explanation: The maximum t value of a concave down parabola for the quadratic equation $ax^2 + bx + c$ can be found using the formula $t = \dfrac{-b}{2a}$, which finds the x coordinate of the vertex of the parabola. In the equation above, a is 3 and $b = 9$ yielding,

$$t = \left(\dfrac{-9}{2(-3)}\right) = \dfrac{-9}{-6} = \dfrac{3}{2}$$

20. **Level:** Hard | **Domain:** GEOMETRY AND TRIGONOMETRY
Skill/Knowledge: Right triangles and trigonometry | **Testing point:** Special triangles

Key Explanation: The triangle PQR is a special triangle. **Choice D** is correct. Triangle PQR is inscribed in a semicircle where the hypotenuse of triangle PQR is the diameter of the circle. This makes angle P a right angle. A triangle has 180 degrees and that would make angle R equal to 30 degrees. Therefore triangle PQR is a special triangle, more specifically a 30 – 60 – 90 special triangle. Since the radius of the circle is $7cm$, this makes the diameter $14cm$. The hypotenuse of triangle PQR is the diameter of the circle. In a 30 – 60 – 90 special triangle, the length of the side opposite the right angle, the hypotenuse, is two times the length of the side opposite the 30–degree angle. This makes side $PQ = 7cm$. The side opposite the 60–degree angle in this special triangle is the length of the side opposite the 30–degree angle times $\sqrt{3}$. Therefore the length of PR is equal to $7\sqrt{3}$.

Distractor Explanation: Choice A is incorrect. This is the diameter of the circle and the value of the length of RQ.
Choice B is incorrect as it is the length of PR.
Choice C is incorrect. This answer is due to a conceptual error confusing the ratios in sides of the 30 – 60 – 90 triangle with the 45 – 45 – 90 special triangle.

21. **Level:** Medium | **Domain:** ALGEBRA
Skill/Knowledge: Linear inequalities in one or two variables | **Testing point:** Absolute value linear inequalities

Key Explanation: Choice B is correct. For the above inequality either $x + 3 > 4$ or $x + 3 < -4$. Solving $x + 3 > 4$ yields $x > 1$. Solving $x + 3 < -4$ yields $x < -7$. **Choice B** is the correct choice as it has the only value in the domain of the range of solutions to the inequality.

Distractor Explanation: Choices A, **C**, and **D** are incorrect as they are not part of the range of solutions to the inequality.

22. **Level:** Easy | **Domain:** ALGEBRA
Skill/Knowledge: Systems of two linear equations in two variables | **Testing point:** Systems of equations

Key Explanation: Choice A is correct. To solve this problem, subtract the two equations.
$3x + 4y = 31 - (2x + 3y = 22)$
$= x + y = 9$, which is **Choice A**.

Distractor Explanation: Choice B is incorrect. This answer is the value of x. **Choice C** is incorrect. This answer is the value of y. **Choice D** is incorrect. It is due to conceptual or miscalculation errors.

This page is intentionally left blank

Chapter 5

....

Practice Test 4

You are about to begin a full-length Practice Test. The test has four modules. The time allotted for each module is marked at the beginning of the module. Work on one module at a time. Use a timer to keep track of the time limits for every module.

Try to take the Practice Test under real test conditions. Find a quiet place to work, and set aside enough time to complete the test without being disturbed. At the end of the test, check your answers by referring to the Answer Key and fill in your raw score in the scorecard below. Also, note down the time taken by you for completing each module.

Pay particular attention to the questions that were answered incorrectly. Read the answer explanations and understand how to solve them.

....

My Score Card (Raw Score)

	Reading and Writing		Math	
	Module 1	Module 2	Module 1	Module 2
Out of	27	27	22	22
My Score	_____	_____	_____	_____
Time Taken	_____	_____	_____	_____

TEST BEGINS ON THE NEXT PAGE

Reading and Writing Test

27 QUESTIONS | 32 MINUTES

1

R.K. Narayan was a pioneer in Indian literature that was written in English. His stories often revolve around common people in the fictional town of Malgudi. His unassuming insights and gently humorous treatment of everyday life and interactions are _____ accessible to the average reader and give his writing a timeless appeal.

Which choice completes the text with the most logical and precise word or phrase?

A) readily

B) anxiously

C) contentedly

D) wryly

2

The following text is adapted from Mother Jones's August 15, 1912 speech to coal miners picketing in Charlestown, West Virginia.

The Governor will get until tomorrow night to get rid of his bloodhounds. We are not going to leave a slave class to the coming generation, and I want to say to you that the next generation will not charge us for what we've done; they will condemn us for what we have left undone.

As used in the text, what does the word "charge" most nearly mean?

A) accuse

B) demand

C) impose

D) assault

3

The number of people in the US with myopia, or nearsightedness, has increased over 16 percent since 1971. However, the problem is much more _____ in Southeast Asia, where an estimated 80 to 90 percent of students with twelve years of schooling have the condition.

Which choice completes the text with the most logical and precise word or phrase?

A) pronounced

B) advocated

C) prescribed

D) articulated

4

The following text is adapted from F. Scott Fitzgerald's 1922 novel, *The Beautiful and the Damned*.

Anthony's recollections of the gallant Ulysses were vivid. After Henrietta Lebrune Patch had "joined another choir," as her widower huskily remarked from time to time, father and son lived up at grampa's in Tarrytown, and Ulysses came daily to Anthony's nursery and expelled pleasant, thick–smelling words for sometimes as much as an hour. He was continually promising Anthony hunting trips and fishing trips and excursions to Atlantic City, "oh, some time soon now;" but none of them ever materialized. One trip they did take; when Anthony was eleven they went abroad, to England and Switzerland, and there in the best hotel in Lucerne his father died with much sweating and grunting and crying aloud for air. In a panic of despair and terror, Anthony was brought back to America, wedded to a vague melancholy that was to stay beside him through the rest of his life.

What is the main purpose of including the information about Adam Ulysses Patch continually promising trips to Anthony?

A) To foreshadow the trip in which Adam Ulysses passes away

B) To indicate the superficial nature of Anthony's father

C) To emphasize the deep interest that Adam Ulysses has for his son

D) To give an indication of Adam Ulysses' vast wealth

CONTINUE ➤

5

The Jiroft culture is a hypothetical society that lived in the third millennium BC in Iran. The first indication of the culture was found in 2001 when scientists evaluated confiscated artefacts, but many were skeptical of the find because it did not have an archaeological context and may contain forgeries. However, the site of Konar Sandal in Iran is now being excavated, and archaeologists have discovered two mounds, a citadel, and tablets with an unknown script that might prove a vital link to understanding whether the Jiroft culture actually existed.

What is the main purpose of the text?

A) It casts doubt on the existence of an ancient culture.

B) It reveals flaws in the theory that an ancient culture existed.

C) It outlines the current understanding of an ancient culture.

D) It presents incompatible findings regarding an ancient culture.

6

The following text is from Virginia Woolfe's 1922 novel, Jacob's Room.

The house was flat, dark, and silent. Jacob was at home engaged upon a chess problem, the board being on a stool between his knees. One hand was fingering the hair at the back of his head. He slowly brought it forward and raised the white queen from her square; then put her down again on the same spot. He filled his pipe; ruminated; moved two pawns; advanced the white knight; then ruminated with one finger upon the bishop. Now Fanny Elmer passed beneath the window.

Which choice best states the main purpose of the text?

A) It hints that Jacob was more intent on the window than on chess.

B) It emphasizes Jacob's desire to improve his chess skills.

C) It shows the intensity with which Jacob concentrated on chess.

D) It establishes that Jacob and Fanny had a quarrel.

Text 1

It is stated that Abraham Lincoln "had an almost morbid dislike to an escort, or guard, and daily exposed himself to the deadly aim of an assassin." ... On more than one occasion he the President had gone through the streets of Washington at a late hour of the night, without escort, or even the company of a servant, walking all the way, going and returning.

Text 2

Bancroft's eulogy on Lincoln never pleased the latter's lifelong friends ... February 16, 1866, David Davis, who had heard it, wrote me: "His analysis of Mr. Lincoln's character is superficial." On the 22nd he again wrote: "Mr. Bancroft totally misconceived Mr. Lincoln's character in applying 'unsteadiness' and confusion to it. Mr. Lincoln grew more steady and resolute, and his ideas were never confused. I thought him always master of his subject. He was a much more self-possessed man than I thought.

Based on the texts, how would the author of Text 2 most likely respond to Lincoln's behaviour as illustrated in Text 1?

A) By conceding the importance of protection but asserting the greater significance of Lincoln's belief that "assassination is always possible"

B) By concurring that Lincoln rarely deviated from his personal convictions and exhibited stability and equanimity.

C) By acknowledging that Lincoln had a morbid dislike of any form of security.

D) By challenging the supposition that Lincoln consistently "exposed himself to the deadly aim of an assassin."

8

Chili *(Capsicum spp.)* is a spice, a fruit widely grown around the world that is recognized for its nutraceutical (nutritional and medicinal) properties and economic value. In Benin, chili is the second cash gardening crop after the tomato. Its annual production is about 47.162 tons. Pepper plants produce the compound capsaicin, possibly to deter mammalian herbivores. In Benin, chili pepper is grown only for food partially in the cultivable lands of the coastal areas, where soil salinity and water irrigation can negatively affect the quantity and quality of the crop, and may also have a strong influence on the concentration of bioactive compounds of vegetables.

According to the text, what is the reason that the chili plant evolved to contain capsaicin in the fruit?

A) It adds flavor to human food dishes.

B) It is a part of herbal medicine remedies.

C) It increases the plant's absorption of nutrients.

D) It protects the plant from predation.

9

The following text is adapted from Herman Melville's 1851 novel, *Moby Dick; or The Whale.*

Now, when I say that I am in the habit of going to sea, I do not mean that I ever go to sea as a passenger. For to go as a passenger you must needs have a purse, and a purse is but a rag unless you have something in it. Besides, passengers get sea-sick—grow quarrelsome—don't sleep——no, I never go as a passenger; nor, though I am something of a salt, do I ever go to sea as a Commodore, or a Captain, or a Cook. I abandon the glory and distinction of such offices to those who like them. I always go to sea as a sailor, because they make a point of paying me for my trouble, whereas they never pay passengers a single penny that I ever heard of.

Based on the text, why does Ishmael avoid traveling aboard ship as a passenger?

A) He does not want excessive responsibilities.

B) He desires reimbursement for his efforts.

C) He sometimes enters periods of deep depression.

D) He hungers for recognition for his efforts.

CONTINUE

10

The following text is adapted from F. Scott Fitzgerald's novel, *The Beautiful and the Damned*.

Early in his career, Adam Patch had married an anemic lady of thirty, Alicia Withers, who brought him one hundred thousand dollars and an impeccable entré into the banking circles of New York. Immediately and rather spunkily, she had borne him a son and, as if completely devitalized by the magnificence of this performance, she had thenceforth effaced herself within the shadowy dimensions of the nursery. The boy, Adam Ulysses Patch, became an inveterate joiner of clubs, connoisseur of good form, and driver of tandems—at the astonishing age of twenty–six he began his memoirs under the title "New York Society as I Have Seen It." On the rumor of its conception, this work was eagerly bid for among publishers, but as it proved after his death to be immoderately verbose and overpoweringly dull, it never obtained even a private printing.

Based on the text, which choice best characterizes Adam J. Patch's wife?

A) powerful

B) captivating

C) diffident

D) animated

11

According to scientist James Clark, explaining the coexistence of species is critical to truly understand forest biodiversity and the forces that sustain or reduce it. According to Clark, "A 'neutral model' hypothesizes that species are so similar it just takes a long time for winners and losers to be sorted out by competition, but eventually the better competitor would drive the other to extinction." The neutral model predicts that the variation among the sites increases over time, as random chance caused different species to go extinct in some areas but not others. Some sites, just by chance, should come to be dominated by one species, while others would come to be dominated by another species. However, the researchers found that variance among the sites did not increase over the millennia, leading them to conclude that stabilizing forces were maintaining forest diversity.

Which hypothetical data, if true, would most weaken Clark's claim that stabilizing forces control biodiversity in a given region?

A) Scientists determine that there is now significantly greater variation between species in three nearby sites than there was 7,000 years ago.

B) A complex study determines that the reason that plant diversity did not greatly alter in one region was because of a local herbivore.

C) Archaeological evidence shows that early humans ate the nuts from a tree that has subsequently gone extinct in a given area.

D) Several researchers conducted a study that determined that one species of tree is extremely susceptible to temperature changes.

12

Nutrients Found Primarily in Animal Tissues

Nutrient	Function	Natural source	Alternate Source
B12	Used by nervous and circulatory systems	Fish, meat, dairy, eggs	Enriched grain products; some nutritional yeast
Creatine	Increases muscle performance	Animal tissue	Supplements; the body naturally makes small amounts
DHA	Mental health and brain development, especially in children	Fatty fish, fish oil	Microalgae
Taurine	Muscle function, bile production	Fish, meat, poultry, dairy products	Synthetic supplements

The vegan diet is one that is chosen by individuals for various reasons, including health and/or ethical reasons. In fact, it is evident that the vegan diet is much more than a diet itself, but has developed into a lifestyle, often associated with animal rights and environmental advocacy as well as a greater concern for physical activity and mindfulness. While many health benefits exist, it is essential for those who are vegan or are planning to become vegan to be educated about potential nutritional deficiencies to prevent adverse outcomes. For example, a vegan who is adverse to taking man–made supplements in any form _____

Which choice most effectively uses data from the table to complete the claim?

A) is likely to suffer from mental health disorders

B) may suffer from insufficient levels of bile

C) may be prone to various heart diseases

D) could succumb to circulatory system disorders

13

West Texas Intermediate is a grade or mix of crude oil. It is also the benchmark for trading U.S. crude oil, which is one of the most heavily traded items in international commodities markets. The term, "West Texas Intermediate," is, therefore, often used to refer to the futures market on the New York Mercantile Exchange. The prices fluctuate wildly with the supply and demand, and higher numbers indicate more trading. While the index for trading was at around 90 at the end of October, 2022, it actually fell around the median values for the year. March 2022 had the highest index of around 120, and the lowest index was, curiously, at the end of September.

Based on the text, what is most likely true about the West Texas Intermediate?

A) The amount of trading increased throughout 2022.

B) At the end of September, 2022, the index was probably around 60.

C) The index increased in March 2022 because of changes at the New York Mercantile Exchange.

D) The index dropped below 20 many times due to low demand for crude oil.

14

Most students have heard of the charismatic 18th president, Ulysses S. Grant. However, the name of his vice president, Schuyler Colfax, has mostly been relegated to history. In reality, he played an important role in passing the 13th Amendment, which abolished slavery. Not only did he actively promote his Abolitionist views, but he also voted in favor of the amendment when it came before the House of Representatives. His decision to vote was notable since the Speaker of the House typically remains silent except in the case of a tie.

The passage implies that Colfax's vote for the 13th Amendment

A) occurred because there was a tie in the House of Representatives.

B) was not considered valid because the Speaker of the House could not vote

C) greatly emphasized Colfax's commitment to the amendment

D) went against the opinions held by President U.S. Grant

15

Rabbits and hares look similar and many people use the names interchangeably, but in reality, there are many biological and behavioral differences. For example, the eyes of baby rabbits take about ten days _____ baby hares to be able to focus and process visual information.

Which choice completes the text so that it conforms to the conventions of Standard English?

A) longer than

B) longer as eyes of

C) longer than those of

D) as long as

16

When the Erie Canal was opened in 1825, it was 40 feet wide and 4 feet deep. Over half the original canal was taken out of use with the 1918 opening of a 120 feet wide and 12 feet deep section that _____ about ten years earlier to accommodate the larger barges of the modern era.

Which choice completes the text so that it conforms to the conventions of Standard English?

A) had been designed

B) had designed

C) designed

D) is designed

17

Unusual additions to a freshwater aquarium include pom-pom crabs, aptly named for the hair-like tufts on their pincers which make the crabs appear to be holding small pom-poms. Growing to about one inch long, _____ but they can be eaten by even small predatory fish.

Which choice completes the text so that it conforms to the conventions of Standard English?

A) a large tank is not required for these crabs,

B) it is not a large tank needed for the crabs,

C) these crabs do not require a large tank,

D) the requirements for these crabs do not include a large tank,

18

Pottery and ceramics are interchangeable words. They both refer to objects which are made from clay that is heated to make it harder. Earthenware is pottery that is baked at a low temperature. The result is porous and brittle. Earthenware is often glazed to enhance _____ durability and capacity to hold water.

Which choice completes the text so that it conforms to the conventions of Standard English?

A) its

B) it's

C) their

D) they're

19

The largest known fish species, the whale shark, is actually a slow–moving filter feeder that primarily subsists on plankton. Therefore, despite its _____ is not a threat to humans.

Which choice completes the text so that it conforms to the conventions of Standard English?

A) size. It

B) size it

C) size—it

D) size, it

20

Judy Blume is the author of many beloved children's _____ *Tales of a Fourth Grade Nothing*. Her frank discussions of childhood anxieties and family issues have made her a target of censors, so along with her writing, she has spent considerable time fighting to protect the freedom of speech.

Which choice completes the text so that it conforms to the conventions of Standard English?

A) stories such as:

B) stories, such as

C) stories, such as,

D) stories. Such as

21

When Austrian painter Gustav Klimt completed *The* _____ it was initially reviled as excessive due to its gold leaf, silver, and platinum. However, it is now considered one of the finest examples of the Art Nouveau style.

Which choice completes the text so that it conforms to the conventions of Standard English?

A) *Kiss (Der Kuss* in German)

B) *Kiss, (Der Kuss* in German)

C) *Kiss (Der Kuss* in German),

D) *Kiss, (Der Kuss* in German),

22

American author and inspirational _____ has shared his optimistic outlook with audiences around the world. His unusual approach to leadership is founded in cultural anthropology rather than business.

Which choice completes the text so that it conforms to the conventions of Standard English?

A) speaker Simon Sinek

B) speaker—Simon Sinek—

C) speaker, Simon Sinek

D) speaker Simon Sinek,

23

_____ slavery was abolished and Black American men were granted the right to vote in the 1860s, rights were slowly taken away so that conditions were inferior for people of color. It took almost 100 years for new federal laws to be passed that prevented discrimination based on race.

Which choice completes the text with the most logical transition?

A) Although

B) Since

C) Hence

D) Because

24

Water is by far the most common drink in the world. The next most popular is coffee, but that beverage is consumed in a variety of different ways. _____, it may be served hot, cold, or with additions such as milk or spices.

Which choice completes the text with the most logical transition?

A) Regardless,

B) Nevertheless,

C) Indeed,

D) Additionally,

25

Edgar Allen Poe's *Murders in the Rue Morgue* is a detective story written in 1841. At the time it was written, it was praised as being exceptionally clever and considered quite a novelty. _____ it is considered the beginning of the detective fiction genre.

Which choice completes the text with the most logical transition?

A) Meanwhile,

B) Nevertheless,

C) Instead,

D) Today,

While researching a topic, a student has taken the following notes:

- Geothermal energy is derived by tapping the heat within the Earth, which does not require fuel and does not vary based on atmospheric conditions.

- The energy does not generate carbon dioxide, greenhouse gasses, or particulate matter that contributes to climate change.

- Geothermal power plants have an 80- to 100-year lifespan and require very little maintenance.

- Not all locations are suitable for geothermal power generation because it would be too labor-intensive to reach underground pockets of sufficient heat.

- Although geothermal plants are often associated with a foul smell, modern filtration systems can reduce that effect.

The student wants to address a common concern for an audience familiar with geothermal energy. Which choice most effectively uses relevant information from the notes to accomplish this goal?

A) Though not all areas are suitable for geothermal plants, it is possible to select ones that are less labor-intensive for erecting facilities.

B) Geothermal energy is good because it comes from the heat from within the earth rather than fuel.

C) Geothermal power plants have longer life spans than other power sources because they can operate up to 100 years.

D) If the proper filtration systems are in place, then geothermal plants will not emit odor-causing gasses or particles that lead to climate change.

27

While researching a topic, a student has taken the following notes:

- The first dynasty of Egypt was the first period after Lower and Upper Egypt were unified into one country by the first ruler.

- The seat of the first dynasty was Thinis.

- The exact dates are unknown, but were centered in the Bronze Age, most likely from 3100 B.C. to 2900 B.C.

- Tombs of the period were mostly made from wood, mud, and bricks; stones were typically used only for decoration, though some tombs were stone.

- The first ruler was Narmer and the last ruler was Qa'a.

The student wants to introduce the first ruler of Egypt to someone unfamiliar with Egyptian dynasties. Which choice most effectively uses relevant information from the notes to accomplish this goal?

A) The rulers in the first dynasty of Egypt reigned from about 3100 B.C. to 2900 B.C., starting with Narmer and ending with Qa'a.

B) Narmer unified Lower and Upper Egypt into one country in around 3100 B.C. and became the first ruler of its first dynasty.

C) Narmer was the first ruler in Egypt during the Bronze Age and his tomb was made of wood, mud, and bricks.

D) The first dynasty of Egypt ruled from Thinis after Narmer joined Upper and Lower Egypt.

No Test Material On This Page

Reading and Writing Test

27 QUESTIONS | 32 MINUTES

1

The following text is adapted from Fyodor Dostoevsky's 1848 novel, *White Nights and Other Stories*.

Suddenly, the inebriated gentleman set off and flew full speed in pursuit of my unknown lady. She was racing like the wind, but the staggering gentleman was overtaking—overtook her. In a flash I was on the other side of the street; in a flash the <u>obtrusive</u> gentleman had taken the position, had fallen back without a word.

As used in the text, what does the word "obtrusive" most nearly mean?

A) obvious

B) conspicuous

C) deplorable

D) inevitable

2

Ocean energy, as all other renewable sources of energy, can contribute to a more sustainable energy supply, but it is not environmentally friendly per se. The activities involved in manufacturing, operation, maintenance, and decommissioning of ocean energy devices will have various effects on the environment. Governments and society need a _____ understanding of the environmental implications of ocean energy systems before ocean energy systems are built, and also to reduce or adjust impacts to acceptable levels.

Which choice completes the text with the most logical and precise word or phrase?

A) vigorous

B) sturdy

C) robust

D) tough

3

The following text is from Charles Dickens's novel Oliver Twist, published serially between 1837 and 1839.

> The donkey was in a state of profound <u>abstraction:</u> wondering, probably, whether he was destined to be regaled with a cabbage-stalk or two when he had disposed of the two sacks of soot with which the little cart was laden; so, without noticing the word of command, he jogged onward.

As used in the text, what does the word "abstraction" most nearly mean?

A) generalization

B) hypothesis

C) intention

D) preoccupation

4

The following text is adapted from Emily Dickenson's *Poems*, published after her death in 1886.

> If I can stop one heart from breaking,
>
> I shall not live in vain;
>
> If I can ease one life the aching,
>
> Or cool one pain,
>
> Or help one fainting robin
>
> Unto his nest again,
>
> I shall not live in vain.

What is the main purpose of repeating the line "I shall not live in vain"?

A) It stresses how strongly the author feels about the subject.

B) It indicates that the author is close to her death.

C) It highlights the futile nature of certain tasks.

D) It shows that the author regrets not accomplishing certain goals.

5

The vegan diet is chosen by individuals for various reasons, including health and ethics. While many health benefits exist, it is essential for those who are vegan or are planning to become vegan to be educated about potential nutrient deficiencies to prevent adverse outcomes. In addition, it is evident that <u>the vegan diet is much more than a diet itself,</u> but has developed into a lifestyle, often associated with animal rights and environmental advocacy as well as a greater concern for physical activity and mindfulness. Further research begs the question of whether the health benefits associated with the diet are solely attributable to the diet or in conjunction with a greater physical activity level and mindful living.

What is the main purpose of including the claim that "the vegan diet is much more than a diet itself"?

A) To show that people who are concerned about protecting animals should consider veganism.

B) To indicate that adopting veganism is a good way for people to help the environment.

C) To imply that many vegans consider factors other than food to be part of being a vegan.

D) To establish that people who are vegans have healthier lifestyles than non-vegans do.

6

Text 1

The Kuiper Belt is a region of space, shaped roughly like a donut, at the far reaches of our solar system. It is located outside the orbit of Neptune and contains over 2,000 identified objects, though scientists speculate that there may be millions more that have not been found yet due to its extreme distance from the sun. In 1930, the dwarf planet Pluto was the first object to be found in the Kuiper Belt, but it took many decades for the second, Pluto's moon, Charon, to be located in 1978.

Text 2

Objects in the Kuiper Belt are rocky bodies made from elements such as iron, and most of the ones found to date also are covered with ice that is composed of water or methane. In fact, some scientists speculate whether Earth's oceans were formed from water ice from comets in the Kuiper Belt. The quantity of ice greatly increases an object's reflectivity, making it easier to isolate objects made of such materials in telescopes that are trained on the distant reaches of our solar system.

Based on the texts, how would the author of Text 2 react to the claim in Text 1 that "there may be millions more that have not been found yet"?

A) The author of Text 2 would say that many of the objects will be hard to find because they are not covered with reflective ice.

B) The author of Text 2 would claim that it is easier to find large objects such as dwarf planets, so the remaining objects must all be small.

C) The author of Text 2 would point out that the objects that have been found are probably closer to the sun than the objects that have not yet been found.

D) The author of Text 2 would argue that the number is greatly elevated over the actual number of objects which are in the Kuiper Belt.

Text 1

Prisons in the 1820s were unregulated and unhygienic, ... Dorothea Dix visited every public and private facility she could access, documenting the conditions she found. She then presented her findings to the legislature of Massachusetts, demanding that officials take action toward reform. Her reports—filled with dramatic accounts of prisoners flogged, starved, chained, and abused by their keepers, and left undressed and without heat or sanitation—shocked her audience and galvanized a movement that succeeded in improving conditions for the imprisoned and insane.

Text 2

Settlement house founder and peace activist Jane Addams (1860-1935) ..., along with a college friend, Ellen Starr, moved in 1889 into an old mansion in an immigrant neighborhood of Chicago. Hull-House, which remained Addams's home for the rest of her life and became the center of an experiment in philanthropy, political action, and social science research, was a model for settlement work among the poor.

Based on the texts, how would Jane Addams in Text 2 most likely respond to Dix's actions to improve the conditions for the imprisoned and insane as illustrated in Text 1?

A) By disputing the idea that Dix could impose reform through documentation and reports instead of physically experiencing the conditions.

B) By assenting the importance of political action in achieving reform but asserting the greater significance of a personal lifetime commitment to a social cause.

C) By corroborating that thorough and honest research combined with political action are necessities when attempting social reform.

D) By contesting the effectiveness of the non-scientific and dramatic nature of Dix's reports in achieving reform.

8

The following text is adapted from Abraham Lincoln's last public address, given April 11, 1965.

The amount of constituency, so to speak, on which the new Louisiana government rests, would be more satisfactory to all, if it contained fifty, thirty, or even twenty thousand, instead of only about twelve thousand, as it does. It is also unsatisfactory to some that the elective franchise is not given to the colored man. I would myself, prefer that it were now conferred on the very intelligent, and on those who serve our cause as soldiers. Still the question is not whether the Louisiana government, as it stands, is quite all that desirable. The question is, "Will it be wiser to take it as it is, and help to improve it, or to reject, and disperse it?" "Can Louisiana be brought into proper practical relation with the Union sooner by sustaining, or by discarding her new state government?"

According to the text, what is one of the controversies regarding Louisiana?

A) Relatively few voters reside within the state

B) The state is much larger than many others in the Union.

C) The proportion of freed slaves is higher than in other states.

D) The state has not agreed to policies accepted elsewhere.

9

It was an audacious idea: To send an unmanned research vehicle called a saildrone on a 13,670-mile journey around Antarctica, at the mercy of the most hostile seas on the planet. In winter. "The assumption was the Southern Ocean would eat the saildrone ... and that would be that," said NOAA oceanographer Adrienne Sutton. "But we were willing to try, given the large role the ocean plays in climate change. Getting the Southern Ocean's carbon balance right is urgently important." The 196-day voyage was the world's first autonomous circumnavigation of Antarctica — a technological feat unfathomable just a decade ago. Until recently, scientists assumed that the Southern Ocean was a big contributor to absorbing the greenhouse gases driving global warming, but shifts in winds and circulation around Antarctica could alter CO_2 uptake from the atmosphere. But researchers had yet to sample vast areas, especially during stormy autumn and winter seasons.

According to the text, what is one of the main goals of launching the saildrone during the winter?

A) To prove that the Southern Ocean was absorbing as much CO_2 as previously estimated

B) To test the limitations of new technology designed to survive harsh conditions

C) To collect data during a time period in which very little research had previously been done

D) To establish whether the Southern Ocean played a vital role in CO_2 absorption

CONTINUE

10

Peanut butter and jelly sandwiches are a nostalgic childhood staple. However, research shows that they can be good for you as well as delicious. Peanut butter is filled with nutrients such as vitamin E, iron, and magnesium. Furthermore, it has a lot of protein and fiber, which helps suppress the appetite so people can lose weight. On top of that, people who eat peanut butter regularly may have other health benefits: _____

Which choice most logically completes the text?

A) one study showed women who ate at least five servings of peanut butter per week were 44 percent less likely to suffer from heart disease.

B) peanut butter is high in calories, so it is advisable to use servings that are 2 tablespoons or less.

C) select natural varieties rather than brands which contain partially hydrogenated oils or other additives.

D) it can be served in a variety of ways from peanut butter curry to spread on fruit to mixing it into a smoothie health drink.

11

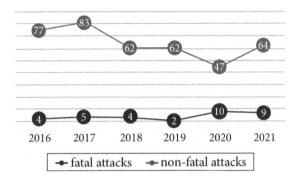

Shark attacks by Year (Global)

fatal attacks   non-fatal attacks

When people envision sharks, they often imagine deadly carnivores that attack people on sight. In reality, sharks tend to avoid encounters with humans unless provoked, and the actual number of deaths per year is typically below 10 for the entire world per year. Of course, it is incorrect to judge the number of dangerous encounters just by looking at deaths. For example, there were 9 deaths from shark attacks in 2021, _____

Which choice most effectively completes the example using data from the graph?

A) but fewer non–fatal attacks than earlier in the decade.

B) down by 1 from the previous year.

C) but there were 64 non–fatal attacks.

D) which was more than in 2018 and 2019 combined.

12

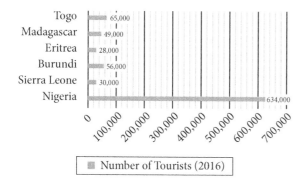

Safari tourism in Africa highlights exotic creatures including elephants, lions, rhinos, hippos, and big game. However, the region is also replete with natural features or attractions that tourists gravitate toward, particularly those in search of outstanding scenic sites or who desire an environmental adventure. There are dozens of awe–inspiring national parks throughout Africa like Mt. Kilimanjaro in Tanzania and Zuma Rock in Nigeria. However, local conditions make it hard to travel in some places. For example, due to the infrastructure for accommodating visitors, travel in Togo in 2016 was: _____

Which choice most effectively uses data from the graph to illustrate the claim?

A) the highest of the selected countries represented in the figure.

B) greater than that of either Burundi or Nigeria.

C) lower than that of Nigeria but higher than that of Eritrea.

D) higher than it had been in the previous year.

13

The following text is adapted from Jane Austin's 1811 novel, *Sense and Sensibility.*

Mrs. Dashwood waited only for the disposal of her effects at Norland before she set off to her new home; and this, as she was exceedingly rapid in the performance of everything that interested her, was soon done. The horses which were left her by her husband had been sold soon after his death, and an opportunity now offering of disposing of her carriage, she agreed to sell that likewise at the earnest advice of her eldest daughter. For the comfort of her children, had she consulted only her own wishes, she would have kept it; but the discretion of Elinor had prevailed. *Her* wisdom too limited the number of their servants to three; two maids and a man, with whom they were speedily provided from amongst those who had formed their establishment at Norland.

Based on the text, what can be inferred about the relationship between Mrs. Dashwood and her oldest daughter?

A) Mrs. Dashwood defers to her daughter's decisions.

B) Mrs. Dashwood usually tells her daughter what to do.

C) Both would prefer living apart from each other.

D) Both feel that the other is acting in error.

14

What can you do to add an extra layer of protection when entering into a business opportunity? Before you buy a franchise, insist on seeing proof in writing for earnings claims, including statements like "Earn up to $10,000 a month!" Phrases like "up to" aren't a way out for the seller. It's an earnings claim and it's your right to demand proof. You should also interview current owners of the seller's business opportunity. Ask the tough questions—like if the information in the disclosure document matches their experience with the company. Listen to sales presentations with a critical ear. They are—of course—trying to sell you something. Finally, if a seller doesn't give you the information you know they have to provide, walk away.

Based on the text, what can reasonably be inferred about the author's opinion concerning franchises?

A) The author feels most franchises do not offer realistic information about their earnings potential.

B) The author feels franchise advertisements usually highlight the best possible scenarios.

C) The author feels there are insufficient laws for the protection of franchise sellers.

D) The author feels that with proper research, an investor can ensure that the business will not fail.

15

The American author Ernest Hemingway, _____ received the 1954 Nobel Prize for Literature, was famous for a very minimalist writing style that is best exemplified in his short novel, *The Old Man and the Sea* about a sailor struggling against a blue marlin.

Which choice completes the text so that it conforms to the conventions of Standard English?

A) he

B) who

C) that

D) whom

16

Carbon emission credit programs are designed to reduce the overall amount of pollution released into the environment by limiting greenhouse gas emissions, encouraging technological innovation, and _____

Which choice completes the text so that it conforms to the conventions of Standard English?

A) it increases competition between enterprises for the credit rights.

B) increasing competition between enterprises for the right to use the credits.

C) the right to use the credits is something enterprises compete for.

D) increased competition between enterprises for the right to use the credits.

17

Most people want to incorporate more exercise into their daily routine, but is there an optimum time for it? According to sports scientists, exercise performance is closely correlated with body temperature, _____ typically peaks in the early evening.

Which choice completes the text so that it conforms to the conventions of Standard English?

A) it

B) when

C) which

D) that

18

Federico Garcia Lorca was one of Spain's foremost poets and was known for _____ classic Spanish forms, but with modern symbolism and individualistic humor. Unfortunately, his career was abruptly cut short by the Spanish Civil War, but his legacy lives on.

Which choice completes the text so that it conforms to the conventions of Standard English?

A) revive

B) revived

C) revival

D) reviving

19

The Similan Islands form an archipelago in the Adaman _____ visitors arrive on speed boats for a day trip, but consider an overnight stay if you want to enjoy the stunning scenery almost completely to yourself.

Which choice completes the text so that it conforms to the conventions of Standard English?

A) Sea. Most

B) Sea, most

C) Sea; and most

D) Sea and—most

20

Modern dance is a contemporary form of expression that evolved from the rigid structure of ballet to become naturalistic, with free and fluid movements that represent _____ feelings.

Which choice completes the text so that it conforms to the conventions of Standard English?

A) ideas emotions and

B) ideas, emotions, and

C) ideas, emotions and,

D) ideas; emotions; and

21

_____ massive stones erected around 2,500 B.C.—is one of the most famous Neolithic monuments in the world, though it was built on the site of a circle made of timber and pounded earth that had been built about 500 years earlier.

Which choice completes the text so that it conforms to the conventions of Standard English?

A) Stonehenge—a ring of

B) Stonehenge, a ring of—

C) Stonehenge, a ring of

D) Stonehenge: a ring of

22

Billy Joel is a singer and songwriter who is best known for the song "Piano Man." He started his music career in earnest when he found he did not have enough credits to graduate high school and claimed he did not care about finishing his education. _____ twenty–five years later he contacted his former school and wrote essays that allowed him to belatedly receive a degree.

Which choice completes the text with the most logical transition?

A) Inevitably,

B) Simultaneously,

C) Consequently,

D) Nonetheless,

23

The largest boat to date to sail the Great Lakes, the Edmund Fitzgerald, sank on November 10, 1975, northwest of Whitefish Point in Lake Superior. _____ its fame, the exact cause of the shipwreck has yet to be determined.

Which choice completes the text with the most logical transition?

A) Because of

B) Despite

C) Indeed,

D) Furthermore,

24

Several international organizations monitor the position of space debris larger than 10 centimeters across to ensure safe space travel. _____ those efforts are not sufficient, as there are about twenty times as many smaller objects that are moving at speeds fast enough to damage even a heavily protected spacecraft.

Which choice completes the text with the most logical transition?

A) However,

B) Likewise,

C) Therefore,

D) Alternatively,

25

While researching a topic, a student has taken the following notes:

- Freshwater tropical fish can tolerate temperatures from 18 to 26 degrees Celsius, so may require a heater in the winter.

- Freshwater tropical fish are often kept in tanks with water plants, but since most eat vegetables as well as meat, they may consume the plants.

- Because ocean water temperatures remain relatively constant throughout the year, saltwater tropical fish must be monitored in a system with less than 2 degrees of variation.

- Saltwater tanks are usually maintained at the proper balance of minerals using synthetic salt.

- Most tropical saltwater aquarium fish are omnivores or scavengers.

The student wants to explain a key difference between the care of tropical saltwater and freshwater fish to an audience that knows very little about fish. Which choice most effectively uses relevant information from the notes to accomplish this goal?

A) Tropical fish, whether freshwater or saltwater, most commonly eat meat, though some include vegetables in their diets.

B) Freshwater fish need to be kept in tanks with plants, though saltwater fish do not.

C) The acceptable temperature variations in a saltwater tank are much lower than what is acceptable for a freshwater tank.

D) Freshwater tropical fish often have plants, but saltwater tropical fish need synthetic salt.

26

While researching a topic, a student has taken the following notes:

- George Elton Mayo was an Australian psychologist, industrial researcher, and theorist who came up with a humanistic theory for management.

- Mayo's theory is based on the idea that repetition of tasks is boring and reduces innovation.

- Mayo's theory offers each worker a significant amount of freedom in completing tasks.

- The teamwork aspects of Mayo's theory can lead to high productivity and communication.

- Some workers feel greater stress and pressure because individual responsibilities are increased in environments where Mayo's theory is applied.

The student wants to introduce Mayo's theory to an audience who wants to increase innovation in the workplace. Which choice most effectively uses relevant information from the notes to accomplish this goal?

A) George Elton Mayo created a theory based on the idea that repetition of tasks is boring, so many companies see little innovation.

B) The theorist George Elton Mayo pointed out that workers given significant freedom complete their tasks and form good teams, but may feel great stress as a result.

C) A theory proposed by George Elton Mayo addresses the question of increasing innovation output by suggesting that workers get more freedom and less repetition in completing tasks.

D) George Elton Mayo's humanistic theory can cause some workers stress, though it is outweighed by the many positive points related to innovation.

27

While researching a topic, a student has taken the following notes:

- The North Pole is located in the Arctic Ocean and temperatures are routinely above freezing in the summer.

- Due to the Earth's axis, there is only one sunset and one sunrise at the poles per year.

- The South Pole is on Antarctica, and research at the Amundsen–Scott South Pole Station has provided compelling evidence about continental drift.

- Ground at the South Pole is about 100 meters above sea level, but there is 2,700 meters of ice, so the high altitude contributes to the arid desert environment.

- The highest temperature recorded at the South Pole was –12.3C, whereas, the lowest was –82.8C.

The student wants to emphasize a way in which the North Pole and South Pole differ from each other. Which choice most effectively uses relevant information from the notes to accomplish this goal?

A) The South Pole has extreme temperatures ranging from –82.8 to –12.3 degrees Celsius, but the North Pole does not.

B) Both the North Pole and the South Pole have only one sunrise and one sunset in a 12–month period.

C) Scientists have studied continental drift at the South Pole, but the North Pole is in the ocean.

D) The temperatures at the South Pole are much colder than at the North Pole, with highs never over –12.3 Celsius at the former and well above freezing at the latter.

STOP

No Test Material On This Page

No Test Material On This Page

Math

22 QUESTIONS | 35 MINUTES

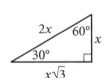

For **multiple–choice questions,** solve each problem, choose the correct answer from the choices provided, and then circle your answer in this book. Circle only one answer for each question. If you change your mind, completely erase the circle. You will not get credit for questions with more than one answer circled, or for questions with no answers circled.

For **student–produced response questions,** solve each problem and write your answer next to or under the question in the test book as described below.

- Once you've written your answer, circle it clearly. You will not receive credit for anything written outside the circle, or for any questions with more than one circled answer.

- If you find more than one correct answer, write and circle only one answer.

- Your answer can be up to 5 characters for a positive answer and up to 6 characters (including the negative sign) for a negative answer, but no more.

- If your answer is a fraction that is too long (over 5 characters for positive, 6 characters for negative), write the decimal equivalent.

- If your answer is a decimal that is too long (over 5 characters for positive, 6 characters for negative), truncate it or round at the fourth digit.

- If your answer is a mixed number (such as 3.!. 2), write it as an improper fraction (7/2) or its decimal equivalent (3.5).

- Don't include symbols such as a percent sign, comma, or dollar sign in your circled answer.

1

Which of the following represents the equation of the graph below?

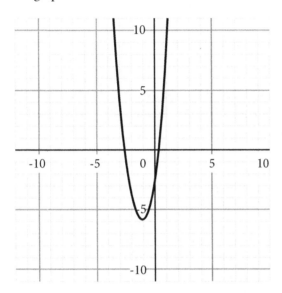

A) $y = 3x^2 - 6x - 3$

B) $y = -3x^2 + 6x - 3$

C) $y = 3x^2 + 6x - 3$

D) $y = -3x^2 - 6x - 3$

2

What is the product of the solutions in the equation below?

$$3x^2 - 12x - 15 = 0$$

3

A standard 52–card deck consists of 13 hearts, 13 spades, 13 cloves, and 13 diamonds. If the first card picked randomly is a heart and is not put back on the deck, what is the probability of picking a second heart card from the deck?

A) $\dfrac{13}{52}$

B) $\dfrac{12}{52}$

C) $\dfrac{12}{51}$

D) $\dfrac{39}{51}$

4

Which expression is equivalent to $6xy(y + 3x) - 2x(3xy + y^2)$?

A) $12xy^2 + 12x^2y$

B) $4xy^2 + 12x^2y$

C) $4xy^2 - 12\ x^2y$

D) $12x^2y - 4xy^2$

5

The price of a dress, which originally cost $200, increased by 15% on 15th May 2021. Mary bought the same dress on the 23rd of May 2021 at a 30% discount. How much did she pay for the dress?

6

If $x^2 - y^2 = 12$ and $x - y = 2$, what is the value of $x + y$?

A) 6

B) 4

C) 2

D) –2

7

What is the value of xy for the system below?

$$2x + y = 2$$
$$3y - x = 20$$

A) –12

B) –2

C) 6

D) –3

8

What is the positive value of x for the following equation?

$$2\,|x + 4| = 12$$

9

A researcher collected a sample of 12 height samples from his local mall and wrote them down in meters.

The data he collected are 1.23, 1.45, 1.67, 1.53, 1.12, 1.23, 1.25, 1.39, 1.73, 1.84, 1.39, and 1.09.

Which of the following statements is correct when he collects a last–minute sample of $2.23m$?

A) The mean and the range will increase and the median and standard deviation will decrease

B) The mean, range, and standard deviation will increase and the median remains the same

C) The mean, range, median, and standard deviation will increase

D) The mean, range, median and standard deviation will decrease

10

A circle is inscribed in a square. If the square has a side length of $14cm$, what is the area of the circle?

A) 196π

B) 49π

C) 14π

D) 98π

11

What is the new *y-intercept* of the function $f(x)$ below if the line is moved 2 units to the left and 1 unit up?

$$f(x) = 3x + 5$$

12

Which of the following coordinates is a solution to the following system of inequalities?

$$-2y > -4$$

$$3x - y > 3$$

A) $(1, 2)$
B) $(1, 3)$
C) $(2, 4)$
D) $(3, 1)$

13

A circle has endpoints of a diameter with the coordinates of $(-6, 10)$ and $(2, 10)$. Which of the following is an equation for the circle?

A) $(x - 2)^2 + (y - 10)^2 = 16$

B) $(x + 2)^2 + (y - 10)^2 = 16$

C) $(x + 2)^2 + (y + 10)^2 = 16$

D) $(x - 2)^2 + (y + 10)^2 = 16$

14

If $f(x) = x + 2$ and $g(x) = 2x + 3$, find $f(g(2))$.

A) 7

B) 4

C) 9

D) 11

15

What is the *y-intercept* of the function below?

$$y = 300^x + 5$$

16

If the shaded region represents the solutions to an inequality, which of the following inequalities is represented by the graph below?

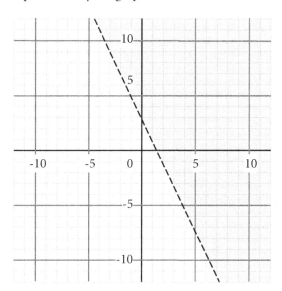

A) $y > 2x + 3$

B) $y > -2x + 3$

C) $y < -x + 3$

D) $y < -2x + 3$

17

Which of the following expressions is represented by the graph below?

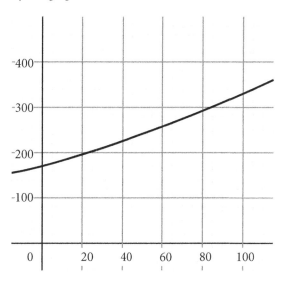

A) $400(1.03)^{0.2x}$

B) $180(0.97)^{0.2x}$

C) $180(1.03)^{0.2x}$

D) $400(0.97)^{0.2x}$

18

If $3x + 2(x + 4y) = ax + by$, what is the value of a?

A) 3

B) 2

C) 4

D) 5

19

Using interval notation, what is the value of y in the inequality below?

$$-3y > -15$$

20

If $sin(3x) = cos(x + 10)$, what is the value of x in degrees?

A) 5°

B) 20°

C) 30°

D) 60°

21

Amanda is planning a trip and decides to save for it. She saves $10 dollars during the first week and doubles the amount she saves every week thereafter. Which type of function below best represents the amount that she will save in a given week?

A) Exponential growth

B) Linear growth

C) Exponential decay

D) Linear decay

22

If $4x + 8 = 24$, what is the value of x?

A) 8

B) 4

C) 3

D) 6

No Test Material On This Page

Math

22 QUESTIONS | 35 MINUTES

DIRECTIONS

The questions in this section address a number of important math skills. Use of a calculator is permitted for all questions.

NOTES

Unless otherwise indicated: • All variables and expressions represent real numbers. • Figures provided are drawn to scale. • All figures lie in a plane. • The domain of a given function is the set of all real numbers x for which $f(x)$ is a real number.

REFERENCE

$A = \pi r^2$
$C = 2\pi r$

$A = \ell w$

$A = \frac{1}{2}bh$

$c^2 = a^2 + b^2$

Special Right Triangles

$V = \ell wh$

$V = \pi r^2 h$

$V = \frac{4}{3}\pi r^3$

$V = \frac{1}{3}\pi r^2 h$

$V = \frac{1}{3}\ell wh$

The number of degrees of arc in a circle is 360.

The number of radians of arc in a circle is 2π.

The sum of the measures in degrees of the angles of a triangle is 180.

For **multiple–choice questions,** solve each problem, choose the correct answer from the choices provided, and then circle your answer in this book. Circle only one answer for each question. If you change your mind, completely erase the circle. You will not get credit for questions with more than one answer circled, or for questions with no answers circled.

For **student–produced response questions,** solve each problem and write your answer next to or under the question in the test book as described below.

- Once you've written your answer, circle it clearly. You will not receive credit for anything written outside the circle, or for any questions with more than one circled answer.

- If you find more than one correct answer, write and circle only one answer.

- Your answer can be up to 5 characters for a positive answer and up to 6 characters (including the negative sign) for a negative answer, but no more.

- If your answer is a fraction that is too long (over 5 characters for positive, 6 characters for negative), write the decimal equivalent.

- If your answer is a decimal that is too long (over 5 characters for positive, 6 characters for negative), truncate it or round at the fourth digit.

- If your answer is a mixed number (such as 3.!. 2), write it as an improper fraction (7/2) or its decimal equivalent (3.5).

- Don't include symbols such as a percent sign, comma, or dollar sign in your circled answer.

1

$7x + 28 = 112$, What is the value of $x + 4$?

A) -4

B) 16

C) 8

D) 12

2

The radius of a ball is three times the radius of its prototype. If the prototype has a volume of $10cm^3$, what is the volume of the ball?

3

If the system of equations below has one solution, what is the value of k?

$$y = 2x + k$$

$$y = x^2 - 10x + 30$$

A) -6

B) 3

C) 6

D) -3

4

If $\dfrac{27^{x-1}}{81^y} = 9$, what is the value of $6x - 8y$?

A) 2

B) 5

C) 4

D) 10

5

If the diagonal of a square is $16\sqrt{2}$, what is the perimeter of the square?

6

Which of the following graphs represents the
equation $12x + 4y = 8$?

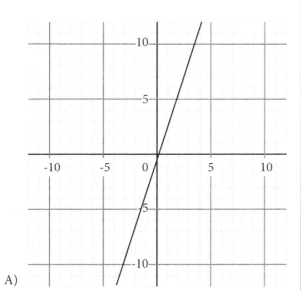

A)

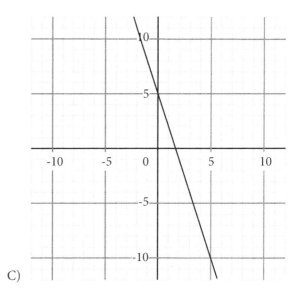

C)

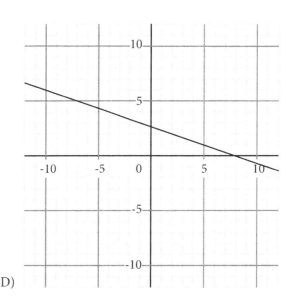

D)

B)

7

If the system of equations below has no solution, what is the value of p?

$$\frac{3}{2}x + 5 = px + \frac{3}{2}$$

8

A researcher created a model $p(x)$, which is a function for the height of a girl in feet. Where t is in years and t is $2 \leq t \leq 5$. If $p(x) = 1.23(1.32)^t$, which of the following best represents the model in m months?

A) $p(x) = 1.23(1.32)^{12m}$

B) $p(x) = 1.23\left(\dfrac{1.32}{12}\right)^m$

C) $p(x) = 1.23(1.32)^{\frac{m}{12}}$

D) $p(x) = 1.23(1.32)^m$

9

If $\dfrac{-2x^2 + 5x + 10}{x - 3} = A + \dfrac{7}{x - 3}$, which of the following expressions best represents A?

A) $-2x - 1$

B) $2x + 3$

C) $-2x - 3$

D) $-2x^2 + 4x + 13$

10

If $3x = -5y$ and $2x + 3y = -1$, what is the value of x?

A) 3

B) −5

C) 2

D) −8

11

What is the greatest possible integer value of k if the quadratic equation below has two distinct solutions?

$$4x^2 - 12x + k = 0$$

12

How many solutions does the equation below have?

$$3(x + 6) + x = 4x + 5$$

A) 0

B) 1

C) 2

D) Infinite

13

Which of the following is equivalent to the expression below?

$$\frac{1}{\dfrac{1}{x-2}+\dfrac{1}{x+2}}$$

A) $\dfrac{x^2-4}{2x}$

B) x

C) $\dfrac{2x}{x^2-4}$

D) $\dfrac{x^2+4}{2x}$

14

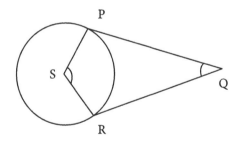

PQ and PR are tangents and points P and R lie on the circle. If $\angle\,PSR = 80°$ and $\angle\,PQR = a\pi$, what is the value of a?

A) $\dfrac{5}{18}$

B) $\dfrac{13}{18}$

C) $\dfrac{5}{9}$

D) 1

15

What is the area of a circle whose circumference is 12π?

16

Which of the following expressions is equivalent to the expression below?

$$3p^{\frac{1}{3}}\sqrt{p}$$

A) $3\sqrt[5]{p}$

B) $\sqrt[6]{3p^5}$

C) $3\sqrt[6]{p}$

D) $3\sqrt[6]{p^5}$

17

What is the volume of a cylinder with a radius of 9 *cm* and a height of 6 *cm*?

A) 270π

B) 486π

C) 81π

D) 108π

18

If lines $3x + 5y = 6$ and $-6x + py = 18$ are parallel, what is the value of p?

A) -10

B) 5

C) 10

D) 3

19

If $3xy(5x + 2) + 2y(3x - 1) = ax^2y + bxy + cy$, what is the value of b?

20

How many solutions does the absolute value equation below have?

$$-2|x + 4| = -8$$

A) 0

B) 1

C) 2

D) Infinite

21

If $xy = 5$ and $x^2 + y^2 = 45$, what is the value of $(x + y)^2$?

A) 9

B) 55

C) 110

D) 35

22

A study was conducted on 1,200 residents in a particular town. 950 of the residents surveyed owned a dog or a cat and the rest owned a different type of pet. If there are 62,500 residents in the town, approximately how many of them own a different type of pet?

A) $62,500$

B) $49,480$

C) $13,020$

D) $61,550$

STOP

This page is intentionally left blank

Answer Key

Reading and Writing

Module 1

Questions	Correct	Mark your correct answers
1.	A	
2.	A	
3.	A	
4.	B	
5.	C	
6.	A	
7.	B	
8.	D	
9.	B	
10.	C	
11.	A	
12.	B	
13.	B	
14.	C	
15.	C	
16.	A	
17.	C	
18.	A	
19.	D	
20.	C	
21.	C	
22.	A	
23.	A	
24.	C	
25.	D	
26.	D	
27.	B	

Module 2

Questions	Correct	Mark your correct answers
1.	C	
2.	C	
3.	D	
4.	A	
5.	C	
6.	A	
7.	C	
8.	A	
9.	C	
10.	A	
11.	C	
12.	C	
13.	A	
14.	B	
15.	B	
16.	B	
17.	C	
18.	D	
19.	A	
20.	B	
21.	A	
22.	D	
23.	B	
24.	A	
25.	C	
26.	C	
27.	D	

Math

Module 1

Questions	Correct	Mark your correct answers
1.	C	
2.	-5	
3.	C	
4.	B	
5.	161	
6.	A	
7.	A	
8.	2	
9.	B	
10.	B	
11.	12	
12.	D	
13.	B	
14.	C	
15.	6	
16.	B	
17.	C	
18.	D	
19.	$(-\infty, 5)$	
20.	B	
21.	A	
22.	B	

Module 2

Questions	Correct	Mark your correct answers
1.	B	
2.	270	
3.	A	
4.	D	
5.	64	
6.	C	
7.	$\frac{3}{2}$ or 1.5	
8.	C	
9.	A	
10.	B	
11.	8	
12.	A	
13.	A	
14.	C	
15.	36π	
16.	D	
17.	B	
18.	A	
19.	12	
20.	C	
21.	B	
22.	C	

1. **Level:** Medium | **Domain:** CRAFT AND
STRUCTURE
Skill/Knowledge: Words in Context

Key Explanation: Choice A is the best answer.
The blank describes the way in which the insights
and treatment of everyday life are "accessible to
the average reader." The passage says the insights
are "unassuming" or "not flamboyant," and the
treatment of everyday life and interactions is
"gently humorous" or "pleasantly funny," which
suggests the stories are probably very easy to read.
Choice A means "effortlessly" or "easily," which
fits the context that the average reader can enjoy
the stories without working hard to understand
them.

Distractor Explanation: Choice B is incorrect
because it refers to being full of worry, but there
is no indication that the average reader would
be worried about stories that are unassuming
and pleasant. **Choice C** is incorrect because the
reader may be content reading the stories, but the
underlined word refers to the "accessibility" of
the stories rather than to the reader. Accessibility
is inanimate and therefore not content. **Choice D**
is incorrect because it refers to dry, ironic humor,
but the passage already states that his humor is
"gentle."

2. **Level:** Medium | **Domain:** CRAFT AND
STRUCTURE
Skill/Knowledge: Words in Context

Key Explanation: Choice A is the best answer
because "charge" is what the next generation will
do to the miners. Choice A means "blame," so
fits the context of saying that the next generation
will not blame the miners for what they have
done. They will only blame the miners for what
is "undone," meaning that they will blame the
miners if the working conditions are still terrible.

Distractor Explanation: None of the other
choices fits the context of explaining what the
next generation will do to the miners. **Choice B**
refers to a strong order or request, but the actions
in "what we've done" and "what we have left
undone" are in the past. **Choice C** refers to forcing
something rather than commenting on something,
and **Choice D** refers to a physical attack rather
than a verbal complaint.

3. **Level:** Easy | **Domain:** CRAFT AND
STRUCTURE
Skill/Knowledge: Words in Context

Key Explanation: Choice A is the best answer.
The underlined word is an adjective which
describes "the problem" as the problem exists in
Southeast Asia. "Pronounced" refers to something
which is conspicuous or noticeable. Therefore, it
fits the context of saying that myopia is a more
noticeable problem in Southeast Asia than in the
US, as such a large percentage of students have it.

Distractor Explanation: None of the other
choices adequately describe "the problem" in
Southeast Asia. **Choice B** refers to supporting a
particular policy, but there is no indication that
people want myopia, as it is a "problem." **Choice C**
refers to something which is ordered to be done,
such as taking a medical prescription. **Choice
D** is incorrect because it refers to how clearly
something is said.

4. **Level:** Medium | **Domain:** CRAFT AND
STRUCTURE
Skill/Knowledge: Text Structure and Purpose

Key Explanation: Choice B is the best answer
because despite promising trips, "none of them
ever materialized." This shows that Ulysses was
more interested in talking than in following

through with his word. That is the action of a "superficial" or "shallow" personality: saying one thing but not caring enough to do it.

Distractor Explanation: Choice A is incorrect because "foreshadowing" involves giving a clue of something that will happen in the future. However, the promised trips never happened, so they do not give any hint that Ulysses would take his son on a trip or that Ulysses would die. **Choice C** is incorrect because, if Ulysses really took an interest in his son, he would follow through on promises and spend time with the boy rather than getting the boy's hopes up and breaking them. **Choice D** is incorrect because the trips would cost a lot of money if the father and son really took them all, but the trips never happened. Therefore, it is possible that the father had very little money and was just talking about places he could only dream of visiting.

5. **Domain:** CRAFT AND STRUCTURE
    Skill/Knowledge: Text Structure and Purpose

    Key Explanation: Choice C is the best answer because the text describes when the Jiroft culture was first proposed and what evidence was available at the time. The text then describes a later finding—the excavations at Komar Sandal—which might strengthen the evidence for such a culture, but the link has not yet been decisively drawn, as the text says "might prove a vital link."

    Distractor Explanations: Choice A is incorrect because the text starts by showing that there was doubt about the culture because the artefacts were not studied where they were found, but the information from Komar Sandal implies that the culture may really have existed. **Choice B** is also incorrect because no "flaws" or "errors" are discussed about the theory; the text only says

that the 2001 artefacts are not strong proof that it existed. **Choice D** is incorrect because there are no "incompatible" or "conflicting" findings, only recent evidence that supplements less strong earlier evidence.

6. **Level:** Hard | **Domain:** CRAFT AND STRUCTURE
    Skill/Knowledge: Text Structure and Purpose

    Key Explanation: Choice A is the best answer. Jacob was looking at the chess board, but uncertain about his moves, fingering his hair and lifting and replacing the same piece before making a few other moves which may or may not have been effective. The end sentence shows what he was actually waiting or hoping for: the sound of Fanny walking by.

    Distractor Explanation: Choice B is incorrect because there is no indication of a desire to get better at chess, only to use time waiting. Though Jacob thinks about his moves, it is unclear whether they are effective or not. **Choice C** is incorrect because Jacob is not "intense" or "concentrating very hard." Instead, he is vacillating over moves and noticing things outside the room. **Choice D** is incorrect because it is clear that Jacob is waiting for Fanny, but not why. There is no clue that there was a "quarrel" or "argument."

7. **Level:** Medium | **Domain:** INFORMATION AND IDEAS
    Skill/Knowledge: Cross–Text Connections

    Key Explanation: Choice B is the best answer because it describes the most likely way that the author of Text 2 most likely respond to Lincoln's behaviour as illustrated in Text 1. According to Text 1, Lincoln was someone who stayed true to his personal convictions despite the concerns of those close to him. Text 2 portrays Lincoln as someone who "grew more steady and resolute, and his ideas were never confused." In both cases, the authors are emphasizing Lincoln's stability and equanimity. The author of Text 2 would agree that Lincoln did not often deviate from his ways.

Distractor Explanation: Choice A is incorrect because nothing in Text 2 suggests that author believed that protection was important. Text 2 is focused on how Lincoln was someone who "grew more steady and resolute, and his ideas were never confused", not on the importance of protection or Lincoln's assassination beliefs. **Choice C** is incorrect because Text 2 doesn't include any information regarding the morbid nature of Lincoln's dislike for personal protection. In fact, Text 2 indicates that the author believes Lincoln to be "steady and resolute, and his ideas were never confused", which Text 1 mirrors by illustrating his constant refusal to be guarded or protected. **Choice D** is incorrect because there's no information in Text 2 suggesting that the author would challenge the supposition that Lincoln consistently "exposed himself to the deadly aim of an assassin." Although Text 1 does indicate that Lincoln regularly ventured out without protection, Text 2 says only that the author believes that Lincoln's character was that of a self-possessed, steady and resolute man. Text 2 doesn't imply that the author doubts that Lincoln consistently put himself at risk of being assassinated.

8. **Level:** Easy | **Domain:** INFORMATION AND IDEAS
    Skill/Knowledge: Central Ideas and Details

    Key Explanation: Choice D is the best answer because "evolved" refers to the changes that the plant underwent over time. The text defines

capsaicin and says that it is mostly contained in the fruit. The speculation is "possibly to deter mammalian herbivores." "Herbivores" are animals that eat plants, so the plants that contained capsaicin "stopped" or "deterred" predators from eating the chili. Over time, the plants with more capsaicin survived.

Distractor Explanation: Choices A and **B** are incorrect because they are uses that chilis have been adapted for by humans but are not why chili plants evolved with capsaicin in their fruit. **Choice C** is not mentioned anywhere in the text.

9. **Level:** Easy | **Domain:** INFORMATION AND IDEAS
    Skill/Knowledge: Central Ideas and Details

    Key Explanation: Choice B is the best answer because "reimbursement" refers to payment, and he explains how much he enjoys getting paid for traveling aboard a ship, "I always go to sea as a sailor, because they make a point of paying me for my trouble."

    Distractor Explanation: Choice A is incorrect because there is no reference to "excessive" or "too much" responsibility for passengers; the narrator does not mention the amount of work. **Choice C** is incorrect because it only describes what happens to passengers, not to Ishmael. **Choice D** is incorrect because the narrator does not want "recognition" or "fame." He indicates that he is happy to leave those "to those who like them."

10. **Level:** Hard | **Domain:** INFORMATION AND IDEAS
    Skill/Knowledge: Central Ideas and Details

    Key Explanation: Choice C is the best answer because Adam's wife, Alicia Withers, is described as "anemic" and "devitalized," which refers to someone who lacks vitality or spirit. She spent her time raising her son out of sight of the general public: "she had thenceforth effaced herself within the shadowy dimensions of the nursery," rather than take an active interest in society or her husband's activities. **Choice C** means "withdrawn" or "not confident," so it describes Alicia well.

Distractor Explanation: Choice A is incorrect because while Alicia had some valuable connections, the passage does not indicate that she used them to her advantage. Therefore, she was not "influential" or "dominant" in manipulating her connections for her own good. **Choice B** refers to being able to attract and hold attention and **Choice D** refers to being very lively, neither of which are consistent with the description of an "anemic" lady who does not leave the nursery.

11. **Level:** Medium | **Domain:** INFORMATION AND IDEAS
    Skill/Knowledge: Command of Evidence (Textual)

    Key Explanation: Choice A is the best answer because Clark bases his claim on the concept that there are few overall changes in the biodiversity of an area. He believes that the neutral model, which is the case if no stabilizing factors exist, would result in more variation because chance is the only thing that affects extinction and replacement of species. Therefore, Choice A gives the scenario in which chance takes a large part, weakening Clark's claim that other forces than chance are at work.

    Distractor Explanation: Choice B can be eliminated as strengthening rather than weakening Clark's claim that stabilizing forces exist. Choice B offers a "stabilizing force" that controls the biodiversity; Clark did not name

the forces, but Choice B shows that at least one exists. **Choice C** does not greatly affect Clark's data in any way. Even if early humans ate nuts, or one species went extinct, the overall biodiversity can remain the same. Clark's theory accounts for contingencies such as extinction as it only shows that stabilizing forces ensure that biodiversity in the region remains approximately rather than exactly the same. **Choice D** does not disprove Clark's theory. If one species is susceptible to heat, it could decrease in number or go extinct, but overall, the plants in a region will still remain in the same balance.

12. **Level:** Medium | **Domain:** INFORMATION AND IDEAS
    Skill/Knowledge: Command of Evidence (Quantitative)

    Key Explanation: Choice B is the best answer because the "alternate source" column on the right-hand side lists only taurine as requiring a "synthetic" or "man-made" supplement. The other nutrients can be at least partly replaced by other sources. The second column of the chart lists "function." The functions of taurine are given as "muscle function, bile production." Someone who does not have enough taurine would therefore, have problems with muscles and bile. **Choice B** refers to "insufficient levels" or "not enough" bile, which relates to problems with producing bile.

    Distractor Explanation: None of the other choices are related to the function of taurine. **Choice A** could be caused by a lack of DHA, which could be replaced using microalgae. **Choices C** and **D** could both be caused by a lack of B12, but that can be replaced using nutritional yeast.

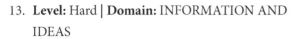

13. **Level:** Hard | **Domain:** INFORMATION AND IDEAS
    Skill/Knowledge: Inferences

    Key Explanation: Choice B is the best answer. The text states that the end of October had "about the middle of the values" at 90. Since the highest values were 30 points greater at 120—in March, the lowest values were probably about 30 points lower. Since 90 was the median the lowest values would be around 60.

    Distractor Explanation: Choice A is incorrect because the amount of trading did not increase over the year if March had a greater index, which shows more trading than September or October. **Choice C** is incorrect because the cause of the index change is only mentioned as changes in supply and demand; there is no discussion of any changes at the New York Mercantile Exchange. **Choice D** is incorrect because if the middle index was 90 and the highest was 120, then it is unlikely that the index dropped below 20 many times; that would greatly change the averages.

14. **Level:** Easy | **Domain:** INFORMATION AND IDEAS
    Skill/Knowledge: Inferences

    Key Explanation: Choice C is the best answer. The passage says that the vote was "notable" or "important" because the Speaker "typically remains silent" or "usually does not vote." In other words, Colfax went against the normal protocol by voting. His decision shows that he was "committed" or "felt strongly" about the amendment to the point of breaking tradition to show his support of it.

    Distractor Explanation: Choice A is incorrect because the passage says that a vote is usually only cast "in the case of a tie." Since Colfax's vote was notable, it probably was not cast under those conditions or it would be considered average or not worth noticing. **Choice B** is incorrect because the passage says that the Speaker usually does not vote, but can if there is a tie. Therefore, it is possible to vote, though it may have been "not valid" or "not acceptable" for other reasons. **Choice D** is impossible to determine because there is not enough information in the passage to determine Grant's views on the subject.

15. **Level:** Medium | **Domain:** STANDARD ENGLISH CONVENTIONS
    Skill/Knowledge: Form, Structure, and Sense

    Key Explanation: Choice C is the best answer. "Longer than" is a comparison which needs to refer to two things that are similar. In the sentence, the thing being compared is "the eyes of baby rabbits." Choice C accurately uses "than" and the comparative form with –er. It also correctly compares the eyes of the baby rabbits with "those"—meaning "the eyes"—of baby hares.

    Distractor Explanation: Choices A and **D** are incorrect because they illogically compare the "the eyes of baby rabbits" with baby hares, not the eyes of baby hares. Furthermore, **Choice D** is incorrect because it shows the same length of time rather than establishing that one event takes ten days more than the other **Choice B** is incorrect because it uses "as" instead of "than" to make a comparison with –er.

16. **Level:** Easy | **Domain:** STANDARD ENGLISH CONVENTIONS
Skill/Knowledge: Form, Structure, and Sense

Key Explanation: Choice A is the best answer. "Had" is used to show that something happened in the past before another action in the sentence; in this case, it shows that the design was made before the opening of the new section. "Been" makes the verb passive, showing that the design of the section was made by someone not mentioned in the passage; the section did not do the designing itself.

Distractor Explanation: Choices B and **C** are incorrect because they are active verbs which erroneously show that the section did the act of designing. **Choice C** is also incorrect because it is the simple past, so does not show that one action occurred before another. **Choice D** is a present–tense verb, so does not fit the context of an action which occurred in the past.

17. **Level:** Medium | **Domain:** STANDARD ENGLISH CONVENTIONS
Skill/Knowledge: Form, Structure, and Sense

Key Explanation: Choice C is the best answer. The beginning of the sentence, "growing to about one inch long," refers to the size of the crab. A modifier like this phrase needs to be followed directly by the noun it modifies. Since **Choice C** starts with "these crabs," it offers the correct order for the modifier and words that follow. In addition, "they" in the second half ("but they… predatory fish") properly refers to the subject of the sentence, "these crabs."

Distractor Explanation: All of the other choices can be eliminated because the preceding modifier, "growing to about one inch long," is not followed

by a logical noun. Since "growing" indicates an animate object, it does not refer to the "large tank" in **Choice A**. **Choice B** starts with the placeholder "it," and **Choice D** illogically makes the modifier refer to "the requirements."

18. **Level:** Easy | **Domain:** STANDARD ENGLISH CONVENTIONS
Skill/Knowledge: Form, Structure, and Sense

Key Explanation: Choice A is the best answer. The subject is the singular "earthenware," as indicated by the singular verb "is." **Choice A** is the singular possessive form showing that the durability and water–holding capacity belongs to the earthenware.

Distractor Explanation: Choice B is incorrect because it is a contraction for "it is" rather than a word showing possession. **Choice C** is incorrect because it is a plural possessive form, but "is" shows that "earthenware" is singular. **Choice D** is incorrect because it is a contraction for "they are."

19. **Level:** Easy | **Domain:** STANDARD ENGLISH CONVENTIONS
Skill/Knowledge: Boundaries

Key Explanation: Choice D is the best answer. The underlined portion connects the modifier "despite its size" with the main clause, "it is not a threat…" A comma needs to follow a modifier at the beginning of the sentence.

Distractor Explanation: Choice A is incorrect because "despite its size" is not a complete sentence; there is no active verb. **Choice B** is incorrect because there should be punctuation separating the main clause "it is not a threat…" from the phrases that modify it. Otherwise, the reader is unsure where one part of the sentence

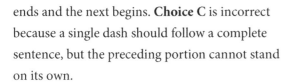

ends and the next begins. **Choice C** is incorrect because a single dash should follow a complete sentence, but the preceding portion cannot stand on its own.

20. **Level:** Medium | **Domain:** STANDARD ENGLISH CONVENTIONS
Skill/Knowledge: Boundaries

Key Explanation: Choice C is the best answer. "such …*Nothing*" adds more information to describe the previous noun, "many beloved children's stories." A comma correctly separates the noun from extra information that describes it but which is not essential for understanding the main part of the sentence.

Distractor Explanation: Choice A is incorrect because a colon should only follow a complete clause, but "such as" leaves the preceding idea unfinished. **Choice C** is incorrect because there should be no comma dividing "such as" from its object, the title of the book. **Choice D** is incorrect because the portion after the period is not a complete idea because there is no verb, so it cannot stand on its own as a sentence.

21. **Level:** Easy | **Domain:** STANDARD ENGLISH CONVENTIONS
Skill/Knowledge: Boundaries

Key Explanation: Choice C is the best answer. Parenthetical information should be treated as if it is part of the noun it describes, so in this case, "*Der Kuss* in German" should follow the same punctuation as "*The Kiss.*" "When…*Kiss*" is a long modifier explaining the time of the main clause, "it was…platinum." A comma should come at the end of a modifier at the start of a sentence. Since the parenthetical information is included as part of the clause, the comma comes after it.

Distractor Explanation: Choice A is incorrect because there is no comma separating the modifier of time from the main clause. **Choices B** and **D** are incorrect because the comma after "Kiss" divides the parenthetical information from the title it describes.

22. **Level:** Medium | **Domain:** STANDARD ENGLISH CONVENTIONS
Skill/Knowledge: Boundaries

Key Explanation: Choice A is the best answer. "Simon Sinek" is necessary in the sentence to know which "American author and inspirational speaker" the sentence is writing about. Therefore, there should be no punctuation dividing the name from the rest of the main clause.

Distractor Explanation: Choice B is incorrect because "Simon Sinek" is not an aside but an essential part clarifying the subject of the sentence. Therefore, it should not be set aside from the main clause. **Choice C** is incorrect because "American author and inspirational speaker" is a subject, not a modifier. If it began with "an" or "the," then it is possible that the description could be used in that way at the start of the sentence. **Choice D** is incorrect because it divides the subject from its verb "has shared."

23. **Level:** Easy | **Domain:** EXPRESSION OF IDEAS
Skill/Knowledge: Transitions

Key Explanation: Choice A is the best answer. The sentence has two parts, one which says that Blacks were granted various rights, but the second part says that conditions grew worse for Blacks and other people of color. **Choice A** is used to show that the main clause occurs in spite of the clause modified by "although." Therefore, it fits the context of showing that conditions were bad in spite of slavery being abolished.

Distractor Explanation: Choices B and **D** can be eliminated because they are used to offer a logical reason for the main clause of the sentence. They do not establish the relationship between the parts of the sentence, because it is not logical that people who are given rights have those rights taken away again. **Choice C** is grammatically incorrect because it is not used to subordinate a clause.

24. **Level:** Easy | **Domain:** EXPRESSION OF IDEAS
    Skill/Knowledge: Transitions

    Key Explanation: Choice C is the best answer. It is used to add information that emphasizes a previous claim, so fits the context of expanding on the claim that coffee is served many ways by giving examples of different ways it is served.

    Distractor Explanation: Choices A and **B** are both used to show that something happens despite something else, so do not fit the context of adding examples to a claim. **Choice D** is used to add more information on a topic, but it does not fit this context because the information should be a new point that is related rather than more details like examples that expand on the original point.

25. **Level:** Medium | **Domain:** EXPRESSION OF IDEAS
    Skill/Knowledge: Transitions

    Key Explanation: Choice D is the best answer. The previous sentence describes how a story was viewed in 1841. The present tense in the following sentence shows that the sentence refers to the current time. **Choice D** correctly warns the reader that the time changes from the past to the present "now."

Distractor Explanation: Choice A is incorrect because it is used to show two things that happen at the same time, but the preceding and following sentences are in the past and present tense, respectively. Therefore, they do not occur simultaneously. **Choice B** is used to show that something happens despite something else. It does not fit the context because it is logical rather than unexpected that a very unusual piece of writing was the beginning of a genre. **Choice C** is used to show an alternative, so is not used to introduce two things that are both true.

26. **Level:** Hard | **Domain:** EXPRESSION OF IDEAS
    Skill/Knowledge: Rhetorical Synthesis

    Key Explanation: Choice D is the best answer. A "common concern" is a worry that people who know about geothermal energy might have. In this case, the worry is the "foul" or "bad" smell, and **Choice D** shows that the smell can be reduced with filters. In addition, **Choice D** highlights another benefit that might be a concern: the plants will also not emit carbon dioxide or other gasses and particles that lead to climate change.

    Distractor Explanation: Choice A is incorrect because the notes do not say how easy it is to select the proper location; the notes only say that some locations are not suitable. **Choice B** is incorrect because the audience already knows what geothermal energy is, so presumably, the information is not new. Furthermore, **Choice B** does not "address" or "answer" a concern or worry; it just explains how the power is generated. **Choice C** is incorrect because the notes do not say how long other power plants last; it is possible that the life cycles of geothermal plants are average or even shorter than other types of energy–producing plants.

27. **Level:** Medium | **Domain:** EXPRESSION OF
IDEAS
Skill/Knowledge: Rhetorical Synthesis

Key Explanation: Choice B is the best answer
because the question asks about the first ruler of
Egypt. **Choice B** provides the most information
about Narmer, including saying that he was the
first ruler. **Choice B** includes relevant details about
his unification of Upper and Lower Egypt and
the approximate time the unification and his rule
began.

Distractor Explanation: Choice A is incorrect
because it describes the first dynasty more than
the first ruler of the dynasty; it provides extra
information at the expense of details that would
add more about Narmer. **Choice C** is incorrect
because the notes do not directly state that
Narmer's tomb was made of these materials, only
that the materials were common for the time. It is
possible that Narmer's was one of the exceptions
made from stone. **Choice D** is incorrect because it
does not explain whether Narmer actually became
the first ruler, so it is unclear who the first ruler
was.

1. **Level:** Hard | **Domain:** CRAFT AND STRUCTURE
Skill/Knowledge: Words in Context

Key Explanation: Choice C is the best answer because it is a strong word that means "disreputable" or "offensive." "Obtrusive" refers to the "gentleman" that was following the girl, and **Choice C** clearly shows that the gentleman was not behaving properly as a gentleman should. **Choice C** conveys distinct contempt for the man's actions.

Distractor Explanation: None of the other choices shows that the narrator took great offense at the gentleman's behavior. **Choice A** means "clear" or "apparent." **Choice B** refers to something that is easy to see or that calls attention to itself. **Choice D** refers to something that is certain to Happen.

2. **Level:** Medium | **Domain:** CRAFT AND STRUCTURE
Skill/Knowledge: Words in Context

Key Explanation: Choice C is the best answer because in the context, the blank describes the understanding that governments and society need before ocean energy deployment takes place. **Choice C** refers to something that is solid and able to withstand outside pressures. It shows that the understanding needs to be complete and not easy to crumble when the pressure of arguments is brought against it.

Distractor Explanation: None of the other choices describe the understanding that governments and society need. **Choice A** refers to a living thing that is healthy and full of energy. **Choice B** refers to something that is physically able to withstand rough treatment. When used to describe something intangible, **Choice D** refers

to something that is strict or uncompromising. It refers to things such as rules rather than the way something is understood.

3. **Level:** Hard | **Domain:** CRAFT AND STRUCTURE
Skill/Knowledge: Words in Context

Key Explanation: Choice D is the best answer. In this context, "abstraction" refers to the "state" or "mood" that the donkey was in. The passage shows that he did not notice "the word of command" but instead "jogged onward" or "continued" because he was wondering whether he would get a cabbage stalk or not. **Choice D** refers to having one's attention focused on something, so fits the context of saying the donkey was paying attention to whether he would get food or not rather than listening to commands.

Distractor Explanation: Choice A is incorrect because it refers to making a judgment based on specific cases, but the donkey is not judging, nor is it making a final decision. **Choice B** refers to a working idea used as the basis for an experiment, but a "state" or "mood" is not a hypothesis. **Choice C** refers to a specific decision, but the donkey has not resolved to do anything, it is just wondering and jogging along.

4. **Level:** Hard | **Domain:** CRAFT AND STRUCTURE
Skill/Knowledge: Text Structure and Purpose

Key Explanation: Choice A is the best answer because "I shall not live in vain" can be paraphrased as "I would have fulfilled a useful purpose before dying." The repetition of this phrase shows that the author feels very strongly or seriously that she should do something useful before she dies, such as helping prevent a person from getting a broken heart or aiding a bird that has fallen from its nest.

Distractor Explanations: Choice B is incorrect because the author is not saying she is about to die, she is saying what she wants to accomplish before dying. **Choice C** is incorrect because the phrase highlights the importance of the tasks, but "futile" means "useless." **Choice D** is incorrect because there is no clue as to whether the author has "accomplished" or "completed" the things she mentions in the poem; she just stresses that they are important things to do.

5. **Level:** Medium | **Domain:** CRAFT AND STRUCTURE
   Skill/Knowledge: Text Structure and Purpose

   Key Explanation: Choice C is the best answer because the author expands on the quote by saying that veganism "has developed into a lifestyle" that incorporates other beliefs, such as animal or environmental activism and concern for physical activity. Therefore, the author is trying to say that the vegan diet includes factors or beliefs that are not solely related to a "diet" or "food."

   Distractor Explanation: Choices A and **B** are incorrect because, while concern for animals and environmental advocacy are often aspects of veganism, on their own, they are not the only reason for including a remark about becoming a vegan. **Choice D** is incorrect because the quote is not comparing vegans and non-vegans. It is broadening the scope of veganism to include aspects that create a lifestyle, not just the food a person eats.

6. **Level:** Medium | **Domain:** CRAFT AND STRUCTURE
   Skill/Knowledge: Cross–Text Connections

Key Explanation: Choice A is the best answer. The author of Text 2 refers to the difficulty of identifying objects that are not covered with ice because such objects do not reflect light. Therefore, the objects that have not been found might not have ice, and therefore, they are harder to see.

Distractor Explanation: Choice B is incorrect because the author of Text 2 does not refer to the size of the object in relation to how easy it is to isolate; it is possible that many large objects that are not covered with ice still have not been found. **Choice C** is incorrect because there is no discussion in Text 2 about the distance from the sun affecting whether it is easy to see objects or not. **Choice D** is incorrect because Text 2 implies that there are objects which have not been located, though there is no clue about how many objects there might be.

7. **Level:** Hard | **Domain:** INFORMATION AND IDEAS
   Skill/Knowledge: Cross–Text Connections

   Key Explanation: Choice C is the best answer because it describes the most likely way that Jane Addams (Text 2) would respond to Dix's actions to improve the conditions for the imprisoned and insane presented in Text 1. According to Text 1, Dix visited every public and private mental illness and prison facility she could to research and document in graphic detail the inhumane conditions, she then took political action and presented the information to legislature of Massachusetts which led to reform. Text 2 indicates that Addams was an advocate for social reform and dedicated her life to political action and social science research that would improve the lives of lower-class slums residents. This suggests that Addams would corroborate or support the methodology and actions used by Dix to achieve social reform.

Distractor Explanation: Choice A is incorrect because nothing in Text 2 suggests that Addams would dispute the effectiveness of research and documentation in achieving social reform. Text 2 confirms that Addams would support this type of action and she practiced it herself. **Choice B** is incorrect because Text 2 doesn't include any information suggesting that Addams placed greater significance on a personal lifetime commitment to social cause than using political action to achieve social reform. **Choice D** is incorrect because there's no information in Text 2 suggesting that Addams would contest or question the effectiveness of Dix's reports in achieving reform. Although Text 2 describes Addams's methodology more scientifically, it doesn't imply that Addams would be against shocking society into reformation using dramatic and emotional information.

8. **Level:** Medium | **Domain:** INFORMATION AND IDEAS
    Skill/Knowledge: Central Ideas and Details

    Key Explanation: Choice A is the best answer because a "controversy" is a "dispute." One point that clouds the debate of whether the state should be invited into the Union is that there are only twelve thousand residents within the state. If there were more, the proper decision might be easier. In Lincoln's words, "The amount of constituency, so to speak, on which the new Louisiana government rests, would be more satisfactory to all, if it contained fifty, thirty, or even twenty thousand, instead of only about twelve thousand, as it does."

    Distractor Explanation: None of the other choices are supported by evidence from the passage. **Choice B** is incorrect because the physical size of the state is not mentioned. As for population, the state is presumably smaller than others in the Union. **Choice C** is incorrect because

it is only established that freed slaves live in the state; no number or percentage is given. **Choice D** is incorrect because there is not enough evidence to determine what policies or laws the state uses.

9. **Level:** Hard | **Domain:** INFORMATION AND IDEAS
    Skill/Knowledge: Central Ideas and Details

    Key Explanation: Choice C is the best answer because the text says that "researchers had yet to sample vast areas, especially during stormy autumn and winter seasons," indicating that the results from the saildrone would fill in the missing information by taking samples during the winter.

    Distractor Explanation: Choice A is incorrect because the saildrone was not launched to prove a point about CO_2 absorption. It was to collect data in order to determine patterns in the times or places that had not previously been studied much. **Choice B** is incorrect because the saildrone was sent to collect data, not to "test limitations." Of course, researchers hoped that it would survive the harsh conditions and did not know if it would, but the main point of the journey was not to see if the saildrone would make it. **Choice D** is incorrect because the passage implies that it was already known that the Southern Ocean played a vital role. The details of that role were not known, so the winter launch was to determine certain details, not to see if it had a role at all.

10. **Level:** Easy | **Domain:** INFORMATION AND IDEAS
    Skill/Knowledge: Command of Evidence (Textual)

    Key Explanation: Choice A is the best answer because the unfinished sentence says that people who eat peanut butter "may have other health benefits." **Choice A** gives a very specific health

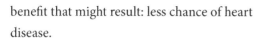

benefit that might result: less chance of heart disease.

Distractor Explanations: None of the other choices gives a specific example to show a health benefit of peanut butter. **Choice B** shows a potential problem: consuming too many calories. **Choice C** explains which types are better than others, but not why. **Choice D** offers serving suggestions but does not explain how nutritious the recipes are.

11. **Level:** Medium | **Domain:** INFORMATION AND IDEAS
    Skill/Knowledge: Command of Evidence (Quantitative)

    Key Explanation: The unfinished sentence is giving an example to illustrate the claim in the previous sentence that "it is incorrect to judge the number of dangerous encounters just by looking at deaths." Therefore, the mission portion should emphasize a point that extends beyond deaths caused by sharks. **Choice C** effectively stresses the point because it shows that there were many more dangerous encounters in the same year, so to estimate the number of attacks, **Choice C** shows that it is better to look at all attacks rather than just fatal ones.

    Distractor Explanations: None of the other choices offer a good example to show that "it is incorrect to judge the number of dangerous encounters just by looking at deaths." **Choice A** is very vague and the reader does not know if the number of non–fatal attacks is high or not. It could be almost identical to the number of deaths. **Choices B** and **D** only offer more detail about deaths, so they do not emphasize how looking at deaths gives an inaccurate idea of the number of dangerous encounters.

12. **Level:** Medium | **Domain:** INFORMATION AND IDEAS
    Skill/Knowledge: Command of Evidence (Quantitative)

    Key Explanation: Choice C is the best answer because the number of tourists in Togo in 2016 was 65,000. That number is lower than the one for Nigeria, 634,000, but higher than the number for Eritrea, 28,000.

    Distractor Explanation: Choice A is incorrect because, although Togo is the top row on the graph, it does not have the greatest number of tourists. That country is Nigeria in the bottom row, which had almost ten times as many visitors. **Choice B** is incorrect because the number for Togo is greater than that for Burundi, 56,000, but lower than that for Nigeria. **Choice D** is impossible to determine because the graph does not give the number of tourists for the previous year.

13. **Level:** Easy | **Domain:** INFORMATION AND IDEAS
    Skill/Knowledge: Inferences

    Key Explanation: Choice A is the best answer because the comment that "an opportunity… kept it" explain that Elinor, the oldest daughter, convinces Mrs. Dashwood to sell the carriage despite the fact that Mrs. Dashwood herself wanted to keep it. In addition, Elinor suggests that Mrs. Dashwood limit their household to three servants. Mrs. Dashwood "defers" or "agrees" to the opinions of her daughter despite some apparent reluctance.

    Distractor Explanation: Choice B is opposite of the relationship portrayed in the passage. **Choices C** and **D** are not supported by any evidence in the text.

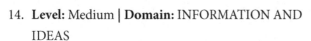

14. **Level:** Medium | **Domain:** INFORMATION AND IDEAS
Skill/Knowledge: Inferences

Key Explanation: Choice B is the best answer because the author warns the buyer to do research and be cautious about any purchase, since sales pitches are by definition, "trying to sell you something." For example, the sales claims may be higher than what an average person is able to earn. Therefore, the sellers are trying to "highlight" or "emphasize" the best possible aspects of the franchise so that you buy into the scheme.

Distractor Explanation: Choice A is incorrect because the author only warns that some claims may be elevated; there is no evidence that "most" are not realistic or tell the truth. **Choice C** is impossible to determine from the text because there is no discussion about laws that protect the seller. **Choice D** is incorrect because the author does not delve into the success or failure of a franchise. The author only indicates that an investor needs to do proper research.

15. **Level:** Easy | **Domain:** STANDARD ENGLISH CONVENTIONS
Skill/Knowledge: Form, Structure, and Sense

Key Explanation: Choice B is the best answer because it is used to introduce a clause that describes the previous person. In this case, it correctly shows that "Ernest Hemingway" was the person that "received the 1954 Nobel Prize for Literature."

Distractor Explanation: Choice A is incorrect because it creates a complete clause that is not subordinated in any way. An idea separated by commas in the middle of another clause must have a word showing how it relates to the other idea. **Choice C** is incorrect because it is used with

objects, not people. In addition, "that" is not used following a comma. **Choice D** is incorrect because it is a pronoun used to show the object of a verb, but the following clause needs a subject. That relationship can be clearly shown by substituting the proper noun into the blank: "Hemingway received the prize."

16. **Level:** Easy | **Domain:** STANDARD ENGLISH CONVENTIONS
Skill/Knowledge: Form, Structure, and Sense

Key Explanation: Choice B is the best answer. The underlined portion is part of a list joined by "and." Each part of such a list needs to have the same grammatical structure. In this case, the first two items are –ing verbs that show the method of the reduction following "by": "limiting… emissions," and "encouraging…innovation." **Choice B** is another –ing verb, so fits the same structure.

Distractor Explanation: All of the other choices can be eliminated because they do not maintain the same structure as the other two items in the list joined by "and." **Choice A** is a complete clause, "it is…." **Choices C** and **D** are noun phrases, "the right…" and "increased competition…."

17. **Level:** Easy | **Domain:** STANDARD ENGLISH CONVENTIONS
Skill/Knowledge: Form, Structure, and Sense

Key Explanation: Choice C is the best answer because it acts as a noun and is used to introduce a clause that describes the previous noun. In this case, **Choice C** shows that body temperature is what peaks in the early evening.

Distractor Explanation: Choice A is incorrect because it forms a comma splice between two

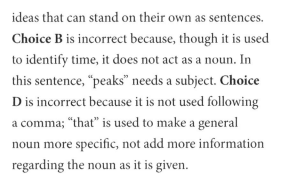

ideas that can stand on their own as sentences. **Choice B** is incorrect because, though it is used to identify time, it does not act as a noun. In this sentence, "peaks" needs a subject. **Choice D** is incorrect because it is not used following a comma; "that" is used to make a general noun more specific, not add more information regarding the noun as it is given.

18. **Level:** Easy | **Domain:** STANDARD ENGLISH CONVENTIONS
Skill/Knowledge: Form, Structure, and Sense

Key Explanation: Choice D is the best answer because the –ing form of a verb is used to create a noun phrase out of an action, and "known for" is a phrasal verb that needs to be followed by a noun.

Distractor Explanation: Choices A and **B** are incorrect because they are verb forms that are not used with "known for." **Choice C** is a noun, but in the sentence, the blank is followed by another noun, "classic Spanish forms." A noun should not be directly followed by another noun without some method of indicating how they are related to each other.

19. **Level:** Easy | **Domain:** STANDARD ENGLISH CONVENTIONS
Skill/Knowledge: Boundaries

Key Explanation: Choice A is the best answer. The information before and after the underlined portion form complete ideas, and can also stand as two complete sentences.

Distractor Explanation: Choice B is incorrect because it creates a comma splice between two independent clauses. One of the clauses needs to be subordinated with a transition word for a comma to be used. **Choice C** is incorrect because

both the portion before and the portion after a semicolon should be an independent clause. However, in this case, "and" subordinates the second half so that it cannot stand on its own. **Choice D** is incorrect because a single dash needs to follow a complete sentence, but the "and" in front of the dash is left hanging.

20. **Level:** Easy | **Domain:** STANDARD ENGLISH CONVENTIONS
Skill/Knowledge: Boundaries

Key Explanation: Choice B is the best answer. When three or more nouns are joined in a list using "and," there should be a comma after all the nouns that precede "and."

Distractor Explanation: All of the other choices can be eliminated because they are not standard punctuation for a list joined by "and." **Choice A** is incorrect because there is no punctuation at all to show where one noun ends and the other begins. **Choice C** is incorrect because there should be a comma after the noun "emotions" but none after "and." **Choice D** is incorrect because semicolons are only used to join items in a list if there are commas within the ideas, but each noun is a single word.

21. **Level:** Medium | **Domain:** STANDARD ENGLISH CONVENTIONS
Skill/Knowledge: Boundaries

Key Explanation: Choice A is the best answer. "a ring of massive stones erected around 2,500 B.C." is added information that describes "Stonehenge." Added information needs to be separated from the main clause "Stonehenge is one of…" using the same punctuation at both ends. In this case, the end punctuation after "2,500 B.C." is a dash, so the added information should also be preceded with a dash.

Distractor Explanation: Choice B is incorrect because the dash divides "of" from its object. The resulting main clause is illogical: Stonehenge, a ring of is one of…." **Choice B** is incorrect because the punctuation needs to be the same at the start and end of information inserted into a sentence's main clause. It is possible to use commas, but there should also be one after "2,500 B.C." In addition, a single dash needs to follow a complete clause, but there is no active verb in the first section. **Choice D** is incorrect because a colon needs to follow an independent clause, but the preceding portion is only a noun.

22. **Level:** Easy | **Domain:** EXPRESSION OF IDEAS
    Skill/Knowledge: Transitions

    Key Explanation: Choice D is the best answer. The previous information says that Joel did not care about finishing a high school degree, but the following says that he later went to the effort of obtaining it. **Choice D** fits that context because it is used to show that the following information happened despite the previous claim. In other words, he finished a degree despite saying he did not care about getting one.

    Distractor Explanation: Choices A and **C** are incorrect because they refer to the following happening as a certain or logical result of the previous claim. However, this text refers to something that happens unexpectedly; Joel got a degree although he said he did not want one. **Choice B** is incorrect because it signifies that the previous and following claims happen at the same time, but in this case, the events occur 25 years apart.

23. **Level:** Easy | **Domain:** EXPRESSION OF IDEAS
    Skill/Knowledge: Transitions

Key Explanation: Choice B is the best answer because it is used to show that something happens even though something else happens. In this case, **Choice B** accurately shows that the main idea of the sentence, not finding the cause of the shipwreck, occurred even though the first idea in the sentence, the fame of the ship, existed. In other words, even though the shipwreck was famous, no one knows why it sank.

Distractor Explanation: Choice A is incorrect because it offers the first idea as a reason for the second, but it is not necessarily reasonable that something very famous is still a mystery. **Choices C** and **D** are incorrect because they do not grammatically fit in the context. They act as separate linking words, so the result is that "its fame" becomes an appositive, but "its fame" is not another way of saying "the exact cause."

24. **Level:** Easy | **Domain:** EXPRESSION OF IDEAS
    Skill/Knowledge: Transitions

    Key Explanation: Choice A is the best answer. The previous portion points out the actions that certain organizations are taking for safety, and the following portion says those actions are "not sufficient" or "not good enough." **Choice A** is used to show a contrast of ideas, so accurately cues the reader that the following idea casts doubt on the first claim.

    Distractor Explanation: Choice B is incorrect because it is used to highlight a similarity, but the preceding and following ideas are opposite as far as ensuring safety for travel in space. **Choice C** is used to show a logical result of the preceding argument, but in this case, the idea that smaller items can cause damage is not a logical result of the previous discussion that steps are taken for safety reasons. **Choice D** is used to show another possibility or choice, so does not fit the context

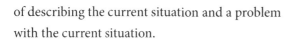

of describing the current situation and a problem with the current situation.

25. **Level:** Medium | **Domain:** EXPRESSION OF IDEAS
Skill/Knowledge: Rhetorical Synthesis

Key Explanation: Choice C is the best answer because the notes say that saltwater tanks can only have a 2–degree Celsius variation, but freshwater tanks can have 8 degrees in variation. Therefore, the range for saltwater tanks is much lower than for freshwater tanks.

Distractor Explanation: Choice A is incorrect because it highlights a similarity rather than a "key difference" between the care of the two types of fish. **Choice B** is incorrect because the passage does not say that freshwater fish "need" or "must" be kept in tanks with plants; it only says that they are frequently kept in such tanks. Furthermore, there is no discussion whether saltwater fish can be kept with plants or not. **Choice D** is incorrect because it only mentions two things from the passage which are not necessarily related to each other and are not opposite in any way; therefore, it does not highlight a crucial difference.

26. **Level:** Medium | **Domain:** EXPRESSION OF IDEAS
Skill/Knowledge: Rhetorical Synthesis

Key Explanation: Choice C is the best answer. The audience is concerned about improving innovation, and **Choice C** directly "addresses" or "responds to" that question by offering a solution based on Mayo's theory: giving workers more freedom.

Distractor Explanation: Choice A is incorrect because it only discusses why innovation does not occur; it does not offer any solutions for increasing

innovation or solving the problem of boredom. **Choice B** is incorrect because it does not show how Mayo's theory affects innovation; it points out a way to get tasks done, but not necessarily in a creative way. Furthermore, it points out a problem that could negate any benefits of the theory. **Choice D** is extremely vague; it says that there are positive points regarding innovation, but the audience does not know what these positive points are. The negative aspect of stress may not outweigh the benefits as far as the audience is concerned; the audience does not have enough information to make a clear judgment.

27. **Level:** Medium | **Domain:** EXPRESSION OF IDEAS
Skill/Knowledge: Rhetorical Synthesis

Key Explanation: Choice D is the best answer because the temperature highs are compared so the reader can see that there is at least a 12–degree difference between the high extremes, which implies a generally large difference between average temperatures at the two poles.

Distractor Explanation: Choice A is incorrect because the temperatures of the North Pole are not given in the notes, so it is possible that the temperatures are just as extreme, though at a higher overall range if the highs are above freezing. **Choice A** does not offer the reader any idea of what the temperatures at the North Pole really are for comparison. For a hypothetical example based on **Choice A**, temperatures at the North Pole could be of a less extreme range, but colder, from –90 to –85 C. **Choice B** is incorrect because it emphasizes a similarity rather than a difference between the places. **Choice C** is incorrect because it does not show how the places are different; the scientists could have studied continental drift from a boat and both locations are in the ocean.

This page is intentionally left blank

1. **Level:** Medium | **Domain:** ADVANCED MATH
   Skill/Knowledge: Nonlinear functions | **Testing point:** Determining the equation of a parabola from its graph

   Key Explanation: Choice C is correct. The general equation of a parabola is given by $y = a(x - h)^2 + k$ where (h, k) is the vertex. Based on the graph, the vertex of the parabola is at $(-1, -6)$. Substituting the coordinate of the vertex to the general equation yields $y = a(x + 1)^2 - 6$. Since the graph opens upward, the leading coefficient is greater than zero. This means that a is positive and based on the choices, a is equal to 3. Substituting 3 to the equation of the parabola yields $y = 3(x + 1)^2 - 6$. Expanding the right side of the equation yields $y = 3x^2 + 6x - 3$.

   Distractor Explanations: Choice A is incorrect and may result from an error in expanding the equation of the parabola. **Choices B** and **D** are incorrect because a is negative, which means that the graph opens downward.

2. **Level:** Easy | **Domain:** ADVANCED MATH
   Skill/Knowledge: Nonlinear functions | **Testing point:** Determining the products of the solutions to a quadratic equation

   Key Explanation: To find the product of the solutions, use the formula $\left(\dfrac{c}{a}\right)$, where a is the coefficient of x^2 and c is the constant. From the given equation $a = 3$ and $c = -15$. Therefore, the product of the solutions is $\left(\dfrac{-15}{3}\right)$, which is equal to -5.

3. **Level:** Medium | **Domain:** PROBLEM-SOLVING AND DATA ANALYSIS
   Skill/Knowledge: Probability and conditional probability | **Testing point:** Calculating probability of simple events

   Key Explanation: Choice C is correct. The probability of a simple event occurring can be calculated using the formula
   $$p = \frac{no.\ of\ favorable\ outcomes}{total\ no.\ of\ possible\ outcomes}.$$ Since a heart is picked at first and is not put back in the deck, there are only 12 hearts left in a deck of now 51 cards. The probability of picking a heart card for the second time would then, therefore, be $\dfrac{12}{51}$, which is 12 heart cards out of the 51 cards on the deck.

   Distractor Explanations: Choice A is incorrect. This would be the probability of picking the first heart from the deck of 52 cards. **Choice B** is incorrect and may result from not subtracting the first card picked from the initial total number of cards. **Choice D** is incorrect because it represents the probability of not picking a second heart.

4. **Level:** Easy | **Domain:** ADVANCED MATH
   Skill/Knowledge: Equivalent expressions | **Testing point:** Matching coefficients

   Key Explanation: Choice B is correct. To solve this, use the distributive property which yields $6xy^2 + 18x^2y - 6x^2y - 2xy^2$. Combining like terms yields $4xy^2 + 12x^2y$.

   Distractor Explanations: Choices A, C, and **D** are incorrect and may result from a conceptual or calculation error.

5. **Level:** Easy | **Domain:** PROBLEM-SOLVING AND DATA ANALYSIS

Skill/Knowledge: Percentages | **Testing point:** Using discounts and percentage increase

Key Explanation: Since the price of the dress first increases by 15%, then it becomes $115\% \times 200 = 230$. Therefore, the price after 15th May is $230. However, she bought it at a discounted price. Applying the discount, the amount that she paid for the dress is $70\% \times 230 = \$161$.

6. **Level:** Easy | **Domain:** ADVANCED MATH

Skill/Knowledge: Nonlinear equations in one variable and systems of equations in two variables

Testing point: Using the difference of two squares to solve a system of equations

Key Explanation: Choice A is correct. The first equation contains the difference of two squares which is in the form of $a^2 - b^2$. This can be factored into $(a + b)(a - b)$.

Therefore,

$(x - y)(x + y) = x^2 - y^2$.

The first equation then becomes $(x - y)(x + y) = 12$. Substituting the value of $(x - y)$ from the second equation into the first equation yields $2(x + y) = 12$.

Dividing both sides of the equation by 2 yields $(x + y) = 6$.

Distractor Explanations: Choice B is incorrect and may result from solving the value of x. **Choice C** is incorrect and may result from solving the value of y. **Choice D** is incorrect and may result from solving the value of $y - x$.

7. **Level:** Medium | **Domain:** ALGEBRA

Skill/Knowledge: Systems of two linear equations in two variables | **Testing point:** Solving system of linear equations for x and y

Key Explanation: Choice A is correct. Solve for the value of x and y by using the elimination method.

Multiplying to the first equation yields $3(2x + y = 2)$ or $6x + 3y = 6$.

Subtracting the second equation from the first equation yields $6x + 3y - 3y + x = 6 - 20$.

Combining like terms yields $7x = -14$. Dividing both sides of the equation by 7 yields $x = -2$. To find y, replace x with the value -2 in the first equation.

This yields $6(-2) + 3y = 6$ or $-12 + 3y = 6$.

Adding 12 to both sides of the equation yields $3y = 18$.

Dividing both sides of the equation by 3 yields $y = 6$.

The value of $xy = (-2)(6) = -12$.

Distractor Explanations: Choices B and **C** are incorrect because these are the values of x and y respectively. **Choice D** is incorrect because it would be the value of $\frac{y}{x}$.

8. **Level:** Medium | **Domain:** ADVANCED MATH

Skill/Knowledge: Nonlinear equations in one variable and systems of equations in two variables

Testing point: Solving absolute value equations

Key Explanation: Isolate the absolute value by dividing both sides of the equation by 2.

This yields $\frac{2|x+4|}{2} = \frac{12}{2}$ or $|x + 4| = 6$.

Solve the values of x by equating the content of the absolute value to the positive and negative values of the constant.

Determine the first value of x using $x + 4 = 6$. Subtracting 4 from both sides of the equation yields $x = 2$.

Determine the second value of x using $x + 4 = -6$. Subtracting 4 from both sides of the equation yields $x = -10$.

Since the problem only requires the positive value of x, the answer is 2.

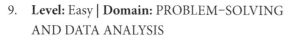

9. **Level:** Easy | **Domain:** PROBLEM-SOLVING AND DATA ANALYSIS
Skill/Knowledge: One-variable data: distributions and measures of center and spread
Testing point: Evaluating and comparing measures of center and spread

Key Explanation: Choice B is correct. The data being added would be an outlier on the higher end of the data set. The add-on changes the maximum of the data set and this would mean that the range would increase. The outlier would also increase the mean. The median will remain the same and will still be 1.39 because it is the 7th number in the new set of data. The standard deviation will increase as the data point is an outlier.

Distractor Explanations: Choices A, C, and **D** are incorrect. They are false statements.

10. **Level:** Medium | **Domain:** GEOMETRY AND TRIGONOMETRY
Skill/Knowledge: Area and volume | **Testing point:** Area of a circle in an inscribed polygon

Key Explanation: Choice B is correct. Since the circle is inscribed in a square, the side length of the square is equivalent to the diameter of the circle. Therefore, if the diameter is 14cm, the radius would be half, which is 7cm. The area would therefore be $7^2\pi$ or 49π.

Distractor Explanations: Choice A is incorrect. It is the area of a circle if the radius is 14cm. **Choice C** is incorrect because this is the circumference of the circle. **Choice D** is incorrect because this is twice the value of the circle's area.

11. **Level:** Hard | **Domain:** ALGEBRA
Skill/Knowledge: Linear functions | **Testing point:** Using linear transformations

Key Explanation: The function $f(x)$ translated 2 units to the left will become $f(x + 2)$.
This yields $y = 3(x + 2) + 5$ or $y = 3x + 11$.
The function $f(x)$ translated 1 unit up will become $f(x) + 1$.
This yields $y = 3x + 11 + 1$ or $y = 3x + 12$.
Therefore, the new y-intercept is 12.

12. **Level:** Medium | **Domain:** ALGEBRA
Skill/Knowledge: Linear inequalities in one or two variables | **Testing point:** Finding the solutions to an inequality

Key Explanation: Choice D is correct. To find the solution, substitute the choices for each inequality and verify if the statements are true or false.
Plugging in **Choice D** (3, 1) to the first inequality yields $(-2)(1) > -4$ or $2 > -4$ which is true.
Plugging (3, 1) into the second inequality yields $3(3) - 1 > 3$ or $5 > 3$ which is also true.
Since both statements are true when the point (3, 1) is plugged into both inequalities, then the correct answer is **Choice D**.

Distractor Explanations: Choice A is incorrect. Plugging in (1, 2) to both inequalities yields $-4 > -4$ and $1 > 3$ which are both false statements.
Choice B is incorrect. Plugging in (1, 3) to both inequalities yields $-6 > -4$ and $0 > 3$ which are both false statements.
Choice C is incorrect. Plugging in (2, 4) to both inequalities yields $-8 > -4$ and $2 > 3$ which are both false statements.

13. **Level:** Medium | **Domain:** GEOMETRY AND TRIGONOMETRY
Skill/Knowledge: Circles | **Testing point:** Using the midpoint formula and the equation of a circle

Key Explanation: Choice B is correct. The standard equation of a circle is given by $(x - h)^2 + (y - k)^2 = r^2$ where (h, k) is the center and r is the radius. The endpoints of the circle are $(-6, 10)$ and $(2, 10)$. The midpoint of these two points would be $\left(\dfrac{-6+2}{2}, \dfrac{10+10}{2} \right) = (-2, 10)$ which is also the coordinates of the center of the circle. The radius of the circle can be solved by calculating the distance between the center and one of the endpoints of the diameter. Substituting $(2, 10)$ and $(-2, 10)$ to the formula $\sqrt{\left(y_2 - y_1\right)^2 + \left(x_1 - x_2\right)^2}$ yields

$\sqrt{\left(10-10\right)^2 + \left(-2-2\right)^2} = 4$

4 would therefore be the radius.
Plugging in the coordinates of the center and the radius to the standard equation yields $(x + 2)^2 + (y - 10)^2 = 16$.

Distractor Explanations: Choices A, C, and D are incorrect and may result due to conceptual errors such as identifying the center from the equation of the circle.

14. **Level:** Medium | **Domain:** ALGEBRA
    Skill/Knowledge: Linear functions | **Testing point:** Finding the value of a composite function

    Key Explanation: Choice C is correct. To solve this, calculate for $g(2)$ first.
    Substituting 2 to $g(x)$ yields $g(2) = 2(2) + 3$ or $g(2) = 4 + 3$.
    Combining like terms yields $g(2) = 7$.
    Since $g(2) = 7$, then $f(g(2)) = f(7)$.
    Substituting 7 yields $f(7) = 7 + 2$ or $f(7) = 9$.

    Distractor Explanations: Choice A is incorrect because this is the value of $g(2)$. **Choice B** is incorrect because this is the value of $f(2)$. **Choice D** is incorrect because this would be the value of $g(f(2))$.

15. **Level:** Medium | **Domain:** ADVANCED MATH
    Skill/Knowledge: Nonlinear functions | **Testing point:** Solving for the *y–intercept* in a nonlinear function

    Key Explanation: The *y–intercept* is when $x = 0$. Substituting 0 for x in the given equation yields
    $y = 300^0 + 5$.
    Any number raised to the power of 0 is equal to 1. The equation becomes, $y = 1 + 5$ or $y = 6$.
    Therefore, the *y–intercept* is 6.

16. **Level:** Easy | **Domain:** ALGEBRA
    Skill/Knowledge: Linear inequalities in one or two variables | **Testing point:** Finding the equation of an inequality from its graph

    Key Explanation: Choice B is correct. The solutions to the inequality are above the line which would mean that the y values are greater. This means that the equation will be in the form of $y > mx + b$. Hence, the possible answer is either **choice A** or **B**. Since the dash line falls down from left to right, the value of the *slope(m)* is negative. Between **Choices A** and **B**, only **Choice A** has a negative slope. Therefore, the graph represents the inequality $y > -2x + 3$.

    Distractor Explanations: Choice A is incorrect because it has a positive slope. **Choices C** and **D** are incorrect because they both use less than symbols for the inequalities.

17. **Level:** Easy | **Domain:** ADVANCED MATH
    Skill/Knowledge: Nonlinear functions | **Testing point:** Finding exponential functions from graphs

    Key Explanation: Choice C is correct. Since the graph rises from left to right, it is an exponential growth function in the form of $f(x) = a(1 + r)^x$ where a is the initial amount, r is the growth rate, and x is the number of time intervals. Since the graph represents an exponential growth function, $(1 + r) > 1$. Hence, the possible answers are **Choices A** or **C** because $1.03 > 1$. To determine the correct answer between **Choice A** and **C**, find the value of a. Looking at the graph, it intersects at $(0, 180)$ which means that the *y-intercept* is 180. Thus, the initial amount is 180 or $a = 180$. Therefore, the correct answer is **Choice C.**

Distractor Explanations: Choices A and **D** are incorrect. They both have *y-intercepts* greater than 180. **Choice B** is incorrect. It represents a decaying exponential function.

18. **Level:** Easy | **Domain:** ALGEBRA
Skill/Knowledge: Linear equations in two variables | **Testing point:** Matching coefficients

Key Explanation: Choice D is correct. To solve this, use the distributive property to simplify the left side of the equation.
This yields $3x + 2x + 8y = ax + by$.
Combining like terms yields $5x + 8y = ax + by$.
Matching the coefficients yields $a = 5$.

Distractor Explanations: Choices A, **B**, and **C** are incorrect and may result from a conceptual or calculation error.

19. **Level:** Easy | **Domain:** ALGEBRA
Skill/Knowledge: Linear inequalities in one or two variables | **Testing point:** Writing the solution of an inequality in interval notation

Key Explanation: To solve for this inequality, divide both sides by –3 which yields $\frac{-3y}{-3} > \frac{-15}{-3}$ or $y < 5$. Since y can be any number less than 5, its value approaches negative infinity. Therefore, the interval notation is $(-\infty, 5)$.

20. **Level:** Easy | **Domain:** GEOMETRY AND TRIGONOMETRY
Skill/Knowledge: Right triangles and trigonometry | **Testing point:** Using trigonometric identities

Key Explanation: Choice B is correct. Since $sin(3x) = cos(x + 10)$, the two angles $(3x)$ and $(x + 10)$ are complementary and add up to 90°.
Therefore, $(3x) + (x + 10) = 90$.
Combining like terms yields $4x + 10 = 90$.
Subtracting 10 from both sides of the equation yields $4x = 80$.
Dividing both sides of the equation by 4 yields $x = 20°$.

Distractor Explanations: Choice A is incorrect and may result from a conceptual or calculation error. **Choice C** is incorrect and may result from solving the value of $(x + 10)$. **Choice D** is incorrect and may result from solving the value of $3x$.

21. **Level:** Easy | **Domain:** ADVANCED MATH
Skill/Knowledge: Nonlinear functions | **Testing point:** Determining the type of equation from data given

Key Explanation: Choice A is correct. Since Amanda doubles the amount of money she will save every week, the amount that she puts in every week grows exponentially. This exponential growth can be represented by the *model* $s = \$10(2)^t$, where t is time in weeks and s is the amount that she will save in the given week.

Distractor Explanation: Choices B and **D** are incorrect. The function is exponential and not linear. **Choice C** is incorrect. The amount she saves per week increases exponentially and does not decrease.

22. **Level:** Easy | **Domain:** ALGEBRA

    Skill/Knowledge: Linear equations in one variable

    Testing point: Solving for x in a linear equation

    Key Explanation: Choice B is correct. The value of x can be solved by subtracting 8 from both sides which yields $4x + 8 - 8 = 24 - 8$ or $4x = 16$. Dividing both sides of the equation by 4 yields $x = 4$.

    Distractor Explanations: Choices A, **C**, and **D** are incorrect and may result from a conceptual or calculation error.

1. **Level:** Easy | **Domain:** ALGEBRA
   Skill/Knowledge: Linear equations in one variable
   Testing point: Solving for x in a linear equation

   Key Explanation: Choice B is correct. To solve for this, start by factoring out the 7 which yields $7(x + 4) = 112$. Then divide both sides of the equation by 7 which yields $(x + 4) = \dfrac{112}{7}$ or $x + 4 = 16$.

   Distractor Explanations: Choice A is incorrect and may result from solving the value of x when $x + 4 = 0$. **Choice C** is incorrect and may result from a miscalculation or conceptual error. **Choice D** is incorrect and may result from only solving for the value of x.

2. **Level:** Medium | **Domain:** GEOMETRY AND TRIGONOMETRY
   Skill/Knowledge: Area and volume | **Testing point:** Using ratios similar figures

   Key Explanation: The ratio of the radius of the ball to that of the prototype is 3 : 1. Since the volume of a sphere is directly proportional to the cube of its radius $(V \propto r^3)$, the ratio of their volumes should be $3^3 : 1^3$ or 27 : 1. And given that the volume of the prototype is $10cm^3$, the volume of the ball will be $27 \times 10 = 270cm^3$.

3. **Level:** Easy | **Domain:** ADVANCED MATH
   Skill/Knowledge: Nonlinear equations in one variable and systems of equations in two variables
   Testing point: Using the discriminant to find the number of solutions of a quadratic equation

   Key Explanation: Choice A is correct. A quadratic with one solution has a discriminant equal to 0 which means $b^2 - 4ac = 0$.

To get the values of a, b, and c, equate the two equations which yield $2x + k = x^2 - 10x + 30$. Subtracting $2x$ and k from both sides of the equation yields $0 = x^2 - 12x + 30 - k$. This means that $a = 1$, $b = -12$, and $c = 30 - k$.

Substituting the values of a, b, and c to the discriminant yields $(-12)^2 - 4(1)(30 - k) = 0$.
Using the distributive property yields $144 - 120 + 4k = 0$.
Combining like terms yields $24 + 4k = 0$.
Subtracting 24 from both sides of the equation yields $4k = -24$.
Dividing both sides of the equation by 4 yields $k = -6$.

Distractor Explanations: Choices B and **D** are incorrect and could be a result of miscalculation or conceptual error. **Choice C** is incorrect because this is the negative value of k.

4. **Level:** Hard | **Domain:** ADVANCED MATH
   Skill/Knowledge: Nonlinear equations in one variable and systems of equations in two variables
   Testing point: Using exponent rules

   Key Explanation: Choice D is correct.
   To solve for this, equate the exponents by making the bases the same. Since 9, 27 and 81 are multiples of 3, then every base will be converted to 3. This yields $9 = 3^2$, $27 = 3^3$, and $81 = 3^4$. Hence the equation will now become $\dfrac{3^{3(x-1)}}{3^{4y}} = 3^2$ or

   $\dfrac{3^{3x-3}}{3^{4y}} = 3^2$.

   Since the terms on the left side of the equation are being divided, the exponents will be subtracted. This yields $3^{3x-3-4y} = 3^2$. Equating the exponents yields $3x - 3 - 4y = 2$. Adding 3 to both sides of the equation yields $3x - 4y = 5$. To find the value of $6x - 8y$, multiply both sides of the equation by

2 which yields $2(3x - 4y) = 2(5)$.
Using the distributive property yields $6x - 8y = 10$.

Distractor Explanations: Choice A is incorrect and may result from solving the value of $\dfrac{6x - 8y}{5}$.
Choice B is incorrect and may result from solving the value of $3x - 4y$. **Choice C** is incorrect and may result from solving the value of $\dfrac{2(6x - 8y)}{5}$.

5. **Level:** Medium | **Domain:** GEOMETRY AND TRIGONOMETRY
Skill/Knowledge: Right triangles and trigonometry | **Testing point:** Using the pythagorean theorem

Key Explanation: The sides of a square are equal. Therefore, if the sides are s, then the diagonal will be $s\sqrt{2}$, which can be proven using the Pythagorean theorem $a^2 + b^2 = c^2$. Since $s\sqrt{2} = 16\sqrt{2}$, then $s = 16$. The perimeter of a square can be found by $4s$ which is $4(16) = 64$.

6. **Level:** Easy | **Domain:** ALGEBRA
Skill/Knowledge: Linear functions | **Testing point:** Matching a linear equation to its graph

Key Explanation: Choice C is correct. Rewrite the given equation into slope–intercept form of $y = mx + b$ where m is the slope of the line and b is the y-intercept.
Subtracting $12x$ from both sides of the equation yields $4y = -12x + 8$.
Dividing both sides of the equation by 4 yields $y = -3x + 2$. Thus, the slope of the line is -3 and a y-intercept of 2. Since the slope is negative, the graph goes down from left to right. Hence, the answer can only be **choice C** or **D**. To determine the correct answer between the two choices, solve for the x-intercept by substituting 0 to y in the

equation. This yields $0 = -3x + 2$. Adding $3x$ to both sides of the equation yields $3x = 2$. Dividing 3 from both sides of the equation yields $x = \dfrac{2}{3}$.
Since **choice C** is the only graph that has a y-intercept of 2, an x-intercept of $\dfrac{2}{3}$, and a negative slope, it is the correct answer.

Distractor Explanations: Choices A and **B** are incorrect because they both represent a linear equation with a positive slope. **Choice D** is incorrect because it has an x-intercept of 6.

7. **Level:** Easy | **Domain:** ALGEBRA
Skill/Knowledge: Systems of two linear equations in two variables | **Testing point:** Working with parallel lines and linear systems with no solution

Key Explanation: To have no solutions means that the lines are parallel and have the same slope. The slope of the first linear equation is $\dfrac{3}{2}$. Since p represents the slope of the second equation, then $p = \dfrac{3}{2}$ which makes both lines parallel.

8. **Level:** Hard | **Domain:** ADVANCED MATH
Skill/Knowledge: Nonlinear functions | **Testing point:** Using exponential growth equation

Key Explanation: Choice C is correct. The original equation requires t in years. Since a year has 12 months, then $\dfrac{m}{12} = t$. This can be best represented by the model in C.

Distractor Explanations: Choices A, **B**, and **D** are incorrect and may result from a conceptual error.

9. **Level:** Medium | **Domain:** ADVANCED MATH

Skill/Knowledge: Equivalent expressions

Testing point: Rewriting the equation and solving for the variable

Key Explanation: Choice A is correct. Solve for A by isolating it and then simplifying the equation. Subtracting $\dfrac{7}{x-3}$ from both sides of the equation yields $\dfrac{-2x^2+5x+10}{x-3} - \dfrac{7}{x-3} = A$

or $\dfrac{-2x^2+5x+3}{x-3} = A$. Factoring the numerator on the left side of the equation yields

$\dfrac{(-2x-1)(x-3)}{x-3} = A$. Canceling out $(x-3)$ yields

$-2x - 1 = A$ or $A = -2x - 1$.

Distractor Explanations: Choice B is incorrect and may result due to calculation errors. **Choice C** is incorrect and may result from solving the value of $-A$. **Choice D** is incorrect. This would be the difference between $-2x^2 + 5x + 10$ and $x - 3$.

10. **Level:** Easy | **Domain:** ALGEBRA
    Skill/Knowledge: Systems of two linear equations in two variables | **Testing point:** Solving the system of linear equations

    Key Explanation: Choice B is correct. Solve the system of equations by solving for y in the first equation and substituting it to the second equation.
    Dividing both sides of the first equation by -5

    yields $-\dfrac{3}{5}x = y$.

    Substituting y to the second equation yields

    $2x + 3(-\dfrac{3}{5}x) = -1$ or $2x - \dfrac{9}{5}x = -1$.

    Combining like terms yields $\dfrac{1}{5}x = -1$.
    Multiplying 5 to both sides of the equation yields

$x = -5$.

Distractor Explanations: Choice A is incorrect. This is the value of y. **Choices C** and **D** are incorrect and may result due to a calculation or conceptual error.

11. **Level:** Hard | **Domain:** ADVANCED MATH
    Skill/Knowledge: Nonlinear equations in one variable and systems of equations in two variables
    Testing point: Using the discriminant to find the number of solutions to a quadratic equation.

    Key Explanation: For a quadratic equation to have two distinct solutions, the discriminant $b^2 - 4ac$ must be positive. In the given equation, $a = 4$, $b = -12$, and $c = k$.
    Substituting the values of a, b and c to get the discriminant yields $(-12)^2 - 4(4)(k)$ or $144 - 16k$. Since the discriminant must be positive, it must be greater than zero which is represented by $144 - 16k > 0$.
    Adding $16k$ to both sides of the inequality yields $144 > 16k$.
    Dividing 16 from both sides of the inequality yields $9 > k$ or $k < 9$.
    The next integer number lower than 9 is 8.
    Therefore, the correct answer is 8.

12. **Level:** Easy | **Domain:** ALGEBRA
    Skill/Knowledge: Linear equations in one variable
    Testing point: Finding the solutions to a linear equation

    Key Explanation: Choice A is correct. Using the distributive property to simplify the equation yields $3x + 18 + x = 4x + 5$ or $4x + 18 = 4x + 5$.
    Subtracting $4x$ from both sides of the equation yields $18 = 5$ or $13 = 0$ which is a false statement.

This implies that there is no solution.

Distractor Explanations: Choice B is incorrect. For a linear equation to have one solution, the value of the variable can be solved. **Choice C** is incorrect. Linear systems do not have 2 solutions. **Choice D** is incorrect. For a linear system to have infinite solutions, the simplified equation must be a true statement.

13. **Level:** Hard | **Domain:** ADVANCED MATH
    Skill/Knowledge: Equivalent expressions
    Testing point: Adding rational expressions with fractions

    Key Explanation: Choice A is correct.
    Simplify the denominator first.

    This yields $\dfrac{1}{x-2} + \dfrac{1}{x+2} = \dfrac{x+2+x-2}{x^2-4} = \dfrac{2x}{x^2-4}$

    Simplifying the whole fraction yields

    $\dfrac{1}{\frac{2x}{x^2-4}} = \dfrac{x^2-4}{2x}$

    Distractor Explanations: Choice B is incorrect and may result from an error in adding the contents in the denominator x. **Choice C** is incorrect because it is only the simplified denominator, not the whole fraction. **Choice D** is incorrect and may result from miscalculation or conceptual errors.

14. **Level:** Hard | **Domain:** GEOMETRY AND TRIGONOMETRY
    Skill/Knowledge: Circles
    Testing point: Using circle theorems and converting degrees to radians

    Key Explanation: Choice C is correct. The measure of a circumscribed angle and its

corresponding central angle are supplementary. Hence, $\angle$ PSR + $\angle$ PQR = 180°.
Substituting the value of the central angle $\angle$ PSR yields 80° + $\angle$ PQR = 180°.
Subtracting 80° from both sides of the equation yields $\angle$ PQR = 100°.
Converting the value of $\angle$ PQR to radians yields
$100° \times \dfrac{\pi}{180°} = \dfrac{5}{9}\pi$. Since $\angle$ PQR = $a\pi$, then $a = \dfrac{5}{9}$.

Distractor Explanations: Choices A, B, and **D** are incorrect and may result from a conceptual or calculation error.

15. **Level:** Easy | **Domain:** GEOMETRY AND TRIGONOMETRY
    Skill/Knowledge: Circles | **Testing point:** Finding the area of a circle given its circumference

    Key Explanation: The circumference of a circle is found by the formula πD where D is the diameter of the circle. Since the circumference is 12π then $D = 12$. The radius is therefore 6, and the area of the circle is $\pi r^2 = \pi(6)^2 = 36\pi$.

16. **Level:** Easy | **Domain:** ADVANCED MATH
    Skill/Knowledge: Equivalent expressions
    Testing point: Converting from exponents to radicals

    Key Explanation: Choice D is correct. Expressing the radical as exponent yields $3p^{\frac{1}{3}}p^{\frac{1}{2}}$. Since the same variables are being multiplied, their exponents will be added.

    Hence, $\dfrac{1}{3} + \dfrac{1}{2} = \dfrac{5}{6}$.

    The expression now becomes $3p^{\frac{5}{6}}$. Converting the exponent back to radical yields $3\sqrt[6]{p^5}$.

Distractor Explanations: Choices A, B, and **C** are incorrect and may result from a conceptual or calculation error.

17. **Level:** Easy | **Domain:** GEOMETRY AND TRIGONOMETRY
    Skill/Knowledge: Area and volume | **Testing point:** Finding the volume of a cylinder

    Key Explanation: Choice B is correct. The volume of a cylinder is found using the formula $V = \pi r^2 h$ where r is the radius and h is the height. Substituting the given radius and height to the formula yields $V = \pi 9^2 6 = 486\pi$.

    Distractor Explanations: Choice A is incorrect and may result from solving the surface area of the cylinder. **Choice C** is incorrect and may result from solving the area of one base of the cylinder. **Choice D** is incorrect and may result from solving the lateral area of the cylinder.

18. **Level:** Hard | **Domain:** ALGEBRA
    Skill/Knowledge: Linear equations in two variables | **Testing point:** Working with parallel lines and their equations

    Key Explanation: Choice A is correct. For lines to be parallel, they must have proportional coefficients of x and y. To make the coefficients of x to be the same, multiply the first equation by –2. This yields $-2(3x + 5y = 6)$ or $-6x - 10y = -12$. Matching the coefficients of y in $-6x - 10y = -12$ and $-6x + py = 18$ yields $p = -10$.

    Distractor Explanations: Choices B and **D** are

incorrect and may result from a conceptual or calculation error. **Choice C** is incorrect. It is the negative of option A.

19. **Level:** Easy | **Domain:** ADVANCED MATH
    Skill/Knowledge: Equivalent expressions
    Testing point: Matching coefficients

    Key Explanation: Using the distributive property, the left side of the equation becomes $15x^2y + 6xy + 6xy - 2y$. Combining like terms yields $15x^2y + 12xy - 2y = ax^2y + bxy + cy$. Matching the coefficients yields $a = 15$, $b = 12$, and $c = -2$. Therefore, b is equal to 12.

20. **Level :** Easy | **Domain:** ADVANCED MATH
    Skill/Knowledge: Nonlinear equations in one variable and systems of equations in two variables
    Testing point: Finding the number of solutions of an absolute value equation

    Key Explanation: Choice C is correct. Isolating the absolute value and simplifying the equation yields $|x + 4| = \dfrac{-8}{-2}$ or $|x + 4| = 4$. Since the absolute value is being compared with a positive number, it has two solutions.

    Distractor Explanations: Choice A is incorrect. For an absolute value to have 0 or no solution, the absolute value should be less than or equal to a negative number. **Choice B** is incorrect. For an absolute value to have 1 solution, it should be equal to zero. **Choice D** is incorrect. For an absolute value to have infinite solutions, it should be greater than a negative number.

21. **Level:** Easy | **Domain:** ADVANCED MATH

Skill/Knowledge: Nonlinear equations in one variable and systems of equations in two variables
Testing point: Using exponent rules and FOILing method to find value of quadratic expression

Key Explanation: Choice B is correct. Expanding the expression $(x + y)^2$ yields $x^2 + 2xy + y^2$.
Since $x^2 + y^2 = 45$, the expression becomes $45 + 2xy$.
Since $xy = 5$, the expression becomes $45 + 2(5)$ or 55.
Therefore, $(x + y)^2 = 55$.

Distractor Explanations:Choice A is incorrect and may result from solving the value of $\dfrac{x^2 + y^2}{xy}$.

Choice C is incorrect and may result from solving the value of $2(x + y)^2$.
Choice D is incorrect and may result from solving the value of $(x - y)^2$.

22. **Level:** Easy | **Domain:** PROBLEM–SOLVING AND DATA ANALYTICS
    Skills/Knowledge: Inference from sample statistics and margin of error | **Testing Point:** Inferring from a sample to a population

    Key Explanation: Choice C is correct. From the data surveyed, $1,200 - 950 = 250$ residents own a different type of pet. We can infer that

    $$\frac{250}{1,200} \times 62,500 = 13,020$$ residents in the town own a different type of pet.

    Distractor Explanations: Choice A is incorrect. This option is the total number of residents in the town. **Choice B** is incorrect. This is the approximate number of residents in the town that own either a dog or a cat. **Choice D** is incorrect. This is the difference between the number of

residents in the survey that owned a cat or a dog and the total number of residents in the town $(62,500 - 950)$.

Chapter 6

Practice Test 5

You are about to begin a full-length Practice Test. The test has four modules. The time allotted for each module is marked at the beginning of the module. Work on one module at a time. Use a timer to keep track of the time limits for every module.

Try to take the Practice Test under real test conditions. Find a quiet place to work, and set aside enough time to complete the test without being disturbed. At the end of the test, check your answers by referring to the Answer Key and fill in your raw score in the scorecard below. Also, note down the time taken by you for completing each module.

Pay particular attention to the questions that were answered incorrectly. Read the answer explanations and understand how to solve them.

My Score Card (Raw Score)

	Reading and Writing		Math	
	Module 1	Module 2	Module 1	Module 2
Out of	27	27	22	22
My Score	_____	_____	_____	_____
Time Taken	_____	_____	_____	_____

TEST BEGINS ON THE NEXT PAGE

Reading and Writing Test

27 QUESTIONS | 32 MINUTES

DIRECTIONS

The questions in this section address a number of important reading and writing skills. Each question includes one or more passages, which may include a table or graph. Read each passage and question carefully, and then choose the best answer to the question based on the passage(s). All questions in this section are multiple–choice with four answer choices. Each question has a single best answer.

1

The idea of a credit card was first proposed in 1887 by Edward Bellamy in a novel titled *Looking Backward*. Different institutions offered cards for limited purposes after that, but the first modern credit card with revolving payments was _____ in 1958 by Bank of America in Fresno, California.

Which choice completes the text with the most logical and precise word or phrase?

A) dispatched

B) issued

C) consigned

D) allocated

2

The following text is adapted from Jane Austen's 1811 novel, Sense and Sensibility.

Mr. John Dashwood told his mother again and again how exceedingly sorry he was that she had taken a house at such a distance from Norland as to prevent his being of any service to her in <u>removing</u> her furniture. He really felt conscientiously vexed on the occasion; for the very exertion to which he had limited the performance of his promise to his father was by this arrangement rendered impractical. Instead, the furniture was all sent around by water.

As used in the text, what does the word "removing" most nearly mean?

A) transferring

B) detaching

C) dismissing

D) separating

3

Caravaggio was an Italian painter active around 1600. His style was very distinct and enchanting, combining realism and high lighting contrasts in a way that added drama and intensity to the scenes portrayed. His <u>peculiar</u> use of shadow was a prime influence on the work of later generations of Baroque artists who also explored artistic extremes.

As used in the text, what does the word "peculiar" most nearly mean?

A) singular

B) abnormal

C) indisposed

D) discernible

4

The parents of the first female self–made millionaire, Madam J. Walker, were slaves, but she made a fortune selling cosmetics and hair care products. Throughout her life, she supported Black organizations and artists. Her philanthropy continued after her death, as two–thirds of her legacy was set aside to _____ charities.

Which choice completes the text with the most logical and precise word or phrase?

A) enforce

B) concede

C) endow

D) accord

5

The following text is adapted from Alexandre Dumas's 1849 novel, *The Three Musketeers*.

It was, then, into the midst of this tumult and disorder that our young man advanced with a beating heart, ranging his long rapier up his lanky leg, and keeping one hand on the edge of his cap, with that half-smile of the embarrassed provincial who wishes to put on a good face. When he had passed one group he began to breathe more freely; but he could not help observing that they turned round to look at him, and for the first time in his life D'Artagnan, who had till that day entertained a very good opinion of himself, felt ridiculous.

What is the main purpose of the underlined portion in the overall structure of the text?

A) It warns the reader of a coming conflict.

B) It indicates a temporal change in the passage.

C) It describes the appearance of a scene.

D) It stresses the emotional state of a character.

6

The following text is from Leo Tolstoy's 1873 novel, "Anna Karenina."

Levin had meant to tell his brother of his determination to get married, and to ask his advice; he had indeed firmly resolved to do so. But after seeing his brother, listening to his conversation with the professor, hearing afterwards the unconsciously patronizing tone in which his brother questioned him about agricultural matters. Levin felt that he could not for some reason begin to talk to him of his intention of marrying. He felt that his brother would not look at it as he would have wished him to.

Which choice best states the function of the underlined sentence in the text as a whole?

A) It explains the purpose of the conversation with the professor.

B) It adds to the sense of inferiority which causes Levin to change his mind.

C) It elaborates on an obstacle preventing Levin from getting married.

D) It introduces a problem that Levin and his brother frequently disagreed about.

7

Text 1

On August 5, 2013, a live television broadcast from London showed two food critics tasting a hamburger patty cooked by chef Richard Geown. The importance of this event was that the hamburger was the first public tasting of cultured meat, meaning meat that was raised from cells in a laboratory. This sample took two years and cost $300,000 to produce, but its creator, Mark Post, is sure there is potential for such foods in the market.

Text 2

Cultured meat is regarded with skepticism in many circles. Will people readily consume animal meat raised in a laboratory? No animals are slaughtered, but the concept is still repulsive to many. Even so, many companies are jumping on the bandwagon to produce different meats, and the first sales occurred in December 2020, when a Singapore restaurant included cultured meat in its offerings.

Which choice best describes the relationship between the texts?

A) Text 1 describes the introduction of a product, and Text 2 explains later developments.

B) Text 1 describes the positive reception of a product, and Text 2 brings up reservations.

C) Both texts refer to the difficulty in creating a new product.

D) Both texts discuss the public's reaction to a new product.

8

Text 1

Prior to 1972, polar bear populations were severely reduced by hunters and trappers, causing concern about the survival of the majestic apex species. However, an international agreement regulating commercial hunting enacted in 1973 changed odds against the hearty animals. Now, the total number of polar bears has rebounded to healthy levels that demonstrate that the species is no longer in imminent danger of extinction.

Text 2

Sea ice is essential for all parts of the polar bear lifecycle—and it is melting at a faster rate than ever before due to climate change. It is important to note that as of 2019, although two of the nineteen known populations increased in numbers, four had declined and there was not enough data on eight.

Based on the texts, after his experiments, how would the author of Text 2 most likely describe the view of the author of Text 1?

A) Limited, because it only addresses one aspect of the threats against polar bears.

B) Inspiring, because it provides evidence that polar bear populations are increasing.

C) Erroneous, because it inaccurately reported the total number of polar bears.

D) Worrisome, because it hints that efforts to protect polar bears are only partially successful.

9

A very rare meteorological event is called
<u>thundersnow.</u> This uncommon event occurs
when there are strong updrafts in cold weather.
The mechanics are basically the same as those
which cause thunderstorms, but the results are
lightning and thunder with falling snow or hail
instead of rain. Thundersnow clouds tend to be
lower than thunderstorm clouds, and the effect is
most common over large bodies of water like the
Great Lakes in the Northwestern United States
and Utah's Great Salt Lake, though they can occur
elsewhere. Often the sounds of the thunder are
muted due to the presence of snow.

What is the main purpose of the text?

A) It explains an unusual phenomenon.

B) It identifies locations to see a phenomenon.

C) It describes why a phenomenon occurs.

D) It outlines a scientific dilemma.

10

This passage is adapted from Mark Twain's 1903
story, "The $30,000 Bequest."

Saladin's wife, Electra, was a capable helpmeet,
although—like himself—a dreamer of dreams and
a private dabbler in romance. The first thing she
did after her marriage was buy an acre of ground
on the edge of the town, and pay cash for it—
twenty-five dollars, all her fortune. Saladin had
less, by fifteen. She instituted a vegetable garden
there, and got it farmed on shares by the nearest
neighbor. Out of Saladin's first year's wage she
put thirty dollars in the savings-bank, sixty out
of his second, a hundred out of his third. By the
time two children had arrived, she banked two
hundred a year from the salary. When she had
been married seven years, she built a pretty and
comfortable house in the midst of her garden-
acre and moved her family in.

What is the main idea of the text?

A) Electra was more capable at finances than her
husband was.

B) Electra and Saladin were too romantic to be
practical.

C) Saladin was taking advantage of Electra's
money.

D) Electra has excellent thrift and planning
ability.

11

John Milton is one of the most famous poets from the 1600s. Though his writing is sometimes archaic to modern readers, the sentiments still ring close to the heart. For instance, he claims at the preface of his 1637 poem "<u>Lycidas</u>" that "the Author bewails a learned Friend": _____

Which quotation from "Lycidas" most effectively illustrates the claim?

A) "YET once more, O ye Laurels, and once more / Ye Myrtles brown, with Ivy never–sear, / I com to pluck your Berries harsh and crude,"

B) "For we were nurst upon the self–same hill, / Fed the same flock by fountain, shade, and rill."

C) "But O the heavy change, now thou art gon, / Now thou art gon, and never must return!"

D) "Fame is the spur that the clear spirit doth raise / (That last infirmity of Noble mind) /To scorn delights, and live laborious days"

12

Training working dogs is a complicated process. Typical pets need to follow commands given by the owners. However, working dogs are also expected to use *selective disobedience*. This term refers to a situation when the dog is given a direct command by the owner which may lead to injury to either the owner or the dog. In such a case, the dog must use its own judgment and disobey rather than blindly following the command that the owner gave it.

Which situation is the best example of selective disobedience as defined in the text?

A) A dog that herds cows rests in the shade of a tree on a hot day while the cows are grazing, even though the owner asked the dog to stand by the cows.

B) A guide dog for the blind refuses to lead the owner onto a street when a truck is approaching and the owner asks to cross.

C) A dog that is trained to rescue victims of earthquakes is approaching a building that may collapse and stops when the owner signals that it is dangerous.

D) A dog trained to help a hearing–impaired owner does not alert the owner when the phone rings and the owner is napping on the couch.

Main Employers of Urban and Regional Planners in the United States, 2018	
Local government	71%
Architectural, engineering, and related services	11
State government	9
Management, scientific, and technical consulting services	3
Federal government	2

Employment of urban and regional planners is projected to grow 11 percent from 2018 to 2028, much faster than the average for all occupations. Demographic, transportation, and environmental changes will drive employment growth for planners. Within cities, urban planners will be needed to develop revitalization projects and address issues associated with population growth, environmental degradation, the movement of people and goods, and resource scarcity. Planners will also be needed as new and existing communities require extensive development and improved infrastructure, including housing, roads, sewer systems, parks, and schools. However, federal, state, and local government budgets may affect the employment of planners in government, because development projects are contingent on available funds.

Based on the text, what can be reasonably inferred about the percentage of urban and regional planners employed by the federal government in the table?

A) The percentage is extremely low because there is very little demand for urban planning outside of large cities.

B) The percentage does not reflect the actual number of planners employed by the federal government compared to those employed in other sectors.

C) The percentage will remain approximately the same level because federal government positions are very stable.

D) The percentage has the potential to decrease if the federal government receives fewer tax dollars and revises its spending plans.

14

The following text is adapted from Mary Wollstonecraft Shelley's 1818 novel, *Frankenstein; Or, the Modern Prometheus.*

We sat late. We could not tear ourselves away from each other nor persuade ourselves to say the word "Farewell!" It was said, and we retired under the pretence of seeking repose, each fancying that the other was deceived; but when at morning's dawn I descended to the carriage which was to convey me away, they were all there—my father again to bless me, Clerval to press my hand once more, my Elizabeth to renew her entreaties that I would write often and to bestow the last feminine attentions on her playmate and friend.

Based on the text, what is most likely true about the narrator?

A) The narrator is a woman who grew up with Elizabeth.

B) The narrator is leaving home for the first time.

C) The narrator was trying to avoid the end of the journey.

D) The narrator will be absent for a long period.

15

Clark and McLachlan examined existing data on pollen from red maple, birch, beech, ash, oak, hemlock and elm trees isolated from cores of lake sediments in southern Ontario. "This record covers about 10,000 years, so if we look at the relative abundance of different species over that time, we can estimate long-term growth rates," said Clark. "What found is huge variability within populations, and this variability means they overlap in ways that determine who's going to win and who's going to lose. And that variability might itself represent a stabilizing mechanism." Clark emphasized that the results from the studies offer cautionary lessons. "Our findings suggest that forest biodiversity has been stabilized in some important ways, so extinction of species should cause us greater concern than if we believed that biodiversity was maintained in the past by continual replenishment of random extinction by generation of new species."

Based on the text, what is one implication of Clark's study regarding the result of biodiversity stabilization?

A) There is a smaller chance of ecosystems collapsing than previously theorized.

B) Extinction is a random event that is compensated for by evolution of new species.

C) As time progresses, fewer new species will evolve than did in the past.

D) An extinction could indicate a larger-scale collapse of the region's equilibrium.

16

Kinkaku-ji, also known as the Golden Pavilion, is one of the most popular tourist sites in Kyoto despite having been completely destroyed in a fire set by an arsonist in 1950; a replica was later rebuilt on the same pattern as the original.

Which choice completes the text so that it conforms to the conventions of Standard English?

A) completely destroying

B) it was destroyed completely

C) to have been completely destroyed

D) having been completely destroyed

17

Many people think of the world's largest cats, lions, and tigers, as living together in the same region. In reality, the only country where they coexist is India, and even there, the two species prefer _____ different habitats.

Which choice completes the text so that it conforms to the conventions of Standard English?

A) extreme

B) extremity

C) extremely

D) extremist

18

First performed in England in 1984, _____ It is most notable because all the cast sing and act their parts on roller skates.

Which choice completes the text so that it conforms to the conventions of Standard English?

A) Richard Stilgoe and Andrew Lloyd Webber wrote the lyrics and music, respectively, for the musical *Starlight Express.*

B) Richard Stilgoe wrote the lyrics for *Starlight Express* and Andrew Lloyd Webber wrote the music.

C) Andrew Lloyd Webber wrote the music and Richard Stilgoe wrote the lyrics for the musical *Starlight Express.*

D) *Starlight Express* is a musical with lyrics by Richard Stilgoe and music by Andrew Lloyd Webber.

19

A survey is a process of collecting a small but representative sampling of responses on a given topic and extrapolating that information to what a larger group might think about it, since many _____ fall into basic patterns when looked at as a whole.

Which choice completes the text so that it conforms to the conventions of Standard English?

A) peoples' opinions

B) people's opinions

C) people's opinions'

D) peoples' opinions'

20

The sousaphone—invented in 1893 by J.W. Pepper at the request of band leader John Philip _____ a brass instrument related to the tuba and often used in marching bands because it is easier to carry and directs sound over the head of other band members.

Which choice completes the text so that it conforms to the conventions of Standard English?

A) Sousa is

B) Sousa is—

C) Sousa, is

D) Sousa—is

21

There has been scholarly debate about the exact definition of Aztec, but it loosely refers to a culture that flourished in Mexico between approximately 1300 and 1521. The Aztec Empire was formed in 1427 of three separate _____ Tlacopan.

Which choice completes the text so that it conforms to the conventions of Standard English?

A) city–states: Tenochtitlan, Texcoco, and,

B) city–states: Tenochtitlan; Texcoco; and

C) city–states Tenochtitlan, Texcoco, and

D) city–states, Tenochtitlan, Texcoco, and

22

In 1961, Jenny Johnson wrote the beloved poem "Warning," which is now best known by its first _____ I am an old woman, I shall wear purple.

Which choice completes the text so that it conforms to the conventions of Standard English?

A) line "when

B) line, "when

C) line, those are "when

D) line, it is "when

23

Many researchers have identified a correlation between the consumption of nuts and longevity. _____ it has yet to be established whether the nuts actually impact lifespan or whether people who already have healthier lifestyles tend to include nuts in their diets.

Which choice completes the text with the most logical transition?

A) Therefore,

B) However,

C) Indeed,

D) Similarly,

24

The Egyptian leader known as King Tut died around 1323 B.C. when he was only 18 or 19 years old. Archaeologists debate over the cause of his death, saying it could have been caused by malaria, a hippopotamus attack, a chariot race injury, or murder. _____ the death was unexpected: he was buried in a tomb that was designed for another person.

Which choice completes the text with the most logical transition?

A) Therefore,

B) As a result,

C) Alternatively,

D) In any event,

25

After Christopher Columbus's ships were stranded in Jamaica, the indigenous people grew tired of providing food and Columbus was worried about the safety of his crew. _____ he used information from an almanac about an upcoming lunar eclipse to intimidate the natives.

Which choice completes the text with the most logical transition?

A) Nevertheless,

B) In other words,

C) Likewise,

D) Therefore,

26

While researching a topic, a student has taken the following notes:

- B.F. Keith lived from 1846 to 1914 and owned and operated hundreds of vaudeville theaters around the United States.

- Keith did not approve of the common theatrical trend of vulgarity and insisted that his performers offered decent acts with no swear words.

- The theaters were lavish and entertained spectators with their palace–like, elegant ornamentation, as opposed to simple structures of older theaters.

- Ushers had authority to remove audience members who heckled the performers.

- Edwin Albee was Keith's invaluable partner and assumed control of the theaters after Keith's death.

The student wants to emphasize what differentiated Keith's theaters from others at the time. Which choice most effectively uses relevant information from the notes to accomplish this goal?

A) B.F. Keith (1846–1914) owned more theaters than others in the era and built ones that were extremely ornamented.

B) Compared to other theaters in that period, B.F. Keith's theaters offered more polite performances and the theaters themselves were very elaborate.

C) B.F. Keith ran vaudeville shows rather than other performances until his death in 1914, when Edwin Albee took over his hundreds of elegant theaters.

D) B.F. Keith disapproved of acts with swear words or audiences that heckled performers, so prohibited those in his gorgeously ornamented theaters.

While researching a topic, a student has taken the following notes:

- There are about 2–4 partial lunar eclipses a year, and they are visible from about half of the Earth.

- Lunar eclipses occur when the Earth is between the Sun and Moon, and therefore casts a shadow across the Moon's surface.

- A blood moon occurs only during a total lunar eclipse and may last up to two hours.

- A total lunar eclipse begins with an increasingly smaller white crescent as more and more light from the Sun is blocked and ends with the reverse, a crescent that grows larger.

- The blood moon occurs only when the entire moon is in shadow.

- The sunrise or sunset that is visible at the edge of the Earth gives the blood moon its red color.

The student wants to explain what a blood moon is to an audience that knows about lunar eclipses. Which choice most effectively uses relevant information from the notes to accomplish this goal?

A) A lunar eclipse is when the shadow of the Earth crosses the Moon, starting with a white crescent, turning into a blood moon, and ending with another crescent.

B) A full lunar eclipse has a phase called the blood moon, which is when the entire Moon is in shadow and the light from around the edges of the Earth color the Moon red.

C) Lunar eclipses happen 2–4 times a year when the Earth passes between the Sun and the Moon, but a total lunar eclipse is called a blood moon.

D) Blood moons occur during a total lunar eclipse when the Earth blocks all but the red light from the Sun, which shines through to color the moon.

No Test Material On This Page

Reading and Writing Test
27 QUESTIONS | 32 MINUTES

DIRECTIONS

The questions in this section address a number of important reading and writing skills. Each question includes one or more passages, which may include a table or graph. Read each passage and question carefully, and then choose the best answer to the question based on the passage(s). All questions in this section are multiple–choice with four answer choices. Each question has a single best answer.

1

Though her invention was originally mocked as foolish, Marion Donovan _____ childcare by inventing the disposable diaper, freeing housewives from hours of labor. In the past, women had to not only clean the diaper but also furniture and clothes when the cloth padding leaked. The disposable diaper's absorbent padding and close–fitting cover completely changed how babies could be raised.

Which choice completes the text with the most logical and precise word or phrase?

A) rebuilt

B) reorganized

C) reclassified

D) revolutionized

2

In the experiment, the date of appearance of the first flowers was noted for each treatment of salt that stressed the plant; thus, the number of days it took for each plant to make its first flower from the start of the stress <u>application</u> was covered. Fruit ripening, number, size, and fresh mass were also evaluated.

As used in the text, what does the word "application" most nearly mean?

A) significance

B) diligence

C) request

D) execution

3

James Abbot McNeill Whistler's famous 1871 painting known as *Whistler's Mother* has been considered one of the classics of American art. Originally titled *Arrangement in Grey and Black #1*, the strong composition of Anna Whistler exemplifies the artist's _____ at manipulating subtle colors.

Which choice completes the text with the most logical and precise word or phrase?

A) susceptibility

B) adroitness

C) engagement

D) diversion

4

The popular 1943 film *Lassie Come Home* was based on a book written in 1940 by Eric Knight about a female dog named Lassie who had a deep emotional connection with the boy who owned her. The fictional dog was <u>supposedly</u> first introduced in an earlier short story that Knight wrote. However, in 1859, Elizabeth Gaskell published "The Half Brothers," a similar short story featuring a dog named Lassie that saved two boys lost in a snowstorm.

What is the main purpose of the underlined portion in the overall structure of the text?

A) It casts doubt on the veracity of a claim.

B) It questions the similarity between two stories.

C) It emphasizes that a character was fictional.

D) It highlights the popularity of an earlier work.

Spike Lee is a movie director known for his nuanced depictions of Black characters, but in the past, movies were far less sensitive about the multiple facets of people of color. The first Black man who starred in a major motion picture was Sam Lucas, who played a role in the 1914 production of *Uncle Tom's Cabin*. Prior to that time, Black characters were played by White actors in face paint. Throughout the following years, Black actors received roles, but primarily as maids, servants, or jungle savages, until the late 19th century, when daring directors pushed the stereotyped boundaries.

What is the primary function of the underlined portion in the overall structure of the text?

A) It hints that a common stereotype is flawed.

B) It offers an example to use as a comparison.

C) It introduces the person who pioneered a change.

D) It brings up a problem that took time to resolve.

Mas Subramanian, a solid–state materials scientist, was trying to create a magnetic substance that could be used in computer hard drives. One of his creations was not at all magnetic, but instead was a bright shade of blue. Subramanian realized that every cloud has a silver lining and started to find ways to market the new pigment. As opposed to most other sources of blue, his material was stable and non–toxic.

What is the main purpose of the phrase "every cloud has a silver lining"?

A) To provide a metaphor showing that the material was gaseous like a cloud

B) To indicate that Subramanian realized that the seeming failure had benefits

C) To establish that the pigment could be used to make silver as well as blue

D) To show that the material could be rendered magnetic by adding other substances

7

Text 1 is adapted from Charles Stearns's 1849 treatise, "The Way to Abolish Slavery."
Text 2 is adapted from Catharine Beecher's 1837 letter, "Slavery and Abolitionism, with
Reference to the Duty of American Females."

Text 1:

The Government of the United States creates no Slaves; it only recognises as lawful the
Slavery existing in the several States, or to use the words of the Constitution, "held to
service or labor, under the laws thereof." The *laws* of the several slave–holding States are
made the standard for the general government's action upon this subject. No quibble can
possibly evade this, for it is not necessary to prove that a runaway Slave justly owes service
to his master, but only if he does, under *the laws of his master.* What then is necessary to
be done to remove this prop from under the colossal statue of Slavery? Plainly, to repeal
all laws recognising its existence.

Text 2:

Now what is it that makes a man cease to be a slave and become free? It is not kind
treatment from a master; it is not paying wages to the slave. It always signifies *that legal*
act, which, by the laws of the land, changes a slave to a freeman. No exception can be
made for those who live in States where the act of emancipation, by a master, makes a
slave the property of the State, to be sold for the benefit of the State.

Which choice best describes how Stearns (Text 1) would most likely react to Beecher's
(Text 2) assertion that some slaves are not freed because they live in states that consider
emancipated slaves the property of the state?

A) Stearns would argue that such a case is only possible with adequate paperwork.

B) Stearns would argue that is one more reason that all slavery laws should be
eliminated.

C) Stearns would argue that slavery is an integral part of the U.S. Constitution.

D) Stearns would argue that if such slaves left the state, they would then be free.

8

Coywolves first appeared in the early part of the 20th century near Canada's Algonquin Provincial Park. They are hybrids between wolves and western coyotes; some studies have also identified genetic material from domestic dogs in coywolves. They are extremely adaptable to a wide variety of habitats and are now flourishing in different areas. Biologists estimate that there may be over one million coywolves dispersed across Eastern North America from Canada to Virginia. In general, the coywolf has a larger body, longer legs, shorter ears, and a larger, stronger jaw than a regular coyote.

Based on the text, what is true about coywolves?

A) They are more common in Canada than other places.

B) They are more closely related to coyotes than wolves.

C) They were hybridized by Canadian people in the early 20th century.

D) They may be found in different environmental conditions.

9

Jessica Nabongo is the first black woman known to have visited all 195 countries in the world; she has been to 10 different territories as well. The last country on her list was the Seychelles, which she visited in 2019. During her travels, she was appalled by the poverty and at the way poor countries supported the burden of the world's waste. Now Nabongo, who is Ugandan–American, is an advocate for ethical and sustainable travel, and has written a book about her adventures called *The Catch Me If You Can*.

According to the text, what is true about Jessica Nabongo?

A) She was born in Uganda and moved to America.

B) She is the author of a book about traveling around the world.

C) She visited 195 countries before visiting 10 territories.

D) She felt that the Seychelles had too much poverty.

10

The automobile company Volkswagen proposed an advertising campaign called The Fun Theory under the assumption that the best way to change people's behaviors was by adding an element of fun. To test the theory, researchers measured the number of passengers in a Swedish subway station who were willing to walk on stairs that made piano sounds for every step as opposed to a regular escalator next to it. Measuring use before and after converting the staircase, results indicated a 66% increase.

Which choice best states the main idea of the text?

A) Volkswagen has created an effective new advertising strategy.

B) People are willing to change behaviors when fun is used as an incentive.

C) More people prefer taking stairs to using an escalator.

D) Staircases should be converted so that they sound like a piano.

11

Argentina's Iguazu National Park contains one of the most spectacular waterfalls in the world. Water drops in multiple cascades up to 80 meters high, forming a crescent about 2,700 meters in diameter. Named a national park in 1934 and a UNESCO World Heritage Site in 1984, the park is considered a world treasure for more than its beauty: _____

Which quotation most effectively illustrates the claim?

A) its conservation has a generous budget and is conducted by rangers and other professionals.

B) it is located on a basaltic line that forms the border between Argentina and Brazil.

C) the spray from the falls creates a unique microclimate with over 2,000 species of plants.

D) most of the region has been severely altered due to logging and agriculture.

12

Total Increase in Iron Content in Cells

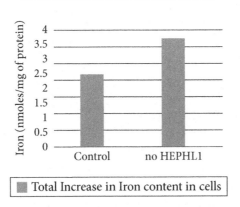

Total Increase in Iron content in cells

Figures adapted from "Biallelic HEPHL1 variants impair ferroxidase activity and cause an abnormal hair phenotype" by Prashant Sharma et al., PLOS Genetics, 2019.

HEPHL1 belongs to a family of proteins known as Multi–Copper Oxidases (MCOs) that catalyze the oxidation of iron so that it can bind to a circulating protein called transferrin which distributes the iron throughout the body. One unique property of MCOs is the presence of three copper–binding sites that can house six copper atoms. To help us explore the physiological consequences of the loss of HEPHL1 activity more thoroughly, we used a gene–targeting approach to make mice with a disrupted *Hephl1* gene. Interestingly, all mice that had a complete deletion of both copies of their *Hephl1* gene had short, curled whiskers throughout their life. We found that the iron uptake increase between the cells of the mouse with no HEPHL1 and the cells of the control mouse was significant: _____ .

Which choice most effectively uses data from the table to complete the statement?

A) about 1.1 nmoles/mg of protein

B) at almost 2.1 nmoles/mg of protein

C) nearly 2.7 nmoles/mg of protein

D) around 3.8 nmoles/mg of protein

13

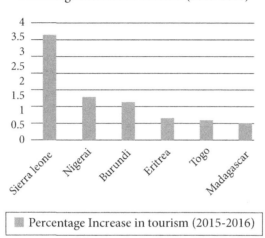

Data for figures is adapted from African Development Bank Group, 2016

Every African country, urban center, or rural village could be, in fact, its own unique tourism magnet. The tourism business, though, is broader than just the sites themselves. Considerations need to be made for transportation, hotels and guest accommodations, and services that link the various components of a trip, such as guide services in national parks or city bus tours. The attractiveness and competitiveness of each tourism destination will depend on the site's quality and accessibility.

Which of the following claims about tourism is best supported by the text and data from the graph?

A) Almost 50% of the visitors who traveled to Africa in 2016 went to Nigeria.

B) Sierra Leone probably invested more in the infrastructure of tourism by 2016 than Togo did.

C) Burundi had over 40% more visitors than Eritrea or Togo in 2016.

D) Eritrea had a greater number of tourists who visited in 2016 than Madagascar did in the same year.

14

The following text is adapted from Jack London's 1903 novel, *The Call of the Wild*.

Buck did not read the newspapers, or he would have known that trouble was brewing, not alone for himself, but for every tide–water dog, strong of muscle and with warm, long hair, from Puget Sound to San Diego. Because men, groping in the Arctic darkness, had found a yellow metal, and because steamship and transportation companies were booming the find, thousands of men were rushing into the Northland. These men wanted dogs, and the dogs they wanted were heavy dogs, with strong muscles by which to toil, and furry coats to protect them from the frost.

Based on the text, what is implied about Buck?

A) He is aboard a steamship headed north.

B) He found gold in the northland.

C) He owns a dog that is needed in the north.

D) He is a strong dog able to tolerate cold.

15

In a powerful 2020 book, Moroccan–American writer Laila Lalami argues the case for citizens that are _____, meaning people who the government accepts as members of the society on one hand, but refuses to grant complete rights to on the other.

Which choice completes the text so that it conforms to the conventions of Standard English?

A) conditions

B) conditional

C) conditionally

D) conditioner

16

Built between 1960 and 1970 in Egypt, the Aswan Dam, now known as the Aswan High Dam, was erected across the Nile River to control flooding, increase water storage, and _____

Which choice completes the text so that it conforms to the conventions of Standard English?

A) generate hydroelectricity.

B) it generates hydroelectricity.

C) hydroelectricity is also generated.

D) to generate hydroelectricity.

17

The Audubon Society was named for one of the most eminent early American ornithologists, John James Audubon. Though Audubon himself made drawings of dead birds, members of the society _____ to the conservation of birds and their habitats.

Which choice completes the text so that it conforms to the conventions of Standard English?

A) is dedicated

B) are dedicated

C) dedicating

D) has been dedicated

18

Almost all of the paintings by the Italian Baroque painter Artemisia Gentileschi feature naturalistic women as the focus. Artemisia herself broke the standard model for women at the time, earning a living as a professional artist. Therefore, it is not surprising that her subjects are also courageous, rebellious, and _____ .

Which choice completes the text so that it conforms to the conventions of Standard English?

A) powerful

B) they have power

C) possess power

D) are powerful

19

Popular since the 1700s, *shichimi* (Japanese for "seven spices") is the name of a spice compound made, as the name suggests, from seven spices, though the exact composition varies.

Which choice completes the text so that it conforms to the conventions of Standard English?

A) *shichimi* (Japanese for "seven spices")

B) *shichimi* , (Japanese for "seven spices")

C) *shichimi* (Japanese for "seven spices"),

D) *shichimi* , (Japanese for "seven spices"),

20

Dinosaurs lived on Earth for about 165 years until the Cretaceous Period, so many of the familiar _____ were actually separated by long periods of time.

Which choice completes the text so that it conforms to the conventions of Standard English?

A) species like stegosaurs and tyrannosaurs

B) species, like stegosaurs and tyrannosaurs

C) species, like stegosaurs, and tyrannosaurs,

D) species like: stegosaurs and tyrannosaurs

21

Saturn's moon Europa has an extremely smooth surface which indicates that there may be a water ocean beneath _____ such an ocean could theoretically exist despite the extremely cold temperatures due to the gravitational pull of Saturn.

Which choice completes the text so that it conforms to the conventions of Standard English?

A) it

B) it,

C) it;

D) it. And

22

The Frank Lloyd Wright building of the Guggenheim Museum is an architectural masterpiece best known for its Grand Ramp, a gentle spiral walkway that leads the visitor to every floor in a stately manner. What is little known is that as the plans evolved over the sixteen years of _____ was eliminated from the design.

Which choice completes the text so that it conforms to the conventions of Standard English?

A) construction, a smaller, much steeper ramp

B) construction a smaller, much steeper ramp,

C) construction a smaller, much steeper, ramp

D) construction a smaller much steeper ramp

23

Seeing eye dogs require the most rigorous training of all forms of working dogs. _____ they must learn to alert their handlers to potential dangers that could hurt the owner but not necessarily the dog, such as walking under a low branch.

Which choice completes the text with the most logical transition?

A) Nevertheless,

B) Therefore,

C) Specifically,

D) Similarly,

24

"Civil disobedience" is a term popularized in the United States by Henry David Thoreau's essay *Civil Disobedience*. That publication inspired Mahatma Gandhi in the 1920s to actively refuse to obey the laws of India in a non–violent way. _____ Martin Luther King, Jr., used similar techniques to promote the Civil Rights Movement in the United States in the 1960s.

Which choice completes the text with the most logical transition?

A) In conclusion,

B) Subsequently,

C) For instance,

D) Nonetheless,

25

Cashews are popular nuts eaten as snacks around the world, but are not sold in the shells, because the shells contain caustic oil compounds that trigger contact dermatitis. _____ the shell creates a rash on the skin.

Which choice completes the text with the most logical transition?

A) In other words,

B) Likewise,

C) Conversely,

D) On the other hand,

26

While researching a topic, a student has taken the following notes:

- Heat islands are urban areas that are 1–7 degrees Fahrenheit hotter than the surrounding areas during the day.

- Nighttime temperatures may be 2–5 degrees hotter

- Heat islands are caused by synthetic materials in buildings and roads that absorb and emit more heat than natural areas like plants or water

- The effect can be mitigated by planting trees

- Lightening the color of surfaces such as roofs can reduce the temperature differences.

- Heat islands do not directly increase global warming but can indirectly do so through factors such as using more air conditioners.

The student wants to offer an audience that does not know what a heat island is some practical solutions for reducing the effect. Which choice most effectively uses relevant information from the notes to accomplish this goal?

A) Heat islands do not increase global warming and their effect can be reduced by using air conditioners.

B) Heat islands, which are urban areas hotter than their surroundings by up to 7 degrees, are caused by using many synthetic materials in buildings and roads.

C) Heat islands are 1–7 degrees Fahrenheit hotter during the day and 2–5 degrees hotter at night, but that effect can be reduced by planting trees.

D) Heat islands, urban areas that are hotter than the surroundings, can be lessened in intensity by steps such as planting trees or painting roofs and other surfaces a lighter color.

27

While researching a topic, a student has taken the following notes:

- Wildlife corridors are areas that are designed to link habitats together.

- The goal is to promote biodiversity and safe movement of species so populations can intermingle and have a larger gene pool rather than become isolated.

- Animals can use wildlife corridors to find food, water, and other resources.

- The concept is consistent with farming, forestry, and conservation efforts because corridors can take different forms.

- Various options include "stepping stones" of native vegetation, bridges for animals to cross roads, and removal of fences around private property.

The student wants to convince people in a farming community to create a wildlife corridor to protect a native species of deer. Which choice most effectively uses relevant information from the notes to accomplish this goal?

A) We can protect the native deer using a wildlife corridor because it can link habitats for the deer to find food and mates while still allowing farmers to do their jobs.

B) We can create a wildlife corridor for the native deer so they can thrive and contribute to conservation efforts in the region.

C) Wildlife corridors are a good solution because they allow the native deer to move around safely, intermingle, and find food, through a system of bridges, native vegetation, and so on.

D) A wildlife corridor can take different forms and achieve the goal of preserving the gene pool of the native deer species.

STOP

No Test Material On This Page

No Test Material On This Page

Math

22 QUESTIONS | 35 MINUTES

The questions in this section address a number of important math skills. Use of a calculator is permitted for all questions.

Unless otherwise indicated: • All variables and expressions represent real numbers. • Figures provided are drawn to scale. • All figures lie in a plane. • The domain of a given function is the set of all real numbers x for which $f(x)$ is a real number.

$A= \pi r^2$
$C = 2\pi r$

$A= \ell w$

$A=\frac{1}{2} bh$

$c^2 = a^2 + b^2$

Special Right Triangles

$V = \ell wh$

$V = \pi r^2h$

$V =\frac{4}{3} \pi r^3$

$V =\frac{1}{3}\pi r^2h$

$V =\frac{1}{3} \ell wh$

The number of degrees of arc in a circle is 360.

The number of radians of arc in a circle is 2π.

The sum of the measures in degrees of the angles of a triangle is 180.

For **multiple-choice questions,** solve each problem, choose the correct answer from the choices provided, and then circle your answer in this book. Circle only one answer for each question. If you change your mind, completely erase the circle. You will not get credit for questions with more than one answer circled, or for questions with no answers circled.

For **student-produced response questions,** solve each problem and write your answer next to or under the question in the test book as described below.

- Once you've written your answer, circle it clearly. You will not receive credit for anything written outside the circle, or for any questions with more than one circled answer.

- If you find more than one correct answer, write and circle only one answer.

- Your answer can be up to 5 characters for a positive answer and up to 6 characters (including the negative sign) for a negative answer, but no more.

- If your answer is a fraction that is too long (over 5 characters for positive, 6 characters for negative), write the decimal equivalent.

- If your answer is a decimal that is too long (over 5 characters for positive, 6 characters for negative), truncate it or round at the fourth digit.

- If your answer is a mixed number (such as 3.!. 2), write it as an improper fraction (7/2) or its decimal equivalent (3.5).

- Don't include symbols such as a percent sign, comma, or dollar sign in your circled answer.

1

Alley bought a piece of land for $47,890. It increased in value every year by 2%. Which of the following best describes the model of the price of the land every year after she bought it if t is the number of years after she bought the land?

A) $47,890(1.02)^t$

B) $47,890 + 0.02^t$

C) $47,890(0.98)^t$

D) $47,890(1.02)^t$

2

If $ax + bx - b + a = 5x - 2$, what is the value of $a^2 - b^2$?

A) 3

B) 5

C) –10

D) –2

3

If one of the solution to the quadratic equation below is $1 + 2\sqrt{k}$, what is the value of k?

$$y = 3x^2 - 6x - 21$$

4

If the length of a rectangle is $6cm$ less than its width x, what is the length of the rectangle given that its area is $27cm^2$?

A) 9

B) 21

C) 6

D) 3

5

Which of the following equations is equivalent to $7x + 14 = 7$?

A) $3x + 6 = 3$

B) $x - 2 = 1$

C) $x = 3$

D) $7x = 7$

6

How many possible integer values of x does the inequality below have?

$$|x + 3| < 7$$

7

The function $p(x)$ is defined by $p(x) = \left(\frac{1}{8}\right)^{-x}$,

what is the value of $p\left(\frac{1}{3}\right)$?

A) 2

B) 512

C) $\frac{1}{2}$

D) $\frac{1}{512}$

8

Which of the following is a factor of
$f(x) = 6x^2 - 17x + 10$?

A) $6x + 5$

B) $x + 5$

C) $x - 2$

D) $x - 5$

9

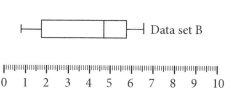

Which of the following is true about the two data sets above?

A) The mean of data set A is less than the mean of data set B

B) Data set A has more values than data set B

C) The median of data set A is greater than the median of data set B

D) The median of data set B is greater than the median of data set A

10

In the xy plane, the graph of the quadratic function f is a parabola with the vertex $(-2, 5)$. The function $g(x)$ is defined when the function $f(x)$ is translated 3 units to the left and 1 unit up. If (h, k) is the vertex of $g(x)$, what is the value of h?

11

For how many points does the line of best fit predict a lower value than the actual point?

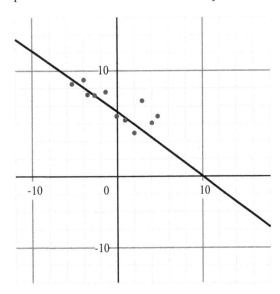

A) 11

B) 5

C) 6

D) 3

12

For all values of $x > 0$, which of the following is equivalent to $\left(x + \sqrt{2}\right)^2 \left(x - \sqrt{2}\right)^2$?

A) $x^2 + 4x + 4$

B) $x^4 + 4x^2 - 4$

C) $2x^2 + 4$

D) $x^4 - 4x^2 + 4$

13

A baker has the graph below which models its daily expenditure for the month of August. Which of the following expressions best describes the equation of the function?

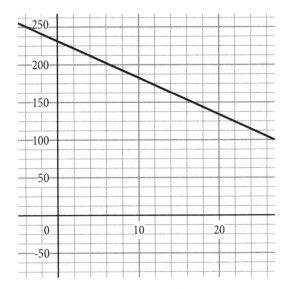

A) $y = 231 - 4.85x$

B) $y = 231 + 0.85x$

C) $y = 4.85x - 231$

D) $y = 4.85x + 231$

14

A school has 24 girls and 20 boys. If $\frac{3}{5}$ of the boys are on the track team and $\frac{3}{4}$ of the girls are not on the track team, what percentage of the students are on the track team? (round off to the nearest whole number)

15

If (a, b) are solutions to the system of inequalities below, what is the minimum value of b?

$$y > 2(x - 2)^2 - 2$$

$$y \geq -1$$

A) 2

B) -2

C) 0

D) -1

16

Which of the following equations is equivalent to $2x^2 + 28x = -98$?

I. $2(x + 7)^2 = 0$

II. $2(x - 7)^2 = 0$

A) I

B) All of them

C) II

D) Neither of them

17

$$3y - 2x = 6$$

$$5y - 4x = 8$$

If the system of equations above has a solution (x, y), what is the value of $2x + y$?

18

A survey was conducted in a school on the change of uniforms. The conclusion of the survey was that 53 students of the 97 students surveyed are in favor of the proposed change. If there are 2,300 students in the school, approximately how many students are not in favor of the change in school uniform?

A) 1,256

B) 1,043

C) 2,300

D) 1,093

19

If the system below has no solution, what is the value of p?

$$y = 3x + 5 - \frac{8}{3}(x + 3) \text{ and } y = px + 4$$

A) 1

B) $\frac{1}{3}$

C) $\frac{5}{3}$

D) $\frac{2}{3}$

20

If the system below has infinite solutions, what is the value of k?

$$y = 5(x - 2) + x + 3 \text{ and } y = k(x - 2) + 2x + 1$$

21

A square is inscribed in a circle. If the circle has a radius of $12cm$. what is the length of one side of the square?

A) 24

B) 12

C) $4\sqrt{3}$

D) $12\sqrt{2}$

22

x	0	1	2	3
y	4	4	4	4

The table above represents the equation $y = 2k$. What is the value of k?

A) 4

B) 2

C) 8

D) 1

No Test Material On This Page

Math

22 QUESTIONS | 35 MINUTES

$A = \pi r^2$
$C = 2\pi r$

$A = \ell w$

$A = \frac{1}{2}bh$

$c^2 = a^2 + b^2$

Special Right Triangles

$V = \ell wh$

$V = \pi r^2 h$

$V = \frac{4}{3}\pi r^3$

$V = \frac{1}{3}\pi r^2 h$

$V = \frac{1}{3}\ell wh$

The number of degrees of arc in a circle is 360.

The number of radians of arc in a circle is 2π.

The sum of the measures in degrees of the angles of a triangle is 180.

For **multiple-choice questions,** solve each problem, choose the correct answer from the choices provided, and then circle your answer in this book. Circle only one answer for each question. If you change your mind, completely erase the circle. You will not get credit for questions with more than one answer circled, or for questions with no answers circled.

For **student-produced response questions,** solve each problem and write your answer next to or under the question in the test book as described below.

- Once you've written your answer, circle it clearly. You will not receive credit for anything written outside the circle, or for any questions with more than one circled answer.

- If you find more than one correct answer, write and circle only one answer.

- Your answer can be up to 5 characters for a positive answer and up to 6 characters (including the negative sign) for a negative answer, but no more.

- If your answer is a fraction that is too long (over 5 characters for positive, 6 characters for negative), write the decimal equivalent.

- If your answer is a decimal that is too long (over 5 characters for positive, 6 characters for negative), truncate it or round at the fourth digit.

- If your answer is a mixed number (such as 3.!. 2), write it as an improper fraction (7/2) or its decimal equivalent (3.5).

- Don't include symbols such as a percent sign, comma, or dollar sign in your circled answer.

1

Which of the following is a solution for the equation below?

$$3x^2 - 19x + 6 = 0$$

A) −6

B) 2

C) $\dfrac{1}{3}$

D) $-\dfrac{1}{3}$

2

In the equation of a circle given below, what would be the value of its diameter?

$$x^2 - 8x + y^2 + 10y = 8$$

A) 7

B) 14

C) 16

D) 49

3

If $f(x) = -2x - 6$, what is the value of $|f(2)|$?

4

Which of the following is equivalent to $tan(90 - x)°$?

A) $\dfrac{sin\,x}{cos\,x}$

B) $\dfrac{cos\,x}{sin\,x}$

C) $\dfrac{cos(90 - x)°}{sin(90 - x)°}$

D) $-tan\,x$

5

Alina started a savings account with $113. She would earn a simple interest of 6.8% on her deposit monthly. The equation below represents the total amount of money $A(t)$ in her savings account in t months. What does 7.684 represent in this context?

$$A(t) = 113 + 7.684t$$

A) The amount of interest earned after t months

B) The total amount in the account after t months

C) The amount of interest earned every month

D) The interest earned every year.

6

The given equation is part of a system of equations. If the system has no solution, which of the following could be the equation of the second line in the system?

$$6x - 3y = 2$$

A) $2x - 3y = 4$

B) $-2x + y = 4$

C) $-2x + y = \dfrac{-2}{3}$

D) $3x - \dfrac{3}{2}y = 1$

7

If $p(x) = 2x^2 - 6x + 5$, what is the value of $p(2)$?

8

Which of the following is the equation of a line that passes through the origin and point $(6, 5)$?

A) $5y = 6x$

B) $6y = 5x$

C) $y = 5x + 6$

D) $y = 6x + 5$

9

Which of the following is the equation of the graph below?

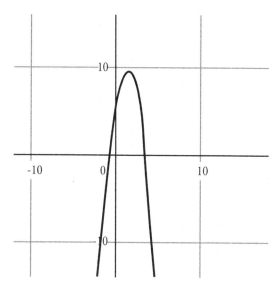

A) $y = 2x^2 - 6x + 5$

B) $y = 2x^2 + 6x + 5$

C) $y = -2x^2 - 6x + 5$

D) $y = -2x^2 + 6x + 5$

10

If a quadrilateral has the following interior angles $x°$, $(x + 40)°$, $(x + 50)°$, $(x - 10)°$, what is the value of x?

11

If triangle ABD is a right triangle, what is the value of sin CAD?

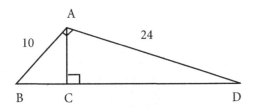

A) $\dfrac{12}{13}$

B) $\dfrac{12}{5}$

C) $\dfrac{5}{13}$

D) $\dfrac{5}{12}$

12

Which of the following expressions is equivalent to $7wp(2w + 5)$?

A) $14w^2p + 35$

B) $14w^2p + 35wp$

C) $14w^2 + 35p$

D) $9w^2p + 35pw$

13

The volume of sphere A is 27 times that of sphere B. If sphere B has a radius of $4cm$, what is the radius of sphere A?

14

A weather forecast report predicted that there is a 43% chance of rain on Monday. The report also indicated that it is twice as likely to rain on Thursday than on Monday. What is the probability that it won't rain on Thursday?

A) 0.43

B) 0.57

C) 0.14

D) 0.86

15

What is the least possible integer value of x for the inequality below?

$$\frac{16^x}{4^x} > 2^6$$

A) 3

B) 4

C) 2

D) 0

16

Given that $3(ax - b) + 4(bx - a) = x - 6$, what is the value of a?

17

What is the volume of a cone with a radius of $12cm$ and a height 6 more than its radius?

A) $2,160\pi$

B) 864π

C) $1,080\pi$

D) 960π

18

What is the slope of the equation of the line below?

$$4x - 3y = 6$$

19

If the circumference of a circle is 20π, what is the value of the angle that is subtended by an arc length of 3π?

20

Thirty students are required to pay a total of p dollars for a field trip. If 28 students paid before the day of the trip, how much was already paid in total?

A) $28p$

B) $\dfrac{14}{15}p$

C) $30p$

D) $\dfrac{p}{30}$

21

If the equation of a circle with a center $(-3, 5)$ and a radius of $6cm$ is written in the form $ax^2 + bx + cy^2 + dy + e = 0$, what is the value of e?

A) 9

B) 36

C) -2

D) 25

22

Which of the choices below is a possible value of x for the given linear inequality?

$$-3(x + 2) < 2(x - 8)$$

A) 1

B) 2

C) 0

D) 3

STOP

This page is intentionally left blank

Answer Key

Reading and Writing

Module 1

Questions	Correct	Mark your correct answers
1.	B	
2.	A	
3.	A	
4.	C	
5.	D	
6.	B	
7.	A	
8.	A	
9.	A	
10.	D	
11.	C	
12.	B	
13.	D	
14.	D	
15.	D	
16.	D	
17.	C	
18.	D	
19.	B	
20.	D	
21.	D	
22.	B	
23.	B	
24.	D	
25.	D	
26.	B	
27.	B	

Module 2

Questions	Correct	Mark your correct answers
1.	D	
2.	D	
3.	B	
4.	A	
5.	B	
6.	B	
7.	B	
8.	D	
9.	B	
10.	B	
11.	C	
12.	A	
13.	B	
14.	D	
15.	B	
16.	A	
17.	B	
18.	A	
19.	A	
20.	A	
21.	C	
22.	A	
23.	C	
24.	B	
25.	A	
26.	D	
27.	A	

Math

Module 1

Questions	Correct	Mark your correct answers
1.	A	
2.	C	
3.	2	
4.	D	
5.	A	
6.	13	
7.	A	
8.	C	
9.	D	
10.	−5	
11.	C	
12.	D	
13.	A	
14.	41	
15.	D	
16.	A	
17.	10	
18.	B	
19.	B	
20.	4	
21.	D	
22.	B	

Module 2

Questions	Correct	Mark your correct answers
1.	C	
2.	B	
3.	10	
4.	B	
5.	C	
6.	B	
7.	1	
8.	B	
9.	D	
10.	70	
11.	A	
12.	B	
13.	12	
14.	C	
15.	B	
16.	3	
17.	B	
18.	A	
19.	54	
20.	B	
21.	C	
22.	D	

1. **Level:** Medium | **Skill/Knowledge:** Words in Context

   Key Explanation: Choice B is the best answer. The blank is a verb that shows what the Bank of America did to the first modern credit card. **Choice B** refers to distributing something for use or sale, so aptly shows that the credit cards were first given out to customers in 1958.

   Distractor Explanations: Choice A is incorrect because it refers to sending something away with a purpose, such as sending an order to an army. It does not refer to selling something or making something available to many people. **Choice C** is incorrect because it refers to putting something into someone's care. **Choice D** refers to distributing the parts of a whole, such as allocating funds.

2. **Level:** Easy | **Domain:** CRAFT AND STRUCTURE
   Skill/Knowledge: Words in Context

   Key Explanation: Choice A is the best answer because "removing" is a verb that shows what Mr. Dashwood cannot do to the furniture. **Choice A** refers to carrying objects from one place to another, which fits the context of saying that Mr. Dashwood cannot "be of service" or "help" his mother move the furniture to a new house that is too far away.

   Distractor Explanation: None of the other choices fits the context of explaining that Mr. Dashwood cannot help take the furniture to a faraway place. **Choices B** and **D** refer to disconnecting something, such as removing a part that is fastened in some way. **Choice C** refers to ordering or sending something away. None of these choices contain the idea of taking the

possessions to a new location.

3. **Level:** Hard | **Domain:** CRAFT AND STRUCTURE
   Skill/Knowledge: Words in Context

   Key Explanation: Choice A is the best answer. "Peculiar" is used to describe Caravaggio's style, which is elsewhere described as "distinct" or "characteristic" of his work. **Choice A** refers to something unique or one–of–a–kind, which fits the context of art that was very notable and later adopted by a different school of artists.

   Distractor Explanation: Choice B is incorrect because it has a negative connotation that implies that the writer does not like it, whereas the writer refers to the work as "enchanting" or "fascinating," indicating that there is a positive quality to it. **Choice C** is incorrect because it relates to feeling unwell or slightly sick, a very different meaning of "peculiar." **Choice D** is incorrect because it refers to something which is possible to see. Although Caravaggio's use of shadows was possible to see, the author is referring to a different, special quality that Baroque artists later used.

4. **Level:** Hard | **Domain:** CRAFT AND STRUCTURE
   Skill/Knowledge: Words in Context

   Key Explanation: Choice C is the best answer. "Endow" refers to formally giving money to someone or something, so fits the context of explaining that much of her "legacy" or "money given to people in a will" went to charities.

   Distractor Explanation: None of the other choices adequately explain what happened between the legacy and charities. **Choice A** refers to forcing someone to comply with laws or rules. **Choice B** refers to surrendering or yielding something, but the charities were not surrendered to anything. **Choice D** is incorrect because it refers to giving power or recognition, not money.

5. **Level:** Hard | **Domain:** CRAFT AND STRUCTURE
    Skill/Knowledge: Text Structure and Purpose

    Key Explanation: Choice D is the best answer. The fact that D'Artagnan notices that people turn around to look stresses that he is very nervous about appearing like an "embarrassed provincial." He realized that they saw through his front and "felt ridiculous." By mentioning the fact that he saw them, it is clear to the reader why his "very good opinion of himself" changed.

    Distractor Explanations: Choice A is incorrect because there is no conflict in the text. **Choice B** is incorrect because a "temporal change" is a shift in time, but the time sequence remains consistent. **Choice C** is incorrect because the reader has no idea what the scene really is; one knows D'Artagnan is walking by a group of people, but there is no clue how many or where they are.

6. **Level:** Medium | **Domain:** CRAFT AND STRUCTURE
    Skill/Knowledge: Text Structure and Purpose

    Key Explanation: Choice B is the best answer. The passage starts by saying that Levin planned to tell his brother about the marriage, and ends by saying he did not because he was afraid his brother would not view it favorably. The underlined portion gives part of the reason Levin changed his mind: his brother used an "unconsciously patronizing tone" or "spoke as if he looked down on Levin without intending to do

so." Therefore, Levin felt "inferior" or "too low" to discuss an important topic.

Distractor Explanation: Choice A is incorrect because the topic of the conversation with the professor is not given; the conversation about agriculture came "afterwards" or "later," and was presumably between Levin and his brother rather than the professor. **Choice C** is incorrect because there is no indication that the conversation about agriculture was an "obstacle" or "barrier" that prevented Levin from getting married; the details could have related to anything agricultural. Instead, the conversation was conducted in a tone which made him feel like he should bring up the topic at a different time. **Choice D** is incorrect because there is no indication that Levin and his brother "frequently" or "often" disagreed about agriculture. In fact, they might not have disagreed in this case, either. The brother just talked in a "patronizing" or "belittling" way.

7. **Level:** Easy | **Domain:** CRAFT AND STRUCTURE
    Skill/Knowledge: Cross–Text Connections

    Key Explanation: Choice A is the best answer because Text 1 describes the "first public tasting of cultured meat" in 2013, and Text 2 explains the "later development" or "thing which occurred afterwards" by saying that the "first sales occurred in December 2020."

    Distractor Explanations: Choice B is incorrect because Text 1 does not actually say how anyone viewed the product, only that it was first tasted on television. **Choice C** is incorrect because only Text 1 says that it was expensive to develop. Text 2 refers to "skepticism" or "concern" about the product, but does not discuss how it was "created" or "made." **Choice D** is incorrect because Text

2 refers to the public's reaction of "skepticism," but Text 1 never says what people other than the creator thought of the product.

8. **Level:** Medium | **Domain:** CRAFT AND STRUCTURE
Skill/Knowledge: Cross–Text Connections

Key Explanation: Choice A is the best answer. Text 1 claims that polar bear populations are not threatened any longer because there was a ban on hunting. However, Text 2 points out that climate change is a severe problem. The author of the Text 2 further distinguishes between changes in different populations, which indicates that while the numbers may be increasing overall, there may be serious losses in genetic diversity if some of the populations die out. Therefore, the author of Text 2 would probably say that Text 1 shows a "limited" or "insufficient" analysis of the complete situation.

Distractor Explanation: Choice B is incorrect because, while Text 1 does say that total numbers have "rebounded" or "returned to previous levels," the author of Text 2 points out that some populations have not. In addition, the author of Text 1 does not mention the problem of global warming, which Text 2 points out is eliminating sea ice essential to the survival of the polar bears. Therefore, the author of Text 2 would probably not find the text "inspiring" or "uplifting," but rather "incomplete" or "in error." **Choice C** is incorrect because, while the author of Text 2 might say that Text 1 is "erroneous" or "wrong" in claiming that polar bears are not "in imminent danger of extinction" or "threatened," the reason is not correct. The author of Text 2 might say that the total number is correct, but it is more important to look at numbers in different populations. **Choice D** is incorrect because Text 1 does not imply that efforts to conserve polar bears are "only partially successful." Rather, Text 1 indicates that efforts were successful and now there is little concern at all. The author of Text 2 would be worried about climate change, not about the positive information regarding hunting given in Text 1.

9. **Level:** Easy | **Domain:** INFORMATION AND IDEAS
Skill/Knowledge: Central Ideas and Details

Key Explanation: Choice A is the best answer. The passage says that thundersnow, a "meteorological event" or "weather phenomenon" is rare, then explains what it is and how it is different from a thunderstorm. Therefore, the main purpose is to introduce a reader to the unusual weather event.

Distractor Explanations: Choice B is incorrect because only one sentence in the passage says that thundersnow is most common over "large bodies of water" and gives examples, but also says that the event occurs elsewhere. There is not enough information to know what kinds of other places are suitable, so **Choice B** is not the main purpose of the passage. **Choice C** is incorrect because "why" or "the reasons for" the effect are not discussed. The passage only says that the formation occurs in the same way that thunderstorms do. **Choice D** is incorrect because a "dilemma" is a problem, but there is no discussion of a problem that needs solved.

10. **Level:** Medium | **Domain:** INFORMATION AND IDEAS
Skill/Knowledge: Central Ideas and Details

Key Explanation: Choice D is the best answer because the passage focuses on how Electra increases her savings from $25 to buy a plot of land to having enough money after seven years to build a house for her family. "Thrift" refers to the ability to manage money well, so accurately describes Electra.

Distractor Explanations: Choice A is incorrect because the text points out that Electra had more money than her husband to begin with, but since she is saving increasing amounts after they got married, he is at least capable of earning money. It is possible he is also saving more on his own, too. **Choice B** is the opposite of the correct answer. The text says that they were romantic, but "practical" refers to making good decisions about everyday life, and the couple save enough for a nice house. **Choice C** is incorrect because there is no indication that Saladin is "taking advantage" or "using" Electra's money; she is saving the money he earned, so he is contributing to the family finances.

11. **Level:** Hard | **Domain:** INFORMATION AND IDEAS
    Skill/Knowledge: Command of Evidence (Textual)

    Key Explanation: Choice C is the best answer. The claim is that the author "bewails" or "expresses great regret" about a friend in the poem. **Choice C** says "thou art gone," meaning "you are no longer here." The following line, "and never must return" gives more of a clue to what happened: if the friend cannot return, he is probably dead. In other words, **Choice C** shows that there was a "heavy" or "horrible" change in that the friend died and the author is very sad.

    Distractor Explanation: Choice A is incorrect because it only refers to picking plants, not to any reason for doing so. **Choice B** is incorrect because it only reinforces that they are friends who "nurst upon the self–same hill" or "grew up together," and

"fed the same flock," meaning that they worked together. The friendship is established but there is no indication of mourning or sorrow. **Choice D** refers to fame, not to friendship or sorrow, so is incorrect.

12. **Level:** Easy | **Domain:** INFORMATION AND IDEAS
    Skill/Knowledge: Command of Evidence (Textual)

    Key Explanation: Choice B is the best answer. "Selective disobedience" is defined as a situation where the dog refuses to do something that the owner orders but which might hurt the dog or the owner. **Choice B** gives just such a situation: if the dog leads the owner onto the street, then the dog, the owner, or both could get hit by a truck. The dog makes a decision to wait rather than allow an injury to happen.

    Distractor Explanations: Choice A is incorrect because there is no indication that an injury would occur if the dog follows the order to watch the cows. If anything, the dog has decided to do something dangerous, as the cows could get lost or cause damage to property. **Choice C** is incorrect because it shows a situation where the dog follows orders, but "selective disobedience" refers to deciding not to follow an order. **Choice D** is incorrect because it is unclear whether the dog is following orders or not. Also, there is no indication that the dog or the person will get harmed if the dog alerts the owner about the ringing phone.

13. **Level:** Medium | **Domain:** INFORMATION AND IDEAS
    Skill/Knowledge: Command of Evidence (Quantitative)

Key Explanation: Choice D is the best answer because the table only includes data for the year 2018. The text warns that "federal, state, and local government budgets may affect the employment of planners in government, because development projects are contingent on available funds." In other words, employment may increase or decrease if available "funds" or "money" changes. "Budgets" are "spending plans," so if the federal government revises or changes its plans due to "fewer tax dollars," the amount of money for employing planners may be lower. Therefore, there is a "potential" or "chance" that there will be fewer planners in the future than listed in the table.

Distractor Explanation: Choice A is incorrect because neither the table nor the text explains where federal planners work; it is possible that they work in large cities. Therefore, there is not enough evidence to say that the percentage is low because of "need" or "demand" in one area or another. **Choice B** is incorrect because, while no exact numbers are given, the table does show the percentages of the total number of planners. Therefore, it is possible to determine which sectors hire more planners than others. The actual number is "reflected" or "indicated" as a comparison. **Choice C** is incorrect because the text does not say that federal government positions are stable. On the contrary, the text says that employment in government positions is variable depending upon budgets, so if the budget changes in any of the levels of government, the percentage of people employed by each sector may also change.

14. **Level:** Medium | **Domain:** INFORMATION AND IDEAS
    Skill/Knowledge: Inferences

Key Explanation: Since the group did not want to say "farewell" and everyone went out to see the narrator off, it is logical to assume that the narrator is not leaving for a brief trip. Since Elizabeth asked for the narrator to write, there will be time to send letters.

Distractor Explanations: Choice A is incorrect because the gender is not given; it is possible that the narrator is a man. **Choice B** is incorrect because the narrator could have traveled before. **Choice C** is incorrect because, while the narrator didn't want to leave the others, it is possible that the narrator was looking forward to the end of the journey and what would happen upon arrival.

15. **Level:** Medium | **Domain:** INFORMATION AND IDEAS
    Skill/Knowledge: Inferences

Key Explanation: Choice D is the best answer because Clark claims, "extinction of species should cause us greater concern than if we believed that biodiversity was maintained in the past by continual replenishment of random extinction by generation of new species." In other words, he feels that if one species goes extinct, it would show that the biodiversity is not being maintained as it should be; the stabilizing forces would no longer be functioning properly. That could indicate a "collapse" or "failure" of the entire system.

Distractor Explanation: Choice A is incorrect because Clark implies that because of stabilization, ecosystems remain in balance, but if one part of the balance is disrupted, the entire system may collapse. Therefore, a total collapse is more likely than if the system is random. **Choice B** is incorrect because it refers to the situation in the neutral theory, not the biodiversity stabilization theory. **Choice C** is incorrect because the stabilization theory proposes that the number of species remains about the same. It is implied that the rate of addition and extinction would therefore be about the same.

16. **Level:** Medium | **Domain:** STANDARD ENGLISH CONVENTIONS
Skill/Knowledge: Form, Structure, and Sense

Key Explanation: Choice D is the best answer because it is a passive past perfect form. That form shows that something else did the act of destroying to the subject; in this case, the arsonist destroyed the pavilion.

Distractor Explanation: Choice A is incorrect because it is an active form, but the pavilion did not do the act of destroying, the arsonist did. **Choice B** is incorrect because "despite" should not be followed by a clause with a noun and verb. **Choice C** is incorrect because "despite" should not be followed by an infinitive verb.

17. **Level:** Easy | **Domain:** STANDARD ENGLISH CONVENTIONS
Skill/Knowledge: Form, Structure, and Sense

Key Explanation: Choice C is the best answer. The underlined portion is a word that modifies "different," which is an adjective. **Choice C** is an adverb, so correctly can be used to describe how different the habitats are.

Distractor Explanation: All of the other choices are incorrect because they are parts of speech which cannot be used to modify an adjective. **Choice A** is another adjective. **Choices B** and **D** are nouns that mean, respectively, "the furthest point" and "a person who had radical views."

18. **Level:** Medium | **Domain:** STANDARD ENGLISH CONVENTIONS
Skill/Knowledge: Form, Structure, and Sense

Key Explanation: Choice D is the best answer. "First performed in England in 1984" is a modifier that describes *Starlight Express*, so it needs to be followed by the noun it modifies. **Choice D** correctly puts the parts of the sentence in order with *Starlight Express* at the start of the main clause.

Distractor Explanation: All of the other choices can be eliminated because "First performed in England in 1984" illogically refers to a person rather than the musical 8 In **Choice A**, the modifier refers to both Stilgoe and Webber. In **Choice B**, it refers to Stilgoe, and in **Choice C** it refers to Webber.

19. **Level:** Medium | **Domain:** STANDARD ENGLISH CONVENTIONS
Skill/Knowledge: Form, Structure, and Sense

Key Explanation: Choice B is the best answer. "People" is plural, and since it ends with an "e," there needs to be an apostrophe and "s" to show that the opinions belong to the people.

Distractor Explanation: Choices A and **D** are incorrect because "peoples'" is not the correct plural apostrophe, as "people" already refers to more than one person. **Choices C** and **D** are also incorrect because "opinions" does not possess anything, so does not need an apostrophe of possession.

20. **Level:** Medium | **Domain:** STANDARD ENGLISH CONVENTIONS
Skill/Knowledge: Boundaries

Key Explanation: Choice D is the best answer. "Invented in…Sousa" is an added piece of information to the main idea that "the sousaphone is a brass instrument…." Such information could be included with commas at each end, in parentheses, or with dashes at each end, but must use the same punctuation at both ends. Since "invented" is preceded by a dash, "Sousa" needs to be followed by one.

Distractor Explanation: Choice A is incorrect because a single dash in a sentence needs to follow a complete clause, but "The sousaphone" is just a noun. **Choice B** is incorrect because "is" is placed in the aside and away from the main clause, leaving the main clause without a verb. That problem can be more easily seen by writing the sentence without the words between the dashes: "the sousaphone is a brass instrument…." **Choice C** is incorrect because it uses a comma rather than a dash, so the punctuation at the start and end of the aside are not consistent.

21. **Level:** Easy | **Domain:** STANDARD ENGLISH CONVENTIONS
Skill/Knowledge: Boundaries

Key Explanation: Choice D is the best answer. "Tenochtitlan, Texcoco, and Tlacopan" are added information to describe the previous noun, "three separate city–states." They are not essential to understand the meaning of the noun, so need to be divided from the noun they refer to with a comma. There should also be a comma after "Tenochtitlan" and "Texcoco" because they are three items in a list joined by "and." Such lists need to have a comma after each item.

Distractor Explanation: In **Choices A** and **B**, a colon is not incorrect after "city–states" because the previous sentence can stand on its own and

the following information adds detail to that sentence. However, **Choice A** is incorrect because "and" in a list is not followed by a comma. **Choice B** is incorrect because single words need to be separated by commas in a list, not by semicolons (semicolons are only used when the items in the list are multiple words with commas). **Choice C** is incorrect because a comma is necessary to divide "city–states" from the names of the city–states; a noun cannot be followed directly by another noun without punctuation showing how they relate to each other.

22. **Level:** Easy | **Domain:** STANDARD ENGLISH CONVENTIONS
Skill/Knowledge: Boundaries

Key Explanation: Choice B is the best answer because a comma needs to divide non–essential information from a noun that it describes. In this case, there is only one first line of the poem, so the actual words in the line are helpful but not necessary to understand the noun.

Distractor Explanation: Choice A is incorrect because there should be a comma after "line" because the words from the poem are not necessary to understand the sentence. **Choices C** and **D** are incorrect because they create a comma splice between two clauses. Both the parts before and after the comma can stand on their own as sentences.

23. **Level:** Easy | **Domain:** EXPRESSION OF IDEAS
Skill/Knowledge: Transitions

Key Explanation: Choice B is the best answer because it is used to show an exception or change the tone of a passage. The preceding sentence says nuts are related to a longer life, but the following says that it is unclear whether the nuts actually cause the longer life. **Choice B** therefore effectively shows that there is doubt related to the first claim.

Distractor Explanation: None of the other choices accurately show that the tone changes between sentences. **Choice A** is used to show the result of the first claim, not to show an exception. **Choice C** is used to emphasize the first point with supporting information. **Choice D** is used to highlight a common idea between two concepts that are related.

24. **Level:** Medium | **Domain:** EXPRESSION OF IDEAS
    Skill/Knowledge: Transitions

Key Explanation: Choice D is the best answer because it is used to show that something happened despite possible ambiguity over previous claims. The previous sentence refers to a range of hypotheses about why King Tut died, which demonstrates ambiguity about the death. The second sentence shows a situation that is common to each of the possible scenarios; the death was fast.

Distractor Explanation: Choices A and **B** are incorrect because they are used to introduce the logical conclusion of a previous claim. However, the fact that the death was fast is not necessarily logical given the options expressed; for example, he could have lived a long time after an injury or illness. **Choice C** is incorrect because it is used to give another option or possibility. However, the following sentence discusses something that is true in all of the cases, not something which is separate from one of the theories. For example, being murdered is a form of unexpected death.

25. **Level:** Easy | **Domain:** EXPRESSION OF IDEAS
    Skill/Knowledge: Transitions

Key Explanation: Choice D is the best answer because it is used to introduce the result of a series of events. In this context, **Choice D** aptly introduces the result of intimidating the natives because Columbus was worried that the natives might harm his crew or stop providing food. If they were intimidated, they would continue giving necessary supplies without rebelling.

Distractor Explanation: Choice A is incorrect because it is used to show that something happens despite something else, but in this case, the second is a direct result of the first. **Choice B** is used to paraphrase the preceding idea, so does not fit the context of continuing a story. **Choice C** is used to identify similarities in a comparison rather than show how one event was stopped by another.

26. **Level:** Medium | **Domain:** EXPRESSION OF IDEAS
    Skill/Knowledge: Rhetorical Synthesis

Key Explanation: Choice B is the best answer because it clearly meets the student's goal of "differentiating" or "showing the contrasts" between Keith's theaters and others. **Choice B** highlights two main differences from the notes. One is that the performances were "polite" because they did not have vulgarity, swear words, or audiences that heckled. The other is that the theaters were elaborate by comparison to "other theaters in that period."

Distractor Explanation: Choice A is incorrect because it only says Keith owned more theaters; there is nothing which shows how those theaters are different from other people's. Keith's theaters were elaborate, but **Choice A** does not show that other theaters were simple. **Choice C** is incorrect because there is no mention of the type of performances that other people's theaters ran; in addition, the fact that Albee took over does not offer a contrast for what happened in other situations. **Choice D** is incorrect because it only says what Keith preferred and did; there is no contrast to show how his decisions led to differences from other theaters.

27. **Level:** Hard | **Domain:** EXPRESSION OF IDEAS
    Skill/Knowledge: Rhetorical Synthesis

    Key Explanation: Choice B is the best answer because it explains what the blood moon is, including when it occurs and how it forms. **Choice B** therefore best accomplishes the goal of educating the audience about a blood moon.

    Distractor Explanation: Choice A can be eliminated because the audience already knows about a lunar eclipse, so does not need more information about how one occurs. **Choice A** mentions a blood moon, but does not help the reader understand what it is or why the moon turns red. **Choice C** is incorrect because according to points 3 and 4, the entire total lunar eclipse is not called a blood moon; a blood moon is only a stage or phase of the process. **Choice D** is incorrect because it erroneously indicates that red light from the Sun shines through the Earth, but instead, the final point shows that the Moon is colored by light that shines around the Earth.

1. **Level:** Medium | **Domain:** CRAFT AND STRUCTURE
Skill/Knowledge: Words in Context

Key Explanation: Choice D is the best answer because the blank portion shows what "Donovan" did to "childcare." **Choice D** refers to a great change or improvement, so fits the context of saying that disposable diapers completely changed the way children could be raised.

Distractor Explanations: None of the other choices accurately show what "Donovan" did to "childcare." **Choice A** refers to putting something back together, but childcare has not been damaged or fallen apart from a better state. **Choice B** refers to changing the structure of an institution or rearranging objects in a place, and **Choice C** refers to changing the name or identification of something.

2. **Level:** Medium | **Domain:** CRAFT AND STRUCTURE
Skill/Knowledge: Words in Context

Key Explanation: Choice D is the best answer because "application" refers to the starting point of the salt stress. **Choice D** refers to the carrying out of a course of action, so aptly shows that the number of days from the action of creating stress until the appearance of the first flowers was recorded.

Distractor Explanation: None of the other choices fits the context of indicating when the salt process began. **Choice A** refers to "meaning" or "importance. **Choice B** refers to putting in hard effort over a long period. **Choice C** refers to asking for something.

3. **Level:** Hard | **Domain:** CRAFT AND STRUCTURE
Skill/Knowledge: Words in Context

Key Explanation: Choice B is the best answer. "Adroitness" means "skill" or "talent," so shows that the composition "exemplifies" or "stands as a model of" the artist's ability to manipulate or control color.

Distractor Explanation: None of the other choices adequately explain what the manipulation of subtle colors refers to. **Choice A** refers to the state of being easily harmed by something, but Whistler was not harmed by the colors. **Choice C** refers to an agreement to do something, such as meet a person. **Choice D** refers to something that distracts from a serious activity.

4. **Level:** Medium | **Domain:** CRAFT AND STRUCTURE
Skill/Knowledge: Text Structure and Purpose

Key Explanation: Choice A is the best answer because "casting doubt" refers to showing that something may not be true; "veracity" is "truth." The underlined word also has the same meaning: it shows that something is said but that there is doubt about whether the claim is true or not. The claim is that Knight created the Lassie character, but the following sentence shows there is doubt: Gaskell wrote about such a character almost a century earlier. In other words, the underlined portion indicates that the author feels that maybe Gaskell was the creator and not Knight, as others said.

Distractor Explanations: Choice B is incorrect because the underlined portion does not "question" or "cast doubt" on the idea that the stories have a lot in common; instead, the underlined portion emphasizes that they are

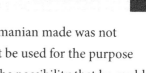

similar by hinting that maybe Knight copied the character. **Choice C** is incorrect because the underlined portion does not modify or cast doubt upon "fictional," it modifies "first introduced." **Choice D** is incorrect because there is no indication that Gaskell's story was popular or widely read at all.

5. **Level:** Medium | **Domain:** CRAFT AND STRUCTURE
   Skill/Knowledge: Text Structure and Purpose

   Key Explanation: Choice B is the best answer because the example is that Lee is a sensitive director who shows "nuances" or "subtleties" about Black characters. The following portion is a "contrast" or "difference" because it shows how other people stereotyped black actors to specific roles or even painted White people to look like Black ones.

   Distractor Explanations: Choice A is incorrect because there is no mention of a stereotype in the underlined portion; the rest of the text points out that Blacks were reduced to stereotypical roles. **Choice C** is incorrect because there is no evidence that Lee "pioneered" or "started" a change; the text only says that his work is different from that of directors in the past. **Choice D** is incorrect because the problem of Black stereotypes is not mentioned in the underlined portion, so the underlined portion does not show that it took time to "resolve" or "fix" it.

6. **Level:** Easy | **Domain:** CRAFT AND STRUCTURE
   Skill/Knowledge: Text Structure and Purpose

   Key Explanation: Choice B is the best answer. "Every cloud has a silver lining" is an idiom which means that everything which at first looks bad actually has something good about it. In this case,

the material that Subramanian made was not magnetic and could not be used for the purpose he wanted, but he saw the possibility that he could "market" or "sell" it and earn money because of its other properties.

Distractor Explanation: Choice A is incorrect because the idiom is not used literally, but figuratively. A "pigment" is a coloring agent like a powder, not a cloud. **Choice C** is incorrect because there is no indication that the pigment could make other colors, only that it was useful for making blue because it had properties most other blues did not. **Choice D** is incorrect because "market the new pigment" shows that Subramanian is taking advantage of or selling the color, not the quality of magnetism. There is no sign that adding something else will make it magnetic after all.

7. **Level:** Medium | **Domain:** CRAFT AND STRUCTURE
   Skill/Knowledge: Cross–Text Connections

   Key Explanation: Choice B is the best answer because Stearns says that slavery is only possible because laws governing slavery exist. The fact that the slave is owned by the state is one piece of legislation, so it supports the claim that slavery continues due to legislation rather than just the wishes of the slave and owner.

   Distractor Explanation: Choice A is incorrect because Stearns says that the law is the only thing to be considered. Therefore, if the law says that emancipated slaves are state property, it doesn't matter if the former slave has any paperwork showing otherwise. **Choice C** is incorrect because Stearns says that the U.S. Constitution supports laws of the states, but does not support slavery *per se*. **Choice D** is incorrect because Stearns says that the slaves are subjected to the laws of their masters. In the scenario given, the master would be the state, so running away would not protect the slave from the laws of that state.

8. **Level:** Easy | **Domain:** INFORMATION AND IDEAS
   Skill/Knowledge: Central Ideas and Details

   Key Explanation: Choice D is the best answer because the passage states that "They are extremely adaptable to a wide variety of habitats" and "are now flourishing in different areas." In other words, coywolves are able to "adapt" or "change" enough to live in many different "habitats" or "natural surroundings." Hence, they are in a range of "environmental conditions."

   Distractor Explanations: Choice A is incorrect because the text offers no comparison of which place has the most coywolves; it only says that they live in many habitats in Canada and other places. **Choice B** is incorrect because there is no indication of how closely related coywolves are to any species; it could be that they have one wolf parent and one coyote parent. **Choice C** is incorrect because the passage only says that coywolves "first appeared" in Canada in the 20th century. It is unclear whether anyone bred them or whether they hybridized naturally in the wild.

9. **Level:** Easy | **Domain:** INFORMATION AND IDEAS
   Skill/Knowledge: Central Ideas and Details

   Key Explanation: Choice B is the best answer because the final sentence says that Nabongo "has written a book about her adventures." Since "her adventures" refers to traveling to all the countries in the world, she is an "author" or "writer" of such a book.

Distractor Explanations: Choice A is incorrect because the text does not say which country Nabongo was born in; the fact that she is Ugandan–American could mean she was born in the U.S. to Ugandan parents. **Choice C** is incorrect because there is no indication of which order Nabongo visited the locations. **Choice D** is incorrect because the text does not give Nabongo's opinion just of the Seychelles, only of her travels in general.

10. **Level:** Easy | **Domain:** INFORMATION AND IDEAS
    Skill/Knowledge: Central Ideas and Details

    Key Explanation: Choice B is the best answer. The first sentence explains the idea of The Fun Theory and the second sentence explains how the company proposed to test the theory. The final sentence gives the results: a large percentage of people changed their behaviors due to the fun factor which was introduced.

    Distractor Explanation: Choice A is incorrect because the passage says that the experiment was designed to test a theory used in an advertising campaign, but does not explain the results of the campaign. It is possible that no additional cars were sold as a result of it. **Choice C** is incorrect because the passage does not say that more people took the stairs than the escalator, only that the use of stairs increased. It is possible that the use of the escalator was still higher than the stairs. **Choice D** is incorrect because there is no discussion that other places should adopt the same type of piano stairs; the passage only says that the stairs were effective in changing behavior in this experiment.

11. **Level:** Hard | **Domain:** INFORMATION AND IDEAS

   Skill/Knowledge: Command of Evidence (Textual)

   Key Explanation: Choice C is the best answer. The claim is that the park is "considered a world treasure for more than its beauty" or "valuable for things other than the way it looks." **Choice C** gives an important reason that people might want to conserve it: the climate is "unique" or "one of a kind" that is high in biodiversity, as illustrated by the huge number of plants in the area.

   Distractor Explanation: Choice A is incorrect because it only says that the site is preserved; it does not give a reason why. **Choice B** is incorrect because there is no reason that a country boundary is a world heritage site of great value; this choice could be acceptable if there were reasons showing why the basaltic line is special, but not as it stands. **Choice D** is incorrect because it gives a reason that the park might have lost value. If the park has also been damaged, then the conservation value is decreased.

12. **Level:** Medium | **Domain:** INFORMATION AND IDEAS

   Skill/Knowledge: Command of Evidence (Quantitative)

   Key Explanation: Choice A is the best answer because the statement describes the "difference in the iron uptake increase." Therefore, the correct answer is derived by subtracting the smaller column from the larger. The smaller column is the control mouse, which has a value of about 2.7. The larger represents the mouse with no HEPHL1 genes, which has a value of about 3.8. The difference is 3.8–2.7=1.1. Even if the values

are changed by a few decimal points, **Choice A** is the closest approximate.

   Distractor Explanation: None of the other choices shows the "difference in the iron uptake increase." **Choice A** would represent a difference larger than 2 of the lines on the y–axis, but there is only one line (the one for 3 nmoles) between the two bars. **Choice C** refers to the total increase for the control mouse, not the difference between the control mouse and the mouse with no HEPHL1. **Choice D** refers to the total increase of the mouse with no HEPHL1.

13. **Level:** Medium | **Domain:** INFORMATION AND IDEAS

   Skill/Knowledge: Command of Evidence (Quantitative)

   Key Explanation: Choice B is the best answer because the graph shows the percentage of increase from the previous year, 2015. The data for Sierra Leone, in the far left–hand column, is just over 120%, but the data for Togo, the second column from the right, says that there was only a growth of just over 20%. The passage points out that quality and accessibility affect whether tourists are attracted to a site or not. Therefore, it is reasonable to assume that the reason for the great increase is that there was a change in infrastructure that made it easier for tourists to visit.

   Distractor Explanation: Choice A is incorrect because the graph compares a percentage increase in tourism, not a percentage of the total tourists. It is unknown how many people went to any given place. **Choice C** is also incorrect because the graph says that Burundi had an increase in visitors of about 40%, which means that it had 40% more than the previous year, not that it had 40% more than other places. **Choice D** is also incorrect because, while there was a greater increase in the number of visitors in Eritrea than in Madagascar, it is unknown what the original number was. It is possible that Madagascar started with a much greater number of tourists in previous years.

14. **Level:** Medium | **Domain:** INFORMATION AND IDEAS
Skill/Knowledge: Inferences

Key Explanation: Choice D is the best answer because the text refers to trouble that was "not alone for himself, but for every tide–water dog." Therefore, Buck probably considers himself to be a "tide–water dog." It is clear he is strong, because the text calls these dogs "strong of muscle and with warm, long hair" and ends by saying that the men wanted dogs that were "heavy dogs, with strong muscles by which to toil, and furry coats to protect them from the frost."

Distractor Explanations: Choice A is not supported by the passage because there is reference to steamships as being currently in the news, but Buck does not know the news. Therefore, he has yet to know about going to the north on a ship. **Choice B** is incorrect because finding "yellow metal"—presumably gold in Alaska—is something that is in the news that Buck does not know about. **Choice C** is incorrect because the text appears to be written from a dog's point of view, as Buck considers himself part of "every tide–water dog."

15. **Level:** Medium | **Domain:** STANDARD ENGLISH CONVENTIONS
Skill/Knowledge: Form, Structure, and Sense

Key Explanation: Choice B is the best answer because it is an adjective, so can correctly be used after the "to be" verb "are" to describe the noun "citizens."

Distractor Explanation: Choice A is a plural noun that refers to circumstances or rules, which does not describe people well. **Choice C** is an adverb, so cannot be used to describe the noun "citizens." **Choice D** is incorrect because it refers to a substance that makes something softer—for example, a fabric softener.

16. **Level:** Easy | **Domain:** STANDARD ENGLISH CONVENTIONS
Skill/Knowledge: Form, Structure, and Sense

Key Explanation: Choice A is the best answer. The underlined portion is one item in a list joined by "and," and such lists need to have the same grammatical structure in each item. The first two items are infinitive verbs that follow "to" and show the purpose of the dam: "control" and "increase." **Choice A** maintains the same structure with the infinitive "generate."

Distractor Explanation: All of the other choices are incorrect because they are not parallel with the other items in the list joined by "and." **Choice B** includes the noun "it." **Choice C** changes the order of the words into a clause, and **Choice D** repeats "to," which is not repeated with "increase water storage."

17. **Level:** Easy | **Domain:** STANDARD ENGLISH CONVENTIONS
Skill/Knowledge: Form, Structure, and Sense

Key Explanation: Choice B is the best answer. The underlined portion is a verb that needs to agree with the subject, which is the plural word "members."

Distractor Explanation: Choices A and D are incorrect because they are singular verbs. Though the preceding word, "the society" is singular, the subject is actually plural, "members of the society." **Choice C** is incorrect because the underlined portion is part of the main clause; "though" subordinates the first half of the sentence. Therefore, an active verb is necessary to make a complete clause, but "dedicating" is a gerund.

18. **Level:** Easy | **Domain:** STANDARD ENGLISH CONVENTIONS
Skill/Knowledge: Form, Structure, and Sense

Key Explanation: Choice A is the best answer. The underlined portion is part of a list of adjectives joined by "and." **Choice A** is parallel with the other adjectives, "courageous" and "rebellious."

Distractor Explanation: All of the other choices can be eliminated because they do not create a parallel list with the adjectives preceding "and." **Choice B** is a complete clause. **Choices C and D** contain verbs.

19. **Level:** Easy | **Domain:** STANDARD ENGLISH CONVENTIONS
Skill/Knowledge: Boundaries

Key Explanation: Choice A is the best answer because parenthetical information should be considered part of the word it refers to in the

sentence and the punctuation should follow the regular punctuation of that part of speech. In this case, the facts in the parentheses describe the subject "shichimi", so should be considered part of the subject. No commas are needed between the subject and the following verb "is."

Distractor Explanation: All of the other choices are incorrect because they include unnecessary commas. In **B** and **D**, the commas separate the noun from the parenthetical information that describe it. In **C** and **D**, the commas divide the subject and its verb.

20. **Level:** Easy | **Domain:** STANDARD ENGLISH CONVENTIONS
Skill/Knowledge: Boundaries

Key Explanation: Choice A is the best answer. "Like stegosaurs and tyrannosaurs" is used to explain what is meant by "familiar species," so does not have to be separated from the sentence with any punctuation.

Distractor Explanation: Choice B is incorrect because "were" is the verb that goes with "familiar species." If there is only one comma, then "like… of time" becomes a modifier of "species" and there is no verb in the main clause. **Choice C** is incorrect because "like stegosaurs and tyrannosaurs" could be separated from "species" and the main sentence with commas at both ends, but in that case, there should be no comma after "stegosaurs." Two nouns joined by "and" should not be separated with punctuation. **Choice D** is incorrect because a colon needs to follow a complete sentence, but the preceding portion has no verb to go with "species."

21. **Level:** Easy | **Domain:** STANDARD ENGLISH CONVENTIONS
Skill/Knowledge: Boundaries

Key Explanation: Choice C is the best answer. The portions before and after the underlined section are both able to stand on their own as sentences, so can be joined with a period or semicolon.

Distractor Explanation: Choice A is incorrect because it creates a run–on. **Choice B** is incorrect because it creates a comma splice. **Choice D** is incorrect because "and" turns the following portion into a dependent clause that cannot stand on its own as a sentence.

22. **Level:** Medium | **Domain:** STANDARD ENGLISH CONVENTIONS
Skill/Knowledge: Boundaries

Key Explanation: Choice A is the best answer. "What is little known is that as the plans evolved over the sixteen years of construction" is a modifier separate from the main idea, "a ramp was eliminated." Additional information needs to be divided from the main clause with a comma, as indicated by the comma after "construction." A comma should also follow "smaller" because it is part of a series of adjectives modifying the verb "ramp."

Distractor Explanation: None of the other choices correctly divides the sentence. **Choices B, C,** and **D** do not have the comma after "construction" that is necessary to identify where the modifier ends and the main clause starts. **Choice B** includes an unnecessary comma after "ramp," separating that noun from its verb, "was

eliminated." The comma after "steeper" in **Choice C** is possible if "much steeper" is used to add description to the word "smaller," but there is still a comma lacking after "construction." **Choice D** is missing all punctuation.

23. **Level:** Medium | **Domain:** EXPRESSION OF IDEAS
Skill/Knowledge: Transitions

Key Explanation: Choice C is the best answer because it is used to give a detail related to a previous claim. In the context, the general idea of rigorous training is expanded upon with an example of one form of such rigorous training: the dog needs to learn to alert the owner in a special circumstance.

Distractor Explanation: None of the other choices establish the relationship that the second sentence gives an example that illustrates the first sentence. **Choice A** is used to show that something happened despite the previous claim. **Choice B** is used to show the result of the previous claim. **Choice D** is used to point out a similarity between two different examples.

24. **Level:** Easy | **Domain:** EXPRESSION OF IDEAS
Skill/Knowledge: Transitions

Key Explanation: Choice B is the best answer because it is used to show that the following thing comes chronologically after the previous discussion. It fits the context of showing that Gandhi used civil disobedience in the 1920s and King used it in the 1960s.

Distractor Explanation: Choice A is incorrect because it is used to introduce the results of an argument, but the fact that King used civil disobedience does not necessarily follow from the points that Thoreau wrote about it and Gandhi practiced it. **Choice C** is incorrect because it is used to give an example. While the following portion is an example of civil disobedience, it is not an example of the previous sentence, Gandhi's use of the technique. Therefore, the transition is misplaced at this point. **Choice D** shows that something happens despite something else. However, King's use of civil disobedience did not necessarily happen because Gandhi used it; King might have drawn some inspiration from the previous event.

25. **Level:** Medium | **Domain:** EXPRESSION OF IDEAS
    Skill/Knowledge: Transitions

Key Explanation: Choice A is the best answer because it is used to offer a paraphrase or different wording of a previous idea. In this case, it offers a simple explanation "the shell creates a rash" to clarify the earlier claim that the shells "trigger contact dermatitis" because of oils that are "caustic" or "cause a burning sensation."

Distractor Explanation: Choice B is incorrect because it is used to show something similar between a comparison of two items that have common elements but that are not the same. It is not used to explain the same idea in different words. **Choices C** and **D** are incorrect because they are used to introduce the opposite possibility, but the context gives different words for the same thing.

26. **Level:** Easy | **Domain:** EXPRESSION OF IDEAS
    Skill/Knowledge: Rhetorical Synthesis

Key Explanation: Choice D is the best answer because it gives a concise definition of "heat islands" for an audience that does not know what they are. **Choice D** then achieves the student's goal of offering solutions by summarizing the fourth and fifth bullet points.

Distractor Explanation: Choice A is incorrect because it mistakenly offers air conditioners as a solution for heat islands, but the notes only say that air conditioners contribute to the problem of global warming. **Choice B** is incorrect because it only explains what heat islands are; it does not offer any solutions as per the student's goal. **Choice C** is incorrect because an audience that does not know what a heat island is will not know the meaning after reading the statement. It does not include the crucial definition that they are hotter urban areas. Though **Choice C** does offer one way to solve the problem, the reader does not know why it helps.

27. **Level:** Hard | **Domain:** EXPRESSION OF IDEAS
    Skill/Knowledge: Rhetorical Synthesis

Key Explanation: Choice A is the best answer because it is the most convincing argument for a farming community: it shows how the deer can be protected, yet it also shows the people that the student is trying to convince that they will not be harmed in the process. The farmers can "do their jobs" rather than lose land or work because of the new plan.

Distractor Explanation: All of the other choices are incorrect because they show how the plan benefits deer, but they do not address the potential concerns of a farming community about such problems as losing part of their property to the corridor or how to continue farming if there are more deer habitats in the area. Therefore, they are not as convincing an argument for the student to use in trying to get the people to agree to a wildlife corridor.

1. **Level:** Easy | **Domain:** ADVANCED MATH
   Skill/Knowledge: Nonlinear functions | **Testing point:** Writing exponential function equation from data

   Key Explanation: Choice A is correct. The initial value of the land is $47,890, which increases by 2% every year. This suggests that the function is exponential growth. The exponential growth formula is $f(x) = a(1 + r)^x$ where a is the initial value, r is the growth rate and x is the time. In this situation, $a = 47,890$, $r = 0.02$, and $x = t$. Substituting these values to the formula yields $f(x) = 47,890(1.02)^t$. Making A the correct option.

   Distractor Explanations: Choices B and **D** are incorrect. These options are linear functions, however, the model equation in the question is exponential. **Choice C** is incorrect. This is a decreasing exponential function since the factor 0.98 is less than 1.

2. **Level:** Medium | **Domain:** ALGEBRA
   Skill/Knowledge: Linear equations in one variable
   Testing point: Matching coefficients

   Key Explanation: Choice C is correct. Grouping the left side of the equation yields $(ax + bx) + (a \quad b) - 5x - 2$. Factoring out x from the first group yields $x(a + b) + (a - b) = 5x - 2$. Matching coefficients and constants on both sides of the equation yields $(a + b) = 5$ and $(a - b) = -2$. Factoring the given expression $(a^2 - b^2)$ yields $a^2 - b^2 = (a + b)(a - b)$. Substituting the values of $(a + b)$ and $(a - b)$ yields $a^2 - b^2 = (5)(-2) = -10$.

   Distractor Explanations: Choice A is incorrect. This is the value of $(a + b) + (a - b)$.
   Choice B is incorrect. This is the value of $a + b$.
   Choice D is incorrect. This is the value of $a - b$.

3. **Level:** Medium | **Domain:** ADVANCED MATH
   Skill/Knowledge: Nonlinear functions
   Testing point: Solving for a quadratic equation using the quadratic formula

   Key Explanation: To solve for this quadratic equation, use the quadratic formula
   $$x = \frac{-b \pm \sqrt{b^2 - 4ac}}{2a},$$
   where $a = 3$, $b = -6$ and $c = -21$.
   Substituting the given values yields
   $$x = \frac{-(-6) \pm \sqrt{(-6)^2 - 4(3)(-21)}}{2(3)} \text{ or } x = \frac{6 \pm \sqrt{288}}{6}.$$
   Simplifying the equation yields $x = 1 \pm \dfrac{12\sqrt{2}}{6}$ or
   $x = 1 \pm 2\sqrt{2}$.
   Matching the two expressions yields
   $1 \pm 2\sqrt{2} = 1 + 2\sqrt{k}$. Therefore, $k = 2$.

4. **Level:** Easy | **Domain:** GEOMETRY AND TRIGONOMETRY
   Skill/Knowledge: Area and volume | **Testing point:** Finding the area of a rectangle

   Key Explanation: : Choice D is correct. The length of the rectangle is $(x - 6)$ and the width is x. The area of a rectangle is given by length $\times$ width which is $x(x - 6) = 27$.
   Using distributive property yields $x^2 - 6x = 27$.
   Subtracting 27 from both sides of the equation yields $x^2 - 6x - 27 = 0$. Solve the quadratic equation either by using the quadratic formula or by using the factor method.
   Factoring $x^2 - 6x - 27 = 0$ yields $(x + 3)(x - 9) = 0$.
   Equating $(x + 3)$ to zero yields $x + 3 = 0$ or $x = -3$.
   Equating $(x - 9)$ to zero yields $x - 9 = 0$ or $x = 9$.
   Since the width cannot be negative, the width would therefore be 9. Solving for the length of the rectangle yields $9 - 6 = 3$.

Distractor Explanations: Choice A is incorrect. This is the value of x or the width of the rectangle. **Choice B** is incorrect and may result from a conceptual or calculation error. **Choice C** is incorrect. This is the difference between the length and the width of the rectangle.

5. **Level:** Easy | **Domain:** ALGEBRA
   Skill/Knowledge: Linear equations in one variable
   Testing point: Solving for x in a linear equation

   Key Explanation: Choice A is correct. Solve for x first in the given equation $7x + 14 = 7$. Subtracting 14 from both sides of the equation yields $7x = 7 - 14$ or $7x = -7$. Dividing both sides of the equation by 7 yields $x = -1$. The equivalent equation will also have the same value of x. Solve the value of x in choice A by subtracting 6 from both sides of the equation which yields $3x = 3 - 6$ or $3x = -3$. Dividing both sides of the equation by 3 yields $x = -1$. Therefore, $3x + 6 = 3$ is equal to $7x + 14 = 7$.

   Distractor Explanations: Choices B and **C** are incorrect. Solving the value of x from both equations yields $x = 3$. **Choice D** is incorrect. Solving the value of x from $7x = 7$ yields $x = 1$.

6. **Level:** Hard | **Domain:** ALGEBRA
   Skill/Knowledge: Linear inequalities in one or two variables | **Testing point:** Solving absolute value inequalities

   Key Explanation: To solve for the values of x, make two inequalities of absolute value for the positive and negative values.

$^+\lvert x+3\rvert < {}^+7$	$-\lvert x+3\rvert < {}^+7$
$x+3 < 7$	$-x-3 < 7$
$x+3-3 < 7-3$	$-x-3+3 < 7+3$
$x < 4$	$-x < 10$, divide both sides by -1

   $x > -10$

   Hence, $-10 < x < 4$. The integers between -10 and 4 are $-9, -8, -7, -6, -5, -4, -3, -2, -1, 0, 1, 2$ and 3.
   Therefore, there are 13 integer solutions in the given inequality.

7. **Level:** Easy | **Domain:** ADVANCED MATH
   Skill/Knowledge: Nonlinear functions | **Testing point:** Finding a value of an exponential function

   Key Explanation: Choice A is correct.

   Substituting $\dfrac{1}{3}$ to the given equation yields

   $$p\left(\frac{1}{3}\right) = \left\{\frac{1}{8}\right\}^{\frac{-1}{3}} = 8^{\frac{1}{3}} = \sqrt[3]{8} = 2$$

   Therefore, $p\left(\dfrac{1}{3}\right) = 2$.

   Distractor Explanations: Choice B is incorrect. This option may be a result of finding $p(3)$. **Choice C** is incorrect and may result from solving the value of $p\left(-\dfrac{1}{3}\right)$. **Choice D** is incorrect. This option may be a result of finding $p(-3)$.

8. **Level:** Medium | **Domain:** ADVANCED MATH
   Skill/Knowledge: Nonlinear functions | **Testing point:** Using the factor theorem

   Key Explanation: Choice C is correct. Factor theorem states that if $f(a) = 0$, then $x - a$ is a factor of $f(x)$. In **Choice C**, $a = 2$. Substituting 2 to the given equation yields $f(2) = 6(2)^2 - 17(2) + 10$. Using distributive property yields $f(2) = 24 - 34 + 10$ or $f(2) = 0$. This means that $x - 2$ is a factor of $f(x)$.

   Distractor Explanations: Choice A is incorrect. Substituting $-\dfrac{5}{6}$ to the given equation yields

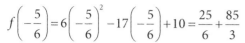

$$f\left(-\frac{5}{6}\right) = 6\left(-\frac{5}{6}\right)^2 - 17\left(-\frac{5}{6}\right) + 10 = \frac{25}{6} + \frac{85}{3}$$

Choice B is incorrect. Substituting –5 to the given equation yields 245. **Choice D** is incorrect. Substituting 5 to the given equation yields 75.

9. **Level:** Easy | **Domain:** PROBLEM–SOLVING AND DATA ANALYTICS
   Skill/Knowledge: One–variable data: distributions and measures of center and spread | **Testing point:** Interpreting box and whisker plots

   Key Explanation: Choice D is correct. The median in a box and whisker plot is represented by the line in the box (interquartile range). From the above, data set A has a median of data set B has a greater median compared to data set A.

   Distractor Explanations: Choice A and **Choice B** are incorrect. The mean and number of data or frequency cannot be found from a box and whisker plot representation. **Choice C** is incorrect. This statement is false.

10. **Level :** Easy | **Domain:** ADVANCED MATH
    Skill/Knowledge: Nonlinear equations in one variable and systems of equations in two variables
    Testing point: Finding the vertex of a parabola through a transformation

    Key Explanation: The vertex of $f(x)$ is (–2, 5). Translating the parabola 3 units to the left and 1 unit up would result in (–5, 6), which is the vertex of $g(x)$.
    Therefore, the value of h is –5.

11. **Level:** Easy | **Domain:** PROBLEM–SOLVING AND DATA ANALYSIS
    Skill/Knowledge: Two–variable data: models and scatterplots | **Testing point:** Using the line of best fit

Key Explanation: Choice C is correct. The points above the line of best fit have a higher value than the values predicted by the line of best fit. There are 6 points above the line.

Distractor Explanations: Choice A is incorrect and may result from counting the total points in the scatter plot. **Choice B** is incorrect and may result from counting the points below the line. **Choice D** is incorrect. This option may result from conceptual errors.

12. **Level:** Easy | **Domain:** ADVANCED MATH
    Skill/Knowledge: Equivalent expressions | **Testing point:** Using the difference of two squared with binomial expressions

    Key Explanation: Choice D is correct. Rewriting the expression $(x+\sqrt{2})^2(x-\sqrt{2})^2$ yields
    $$\left[(x+\sqrt{2})(x-\sqrt{2})\right]^2.$$
    Using $(a + b)(a - b) = a^2 - b^2$ yields
    $\left[(x+\sqrt{2})(x-\sqrt{2})\right]^2 = (x^2 - (\sqrt{2})^2)^2$. Simplifying the radicals yields $(x^2 - 2)^2$. Expanding the expression yields $x^4 - 4x^2 + 4$.

    Distractor Explanations: Choices A, B, and C are incorrect and may result from a conceptual or calculation error

13. **Level:** Easy | **Domain:** ALGEBRA
    Skill/Knowledge: Linear functions | **Testing point:** Finding the equation of a line from a graph

    Key Explanation: Choice A is correct. The graph decreases from left to right. This means that the line has a negative slope. Looking at the choices, only **Choice A** has a negative slope of –4.85. Therefore, $y = 231 - 4.85x$ is the equation of the graph.

Distractor Explanations: Choices B, C, and **D** are incorrect. These equations have positive values of slopes.

14. **Level :** Medium | **Domain:** PROBLEM SOLVING AND DATA ANALYSIS

    Skill/Knowledge: Percentages | **Testing point:** Using proportions and percentages

    Key Explanation:

	Girls	Boys
On the track team	6	$\frac{3}{5} \times 20 = 12$
Not on the track team	$\frac{3}{4} \times 24 = 18$	8
	24	20

From the table, the number of students on the track team would be $6 + 12 = 18$ out of the 44 students. In percentage form this would be $\frac{18}{44} \times 100 = 40.909\%$ or 41% rounded off to the nearest whole number.

15. **Level:** Easy | **Domain:** ADVANCED MATH

    Skill/Knowledge: Nonlinear equations in one variable and systems of equations in two variables

    Testing point: Solving for quadratic and linear inequalities

    Key Explanation: Choice D is correct. The inequality $y > 2(x - 2)^2 - 2$ has a graph of parabola. This means that it is in the form $y > a(x - h)^2 + k$ where (h, k) is the vertex. Hence, the vertex is at $(2, -2)$. Since the value a is positive, the parabola opens upwards. This means that the lowest point of the graph is the vertex. Hence, the value of y must be greater than -2.

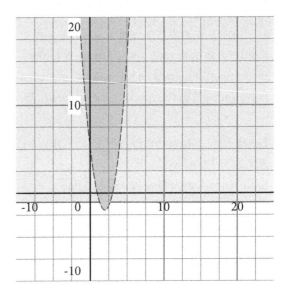

However, the second inequality states that $y \geq -1$, making -1 the least value of y.

Distractor Explanations: Choices A and **C** are incorrect. These are solutions to the system. However, they are not the least value of y. **Choice B** is incorrect. The option is not part of the solutions of the system.

16. **Level:** Hard | **Domain:** ADVANCED MATH

    Skill/Knowledge: Equivalent expressions |

    Testing point: Factoring a quadratic

    Key Explanation: Choice A is correct. Adding 98 to both sides of the equation yields $2x^2 + 28x + 98 = 0$. Factoring out 2 yields $2(x^2 + 14x + 49) = 0$. Using the model $(a + b)^2 = a^2 + 2ab + b^2$, the expression $(x^2 + 14x + 49)$ can be written as $(x + 7)^2$. Hence, the equation becomes $2(x + 7)^2 = 0$. Therefore, only equation 1 is equal to the given equation.

    Distractor Explanations: Choices B and **C** are incorrect. This is because equation two is not equivalent to the given equation. **Choice D** is incorrect. This is because only equation 2 is not equivalent and not both of them.

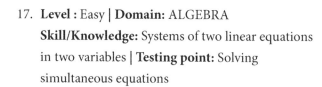

17. **Level :** Easy | **Domain:** ALGEBRA
Skill/Knowledge: Systems of two linear equations in two variables | **Testing point:** Solving simultaneous equations

Key Explanation: The system of equations above can be solved either by substitution or elimination. Using elimination method, the 1st equation is multiplied by 2 which yields $2(3y - 2x = 6)$ or $6y - 4x = 12$.
Subtract the two equations yields $y = 4$.
Substituting the value of y to the first equation yields $3(4) - 2x = 6$ or $12 - 2x = 6$.
Adding $2x$ and subtracting 6 from both sides of the equation yields $12 - 6 = 2x$ or $6 = 2x$.
Dividing both sides of the equation by 2 yields $3 = x$ or $x = 3$.
Therefore, $2x + y$ is $2(3) + 4 = 6 + 4 = 10$.

18. **Level :** Medium | **Domain:** PROBLEM SOLVING AND DATA ANALYSIS
Skill/Knowledge: Inference from sample statistics and margin of error | **Testing point:** Making inferences from sample to population

Key Explanation: Choice B is correct. From the survey, $\dfrac{53}{97}$ of the students surveyed are in favor of changing the school uniform. This means that $97 - 53 = 44$ or 44 of 97 students are not in favor of changing the school uniform. To approximate the number of students in school that are not in favor of the change would be $\dfrac{44}{97} \times 2{,}300 = 1{,}043$.

Distractor Explanations: Choice A is incorrect. This would be the approximate number of students in school that are in favor of the change in uniform. **Choice C** is incorrect. This is the total number of students in the school. **Choice D** is incorrect. This option may result from miscalculation or conceptual error.

19. **Level :** Easy | **Domain:** ALGEBRA
Skill/Knowledge: Systems of two linear equations in two variables | **Testing point:** Working with systems of linear equations with no solution

Key Explanation: Choice B is correct. A system of equations with no solutions means that the lines are parallel. They have the same slope but different y intercepts. Using distributive property yields

$$3x + 5 - \frac{8}{3}x - 8 = px + 4$$

Simplifying the left side of the equation yields $\dfrac{1}{3}x - 3 = px + 4$. Matching the coefficients of x yields $p = \dfrac{1}{3}$.

Distractor Explanations: Choices A, **C** and **D** are incorrect. These options would result in having a system of equations with one solution.

20. **Level :** Medium | **Domain:** ALGEBRA
Skill/Knowledge: Linear equations in two variables | **Testing point:** Solving a system of equations with Infinite solutions

Key Explanation: A system of equations with infinite solutions are equations of the same line and have both the same slope and y–intercept. Using distributive property yields $5x - 10 + x + 3 = kx - 2k + 2x + 1$.
Combining and grouping like terms yields $6x - 7 = (kx + 2x) + (-2k + 1)$.
Matching the constants yields $-7 = -2k + 1$.
Adding 7 and $2k$ to both sides of the equation yields $2k = 8$.
Dividing both sides of the equation by 2 yields $k = 4$.

21. **Level :** Easy | Domain: GEOMETRY AND TRIGONOMETRY

    Skill/Knowledge: Lines, angles, and triangles | **Testing point:** Working with inscribed shapes and special triangles

    Key Explanation: Choice D is correct. The diameter of the circle is equal to the diagonal length of the square. The diameter is $12 \times 2 = 24$ *cm*, which means that the diagonal of the square is also 24. And since the diagonal length is equal to $s\sqrt{2}$ where s is the side length of the square, then $s\sqrt{2} = 24$. Solving for *s* by dividing both sides of the equation by $\sqrt{2}$ yields $s = \dfrac{24}{\sqrt{2}}$ Rationalizing the denominator yields

    $s = \dfrac{24}{\sqrt{2}} \times \dfrac{\sqrt{2}}{\sqrt{2}} = \dfrac{24\sqrt{2}}{2} = 12\sqrt{2}$. Therefore, $s = 12\sqrt{2}$

    Distractor Explanations: Choice A is incorrect. This is the value of the diameter of the circle. **Choice B** is incorrect. This is the value of the radius of the circle. **Choice C** is incorrect. This option would be a result of misconception and conceptual error.

22. **Level :** Hard | **Domain:** ALGEBRA

    Skill/Knowledge: Linear equations in two variables | **Testing point:** Determining the equation of a line from data

    Key Explanation: Choice B is correct. The value is constant for all values of *x* given; thus the equation of the line would be $y = 4$. Substituting the value of *y* to the given equation yields $4 = 2k$. Dividing both sides of the equation by 2 yields $2 = k$ or $k = 2$.

    Distractor Explanations: Choice A is incorrect. This is the value of the constant 2k. **Choices C**

and **D** are incorrect. These options may be due to conceptual and miscalculation errors.

1. **Level:** Medium | **Domain:** ADVANCED MATH
Skill/Knowledge: Nonlinear equations in one variable and systems of equations in two variables
Testing point: Solving quadratic equations

Key Explanation: Choice C is correct. Quadratic equations can be solved either by using the quadratic formula or by solving using the factor method.

Using the factor method, first find the product of the highest degree term and the constant which will be $3x^2 \times 6 = 18x^2$.

The factors of $18x^2$ that will add up to be equal to the middle term $-19x$ are $-x$ and $-18x$.

Splitting the middle term yields $3x^2 - x - 18x + 6 = 0$.

Grouping the equation yields $(3x^2 - x) - (18x - 6) = 0$.

Factoring the equation yields $x(3x - 1) - 6(3x - 1) = 0$.

Factoring out $(3x - 1)$ yields $(3x - 1)(x - 6) = 0$.

Equating $(x - 6)$ to zero yields $x - 6 = 0$ or $x = 6$.

Equating $(3x - 1)$ to zero yields $3x - 1 = 0$ or $x = \frac{1}{3}$.

Since $\frac{1}{3}$ is in the options, then **Choice C** is the correct answer.

Distractor Explanations: Choice A is incorrect. This is the negative value of the solution $x = 6$.
Choice B is incorrect. This is the value of the products of the solutions/roots which is $\frac{c}{a}$.
Choice D is incorrect. This is the negative value of the solution $x = \frac{1}{3}$.

2. **Level:** Medium | **Domain:** GEOMETRY AND TRIGONOMETRY
Skill/Knowledge: Circles | **Testing point:** Completing the square and using the equation of a circle

Key Explanation: Choice B is correct. Diameter is twice the radius. To find the radius of the circle, rewrite the given equation in standard form $(x - h)^2 + (y - k)^2 = r^2$ where (h, k) is the center of the circle and r is its radius. Completing the squares yields $(x-4)^2 - \left(\frac{-8}{2}\right)^2 + (y+5)^2 - \left(\frac{10}{2}\right)^2 = 8$ or $(x-4)^2 - 16 + (y+5)^2 - 25 = 8$. Adding 25 and 16 to both sides of the equation yields $(x - 4)^2 + (y + 5)^2 = 8 + 25 + 16$ or $(x - 4)^2 + (y + 5)^2 = 49$. Since $r^2 = 49$, then $r = 7$. The diameter would then be $2(7) = 14$.

Distractor Explanations: Choice A is incorrect. This is the value of the radius of the circle given above. **Choice C** is incorrect. This assumes that 8 is the radius of the circle and that the diameter would be $2(8) = 16$. **Choice D** is incorrect. This can be a result of not getting the square root of the constant in the equation.

3. **Level:** Easy | **Domain:** ALGEBRA
Skill/Knowledge: Linear functions | **Testing point:** Solving for the absolute value of a linear function $f(x)$, given x

Key Explanation: To find $f(2)$, substitute 2 in place of x in the equation which yields $f(2) = -2(2) - 6$.
Simplifying the equation yields $f(2) = -4 - 6$ or $f(2) = -10$.
$|f(2)|$ is the absolute value of $f(2)$.
Therefore, $|-10| = 10$.

4. **Level:** Hard | **Domain:** GEOMETRY AND TRIGONOMETRY
Skill/Knowledge: Right triangles and trigonometry | **Testing point:** Using trigonometric identities

Key Explanation: Choice B is correct. Converting the tangent function to sine and cosine functions yields $\tan(90-x)° = \dfrac{\sin(90-x)°}{\cos(90-x)°}$. Since the sine of an angle is equal to the cosine of its complementary angle and vice versa, $\sin x = \cos(90-x)$ and $\cos x = \sin(90-x)$. Substituting the equivalent identities yields $\tan(90-x) = \dfrac{\cos x}{\sin x}$. Therefore, the correct answer is **Choice B**.

Distractor Explanations: Choices A and C are incorrect and may result from solving the equivalent identity of $\tan x$ and $\dfrac{1}{\tan x}$ respectively. **Choice D** is incorrect and may result from solving the equivalent identity of $\tan(-x)$.

5. **Level:** Easy | **Domain:** ALGEBRA
   Skill/Knowledge: Linear functions | **Testing point:** Meaning in context in linear equation

   Key Explanation: Choice C is correct. Alina earns an interest monthly based on her deposit. This makes the model equation for her savings account linear. 7.684 in this context, is the amount of interest she earns monthly which can be obtained by multiplying the interest rate with the principal amount. This yields $(6.8\% \times 113) = 7.684$. Thus making option C correct.

   Distractor Explanations: Choice A is incorrect. The amount of interest earned after t months would be represented by $7.684t$. **Choice B is** incorrect. The total amount in the account after t months would be represented by the function $A(t)$. **Choice D is incorrect.** The interest earned per year is $92.208.

6. **Level:** Medium | **Domain:** ALGEBRA
   Skill/Knowledge: Systems of two linear equations in two variables | **Testing point:** Finding equation that makes system have no solutions

Key Explanation: Choice B is correct. A system of equations with no solution are systems that have parallel lines and therefore have the same slope and different y-intercepts. To find the slope and y-intercept of the given equation, the equation has to be in the slope–intercept form $y = mx + c$. Subtracting $-6x$ from the equation yields $-3y = -6x + 2$. Dividing -3 from both sides of the equation yields $y = 2x - \dfrac{2}{3}$. The slope is 2 and the y-intercept is $-\dfrac{2}{3}$.

Rewriting **Choice C** in slope intercept form yields $y = 2x + 4$. Since it has the same slope and different y-intercept with the given line, both lines are parallel and will have no solutions.

Distractor Explanations: Choice A is incorrect. The line has a different slope of $\dfrac{2}{3}$, which makes the system have one solution. **Choices C and D** are incorrect. Both lines have a slope of 2 and y-intercept is $-\dfrac{2}{3}$ which is the same as the given line. Hence, both lines are collinear which makes the system have infinite solutions.

7. **Level :** Easy | **Domain:** ADVANCED MATH
   Skill/Knowledge: Nonlinear functions | **Testing point:** Solving for $p(x)$ given x in a quadratic function

   Key Explanation: To find $p(2)$, substitute 2 in place of x. This yields $p(2) = 2(2)^2 - 6(2) + 5$. Simplifying the equation yields $p(2) = 8 - 12 + 5$ or $p(2) = 1$.

8. **Level:** Easy | **Domain:** ALGEBRA
   Skill/Knowledge: Linear equations in two variables | **Testing point:** Finding the equation of the line given two points

Key Explanation: Choice B is correct. To find the equation of the line, first find the slope of the line. Substituting (6, 5) and (0, 0) to the slope formula

$m = \dfrac{y_2 - y_1}{x_2 - x_1}$ yields $m = \dfrac{0-5}{0-6} = \dfrac{5}{6}$. Substituting the

slope to the slope–intercept form $y = mx + b$ yields

$y = \dfrac{5}{6}x + b$. Since the line passes through the

origin, the y-$intercept$ is zero which means $b = 0$.

Hence, the equation of the line is $y = \dfrac{5}{6}x$ or

$6y = 5x$, which makes B the correct option.

Distractor Explanations: Choice A is incorrect and may result from finding the equation of the line that passes through the origin and point (5, 6). **Choices C** and **D** are incorrect. These lines do not pass through the origin and point (6, 5).

9.   **Level:** Easy | **Domain:** ADVANCED MATH
     Skill/Knowledge: Nonlinear functions | **Testing point:** Determining a quadratic equation from its graph

Key Explanation: Choice D is correct. The graph opens downwards and this makes a (the coefficient of x^2) negative. Hence, the possible answer is either **choice C** or **D**. To determine which is correct between **choice C** and **choice D**, check the

value of h for each equation using the formula $\dfrac{-b}{2a}$

where b is the coefficient of x. Since the vertex of the graph is in the first quadrant, then h must be

positive. Solving h in **Choice C** yields $\dfrac{-(-6)}{2(-2)}$ or

$-\dfrac{3}{2}$. Hence, **Choice C** is incorrect. Solving h in

choice D yields $\dfrac{-(6)}{2(-2)}$ or $\dfrac{3}{2}$. Therefore, **Choice D**

is the correct answer.

Distractor Explanations: Choices A and **B** are incorrect. The graph of these equations opens upwards since the coefficient of x^2 is positive. **Choice C** is incorrect because the value of h is negative.

10. **Level:** Easy | **Domain:** GEOMETRY AND TRIGONOMETRY
     Skill/Knowledge: Lines, angles and triangles | **Testing point:** Using the sum of the interior angles of a polygon formula

Key Explanation: A quadrilateral is a four sided figure. The sum of the interior angles can be found by $180(n-2)$ where n is the number of sides. Substituting 4 yields $180(4 - 2) = 360°$. Adding the given angles yields $x + x + 40 + x + 50 + x - 10 = 360$. Combining like terms yields $4x + 80 = 360$. Subtracting 80 from both sides of the equation yields $4x + 80 - 80 = 360 - 80$ or $4x = 280$. Dividing both sides of the equation by 4 yields $x = 70°$.

11. **Level:** Medium | **Domain:** GEOMETRY AND TRIGONOMETRY
     Skill/Knowledge: Right triangles and trigonometry | **Testing point:** Using SOHCAHTOA in similar right triangles

Key Explanation: Choice A is correct. Triangle ABD and Triangle ACD are similar right triangles. This makes angle CAD and angle DBA equal. Therefore, sin CAD = sin DBA.

Since sin $DBA = \dfrac{O}{H} = \dfrac{AD}{BD}$, then sin $CAD = \dfrac{AD}{BD}$

BD is the hypotenuse for triangle ABD which can be calculated using Pythagorean Theorem $a^2 + b^2 = c^2$, where a and b are the legs and c is the hypotenuse of the right triangle. Applying this to triangle ABD yields $AB^2 + AD^2 = BD^2$. Substituting the values of AB and AD yields $10^2 + 24^2 = BD^2$. Simplifying the left side of the equation yields $676 = BD^2$. Getting the square root of both sides of the equation yields $\sqrt{676} = BD$ or $26 = BD$. Substituting the value of AD and BD to $\sin CAD = \dfrac{AD}{BD}$ yields $\sin CAD = \dfrac{24}{26}$ or $\sin CAD = \dfrac{12}{13}$.

Distractor Explanations: Choice B is incorrect. This option is the value of $\tan CAD$. **Choice C** is incorrect. This option is the value of $\cos CAD$. **Choice D** is incorrect. This option is the value of $\tan CDA$.

12. **Level:** Easy | **Domain:** ADVANCED MATH
    Skill/Knowledge: Equivalent expressions |
    Testing point: Using the distributive property

    Key Explanation: Choice B is correct. Using distributive property yields $7wp(2w) + 7wp(5)$. Simplifying the expression yields $14w^2p + 35wp$.

    Distractor Explanations: Choices A, C, and **D** are incorrect and may result from a conceptual or calculation error.

13. **Level :** Easy | **Domain:** GEOMETRY AND TRIGONOMETRY
    Skill/Knowledge: Area and volume | **Testing point:** Using volumes of similar shapes

    Key Explanation: The ratio of volume of sphere A and sphere B is $27 : 1$. The ratio of the radius would be $\sqrt[3]{27} : \sqrt[3]{1} = 3 : 1$.
    Sphere B has a radius of 4 *cm*.
    Applying the ratio of 3 : 1, this would make the radius of sphere A $3 \times 4 = 12$.

14. **Level:** Hard | **Domain:** PROBLEM-SOLVING AND DATA ANALYSIS
    Skill/Knowledge: Probability and conditional probability | **Testing point:** Calculating probabilities

    Key Explanation: Choice C is correct.

	Rain	No rain
Monday	43%	57%
Thursday	86%	14%

    Probability is equal to one or 100% (if in percentage form), therefore the chance that it won't rain on Monday will be 100% – 43% = 57%. Since it is twice as likely to rain on Thursday than on Monday, the chance that it will rain on Thursday will be 2(43%) = 86%. Hence, the chance that it would not rain on Thursday is 100% – 86% = 14% or 0.14.

    Distractor Explanations: Choice A is incorrect. This is the value of the probability that it would rain on Monday. **Choice B** is incorrect as this is the chance that it would not rain on Monday. **Choice D** is incorrect as this is the chance that it would rain on Thursday.

15. **Level:** Hard | **Domain:** ADVANCED MATH
    Skill/Knowledge: Nonlinear equations in one variable and systems of equations in two variables
    Testing point: Solving nonlinear inequalities

    Key Explanation: Choice B is correct. To solve the following system, the bases have to be the same. Since 16 and 4 are multiples of 2, 16^x becomes 2^{4x} and 4^x becomes 2^{2x}. This yields $\dfrac{2^{4x}}{2^{2x}} > 2$. Since the terms on the left side of the inequality are divided, their exponents will be subtracted which will yield $2^{4x-2x} > 2^6$ or $2^{2x} > 2^6$. Since the bases are the same, then $2x > 6$. Dividing both sides of the inequality by 2 yields $x > 3$. 4 is the next integer greater than 3.

Distractor Explanations: **Choices A, C**, and **D** are incorrect as they are all less than 3 or equal to 3.

16. **Level :** Hard | **Domain:** ADVANCED MATH
    Skill/Knowledge: Equivalent expressions |
    Testing point: Matching coefficients and solving systems of equations

    Key Explanation: Using distributive property yields $3ax - 3b + 4bx - 4a = x - 6$.
    Grouping like terms yields $(3a + 4b)x + (-3b - 4a) = x - 6$. Matching the coefficients of x and the constants to make two equations yields $3a + 4b = 1$ and $-4a - 3b = -6$. Using the elimination method to find the value of a and b, multiply the 1st equation by 4 and the 2nd equation by 3. This yields $4(3a + 4b = 1)$ or $12a + 16b = 4$ and $3(-4a - 3b = -6)$ or $-12a - 9b = -18$. Adding the two equations yields $7b = -14$. Dividing both sides of the equation by 7 yields $b = -2$. Substituting the value of b to the 1st equation yields $3a + 4(-2) = 1$ or $3a - 8 = 1$. Adding 8 to both sides of the equation yields $3a = 9$. Dividing both sides of the equation by 3 yields $a = 3$.

17. **Level:** Easy | **Domain:** GEOMETRY AND TRIGONOMETRY
    Skill/Knowledge: Area and volume | **Testing point:** Finding the volume of a cone

    Key Explanation: Choice B is correct. The volume of a cone is given by the formula $\left(\dfrac{1}{3}\pi r^2 h\right)$ where r is the radius and h is the height. Since the height is 6 more than the radius, $h = 12 + 6 = 8$. Substituting the values to the formula yields $\dfrac{1}{3}\pi(12)^2(18) = 864\pi$.

Distractor Explanations: **Choice A** is incorrect because this gives the volume of a cylinder with the given parameters. **Choices C** and **D** are incorrect. These options may result from miscalculation or by using the wrong formula.

18. **Level:** Easy | **Domain:** ALGEBRA
    Skill/Knowledge: Linear equations in two variables | **Testing point:** Finding the slope of a line from an equation

    Key Explanation: Choice A is correct. To find the slope of the line, rewrite the equation in slope intercept form $y = mx + c$, where m is the slope and c is the y-intercept. Adding $3y$ and subtracting 6 from both sides of the equation yields $4x - 6 = 3y$. Dividing both sides of the equation by 3 yields $\dfrac{4}{3}x - 2 = y$ or $y = \dfrac{4}{3}x - 2$. Therefore, the slope of the line is $\dfrac{4}{3}$.

Distractor Explanations: **Choice B** is incorrect because this is the coefficient of x when the equation of the line is in general form. **Choices C** and **D** are incorrect and may result from a conceptual or calculation error.

19. **Level :** Medium | **Domain:** GEOMETRY AND TRIGONOMETRY
    Skill/Knowledge: Circles | **Testing point:** Calculating angle measure given arc length

    Key Explanation: The arc length is a fraction of the circumference. The arc would therefore be $\dfrac{3\pi}{20\pi} = \dfrac{3}{20}$.
    Multiplying it to the full angle of a circle yields $\dfrac{3}{20} \times 360° = 54°$.

20. **Level:** Easy | **Domain:** PROBLEM SOLVING AND DATA ANALYSIS
Skill/Knowledge: Ratios, rates, proportional relationships, and units | **Testing point:** Using inverse proportions

Key Explanation: Choice B is correct. The price per student would be $\frac{p}{30}$. If 28 students paid before the day of the trip, then this can be represented by $\frac{p}{30} \times 28 = \frac{28p}{30}$ or $\frac{14}{15p}$.

Distractor Explanations: Choices A and **C** are incorrect and may result from assuming that p is the price per student. **Choice D** is incorrect and may result from solving the price per student.

21. **Level:** Hard | **Domain:** GEOMETRY AND TRIGONOMETRY
Skill/Knowledge: Circles | **Testing point:** Finding the equation of a circle

Key Explanation: Choice C is correct.
The standard form of the equation of a circle is $(x - h)^2 + (y - k)^2 = r^2$, where (h, k) is the center of the circle and r is the radius. Substituting the given data yields $(x + 3)^2 + (y - 5)^2 = 6^2$.
Expanding the equation yields
$x^2 + 6x + 9 + y^2 - 10y + 25 = 36$.
Subtracting 36 from both sides of the equation yields $x^2 + 6x + y^2 - 10y + 34 - 36 = 0$.
Matching the constant in $x^2 + 6x + y^2 - 10y - 2 = ax^2 + bx + cy^2 + dy + e$ yields $e = -2$.

Distractor Explanations: Choices A and **D** are incorrect. These options may result from conceptual errors. **Choice B** is incorrect. This is the value of $r^2 = 6^2 = 36$, however it is not the value of e.

22. **Level:** Medium | **Domain:** ALGEBRA
Skill/Knowledge: Linear inequalities in one or two variables | **Testing point:** Solving for a linear inequality

Key Explanation: Choice D is correct. Using distributive property yields $-3x - 6 < 2x - 16$. Adding 6 and subtracting $2x$ from both sides of the inequality yields $-3x - 6 - 2x + 6 < 2x - 16 + 6 - 2x - 5x < -10$. Dividing both sides of the inequality by -5 yields $x > 2$. Since 3 is greater than 2, it is the correct answer.

Distractor Explanations: Choices A, B and **C** are incorrect. These values are less than or equal to 2.

Made in United States
Orlando, FL
08 June 2023

33940835R00222